Collaborative *Dubliners*

Irish Studies

James MacKillop, *Series Editor*

Collaborative
Dubliners

Joyce in Dialogue

Edited by Vicki Mahaffey

SYRACUSE UNIVERSITY PRESS

First Edition 2012
16 17 18 19 20   6 5 4 3 2

∞ The paper used in this publication meets the minimum requirements of the American
National Standard for Information Sciences—Permanence of Paper for Printed Library
Materials, ANSI Z39.48–1992.

The chapter "Reopening 'A Painful Case,'" by Paul K. Saint-Amour and Karen R. Lawrence,
previously appeared in *Who's Afraid of James Joyce?* by Karen R. Lawrence (Gainesville:
University Press of Florida, 2010) and is republished here in slightly revised form with
permission.

For a listing of books published and distributed by Syracuse University Press,
visit www.SyracuseUniversityPress.syr.edu.

ISBN (cloth): 978-0-8156-3270-2   (e-book): 978-0-8156-5176-5
ISBN (paper): 978-0-8156-3269-6

Library of Congress Cataloging-in-Publication Data

Collaborative Dubliners : Joyce in dialogue / edited by Vicki Mahaffey. — 1st ed.
    p. cm. — (Irish studies)
  Includes bibliographical references and index.
    ISBN 978-0-8156-3270-2 (cloth : alk. paper) — ISBN 978-0-8156-3269-6 (pbk. : alk.
paper) 1. Joyce, James, 1882–1941. Dubliners.   2. Dublin (Ireland)—In literature.
3. Dialogue in literature.   I. Mahaffey, Vicki.
  PR6019.O9D8684 2012
  823'.912—dc23   2012002070

Manufactured in the United States of America

To Joe, who blazed the way

Contents

Acknowledgments

I am grateful to Tania Lown-Hecht for her insightful and efficient editorial help in preparing the final manuscript for the press and compiling the index, to Claire Barber for her expert proofreading, and to the University of Illinois Faculty Research Board for a grant to help finish the editing. I would also like to acknowledge the many fruitful dialogues that helped make this book even more rewarding to produce: dialogues with the exceptionally knowledgeable and responsive acquisitions editor Jennika Baines at Syracuse University Press, as well as with those who read and commented on parts of the manuscript as it progressed, Joe Valente and Amanda Dennis. The dedication of the book commemorates thirty years of ongoing, illuminating dialogue about Joyce with someone who first demonstrated to me through his own work the rewards of collaboration.

Contributors

DEREK ATTRIDGE teaches at the University of York, England, and is a Fellow of the British Academy. He is the author or editor of several books on Joyce, including *Joyce Effects: On Language, Theory, and History* (2000), *Semicolonial Joyce* (with Marjorie Howes) (2000), *Peculiar Language: Literature as Difference from the Renaissance to James Joyce* (2004), *The Cambridge Companion to Joyce* (2nd ed., 2004), *James Joyce's "Ulysses": A Casebook* (2004), and *How to Read Joyce* (2007). Other books include *The Singularity of Literature,* which won the ESSE Prize in 2006. His most recent publication is *Reading and Responsibility: Deconstruction's Traces* (2010), and he has coedited *Theory after "Theory"* (2011) and *The Cambridge History of South African Literature* (2012).

MARGOT GAYLE BACKUS is Associate Professor of English at the University of Houston, where she teaches Irish literature and literary modernism. She has published articles in journals including *Signs, Cultural Critique, American Imago, Interventions,* and *ELH.* Her study *The Gothic Family Romance: Heterosexuality, Child Sacrifice, and the Anglo-Irish Colonial Order* (1999) won the 2001 American Conference for Irish Studies' prize for an outstanding first book. She was the Irish American Cultural Institute's 2007–8 Research Fellow at the National University of Ireland–Galway's Irish Studies Centre. Her book *Odd Jobs: James Joyce and the Work of Scandal* is forthcoming.

RICHARD BROWN is Reader in Modern Literature in the School of English at the University of Leeds. His most recent published books on Joyce are *A Companion to James Joyce* (2008), which offers essays by leading experts on a range of texts and topics with a global reach, and *Joyce, "Penelope," and the Body* (2006), a collection of essays concentrated on the final episode of *Ulysses* in relation to the body theme. His highly regarded *James Joyce and Sexuality* (1981) was followed by *James Joyce: A Postculturalist Perspective* (1992). He has completed a new monograph on Joyce and English literature and is currently working on representations of the body in modernism. He cofounded and remains coeditor of the *James Joyce Broadsheet,* a specialist review on Joyce that has appeared three times a year since 1980, and he is the author of more than fifty articles and book chapters on Joyce and other modern and contemporary writers, including Seamus Heaney, Martin Amis, Ian McEwan, and Bob Dylan.

GABRIELLE CAREY was born in Sydney and published her first coauthored novel, *Puberty Blues,* at the age of twenty. Carey is the author of fiction and nonfiction books, including *In My Father's House, The Borrowed Girl, So Many Selves,* and *Waiting Room.* She teaches writing at the University of Technology, Sydney, and for the past seven years she has coordinated Australia's only *Finnegans Wake* reading group.

GREGORY CASTLE is Professor of British and Irish Literature at Arizona State University. He has published *Modernism and the Celtic Revival* (2001), *Reading the Modernist Bildungsroman* (2006), and *The Blackwell Guide to Literary Theory* (2007). He has also edited *Postcolonial Discourses* (2000) and *The Encyclopedia of Literary and Cultural Theory,* vol. 1, *Literary Theory from 1900 to 1966* (2011). He has published numerous essays on Joyce, Yeats, Wilde, and other Irish writers and is currently working on *Inventing Souls: The Pedagogies of Irish Revivalism,* a study of misrecognition and political education in Irish revivalism.

KATHRYN CONRAD is Associate Professor of English at the University of Kansas, where she teaches courses on Joyce as well as on British and Irish literature, Northern Ireland, and queer theory. She has published on a number of subjects, including Joyce, Irish feminism, queer politics, mural photography, discriminatory surveillance, and Northern Irish counterpublics, and is the author of *Locked in the Family Cell: Gender, Sexuality, and Political Agency in Irish National Discourse* (2004). Her current research deals with surveillance and epistemology.

KIMBERLY J. DEVLIN is Professor of English at the University of California, Riverside. She is the author of *Wandering and Return in "Finnegans Wake"* (1991) and *James Joyce's Fraudstuff* (2002). Her articles on Joyce have appeared in *PMLA, Novel, James Joyce Quarterly,* and several essay collections. She has coedited *Joycean Cultures/Culturing Joyces* (1998) and *"Ulysses"—En-gendered Perspectives* (1999).

MARIAN EIDE is Associate Professor of English and Women's and Gender Studies at Texas A&M University and is author of *Ethical Joyce* (2002 and 2008). She has published widely on James Joyce, including "The Woman of the Ballyhoura

Hills: James Joyce and the Politics of Creativity," in *Twentieth-Century Literature* (reprinted in the Norton Critical Edition of James Joyce's *A Portrait of the Artist as a Young Man*). She is currently working on a book manuscript on political violence in twentieth-century aesthetics.

MAUD ELLMANN is Randy L. and Melvin R. Berlin Professor of the Development of the Novel in English at the University of Chicago; she was previously the Donald and Marilyn Keough Professor of Irish Studies at the University of Notre Dame. Her publications include *The Poetics of Impersonality: T. S. Eliot and Ezra Pound* (1987), *The Hunger Artists: Starving, Writing, and Imprisonment* (1993), *Psychoanalytic Literary Criticism* (1994), *Elizabeth Bowen: The Shadow Across the Page* (2003, winner of the Crawshay Prize from the British Academy), and *The Nets of Modernism: Henry James, Virginia Woolf, James Joyce, and Sigmund Freud* (2010).

ANNE FOGARTY is Professor of James Joyce Studies at University College, Dublin, and President of the International James Joyce Foundation. She is director of the UCD James Joyce Research Center and editor of the *Irish University Review*. She is coeditor with Timothy Martin of *Joyce on the Threshold* (2005) and with Morris Beja of *Bloomsday 100: Essays on "Ulysses"* (2009). With Luca Crispi she is editor of the newly founded *Dublin James Joyce Journal*. She is currently writing a study of the historical and political dimensions of *Ulysses*, titled *James Joyce and Cultural Memory: Reading History in "Ulysses."* She has edited special issues of the *Irish University Review* on Spenser and Ireland, Lady Gregory, Eiléan Ní Chuilleanáin, and Benedict Kiely and has published widely on aspects of contemporary Irish fiction and poetry. She has codirected two international Joyce symposia and has been academic director of the Dublin James Joyce Summer School since 1997. She is the recipient of the 2008 Charles Fanning Prize in Irish Studies awarded by the Southern Illinois University Carbondale, for her contributions to the field.

ANDREW GIBSON is Research Professor of Modern Literature and Theory at Royal Holloway, University of London, and a member of the Conseil Scientifique of the Collège International de Philosophie in Paris. He is a member of the editorial board of the *James Joyce Quarterly*, director of the "London University (Charles Peake) Seminar for Research into *Ulysses*" and codirector of the "London University Seminar for Research into *Finnegans Wake*." His many publications include *Joyce's Revenge: History, Politics and Aesthetics in "Ulysses"* (2002) and *James Joyce: A Critical Life* (2006). He is coeditor with Len Platt of *Joyce, Ireland, Britain* (2006) and author of *Beckett and Badiou: The Pathos of Intermittency* (2006) and *Samuel Beckett: A Critical Life* (2010). He is currently completing *The Strong Spirit: History,*

Politics, and Aesthetics in Joyce's Writings, 1898–1915. His *Intermittency: The Concept of Historical Reason in Recent French Philosophy* appeared in January 2012.

MICHAEL PATRICK GILLESPIE is Professor of English at Florida International University in Miami. He had previously taught at Marquette University, where he held the Louise Edan Goeden Chair in English. Gillespie has published twenty books and sixty articles on Joyce, Oscar Wilde, William Kennedy, chaos theory, and Irish film, including *Reading the Book of Himself* (1989), *Oscar Wilde and the Poetics of Ambiguity* (1996), *Reading William Kennedy* (2001), *The Aesthetics of Chaos* (2003), *Critical Companion to James Joyce* (2006), *The Myth of an Irish Cinema* (2008), and his compilation of early Joyce criticism, *Foundational Essays in James Joyce Studies* (2011). Currently, he is working on a study of Joyce and exile and on developing backspin on balls pitched to the green.

MICHAEL GRODEN is Distinguished University Professor in the Department of English at the University of Western Ontario. He is the author of *"Ulysses" in Progress* (1977) and *"Ulysses" in Focus: Genetic, Textual, and Personal Views* (2010), general editor of *The James Joyce Archive* (63 vols., 1977–79), and coeditor of *The Johns Hopkins Guide to Literary Theory and Criticism* (1994, 2nd ed. 2005) and *Genetic Criticism: Texts and Avant-Textes* (2004).

JAMES HANSEN is Associate Professor of English and Critical Theory at the University of Illinois. He is the author of *Terror and Irish Modernism: The Gothic Tradition from Burke to Beckett* (2009) and coeditor with Matthew Hart of *Contemporary Literature and the State* (2008). His articles have appeared in such journals as *New Literary History, Studies in Romanticism,* and *Contemporary Literature.*

R. BRANDON KERSHNER is Alumni Professor of English at the University of Florida. He is the author of *Dylan Thomas: The Poet and His Critics* (1977), *Joyce, Bakhtin, and Popular Literature* (1989), and *The Twentieth-Century Novel: An Introduction* (1997). He is also the editor of the Bedford Books edition of Joyce's *A Portrait of the Artist as a Young Man* (2006) and of *Joyce and Popular Culture* (1996). He has published some forty articles and book chapters on various aspects of modern literature and culture and a similar number of reviews and poems. *Joyce, Bakhtin, and Popular Literature* won the 1990 award from the American Conference for Irish Studies as the best work of literary criticism in the field. Kershner is a member of the Board of Advisory Editors of the *James Joyce Quarterly* and was recently reelected to the Board of Trustees of the International Joyce Foundation. His book-length study *The Culture of Joyce's "Ulysses"* was published in 2010.

KAREN R. LAWRENCE became the tenth president of Sarah Lawrence College in August 2007. She has served as president of the International James Joyce Foundation and the International Society for the Study of Narrative. She has written or edited seven books on literature and has published widely in leading academic journals. Her books include *The Odyssey of Style in "Ulysses"* (1981), *Penelope Voyages: Women and Travel in the British Literary Tradition* (1994), *Transcultural Joyce*, and *Decolonizing Tradition: New Views of 20th-Century "British" Literary Canons* (1998). Two new books were published in 2010: *Techniques for Living: Fiction and Theory in the Work of Christine Brooke-Rose* and *Who's Afraid of James Joyce?*

JENNIFER LEVINE is Senior Lecturer in the Literary Studies Program at the University of Toronto and cross-appointed to the English Department. Her essays on Joyce have appeared in *The Cambridge Companion to James Joyce, Quare Joyce, Joyce in the Hibernian Metropolis, PMLA, James Joyce Quarterly,* and *Novel.* Most recently, she has written on travel narratives and is beginning work on a translation of the Uruguayan writer Tomás de Mattos's *La fragata de las mascaras.* Her deepest interest is in teaching.

BARBARA LONNQUIST is Associate Professor of English at Chestnut Hill College in Philadelphia, where she teaches nineteenth-century to contemporary British and Irish literature. She has written on Joyce and Woolf as "two-tongue common readers," on Cleopatra and romantic precursors of the female vampire, and on the Easter Rising in Yeats, Joyce, and Edna O'Brien.

MARY LOWE-EVANS, Professor Emerita, Department of English and Foreign Languages at the University of West Florida in Pensacola, now resides in Memphis, Tennessee. She is the author of *Crimes Against Fecundity: Joyce and Population Control* (1989) and *Frankenstein: Mary Shelley's Wedding Guest* (1993) and volume editor of *Critical Essays on Mary Wollstonecraft Shelley* (1998). She has contributed articles and reviews to the *James Joyce Quarterly,* the *Journal of Modern Literature, Studies in Short Fiction, English Literature in Transition,* and *Studies in the Novel.*

VICKI MAHAFFEY is the Thelma and Clayton Kirkpatrick Professor of English and Gender and Women's Studies at the University of Illinois. She is the author of *Reauthorizing Joyce* (1988), *States of Desire: Wilde, Yeats, Joyce, and the Irish Experiment* (1998), and *Modernist Literature: Challenging Fictions* (2007). She is currently completing a book called *The Joyce of Everyday Life.*

MARGOT NORRIS is Chancellor's Professor of English and Comparative Literature at the University of California, Irvine, where she teaches modern literature. She is the author of four books on James Joyce, including *The Decentered Universe of "Finnegans Wake"* (1976), *Joyce's Web: The Social Unraveling of Modernism* (1992), *Suspicious Readings of Joyce's "Dubliners"* (2003), and a study of the 1967 Joseph Strick film *Ulysses* (2004). She has also published *Beasts of the Modern Imagination: Darwin, Nietzsche, Kafka, Ernst, and Lawrence* (1985) and *Writing War in the Twentieth Century* (2000).

MARK OSTEEN is Professor of English and Director of Film Studies at Loyola University in Maryland. He is the author of *The Economy of "Ulysses": Making Both Ends Meet* (1995) and *American Magic and Dread: Don DeLillo's Dialogue with Culture* (2000) and the editor or coeditor of five other books, including *The Question of the Gift* (2002) and *Autism and Representation* (2008). His memoir, *One of Us: A Family's Life with Autism,* appeared in 2010. He has completed a book titled *The Big Night: Film Noir and American Dreams.*

VINCENT P. PECORA is the Gordon B. Hinckley Professor of British Literature and Culture at the University of Utah. He is the author of *Self and Form in Modern Narrative* (1989) and *Households of the Soul* (1997) and the editor of *Nations and Identities: Classic Readings* (2001). His most recent book is *Secularization and Cultural Criticism: Religion, Nation, and Modernity* (2006). He is currently at work on a book about the necessarily unfinished character of secular modernity.

JEAN-MICHEL RABATÉ is the Vartan Gregorian Professor in the Humanities at the University of Pennsylvania. Cofounder and curator of the Slought Foundation in Philadelphia, he is a senior editor of the *Journal of Modern Literature.* A fellow of the American Academy of Arts and Sciences, he has authored or edited more than thirty books on modernism, psychoanalysis, contemporary art, and philosophy. Recent titles are *Lacan Literario* (2007), *1913: The Cradle of Modernism* (2007), *The Ethic of the Lie* (2008), and *Etant donnés: 1) l'art, 2) le crime* (2010). He is currently editing a collection of essays on modernism and theory. He is the president of the Samuel Beckett Society and working on a book on Samuel Beckett and philosophy.

MARILYN REIZBAUM is Professor of English at Bowdoin College. Her scholarship is in the areas of modernisms, contemporary Scottish and Irish literatures and film, and Jewish cultural theory. She is the author of *James Joyce's Judaic Other* (1999) and numerous essays on Joyce, and she is coeditor with Kimberly J. Devlin of *"Ulysses"— En-gendered Perspectives: Eighteen New Essays on the Episodes* (1999). Recent essays include "They Know Where They're Going: Landscape and Place in Scottish Cinema" (2009), "Wall-Loving: The Architecture of German Film Before and After

Unification" (2008), "Gender and Nationalism in Scotland and Ireland: Making and Breaking the Waves" (2005), "Yiddish Modernisms: Red Emma Goldman" (2005), and "Max Nordau and the Generation of Jewish Muscle" (2004). This last essay is part of her current book project, *Jews, Scientism, and Modern Arts*. She is a contributor to the forthcoming *Edinburgh Companion to Muriel Spark*.

PAUL K. SAINT-AMOUR is Associate Professor of English at the University of Pennsylvania and has been a fellow at the Stanford Humanities Center, the Society for the Humanities at Cornell, and the National Humanities Center. His book *The Copywrights: Intellectual Property and the Literary Imagination* (2003) won the MLA Prize for a First Book. He recently completed an edited collection, *Modernism and Copyright* (2010), and is at work on a monograph titled *Archive, Bomb, Civilian: Modernism in the Shadow of Total War*. He coedits, with Jessica Berman, the Modernist Latitudes book series.

JILL SHASHATY is a doctoral candidate at the University of Pennsylvania. She earned a BA in English from Georgetown University and an M.Div. with a concentration in social and environmental ethics from Vanderbilt Divinity School. Her dissertation focuses on utopian thought as a mode of historical consciousness in nineteenth-century America. Her other research interests include American Indian literatures, Irish modernism, the nineteenth-century novel, genre theory, and historical fiction.

CAROL LOEB SHLOSS, Professor of English at Stanford University, spent the 2007–8 academic year as the Ellen Andrews Wright Senior Fellow at the Stanford Center for the Humanities. The author of five books, numerous essays on literary modernism, and the recipient of a Collaborative Research Grant to do further work on the unpublished work of James Joyce, she is currently at work on the second volume of a trilogy, *Modernism's Daughters*, about Lucia Joyce, Mary de Rachewiltz, Anna Freud, and the issues of inheritance that modernism poses to succeeding generations. Along with Paul K. Saint-Amour, Robert Spoo, and Michael Groden, she served on the International James Joyce Foundation's Commission to examine James Joyce and Copyright, whose work is published in a recent issue of the *James Joyce Quarterly*. She is also the first modernist scholar successfully to sue a literary estate over the issue of fair use in *Shloss v. The Estate of James Joyce*.

JOSEPH VALENTE is Professor of Global Literature and Culture at SUNY–Buffalo. He is the author of *James Joyce and the Problem of Justice: Negotiating Sexual and Colonial Difference* (1995) and *Dracula's Crypt: Bram Stoker, Irishness, and the Question of Blood* (2002). He has also edited a number of volumes, including *Quare*

Joyce (1998) and a recent special issue of *Eire-Ireland* on Irish cities. His new book is titled *The Myth of Manliness in Irish National Culture, 1880–1922* (2011).

DAVID WEIR is an independent scholar living in New York City who happens to teach at the Cooper Union. His work on James Joyce includes numerous articles and notes in the *James Joyce Quarterly;* a monograph, *James Joyce and the Art of Mediation* (1996); and two other books in which the work of Joyce figures, *Decadence and the Making of Modernism* (1995) and *Anarchy and Culture: The Aesthetic Politics of Modernism* (1997). He is presently contemplating a book on Joyce and Proust and is looking for someone to talk him down.

Abbreviations

References to Joyce's writing are abbreviated and cited parenthetically. In the case of *Ulysses*, page and line numbers, separated by a period, are cited. In the case of *Finnegans Wake*, page and line numbers, separated by a period, are cited. Standard editions and abbreviations used are as follows:

BK *My Brother's Keeper: James Joyce's Early Years*. Edited by Richard Ellmann. New York: Viking, 1958.

CM *Chamber Music*. Edited by William York Tindall. New York: Columbia Univ. Press, 1954.

CW *The Critical Writings of James Joyce*. Edited by Ellsworth Mason and Richard Ellmann. New York: Viking, 1959.

D *Dubliners*. New York: B. W. Huebsch, 1916.

E *Exiles*. New York: Viking, 1951.

FW *Finnegans Wake*. 1939. Reprint, New York: Viking, 1967.

Letters I, II, III *Letters of James Joyce*. Vol. 1 edited by Stuart Gilbert. New York: Viking, 1957; reissued with corrections, 1966. Vols. 2–3 edited by Richard Ellmann. New York: Viking, 1966.

P *A Portrait of the Artist as a Young Man*. 1964. Edited by Jeri Johnson. Oxford: Oxford Univ. Press, 2000.

SH *Stephen Hero*. Edited by Theodore Spencer, John J. Slocum, and Herbert Cahoon. New York: New Directions, 1963.

SL *Selected Letters*. Edited by Richard Ellmann. New York: Viking, 1975.

U *Ulysses: A Critical and Synoptic Edition*. Prepared by Hans Walter Gabler with Wolfhard Steppe and Claus Melchior. New York: Garland, 1984.

Collaborative *Dubliners*

Introduction

VICKI MAHAFFEY AND JILL SHASHATY

In the autumn of 2005, Jill wrote an essay arguing that the stories in "Dubliners" functioned as dialogical tools for teaching, like parables (Shashaty 2010). Vicki asked Jill to collaborate with her on the introduction to this collection of essays, since the collection was built around the idea of dialogue. Vicki wanted to intertwine Jill's argument about parables as a literary genre with work she was doing on the dialogical teachings of Paulo Freire and Socrates. Our collaboration was based on a shared interest in education through dialogue, and we enjoyed being able to do what Freire recommends: to act as a student-teacher team working together to solve a common problem.

To "collaborate" is literally to work or labor together. The word didn't take on overtones of sleeping with the enemy until World War II, when in 1940 the Vichy government in France was charged with collaborating with, or selling out to, the Nazis to protect their own interests. The title of this collection, *Collaborative Dubliners,* plays on both meanings. First, it refers to the characters in Joyce's collection, characters that Joyce portrays as unconsciously "collaborating" with the enemy insofar as they have internalized the values of the imperial power, including the denigration of the indigenous Irish as helpless, lazy, and incapable of governing themselves. The title also—less pejoratively—identifies the approach the contributors are taking to *Dubliners* as a collection; we have agreed to "work together," to record our dialogues (or in some cases the consensus that resulted from them) as

1

we tried to construct new meanings from these parabolic narratives, these encrypted "codifications" that turn the banal and the ordinary into challenging opportunities for fresh self-awareness. The effect we tried to achieve might be described musically: instead of one note, each of these essays strikes a chord, which is in some cases dissonant and in others harmonic. We hope that chord may inspire readers to design their own counterpoint in response, generating an increasingly polyphonic legacy of interpretation.

The purpose of this project was to produce a new way of doing literary criticism based on dialogue, interplay, and an explicit acknowledgment of a range of possible ways of "framing" interpretations. The method is designed to be inclusive, even inspirational, to a wide range of readers. The goal is to offer an introduction to Joyce's *Dubliners* (his most widely taught work) that is interesting and accessible to a large audience while utilizing the knowledge and precision that come with expertise. Part of what gives academic criticism its edge is the critic's dependence upon a specific theoretical or historical methodology or frame of reference. Here, the object was to retain the power of the individual critic's methodological approach while challenging the narrowness of a single point of view. Whenever possible, two Joyce specialists with different orientations toward the material were paired together: for example, a poststructuralist is linked with a textual scholar, someone who does French psychoanalytic theory with a historicist, a feminist biographer with a feminist who specializes in psychoanalysis. The idea was to create a situation in which each critic had to negotiate with a different set of assumptions in a collaborative effort to create a more elastic, responsive, capacious reading of the text. The contributors to this volume range in age from graduate students to chaired professors, and they come from seven different countries (England, Ireland, the United States, France, Australia, Canada, and South Africa). Our intent was to produce conflicts, critical aporias designed to be provocative but not fractious, in order to spark even more varied responses in readers.

As professional critics, the contributors to this volume understand that these stories mediate between past and future, Ireland and other countries, the known and the unknown. Like miniature time capsules, the tales contain "clues" that offer interpreters of the future a means of understanding what an older generation learned to see. Of course, Joyce's tales do not deliver

such insights directly; instead, they offer readers the means of (re)construct-
ing them in relation to their own experience, their own personal and cultural
circumstances. These stories, then, serve as prompts for dialogue. As we enter
into ghostly conversations with the printed characters on the pages of Joyce's
book, the ghosts within ourselves emerge almost antiphonally so that they
can be identified, and perhaps even exorcised. As we watch Joyce's characters
lapse into hopelessness, feeling, like Bob Doran, "more helpless than ever"
(*D*, 81), or exclaiming with Eveline, "It was impossible" (*D*, 48), or with
Little Chandler, "It was useless" (*D*, 102), we are offered the opportunity to
realize that each of these characters has just submitted to circumstance with
the passivity born of hopelessness. Instead of seeing their circumstances as
constructed, Joyce's characters, one after another, bow to forces they believe
to be too strong for them, like the "force that pushed [Bob Doran] downstairs step by step" (*D*, 81). The failure of almost all of the protagonists to
see their situations as ones to which they unconsciously contribute invites
readers to adopt an alternative perspective: readers are challenged to view
these constellations of concrete sociohistorical circumstances as what Brazilian educator Paulo Freire calls "limit-situations" that are capable of being
changed. But that perspective is available only to those interested in using
this volume to get a good look at themselves in what Joyce significantly
described as his "nicely polished looking-glass."

THE SPARE STORIES of Joyce's *Dubliners* spring onto the page apparently
denuded of context. Each story functions like a narrative "body" unclothed
by a narrator's conclusions, bare of significance and apparently devoid of
implication. Such uncustomary narrative nakedness inspires in first-time
readers the same blend of interest, discomfort, and even disgust that might
be evoked by a glimpse of the naked bodies of strangers. What is a reader to
do with such apparently unprocessed information? With the sudden, shocking revelation of little truths usually draped by (narrative and social) conven-
tion? With the sight of imperfections that individuals are usually ashamed to
admit even to themselves, much less display to the eyes of people they have
never met?

The query these stories pose to readers is essentially the one that Robert
Frost beautifully attributed to the oven bird in his sonnet of the same name.

The bird "frames in all but words" one haunting question: "what to make of a diminished thing"? The oven bird is also known as a "teacher" bird, like his mellifluous counterpart, the poet. The midsummer song that poet and bird share addresses the imminence of loss: specifically, the loss of spring's abundance, the inevitability of the coming fall. According to the poem's speaker, the oven bird differs from other (now silent) birds in "that he knows in singing not to sing." This understanding—that the most moving communication is about the impossibility of communication, just as the most beautiful singing is about silence—shapes the enigmatic technique Joyce uses in *Dubliners:* in narrating he knows not to narrate, not to build to an explanatory climax. Instead, he writes prose "sonnets" that prompt the reader to contemplate the spectacle of diminishing life and to wonder what to make of it. The puzzling, apparently artless, but carefully structured design of the stories has the potential to awaken both melancholy and wonder. Again, another Frost poem helps us find language for Joyce's design. "Design" asks what brought a white spider carrying a dead white moth onto a white heal-all, and the wittily paradoxical answer—given that "appall" means to make white—is "What but design of darkness to appall? / If design govern in a thing so small." Design certainly governs each small building block in Joyce's collection, and the "design" of the whole is to appall the reader with the darkness of the unenlightened self's complicity in its own entrapment. Joyce would shock his readers out of submitting to their own despair by showing them just what such submission looks like.

What we would like to do in this introduction is to alter the unconscious assumptions many readers have about the structure and purpose of stories by relating these particular stories to parables and to what Paulo Freire, in *The Pedagogy of the Oppressed,* called "codifications." If we modify the genre of the tales in this way, reconfiguring them as part of a pedagogical tradition that is designed to inspire dialogue, it may become clearer why we have chosen to respond to the stories, not with "lectures," but with collaborative critical discussions that may even contain productive disagreements. These stories are miniature representations of a reality shaped by human desires and fears; they are the product of individual psychologies, national histories, and colonial politics that are at once highly particular and at the same time structurally familiar. They present us with a set of problems designed to stimulate and mediate a dialogue with the reader, and the subject of that dialogue is how the unconscious minds of individuals may collaborate to confirm—and thereby perpetuate—their own helplessness. Moreover, since the illusion of helplessness is compounded by isolation, the communal or social aspect of dialogue helps to mitigate that isolation.

What kind of communication does *Dubliners* offer? The book does not subscribe to a view of writing as "mental telepathy," in which thoughts and feelings are "magically" transferred from the mind of the author to that of the reader. This is the view of writing that thrills Briony, the thirteen-year-old protagonist of Ian McEwan's *Atonement,* and many readers might agree with her. Briony marvels, "Reading a sentence and understanding it were the same thing; . . . Nothing lay between them. There was no gap during which the symbols were unravelled" (2001, 33). In Briony's experience, however, as opposed to her writing, there *is* a critical gap between perceiving and understanding; it is by willfully closing (or denying) that gap that she precipitates the tragedy that her subsequent writing tries to reverse or palliate. In *Dubliners,* Joyce (like McEwan and unlike the younger Briony) insists upon that gap between reading and understanding, identifying it—and not the narrative surface itself—as the "magical" space where new understanding may be born. Fictions reproduce themselves in readers, often with destructive effects, as we can see most memorably in the adventures of Flaubert's Emma Bovary, especially in the series of disastrous love affairs inspired by all the literature of passion and romance she has avidly consumed. Arguably, it is only by problematizing reality, by exposing it as socially constructed (at least in part) and therefore capable of change, that writers can give readers the opportunity to revise their habitual ways of seeing, to drive a wedge between past and future where reevaluation might occur. In order to open such a gap between fact and meaning, Joyce designs his stories as problems. Their literal meaning is vivid and clear; what is not immediately apparent is their significance. In that puzzling gap lurks the threat and the promise of a newly demythologized conception of the self, a self that—once free from the mythology that "fixes" it (polishes and simultaneously immobilizes it)—can change.

The stories in *Dubliners* challenge readers to understand not only why Joyce may have shaped them as he did, but also how to devise a method for understanding them that may also be applied to readers' own lives. Instead of functioning as a mode of "telepathy," as a naive writer like Briony might expect them to do, the stories are designed to initiate a dialogue with the reader as he or she attempts to decode them and to measure each successive attempt against the evidence on the page and against her own lived experience. The stories stimulate boredom *or* curiosity; the curious reader returns to the text with a hypothesis to be tested, thereby sparking fresh questions. The process these stories may potentially set in motion is therefore pedagogical without being didactic: they continue a dialogical tradition of pedagogy that dates back to Socrates. Socrates used the aporia—an apparently insoluble dilemma—to motivate students to reexamine their assumptions in a way that anticipates Joyce's use of stories. In classical rhetoric, aporia (literally "without passage") designates a way of placing a claim in doubt by generating arguments on both sides of an issue. It therefore simulates a stalemate buttressed by opposing points of view—a powerful contradiction that Socrates believed to be generative. New (or revised) ideas are produced not through instruction, but through a frustrating encounter with a problem or contradiction that both demands and resists easy resolution.

Socrates characterized his method not only as a dialectical pedagogy but also as a form of midwifery: he helped to bring forth new ideas. As Stephen puts it in the "Scylla and Charybdis" episode of *Ulysses*, Socrates learned dialectics from his "shrewish" wife, Xanthippe, and from his (midwife) mother he learned "how to bring thoughts into the world" (*U*, 9.235–56). The implicit connection between dialogue and midwifery allows us to imagine a pedagogical dynamic in which the text functions as a repository of embryonic possibilities.[1] Only the reader can give birth to one or more of those

1. See Plato's *Theaetetus*, translated by F. N. Cornford, for Socrates' explanation of how his ministrations as a teacher show that he practices his mother's art of midwifery. According to Socrates, his "art of midwifery is in general like [that of female midwives]; the only difference is that my patients are men, not women, and my concern is not with the body but with the soul that is in travail of birth. And the highest point of my art is the power to prove by every test whether the offspring of a young man's thought is a false phantom, or instinct with life and truth." Socrates goes on to explain that he also disposes of misbirths like a midwife, requesting that Theaetetus not be angry with him if he does so: "People have often felt like

potential conceptions, with the help of the author, whose aid—in the form of contextual information from letters and other works—helps the reader "deliver" new ideas. Or, if we frame the author-reader conversation as a dialectic, we can see that although the author may be in virtual dialogue with the reader, that dialogue is mediated by the text and conditioned by varying geographical and temporal contexts, which means that if the text is crafted carefully enough, the dialectic will be capable of producing new syntheses in different times (and places), perhaps indefinitely. In other words, the reader and her context are the only terms in the dialectic that are variable.

When applied to reading, Socrates's theory might be described as follows: the mediating text serves as the repository of "seminal stimuli" that may prompt a responsive reader to conceive new thoughts that he or she must develop, with labor, in order to "deliver" them into living, productive ideas. Alternatively, the text works as the antithetical "other," challenging the reader's assumptions and provoking him or her into a dialectical exchange that may produce an impasse, which in some cases, over time, may inspire unexpected syntheses.[2] The stories are puzzles carefully designed to motivate the reader-cum-student to find a specific, *verifiable* answer to the problem being presented, using a method that can also be applied to other situations. Such a pedagogical method was used in illuminating ways in a fraught political context by twentieth-century Brazilian educator Paulo Freire, who was imprisoned and later exiled as a political threat to the fascist military regime in Brazil because of his success in making peasants not only literate, but also critically astute and willing to take collaborative action to improve their living conditions.[3] According to the Brazilian government, he

---

that toward me and been positively ready to bite me for taking away some foolish notion they have conceived. They do not see that I am doing them a kindness. They have not learned that no divinity is ever ill-disposed toward man, nor is such action on my part due to unkindness; it is only that I am not permitted to acquiesce in falsehood and suppress the truth." I am grateful to Sheila Murnaghan for this reference.

2. Paulo Freire connects liberation with both pedagogy and childbirth as well. He argues, "Liberation is thus a childbirth, and a painful one" (1970, 49).

3. See the discussion of Freire's career in Herzog 1994, 24.

was turning people into revolutionaries simply by teaching them how to read more independently and honestly.

Freire's pedagogical method helps to illuminate one particular facet of the way Joyce conceived *Dubliners* at the beginning of the twentieth century. The first stories of *Dubliners* were published as the creations of "Stephen Daedalus," a character loosely modeled on Joyce himself, who in *A Portrait of the Artist as a Young Man* proclaimed a desire to forge "the uncreated conscience of [his] race" (*P*, 213).[4] The mature Joyce, while distancing himself from Stephen's self-protective hauteur, seems to have sympathized with and even shared Stephen's artistic objective: to inspire his readers to generate greater self-awareness and the ethical responsibility that attends it.[5] Joyce wrote to the publisher of *Dubliners* that his collection served as a "nicely polished looking-glass" in which the Irish people might see themselves (*Letters I*, 64). What he may have meant can be illuminated by a comparison with the methods and aims of Freire: Freire set out to instigate a process that he called "conscientization" in Brazilian peasants, a purpose comparable to Stephen's (and the mature Joyce's) angry desire to "create" a conscience in the Irish. Conscientization, for Freire, involves "learning to perceive social, political and economic contradictions, and to take action against the oppressive elements of reality" (1970, 35);[6] it is therefore "a movement from a dominated consciousness to a critically active consciousness" (Herzog 1994, 24). Freire argued that indoctrinated people must learn to perceive contradictions because "oppressive reality absorbs those within it and thereby acts to submerge human beings' consciousness" (1970, 51).

Freire's contradictions function like Socrates's aporia, although Freire lays more stress on the sociopolitical implications of an awakened conscience. Freire understands dialogical education as implicitly revolutionary, which can help us appreciate why Joyce claimed that *Dubliners* constituted

4. All subsequent references to *A Portrait of the Artist as a Young Man* will be to the J. Joyce 2000 edition unless otherwise indicated.

5. "Conscience" designates an ethical and moral ability to differentiate right from wrong, but one of its obsolete meanings is "consciousness; self-knowledge."

6. In this edition, the term *conscientization* is not translated, but is identified as *conscientização*.

a "first step towards the spiritual liberation of [his] country."[7] Like Joyce's before him, Freire's methods of sensitizing readers to the contradictions in the dominant ideology rely heavily on dialogue (rather than narration). He encourages "students" to work *with* their "teachers" to perceive and solve the problems in the construction of the social conditions that limit them.[8] Similarly, readers of *Dubliners* are asked to join the author in a scrupulous analysis of the paralysis—rooted in hopelessness—that precludes characters (like many of the readers they mirror) from seeing themselves accurately, and so from acting with a greater degree of freedom.

Freire's way of distinguishing between the animal and the human in relation to their respective environments helps to clarify the way in which critical reflection can serve as the first step toward psychic liberation. Freire argues that the animal is part of his environment.[9] The animal cannot reflect on that environment, which means that he cannot transform it; instead, he must learn to adapt to it.[10] If the environment stops yielding food, an animal cannot decide to grow corn (thereby changing the environment); he can only find a new habitat. The human, in contrast, *can* interact with her environment; she can both reflect on and strategically transform some (but not all) of the objective circumstances that limit her. In a social situation of

7. Letter to Grant Richards, May 20, 1906 (*SL*, 88). Stephen Dedalus's revolutionary tendencies are made apparent (framed by ironic self-awareness) in a diary entry at the end of *A Portrait of the Artist as a Young Man*, when he describes himself talking to E. C., his love interest: "I made a sudden gesture of a revolutionary nature. I must have looked like a fellow throwing a handful of peas into the air" (213).

8. Freire calls teachers "teacher-students" and students "student-teachers" to emphasize the similarity between them in their shared problem-solving mission. He argues, "Education must begin with the solution of the teacher-student contradiction, by reconciling the poles of the contradiction so that both are simultaneously teachers *and* students" (1970, 72).

9. "Organically bound to their prop, animals do not distinguish between themselves and the world" (ibid., 100).

10. "Accordingly, animals are not limited by limit-situations—which are historical—but rather by the entire prop. And the appropriate role for animals is not to relate to their prop (in that event, the prop would be a world), but to adapt to it. . . . Their productive activity is subordinated to the satisfaction of a physical necessity which is simply stimulating, rather than challenging" (ibid.).

oppression, however, the human being's ability to transform her environment is constrained by her unconscious identification with her oppressor. Similarly, her oppressor is bound by the need to ensure her continuing docility, which he does primarily through indoctrination (a form of education).[11] Indoctrination produces hopelessness, because it teaches subordinate groups that they are both defective and powerless. In other words, through indoctrination, subdominant populations are reduced to the state of animals (or small children), led to believe that they cannot change their world and must simply adapt to it. The refrain of "it was useless" that runs throughout *Dubliners* accents the hopelessness that characterizes psychic oppression—and psychic oppression is what allows political or military oppression to continue when physical violence is not actively in use.

Liberation, according to Freire, begins with awareness, "acts of critical cognition," which differ significantly from docile or even receptive listening. And critical cognition is possible only if the subject is able to recognize and thereby question her unconscious identification with the oppressor (as well as with the environment shaped by oppression), thereby gaining perspective on herself and her world. What makes that critical distance so difficult to achieve is the compound construction of the colonized subject. Freire, like many postcolonial critics, notes that the colonized subject is divided,[12] that the oppressors have deposited their views and values in her, much as a parasite lives within a host. Because the oppressed have learned to identify with and even admire the oppressor who lives psychically within them, "having internalized the image of the oppressor and adopted his guidelines" (Freire 1970, 47), they will desire authentic existence and freedom, but they will also fear it. The fear stems from a fear of ejecting the familiar image of the

11. Freire also argues that oppressors are limited by their possessiveness, their tendency to transform everything into an object they can own and dominate: "In the egoistic pursuit of *having* as a possessing class, [the oppressors] suffocate in their own possessions and no longer *are;* they merely *have*" (ibid., 59).

12. Compare W. E. B. DuBois, in *The Souls of Black Folk,* who argues that the American Negro is plagued by "double consciousness": "One ever feels his twoness,—an American, a Negro; two souls, two thoughts, two unreconciled strivings; two warring ideals in one dark body, whose dogged strength alone keeps it from being torn asunder" (1965, 215).

oppressor and "replacing it with autonomy and responsibility" (ibid.); it is a fear of recognizing and resolving the (unconscious) psychic ambivalence that justifies their immobility. As Freire explains, "The oppressed, who have adapted to the structure of domination in which they are immersed, and have become resigned to it, are inhibited from waging the struggle for freedom so long as they feel incapable of running the risks it requires. Moreover, the struggle for freedom threatens not only the oppressor, but also their own oppressed comrades who are fearful of still greater oppression" (ibid.). To reject the oppressor within is to give up "the illusion of acting through the action of the oppressors" and to replace that illusion with action that is deliberately chosen, in readiness to accept the consequences of that action. It is to speak out instead of "being silent, castrated in their power to create and re-create, in their power to transform the world" (ibid., 48). So when, in "After the Race," the narrator describes "clumps of people" in Dublin raising "the cheer of the gratefully oppressed" (*D*, 49), he is registering a perception that Dubliners, like most colonized people who have been shaped by indoctrination, feel unconsciously indebted to those who have relieved them of their freedom and responsibility, because they have "learned" that on their own they would be incapable of wielding such freedom effectively.

Would-be liberators or educators cannot succeed in creating a conscience by simply explaining the nature of oppression, because the oppressed, as they listen to these explanations, must sustain their passive position in doing so.[13] Instead, Freire argues that the oppressed must be stimulated "to participate

13. "Attempting to liberate the oppressed without their reflective participation in the act of liberation is to treat them as objects which must be saved from a burning building" (Freire 1970, 65). Freire devotes most of his second chapter to differentiating between two kinds of education: what he calls a "banking concept," in which educators "deposit" their ideas in the (presumptively empty) minds of their students, a process that leaves no room for creativity, and "problem-posing" education, which "affirms men and women as beings in the process of *becoming*—as unfinished, uncompleted beings in and with a likewise unfinished reality. . . . The unfinished character of human beings and the transformational character of reality necessitate that education be an ongoing activity" (ibid., 84). When students are encouraged (through dialogue and a mediating text or image) to meet the challenge of the limits that circumscribe their creativity, they begin to demythologize their reality.

in developing the pedagogy of their liberation" (1970, 48); they must discover for themselves that liberation is desirable, and do so as subjects, not as objects (ibid., 67). What they are fighting for is the "freedom to create and to construct, to wonder and to venture," and this cannot be achieved by quietly listening (or reading) (ibid., 68). Freire's way of bypassing this difficulty was to use a carefully chosen "problem-posing" or enigmatic work of art—he used visual images—to inspire active dialogue. If the image was related to problems in the larger culture, the person decoding it would find it easier to decode or demystify his culture at the same time. (Cultural decoding enabled those individuals that Freire called "the oppressed" to see *both* themselves and the oppressors as dehumanized by their relationship [1970, 58].) This puzzling artwork (which Freire calls a "codification") has the potential to inspire reflection, to act as a mirror (like Joyce's nicely polished looking-glass). This mirror may reveal an image of the beholders as emotionally and economically dependent upon the very beings they despise and envy. As Freire explains, the "subject must recognize himself in the object (the coded concrete existential situation) and recognize the object as a situation in which he finds himself" (1970, 105). More accurate self-perception may in turn enable the oppressed to "perceive the reality of oppression not as a closed world from which there is no exit, but as a limiting situation which they can transform" (ibid., 49). This is also one of the functions that the stories of *Dubliners* were designed to serve: to be enigmatic yet recognizable re-presentations of the social environment. Joyce, however, treats limiting circumstances not as a punishment that the inhabitants deserve because of their inadequacies, but as a problem that can be addressed only through a demystification of the individual's unconscious complicity with the forces that limit him.

Freire's pedagogical method turns out to be a thoughtful, extended process that begins with a group of "teachers" who begin by trying to learn about the lives of the people they would "instruct." They immerse themselves in these people's day-to-day lives, trying both individually and collectively to understand the unique symbolic "language" they use to express their cultural experience. Each "teacher" repeatedly formulates his impressions, checking them against the perceptions of others in the group and also against subsequent experiences. It is only then that the instructors choose a "codification," a work of art akin to those cultural experiences, that serves to re-present those experiences not as givens but as problems to be reevaluated and solved. When people try to decode a problem in a group, the experience of other points of view prompts them to reconsider their previous considerations (ibid., 112). It is by stimulating new perceptions of a previous perception and "knowledge of the previous knowledge" that people learn to see themselves differently (ibid., 115). Freire argues that education is "sympathetic" in the etymological sense of the word (people sorrowing together about their circumstances), and when everyone involved approaches a given problem with humility, everyday reality takes on new aspects; it "stops looking like a blind alley" (ibid., 90, 108, 105–6). Instead, what used to be an unsurpassable limit takes on the appearance of a threshold of untested possibilities (ibid., 99).

One of the most important prerequisites for engaging in dialogue is an awareness of how easy it is to "project ignorance onto others" without perceiving one's own (ibid., 90). Joyce's Leopold Bloom makes a similar assertion in the "Cyclops" episode of *Ulysses* when he remarks, "Some people . . . can see the mote in others' eyes but they can't see the beam in their own" (*U*, 12.1237–38). The first enemy that Freire and his team of educators must fight is not the oppressor (or England, in Joyce's case), but hopelessness, which they describe as "a form of silence, of denying the world and fleeing from it" (1970, 91). They, like Joyce when he depicts his city of wistful yet ultimately despairing inhabitants, are using recognizable yet puzzlingly artful "mirrors" to stimulate new reflections that can be developed through discussion. Such discussions are optimally conducted with hope, curiosity, humility, and determination. The interlocutors "are neither ignoramuses nor perfect sages"; instead, they are "only people who are attempting, together, to learn more than they now know" by engaging in critical thinking (ibid., 90). Such discussion "becomes a common striving towards awareness of reality and towards self awareness" (ibid., 107). As Freire insists, "I cannot think *for others* or *without others,* nor can others think *for me.* Even if the people's thinking is superstitious or naïve, it is only as they rethink their assumptions in action that they can change. Producing and acting upon their own ideas—not consuming those of others—must constitute that process" (ibid., 108).

What readers sometimes fail to realize about *Dubliners* is that the stories are not only an end in themselves, but also a means to other ends. As we have been arguing, one such end is to prompt the reader to see herself—and perhaps her own moments of hopelessness—in a new light, the light reflected (and refracted) by these stories of failed yearning. Joyce's work, then, can be seen as an effort to mediate (and perhaps even remediate) the de facto relation between the individual and his or her social and material circumstances. His aim is to show ordinary citizens exactly where and how hope founders, and beyond that to instigate political and social change, which he, like Freire after him, believes begins with greater cognitive freedom in individuals.

At this point, our argument takes a controversial turn, as we widen the frame of analogues to Joyce's *Dubliners* to include the parables of Jesus of Nazareth. We want to make it clear at the outset that we are examining these parables not in a religious context but in a literary and political one. Our approach to the topic of historical Christianity is not doctrinal, but secular. We concur with Hannah Arendt in *The Human Condition* when she advocates extending political analysis to include events that have been understood in primarily religious terms:

> It has been in the nature of our tradition of political thought . . . to exclude from articulate conceptualization a great variety of authentic political experiences, among which we need not be surprised to find some of an even elementary nature. Certain aspects of the teaching of Jesus of Nazareth which are not primarily related to the Christian religious message but sprang from experiences in the small and closely knit community of his followers, bent on challenging the public authorities in Israel, certainly belong among them, even though they have been neglected because of their allegedly exclusively religious nature. (1958, 238–39)

The public authorities that Jesus and his followers challenged were not only the Jewish leaders of the synagogue; they also included, less directly, the Romans who were occupying Israel. Their challenges to orthodoxy were nonviolent ones that advocated inner self-development and a reversal of religious exclusivity or intolerance, but the popularity of the group's teachings made the authorities see them as politically subversive, a view that culminated in the ringleader's execution.

In an influential book, *Parables as Subversive Speech: Jesus as Pedagogue of the Oppressed*, William Herzog argues that Freire's codifications were analogous to Jesus's parables (1994, 16): "Living in a visual culture, Freire used pictures as codifications; Jesus, who lived in an oral culture, used storytelling" (ibid., 27–28). We would extend Herzog's account to say that Joyce used written literature in a similar way. Herzog claims that the purpose of Jesus's parables has often been misunderstood: "The parable . . . was not primarily a vehicle to communicate theology or ethics but a codification designed to stimulate social analysis and to expose the contradictions between the actual situation of its hearers and the Torah of God's justice" (ibid., 28). Like Freire, he argues that coded works of art can help readers and listeners to "disclose and explore . . . larger social, political, economic, and ideological systems" (ibid., 7). Because codifications are "narrative snapshots of everyday life" (ibid.), they encourage listeners (or readers) to reflect on their relation to their own experience. "As conversation moves from description to analysis, the learners leave the surface structure and begin to explore the deep structure of the codification" (ibid., 20–21). Herzog pays particular attention to Freire's reliance on what he called "generative words," words that are "charged with existential meaning and phonetically rich" that give expression to the speakers' "thematic universe" (ibid., 19–20) to stimulate deeper awareness. Joyce's *Dubliners* likewise relies on "generative words." Words like *chandler* and *lamp* in "A Little Cloud" expand and interconnect with the name *Ignatius* (fiery) and the *cloud* of the title, and ultimately engage a larger buried context in the Hebrew scriptures and in Dante's *Inferno* to provide a surprisingly coherent cultural context for Little Chandler's seemingly ordinary dilemma. In their essay on "A Painful Case," Paul Saint-Amour and Karen Lawrence show that the word *case* operates as another such generative node. The famous words on the first page of *Dubliners—gnomon, simony,* and *paralysis*—work the same way.

Freire helps to illuminate the implicitly political dimension of Joyce's writing. It is political not in the usual sense but in its capacity to prompt individuals to reexamine their foundational assumptions about their relation to the world, a reevaluation that may generate a desire to change their circumstances through action. Interestingly, a theological context for understanding *Dubliners* works in much the same way as Freire's revolutionary one: if we understand the stories as part of an ancient pedagogical tradition associated with spiritual teaching—specifically, the tradition of teaching through parables—we see that the stories "teach" in much the same way, that is, by presenting narrative "problems" designed not to indoctrinate, but to awaken critical acumen and to promote new self-awareness.[14] Critics are well aware that Joyce's metaphors for his artistic techniques were drawn from Christianity, most notably the notion of epiphany (which Joyce turned into a literary form) and the suggestion that the stories in *Dubliners* were *epicleti*,[15] but few have attended to Joyce's suggestion that his short stories are also parables. Joyce makes this connection in the "Aeolus" episode of *Ulysses* by fictionally restaging the origin of *Dubliners* (when George Russell asked Joyce for a piece to publish in the *Irish Homestead*). In "Aeolus" editor Myles Crawford asks Stephen to contribute to his paper: "I want you to write something for me, he said. Something with a bite in it. You can do it. I see it in your face" (*U*, 8.616–17). A few minutes later, Stephen, after thinking "Dubliners" to himself (*U*, 8.922), recites to Professor McHugh a parable, "*A Pisgah Sight of Palestine or The Parable of the Plums*" (*U*, 8.1057–58), which is similar in gnomic specificity to the stories Joyce wrote for *Dubliners*. In *Finnegans*

14. See Jill Shashaty, "Reading *Dubliners* Parabolically," *James Joyce Quarterly* 47, no. 2 (2010).

15. Joyce wrote a series of epiphanies, which were short sketches illustrating or possibly precipitating a moment of revelation, and he had Stephen Daedalus propound a theory of epiphany in *Stephen Hero* (*SH*, 211–13). Some of his epiphanies were woven into *A Portrait of the Artist as a Young Man*. Joyce referred to the early stories of *Dubliners* as *epicleti* in a letter to Constantine Curran in August 1904. As Robert Scholes and A. Walton Litz have explained, *epiklesis* is a term used in the Eastern church referring to the invocation of the Holy Ghost to transform the bread and wine into the body and blood of Christ. The Greek word also means "reproach" or "imputation" (1996, 247–53). According to *The Catholic Encyclopedia, epiklesis* is actually a prayer that occurs in all Eastern liturgies and used to be part of Western ones as well "in which the celebrant prays that God may send down His Holy Spirit to change this bread and wine into the Body and Blood of His Son. This form has given rise to one of the chief controversies between the Eastern and Western Churches, inasmuch as all Eastern schismatics now believe that the Epiklesis, and not the words of Institution, is the essential form (or at least the essential complement) of the sacrament" (http://www .newadvent.org/cathen/05502a.htm). Although Joyce rejected the Catholic Church and gave up his youthful belief in its teachings, he, like Stephen Dedalus in *A Portrait of the Artist as a Young Man*, arguably remained "supersaturated with the religion in which [he] say[s] [he] disbelieve[s]" (*P*, 202).

Wake, the narrator refers to the fable based on Aesop's fable "The Fox and the Grapes" ("The Mookse and the Gripes") as a "fabulist's parable" (*FW,* 152), one that contains a character, Nuvoletta (which means "little cloud"), who appears in a story that parallels that of "A Little Cloud" in *Dubliners.*

As a genre, parables work much like aporia in Socratic dialogues, dialectic oppositions, or Freire's "codifications." Parables are simple, brief narratives that conclude not with a resolution to the conflicts they present, but with a puzzle. As a narrative unit, a parable is distinctly unsatisfactory. It leaves the reader with a crux—a narrative dilemma without a solution to be found directly within the parable itself. A parable shares with Joyce's *Dubliners* the feeling of nakedness or denuded context we discussed earlier: it is an incomplete text that relies on its audience to process the bare, bewildering information it presents. Consider the parable of the vineyard workers from the Christian scriptures, which relates a tale about unemployed workers waiting in the marketplace for hire. As the day progresses, a vineyard owner hires several workers every few hours, even into the late afternoon, but at the end of the day pays each one the same wage. This, the parable tells us enigmatically, is what the Kingdom of God is like. Such a story immediately raises a host of questions: Is this fair? Is the owner generous or inconsiderate? How should the workers respond? And most important, what does such a parable suggest about the Kingdom of God? Choose any story from *Dubliners* and a similar list of narrative questions will quickly grow. Why is the priest in "The Sisters" laughing in his confession box? Why is the story titled "The Sisters"? What does the boy in "An Encounter" believe that green eyes signify? Where does the slavey get the gold coin she gives to Corley in "Two Gallants"?

Parables become dialogic teaching tools rather than didactic lessons because these sorts of narrative cruxes necessarily generate discomfort in the audience—confusion, embarrassment, frustration, disappointment—which in turn produces dialogue to resolve (or even simply relieve) that discomfort. Such audience responses thus function as hooks that may draw readers and listeners into the narrative in order to grapple with the contradictions parables contain. What is true of parables is true of Joyce's *Dubliners* as well: the stories yield little until audiences engage their narrative cruxes. Such engagement can happen in many ways: a nagging debate in a single reader's own mind, a piece of responsive writing, a conversation between readers, a classroom debate, even a newfound sense of curiosity that leads someone to approach a particular story and now other narratives (whether fictional or not) more critically. (Jennifer Levine's response to Andrew Gibson's essay in the response to "Ivy Day in the Committee Room" is a wonderful illustration of how readers may collectively respond to a puzzling piece of writing.) Like Freire's codifications, parables are not didactic because a parable refers to no overarching authority with predetermined answers. Authority resides in textually generated dialogue and is always contingent on how well that dialogue reflects the integrity of the parable, the life experiences of the audience, and openness to new ways of thinking.

It is important to stress that parables are not allegories (and neither are the stories in *Dubliners*). Allegories are stories whose significance can be determined by a single predetermined referent. Knowledge of the referent becomes the key that reveals connections among the story's disparate elements and unlocks its mysteries. Instead, parables are metaphors in which the relationship between the story and its significance (its referent) shifts with each new reading, with each new conversation about the parable. As audiences engage a parable, or the stories in *Dubliners,* the narrative and its significance define and redefine one another in a dynamic, open-ended process worked out through dialogue. To observe that Joyce designed *Dubliners* as a series of parables, then, is to appreciate the gap each one contains between its facts and its potential meaning, its multiple applications. This gap is a lure that invites readers into the stories to create new meanings out of the problems it presents. As Walter Benjamin observes in his essay "The Storyteller," it is precisely in not explaining a story that a storyteller ensures its germinative power by providing ample opportunity for fresh interpretations amid new readerships, cultures, and moments in history.[16]

The stories of Joyce's *Dubliners* resemble parables in content as well as in structure. Despite the great age of the parable genre and its appearance

16. Benjamin writes, "It is half the art of storytelling to keep a story free from explanation as one reproduces it." The story relates with accuracy, but "it is left up to [the reader] to interpret things the way he understands them, and thus the narrative achieves an amplitude that information lacks" (1968, 89).

across cultures, its central subject matter is arguably the frustration of desire. Characters dramatize this frustration as their hopes and ideals are thwarted by oppressive conditions and their own failings. Audiences experience this frustration when they attempt to locate justice or redemption in the disordered world the parable presents. Ideally, readerly frustration inspires a combination of curiosity and dialogue that will illuminate the mechanisms of oppression the story contains. This process can unveil the inner workings of both social oppression and psychic submission, and in some cases, by shedding light on this destructive relationship, can help a reader to derail it. Like Freire's pedagogical method, parables and the stories in *Dubliners* invite audiences into frustrated, paralyzed lives in order to bring the psychic, social, and political structures of frustration and paralysis to light. The hope is that understanding may produce motivation: the motivation to try to dismantle such structures—not in the fictional world, but in the reader's.

What Herzog, Freire, Socrates, and Jesus all help readers to understand is that dialogical pedagogy is considered a danger to the status quo. Socrates and Jesus were both killed, and Freire was imprisoned and exiled, for their ways of teaching people to "read." Joyce, we would argue, modeled his own teaching on such examples. Like Freire, he used the vocabulary of actual Dubliners "as a tool of social analysis" so that as people learned to read the stories, they could simultaneously learn "to read their culture, including its systems of domination, exploitation, and marginalization" (Herzog 1994, 19). Moreover, by reading *Dubliners,* we can not only learn about the specific systems of domination in place in Ireland at the turn of the last century, but also apply what we learn to systems of domination in our own cultures, especially those systems that are racial, sexual, and economic.

Freire believed that "all true education involves the complementary acts of denunciation and annunciation, denouncing oppression in all its forms and announcing a new future" (ibid., 22). Such a statement gives new meaning to the symbolic overtones of the two male characters, Michael and Gabriel, who preside over the last great story in *Dubliners,* "The Dead." Michael was the archangel of denunciation: he fought Satan and barred Adam and Eve from returning to the Garden of Eden. Michael Furey, too, enters the story as an implicit denunciation of Gabriel's self-satisfaction. Gabriel, in contrast, is the archangel of the Annunciation, who was sent to Mary to tell her that she was bearing the child of God.[17] This last story, like *Dubliners* itself, stages a mighty contest between denunciation and annunciation that cannot finally be decided, because it is the reader's part to enter into conversations that may help him or her do both: to labor with others in an effort to figure out what to denounce and announce in the present and in countries other than late-nineteenth-century Ireland. In their essay "Dead Again," Margot Norris and Vincent Pecora illustrate their long effort to appreciate the perfect balance of opposed possibilities that concludes "The Dead." "The Dead" ends with dawn, but it is a dawn in which darkness and light are marbled together in equal measure. It is the reader who decides (usually unconsciously) whether the book conveys hope or despair. What Pecora and Norris demonstrate is that it conveys both.

By concluding *Dubliners* with "The Dead," Joyce makes a powerful suggestion that dialogue is inevitable, especially when individuals try to avoid it. The inescapability of dialogue (here, dialogue with the dead) implicitly suggests that it is preferable to pursue dialogue actively when productive, collaborative exchange is still possible, instead of waiting until one is haunted by the echoes of communications one has missed. "The Dead" is concerned with a ghostly visitation that comes to Gretta through music (Bartell D'Arcy's singing of "The Lass of Aughrim"), and then to Gabriel through Gretta. But there are two additional ghostly dialogues buried in allusions to poetry and music, especially to two particular poems by Robert Browning and Thomas Moore. When mentally rehearsing the speech that he plans to give after dinner, Gabriel worries that the lines he had planned to quote from Robert Browning "would be above the heads of his hearers," and he reflects, "Some quotation that they could recognise from Shakespeare or from the Melodies would be better" (*D*, 221). Later, we learn that Gabriel published a review of Robert Browning's poems in the *Daily Express* and that Miss Ivors is enthusiastic about the review, if not its venue. Finally, the story reverberates with one of the sentences about Browning that Gabriel had written in his review: "*One feels that one is listening to a thought-tormented music*" (*D*, 238), a locution that later inflects Gabriel's powerful erotic and aesthetic

---

17. Florence Walzl (1966) wrote on this "angelic" opposition many years ago.

response to Gretta when she is listening to the music on the stairs and he longs to paint her in that attitude, titling the painting *"Distant Music"* (*D*, 260–61). Still later, language from a letter he had written to Gretta years earlier also comes to him like "distant music" (*D, 266*).

The "distant music" from Browning that runs through "The Dead" like a haunting score quite possibly takes its source from one of Browning's most influential poems about such music, "A Toccata of Galuppi's." The poem is a dramatic monologue from *Men and Women* spoken by a living scientist to a dead Venetian composer, Baldassaro Galuppi, while he listens to Galuppi's music. The scientist begins by dismissing the music as "old," far away, concerned with young flirtatious couples, now dead. As he listens, the flirting couples come alive in his imagination, and he conceives the music as talking to them of their mortality, offering them sympathy, inciting them to live in the moment. At the end of the poem, the dead Galuppi's voice speaks, like a "ghostly cricket," directly to the scientist, agreeing that Venice and its former occupants are dead and ironically assuring the scientist that he will "not die, it cannot be!" Galuppi's question is about the soul and what comes of it after life ends, but what is most important to Joyce's story is the effect his visitation produces on the scientist who listened to him. The dead have become "dear" ("Dear dead women, with such hair, too—") and their vitality greater than that of the speaker, who reports feeling "chilly and grown old." The living man suddenly experiences himself as less alive than the laughing, flirting crowds of a bygone Venice.

Gabriel's allusion to Thomas Moore as a possibly preferable substitute for Robert Browning might seem insignificant were it not for the fact that "The Dead" is often said to have been named after one of the songs in Thomas Moore's *Irish Melodies:* "O Ye Dead!" Joyce's brother Stanislaus had heard the song performed by the Irish baritone Henry Plunket Greene in 1905, and Joyce asked for a copy and learned to sing it.[18] Like Browning's poem "A Toccata of Galuppi's," "O Ye Dead!" records a musical dialogue

18. Kevin McDermott and Ralph Richey have recorded the version of "O Ye Dead!" that was performed by Henry Plunket Greene in *More Music from the Works of James Joyce* (Sunphone Records, 2006).

between living and dead. In the first verse, the living ask the dead why they have left their graves to haunt the spot where the people who mourned them lie dead. In the second verse, the dead eerily answer that they have come back as shadows to taste the sensual delights of life ere they "freeze mid Hecla's snows" (Hekla is a snow-covered volcano in Iceland; William Blake presents it as the realm of winter in "To Winter").

"The Dead," then, stages a whole series of dialogues or perhaps contests between living and dead that prompt us to ask, who is most "alive" to the sights and sounds of sensual life, those persons who take them for granted or those who miss them? Gabriel faces Michael, pitting beginnings (or birth) against endings (or death); living and dead speak to one another through music not only as Gretta listens to "The Lass of Aughrim," but also as the scientist listens to Venetian music in Browning's poem and as the living sing out to the dead in Moore's melody. Finally, a dead author is talking to a living reader through the medium of Joyce's text, asking, perhaps, if the reader is as alive as he or she may think. What does it mean to be alive? Can one answer this question without dialogue?

TO RETURN TO Ian McEwan's *Atonement,* we could say that what McEwan calls Briony's crime is a very common maneuver in reading: readers tend to substitute what they think they *know* for what they claim they have *seen.* In fact, this certainty takes the place of what the readers *have not* seen: the challenge is to see what does not fit into the narrative patterns of expectation that are already in place. Like Briony, readers often see what they expect to see, things that play into the "story" of life they are constructing. The price and consolation of rewriting reality in this way are that it protects the subject against chaos, against change, and against seeing and hearing something new and potentially disturbing (as a child, Briony was exceptionally neat and orderly in her habits). Joyce, like McEwan, might call the understandable and ignorant impulse to make the world conform to one's private story a crime against reality, against others, and against the self. As he once wrote in defense of the technique he used to write *Dubliners,* it is vital to adhere to factual truth, however uncomfortable that truth may be: "He is a very bold man who dares to alter in the presentment, much less to deform, whatever he has seen and heard" (*Letters II,* 134).

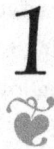

Silence and Fractals in "The Sisters"

MICHAEL GRODEN AND VICKI MAHAFFEY

Mike and Vicki agreed to write two independent ten-page essays on "The Sisters" and to exchange them. They met in a Pizza Express in the Bloomsbury section of London to comment on one another's drafts. Vicki liked Mike's essay, but Mike had reservations about Vicki's: she had outlined a way of understanding the damage that the story alludes to but does not identify, which is exactly what Mike discouraged readers from doing. Moreover, Vicki's tone was passionate, in sharp contrast to the dispassionate observational acuity that Mike appreciated in the boy and believed the critic should emulate. Vicki ruminated over Mike's comments for several months, trying to find a way of approaching the story that might accommodate both their perspectives. This essay is the result of that process.

At the gateway of *Dubliners* we find this spare, narratively uneventful story about death and damage told from the sharply perceptive yet uncomprehending perspective of a young boy. We may well look for a Dantean inscription above this "door" to a collection of stories about Dublin:

> *Per me si va ne la città dolente.*
> *Per me si va ne l'etterno dolore*
> *Per me si va tra la perduta gente.*
> *Giustizia mosse il mio alto fattore*
> *fecemi la divina podestate,*
> *la somma sapienza e'l primo amore.*

> Through me you go to the grief-wracked city.
>
> Through me to everlasting pain you go.
>
> Through me you go and pass among lost souls.
>
> Justice inspired my exalted Creator.
>
> I am a creature of the Holiest Power,
>
> of Wisdom in the Highest and Primal Love.

The inscription ends with the famous words "*Lasciate ogne speranza, voi ch'intrate,*" which is usually translated, "Abandon all hope, ye who enter here" (Alighieri 2006, 20–21).[1] The reader of "The Sisters" is indeed entering a "grief-wracked city," the hopelessness of which is marked in the first sentence: "There was no hope for him this time." In order to explore this urban underworld of stagnation and despair with the requisite sympathy and clarity of mind (with what Dante calls Love as well as Justice), its readers, like its characters, must be willing to postpone the consolation of meaning, defined as a conceptual framework that arranges isolated perceptions into larger patterns. If this hope for immediate apprehension of meaning is not left at the door, readers will be effectively barred from entering the collection of stories, for "The Sisters" is its portal.

Although meaning has been banished from the consciousness of both characters and narrators, the narrator's responses to sensual stimuli are almost preternaturally acute, and readers would do well to imitate that heightened sensitivity to sight and hearing. Joyce's underworld is not just the city of Dublin at the turn of the century, but the unconscious minds of his characters. In order to see beneath the textual surface, readers must sharpen their perceptions and delay judgment, reading the silences as well as the words and looking for the geometries of fact and feeling that subtend what is consciously expressed.

Readers of "The Sisters" are immediately confronted with a dilemma, then: given the reluctance of the narrator to explain what is going on, whether to himself or to an imagined audience, is the reader being prompted to generate explanations or to resist them (remembering that to resist explanation

---

1. Kirkpatrick translates the last line of the inscription differently: "Surrender as you enter every hope you have."

is to accept the almost surgical delineation of irreparably damaged lives)? Alternatively, if we are prompted to do both, to understand and accept the inevitability of such damage under the prevailing conditions, how might we—with the equal measures of justice and love that characterized the creator of Dante's hell—scrupulously create a context for passing through and beyond the specter of characters hopelessly trapped in their ordinary lives? This interpretive crux is mirrored by what might be called an affective one concerning our reaction to the priest in the story: to what extent do we respect and even admire the priest's fatherly "wish" for the boy, his willingness to mentor him, and to what extent do we interrogate and perhaps deplore the implications of what he has communicated?

The two authors of this essay initially took opposite approaches. Mike underscored the story's insistence on tracing—both in itself and in the figure of the dead priest—what Euclid called a "gnomon." He pointed out that this geometrical figure of a parallelogram that has had a smaller parallelogram removed from one of its corners can be described as either "incomplete" (a parallelogram is "missing," requiring the reader to complete it)[2] or "damaged" (with the emphasis falling on the figure that remains, requiring only that the reader register the damage and acknowledge its irreparability).[3] Mike offers the example of how the boy in the story, alone in his bedroom after listening to Old Cotter utter several pronouncements that trail off without conclusion (indicated in the printed text by ellipses), "puzzled [his] head to extract meaning from his unfinished sentences" (*D*, 11). The boy does not

2. Margot Norris refers to what she calls the "familiar notion of gnomonic interpretation" of the stories in *Dubliners:* "The stories are incomplete and require interpretative activity to complete them" (2003, 2–3).

3. Mike cites two different formulas for defining a gnomon: the *Oxford English Dictionary*'s definition of it as incomplete ("the geometric figure that remains after a parallelogram has been removed from a similar but larger parallelogram with which it shares a corner," cited in Herring 1982, 134), and J. Cirlot's characterization of the gnomon as "damaged" in his *Dictionary of Symbols* (quoted in Jackson and McGinley 1993, 11). This second view is underscored by the way the *American Heritage Dictionary* defines *gnomon*, as "the geometric figure that remains after a parallelogram has been removed from a similar but larger parallelogram with which it shares a corner."

try to complete the sentences but merely attempts to draw out—extract—a meaning from the fragments he heard. Here, the text offers one model for how we might go about interpreting it, one that respects its status as a "gnomon" and accords with Derek Attridge's argument that "there is sometimes a virtue in not interpreting"; "responding fully to a text can mean allowing its otherness to remain other, unassimilable, unconceptualizable, irreducible, resistant" (Attridge 2000, 51). Accepting the priest as simply damaged allows us to temper our expectations of him, thereby leaving us freer to sympathize with the boy, who has just lost the only "father" the story suggests that he has.

Mike also proposed reading the story through the boy's silences, his refusals to speak or to explain, to fill in the "missing corner" of a gnomon, his uncompromising insistence on seeing "nothing that is not there" and "the nothing that is" (Stevens 1990). Jean-Michel Rabaté underscores the difference between the boy who observes and the adult who narrates when he argues that the boy is not a narrator but an interpreter (the implication being that it is only the adult who narrates [1982, 21]), in contrast to his adult counterpart, whose narration is marked by a "refusal to interpret" this story from his childhood (Norris 2003, 20). In order to note the changing quality of the boy's silences, it is helpful to separate the story into six scenes: in three of the scenes he is alone (the first scene, in which he stands before Father Flynn's house looking for a sign that the priest has died; the third scene, when he is in his bedroom after listening to Old Cotter and his aunt and uncle discussing the priest's death; and the fourth scene, the next morning returning to Father Flynn's house and reading the sign announcing his death). In the other three, he is with other people (the second scene, in his home with his aunt, uncle, and Old Cotter, when he learns about the priest's death; the fifth scene, in Father Flynn's room with his aunt and the priest's sister Nannie as they observe the corpse in the coffin; and the sixth scene, downstairs in the Flynns' home with his aunt, Nannie, and the priest's other sister, Eliza). Two of the scenes in which he is with other people (the second and sixth) are presented as quoted conversations interspersed with the narrator's observations and comments, whereas the fifth scene, like the three in which the boy is alone, consists entirely of narration.

In the scenes where the boy is with other people, he is, as has often been noted, almost completely silent. Except for two questions near the beginning of the scene with Old Cotter—"Who?" and "Is he dead?" (*D*, 10)—the boy says nothing aloud anywhere in the story. His silence seems to change as the story progresses: in the first scene it is angry; in the second it becomes more bewildered and conflicted; and finally in the third it is opaque as the narration offers a neutral chronicle, a Joycean epiphany, without any clues to the boy's mental state at the time.

If we note the shifts in the boy's silences, from anger to the awkwardness born of bewilderment, to oblique refusal to comment, we see the boy change. The silences progress, and at the end of the story the boy has become an observer and reporter, a narrator without comment who can become, like Stephen Daedalus in *Stephen Hero*, an objective recorder of epiphanies, what *he* calls "the most delicate and evanescent of moments" (213). As "The Sisters" moves from one scene to the next, the focalization remains constant (everything is seen through the boy's eyes), as do the narrative voice and person (the first-person voice of the older man narrating an event from his childhood). Unexpectedly, though, the relation between the perceiver and what he is recounting does change, gradually growing more distant, even clinical. The final scene of the story resembles Stephen's description of "dramatic" art.[4] We have the rudiments of Stephen Dedalus's personality here—his precision, his analytical clarity, perhaps also his aloofness—even if only the rudiments. (A detail from the version of the story first published in the *Irish Homestead* is pertinent here: "The Sisters" as it was published there was attributed to "Stephen Daedalus," with Joyce spelling the surname as it was spelled in *Stephen Hero*.)[5]

The boy's gradual change from a reactive participant to a detached observer is clear if we examine the three scenes in which he is silent in the company of others more closely. In the first scene, we see the boy's increasing

---

4. "The dramatic form is reached when the vitality which has flowed and eddied round each person fills every person with such vital force that he or she assumes a proper and intangible esthetic life. The personality of the artist, at first a cry or a cadence or a mood and then a fluid and lambent narrative, finally refines itself out of existence, impersonalises itself, so to speak" (*P*, 180–81).

5. "The *Irish Homestead* Version of 'The Sisters,'" in J. Joyce 2000a, 190. All subsequent quotations from the *Irish Homestead* will be from this edition.

silent anger as Old Cotter utters his opinions—"I think it was one of those
. . . peculiar cases. . . . But it's hard to say . . ."; "It's bad for children. My
idea is: let a young lad run about and play with young lads of his own age
and not be . . ."; "When children see things like that, you know, it has an
effect . . ." (D, 10–11). The boy relates, "I knew that I was under observation so I continued eating as if the news had not interested me"; "I felt that
his little beady black eyes were examining me"; "I crammed my mouth with
stirabout for fear I might give utterance to my anger. Tiresome old red-nosed
imbecile!" (D, 11). He attributes his anger to Old Cotter's "alluding to me
as a child" (D, 11), but he has been caught off guard by hearing about the
priest's death from adults after he spent days walking by the priest's window
to find it out for himself.[6] The anger is partly annoyance, then, but it is also
a finely calibrated and psychologically realistic response to the fact that he
has lost a "father."

In the next scene in which the boy is silent before others (the fifth scene
of the story, when he, his aunt, and Nannie enter the room where the priest's
body is lying), his silence is attributable to discomfort and the requirements
of propriety; he is overwhelmed by the solemnity of the occasion. Silent
because "it would have been unseemly to have shouted" at the presumably
deaf Nannie (D, 15), the boy kneels with the women at the foot of the bed
but is unable to pray. The narrator states that he was distracted by "the old
woman's mutterings" as she prayed and that he noticed "how clumsily her
skirt was hooked at the back and how the heels of her cloth boots were trod-
den down all to one side" (D, 16), but a larger distraction is the presence of
the corpse of this man who made such a strong and ambivalent impression
on him while he was alive and whose death has filled him with such powerfully conflicting feelings, not to mention the presence of death itself. The
boy's anger at Old Cotter from the first scene does not seem to carry over
here, even though some critics have read the boy's remarks about Nannie's

6. In the *Irish Homestead* version, the narrator explicitly attributes his anger to the fact
that Old Cotter learned about the priest's death before he did: "It is often annoying the way
people will blunder on what you have elaborately planned for. I was sure he would die at night"
(ibid., 191).

clumsily hooked skirt and worn-down boots as an indication that it has. Rather, in an awkward situation, full of implied ritual and solemnity that make him uncomfortable, the boy seems to follow the lead of the adults around him: his aunt "shook hands" with Nannie "for all" instead of talking to her (*D*, 15);[7] and he enters the room where the priest's body is laid "on tip-toe" (*D*, 15), an unnecessary precaution with a dead body and a deaf sister. As Hugh Kenner has noted, the boy seems to focus on the skirt and boots because "everything that is not of the order of boot-heels is vague, suggestive, and a little frightening"; as with the priest's teachings, which seem confined to facts and details and to rote answers to questions, "everything beyond the level of reality represented by boot-heels is vaguely dangerous: for a grown-up too dangerous to bear thinking about, though a child may feel the fascination of evil, and if unusually tenacious may grow up capable of recording it" (1955, 51–52).

In the third "social" scene (the last scene of the story, in which the boy's aunt converses with Father Flynn's other sister, Eliza), both the boy and Nannie are silent. The boy has become detached without losing any of his capacity for sharp observation; like his mentor, he has become "scrupulous" in his narration. As in the first scene, the conversation is full of gnomonic ellipses, with the aunt unable or unwilling to say "die"—"Did he . . . peacefully?" (*D*, 17)—and Eliza repeatedly offering her own "unfinished sentences" as she tells about Father Flynn's breakdown after the chalice broke: "It was that chalice he broke . . ."; "But still . . ."; "wide-awake and laughing-like softly to himself. . . . So then, of course, when they saw that, that made them think that there was something gone wrong with him . . ." (*D*, 20). The boy reports Eliza's mistaken word choices—"*Freeman's General*" instead of "*Journal*" (*D*, 18), "the rheumatic wheels" instead of "pneumatic" (*D*, 19)—as well as her accidental double entendre when she says that her brother's "life was, you might say, crossed" (*D*, 19). All these mistakes, and Eliza's generally poorly educated talk, are reported without comment. The narrator notes that he accepted the offer of sherry but did not eat any

---

7. In the *Irish Homestead* version, Nannie is described as "almost stone deaf," and "it was no use saying anything to her" (ibid., 192).

of the crackers Nannie offered to him "because I thought I would make too much noise eating them," a refusal that he feels made Nannie "somewhat disappointed" (D, 16; Nannie, like the priest, is "disappointed" and hence "crossed," both in the Christian sense of bearing a cross or burden but also in the sense that her desires have been crossed or resisted). Later, the boy walks again to the table with the sherry and crackers and "tasted my sherry and then returned quietly to my chair in the corner," where, with his aunt, he "waited respectfully" for Eliza to resume speaking (D, 19).[8]

Mike modeled his own interpretive methodology on that of the boy at the end of the story: he refused to fill in the blanks, to diagnose or heal the damage to priest or text. Instead, he uncompromisingly registers the fact of imperfection and does not allow that fact to obscure the boy's gratitude to the priest, however ambivalent that gratitude may be. That same method—of registering what is missing, without using it to reconfigure the story as it stands—can be applied to an examination of the textual history of "The Sisters." It is often said that "The Sisters" is gnomonic in its ellipses, but it is also gnomonic in lacking such other missing elements as narrative connections and explanatory or directive remarks. Joyce's revisions to the story between its appearance in the *Irish Homestead* and its final form show that, although much was added to the story, some things were, gnomonically, taken away. Joyce added the three words the boy obsesses over (*paralysis, gnomon, simony*), the dream, the details about what the priest taught him, and the sense of freedom he feels following the priest's death. But he also removed a great deal: the boy's feeling that some kind of Providence was directing him to the priest's house each night ("Three nights in succession I had found myself in Great Britain-street at that hour, as if by Providence" [J. Joyce 2000a, 190]), the priest's misogynistic dismissal of women and his own silence in relation to them ("He had an egoistic contempt for all women-folk, and suffered all their services to him in polite silence" [ibid., 192]), a fuller picture of Old Cotter ("Old Cotter is the old distiller who owns the batch of prize setters" [ibid., 190]), Nannie's deafness, and the boy's explanation

---

8. As in the other two cases, the *Irish Homestead* offers a fuller explanation: Nannie was silent, and "I said nothing either, being too young" (ibid.).

that he stayed silent at the end because he was a boy. These details that Joyce removed, once known, cannot be forgotten (Jerome McGann has remarked that if you know the thirty-line version of Marianne Moore's poem "Poetry," you supply the rejected version as an virtual alternative, a "close encounter of a third kind," when you read the revised three-line version [1988, 87]), but they also cannot be put back in to the extent that they serve as explanations, or fill in the missing corner. They may be compatible with the details in the finished story (the priest's apparent neglect of his serving sisters, the need to speak very loudly to Nannie), but they are not the only possible explanations.

In this sense J. E. Cirlot's definition of a "gnomon" as a "damaged rectangle" is intriguing and appropriate. "The Sisters" is full of damaged characters, the priest especially but also the sisters and the boy, and even the story itself may be seen as damaged. The impulse is to try to heal, to cure, and understandably much criticism of the story tries to restore the missing corner, to turn the gnomon back into the parallelogram. But it seems to Mike that there is no "answer" to the gaps in "The Sisters"; to provide one is the equivalent of filling in the corner of the gnomon. Rather, reading is a process of understanding the nature of the gap, the wound, the damage. Father Flynn suffered a breakdown, and its nature—physical, mental, moral, or a combination of two or more of these—remains unspecified. His sisters experienced the breakdown of a brother who had honored the family by entering the priesthood but whose collapse and neglect probably disappointed them, just as he had been disappointed by his life and the church. The boy faces the death of an older man who was obviously extremely important to him as a father figure and an authority who had introduced him to church mysteries, but who had also filled him with ambivalence toward both his teachings and his very being. "The Sisters" presents these situations with a combination of compassion and objective clarity, even coldness (Joyce referred to the stories in *Dubliners* as "my nicely polished looking-glass" [*Letters I*, 64]). The narrative point of view is similar to the perspective in the first chapters of *A Portrait of the Artist as a Young Man* (specifically, the final scene in "The Sisters" resembles the three "He was sitting" vignettes in chapter 2 of *Portrait* [*P*, 56–57]). Mike agrees with Kenner that the boy's emphasis on the importance of mundane details like dresses and boots is a safe alternative to impenetrable and inscrutably dangerous mysteries. Out of respect for the stringency of Joyce's realism, it is crucial that readers not restore the gnomon to the parallelogram it once was.

VICKI'S INITIAL APPROACH was at odds with Mike's: she aimed to design an interpretive context that illuminates the nature of the damage the story registers, drawing that context not only from the details of the story but also from its similarity to the one that follows ("An Encounter"). Constructing a heuristic solution to the textual puzzle allows the reader (not the characters) to imagine possible ways out of the "maze" of textual or quotidian experience without denying the configuration of frustrating events on the page.[9] Although "The Sisters" seems to focus on the informal, parochial tutoring of a young boy by a "retired" priest, it actually provides a broader prototype of a typical Irish Catholic education and its effects, which may even be extended to any kind of education designed to socialize as it instructs. The story's effect on readers is utterly predictable: very few readers win meaningful independence from the boy's confused perspective because they unconsciously rely on the habit of identifying themselves with the narrator. Most readers, then, will feel ambivalent about the priest: they know that he seems strange and that he did some things (such as breaking a chalice and being found laughing in a confession box in the middle of the night) that may have hastened his retirement from active duty to his parish. But many readers also empathize with what they perceive to be the priest's crisis of faith, his situation as "a disappointed man" who was "crossed," and they respect his determination to help the boy learn. Few first-time readers see the eponymous sisters as important; on the contrary, many (like the boy) dismiss them as poorly dressed and ignorant, in light of their verbal errors. Most readers respond to Old Cotter with the boy's impatience, and they finish the story as puzzled as their guide, the boy narrator. Everything feels unfinished or incomplete, like the "gnomon" itself.[10]

9. Paulo Freire refers to such heuristic "solutions" as probing the "untested feasibility" that lies beyond a situation that limits individuals (2000, 113).

10. For Vicki's initial approach to "The Sisters," see Mahaffey 2007. The description of her initial reading is an elaboration of what was printed there.

Like Mike, Vicki views the story as a kind of mystery, with some "wrong" or "crime" or even "sin" lying at the heart of it. The main indication that the priest has somehow wronged the boy comes from the boy's sensation when he is on the threshold of sleep that the priest is trying to confess something to him; the two have exchanged roles, and the priest is asking the boy for absolution:

> In the dark of my room I imagined that I saw again the heavy grey face of the paralytic. I drew the blankets over my head and tried to think of Christmas. But the grey face still followed me. It murmured; and I understood that it desired to confess something. I felt my soul receding into some pleasant and vicious region; and there again I found it waiting for me. It began to confess to me in a murmuring voice and I wondered why it smiled continually and why the lips were so moist with spittle. But then I remembered that it had died of paralysis and I felt that I too was smiling feebly as if to absolve the simoniac of his sin. (*D*, 11–12)

The boy identifies the priest's sin as simony, a worldly trafficking in sacred things, and his disease as paralysis, an immobility of the body that results from lack of local muscle control. Instead of facilitating a sacramental transformation of the ordinary into the divine, as in the celebration of the Eucharist, the priest as simoniac is guilty of the opposite transformation: he has taken holy mysteries—such as grace or absolution—and made them into ordinary (and marketable) indulgences.

Paralysis is meaningful as the disease that killed the priest because of the way it weakens an individual's physical power: it designates a loss of control over the local muscles on which larger movements depend. Loss of local control is not only a bodily ill, however; it is also a mental and psychological problem that affects readers when they disregard specific details in an effort to affirm some intuitive or expected meaning. One example of a detail easily overlooked is the name of the street where the priest lives—Great Britain Street. If an Irish priest is said to live on Great Britain Street, it would seem to imply that the Catholic establishment in Ireland is complicit with Britain's imperial authority. It is likewise easy to forget that the priest lives over a shop registered as selling "drapery," although what is sold there are primarily umbrellas and children's bootees (*D*, 12). In ordinary usage, "drapery"

simply designates cloth and dry goods, but the word also connotes conceal-
ment, and the goods in the shop are primarily protective items (umbrellas
and boots, like the "Wellingtons" Gabriel advocates in "The Dead"). Drapery in another sense appears in the boy's dream as the long velvet curtains
he associates with Persia. What might the priest be hiding or protecting,
and why? How might Joyce's purpose be related to the purpose of the other
James, the Reverend James Flynn in the story?

In order to understand the boy's unconscious feeling that the priest has
wronged him, it is necessary to analyze the effect that the priest's lessons
have had on the boy: they have simultaneously enlarged and constrained his
relation to the world of knowledge. Some of the stories the priest told him
were romantic—stories about the catacombs and Napoleon Bonaparte. But
most of what he teaches the boy is technical, even scrupulous: Flynn teaches
him to pronounce Latin properly, to recite responses to the Mass, to discern
fine, even hairsplitting, distinctions between mortal and venial sins. Father
Flynn is teaching the boy about the letter (rather than the spirit) of the
law, which according to Saint Paul in 2 Corinthians "killeth."[11] That Joyce
seems to be associating this kind of exegesis with death is indicated by the
inadvertently morbid puns with which the boy's language is sprinkled: "The
duties of the priest towards the Eucharist and towards the secrecy of the
confessional seemed so *grave* to me that I wondered how anybody had ever
found in himself the courage to *undertake* them" (D, 14; emphasis added).
Father Flynn has also taught the boy not to try to understand the mystery
of faith for himself, but to rely on the interpretations of others, especially
the ones found in canon law. He has taught him obedience, in the form of
deference to his superiors and contempt for those individuals he considers
inferior. The price of this obedience is a kind of muteness; the boy has lost
confidence in his own ability to interpret or understand ideas in relation to
his own experience. He recalls, "I was not surprised when he [the priest]
told me that the fathers of the Church had written books as thick as the *Post
Office Directory* and as closely printed as the law notices in the newspaper,
elucidating all these intricate questions. Often when I thought of this I could

11. "The letter killeth, the spirit giveth life" (2 Cor. 3:6).

make no answer or only a very foolish and halting one upon which he used to smile and nod his head twice or thrice" (*D,* 14). The labyrinthine complexity of the law that this priest enforces makes the boy feel stupid, and the priest smiles and nods in apparent approval of the boy's insecure, hesitant responses. Readers often fail to remark this fact because it seems normal to feel helpless before the immense scholarly knowledge of a given subject, but the story suggests that the priest has injured the boy by making him feel that his inadequacy is a cause for shame (rather than an opportunity to learn) and by encouraging him—through his own example—to feel better about this shameful inadequacy by registering the greater inadequacy of others, such as the inferiority of the eponymous sisters. The boy learns to think of all the knowledge he cannot hope to comprehend as proof of his own shortcomings, when it could just as easily be regarded as an exciting frontier.

Such a reading suggests that the priest has wronged the boy by teaching him that he knows nothing, which in turn makes him *feel* less. We see it first in the boy's recollection of the priest's teachings, especially when the boy learns to relinquish his "simple" understanding of the tenets of the church, replacing it with awe at "complex mysteries" that he could not hope to fathom (*D,* 14). His answers become "foolish and halting," and the priest smiles and nods at the boy's new hesitancy. The effect of his education on his emotions is apparent in his realization that, strangely, he is not "in a mourning mood" when he sees the actual evidence of the priest's death on the door knocker of his house. Instead, he feels "a sensation of freedom" (*D,* 13). We see further evidence of the boy's emotional vacuity when he cannot pray at the foot of the priest's bed because he cannot "gather [his] thoughts"; "the old woman's mutterings" distracted him (*D,* 15). Nannie can pray, but the boy cannot focus or even feel, and once again he imagines his mentor smiling at this fact (*D,* 16). Something—and Vicki argues that it is the tutelage of Father Flynn—has caused the boy to change; he no longer feels excited interest in Old Cotter's stories, registering instead only contempt for his nose, reddened by drinking (*D,* 10–11). We see in him no sign of wonder or gratitude. He exhibits none of the caring devotion that characterizes the eponymous sisters. Although they are exhausted and bereft, the boy shows no sympathy for them; instead, he regards Nannie merely as a distraction, her prayers an "old woman's mutterings" and her skirt "clumsily" hooked

(*D*, 16). "The Sisters" shows—through the contrast between the boy and the sisters—how individuals are often "educated" to give up individual interpretive agency and submit to the judgment of others, and it reveals how the acceptance of interpretive helplessness can initiate the educated into a culture of isolation, injustice (for which we compensate by being petty in turn), and finally apathy.

The lesson of "The Sisters" is further illuminated by the story that follows it in *Dubliners,* "An Encounter." Both stories are dominated by "teachers": one a priest, the other commonly identified as a pederast. It is tempting to dismiss or condemn these two men as deviant ("there was something gone wrong with" them [*D*, 20]). However, by deploring the emptiness of the priest's faith (his chalice "empty" and "broken," his confession box the site of private laughter), or by stressing the potentially threatening queerness of the "old josser" in "An Encounter," one may overlook the immense power of both men as normative representations of cultural authority in general, and of cultural education in particular. Both men have a profound impact on the boy, an impact he fails to understand but nonetheless acutely registers. The priest and the pederast are both father figures and teachers, representing two sides of the same Oedipal-cultural configuration: the priest is the one who forbids access to enjoyment and self-enlightenment by demonstrating the great difficulty of understanding the mysteries of church doctrine and discouraging the boy from trying. Instead of appreciation, he teaches denigration, meanness: the boy learns from him to look down on others such as Old Cotter and the sisters. The pederast in "An Encounter," who encourages the boys to recognize and indulge in the eroticism of fighting boys and touching girls, embodies the other side of the Father. Vicki's contention is that these two men personify the same apparently contradictory but actually unified cultural and patriarchal directive, which the boy accordingly learns: you can compensate for your own inadequacies by focusing on the weaknesses of others, alternately deprecating them and enjoying them, punishing them and taking advantage of them. This directive is powerful, made even more so by the priest's death, because a dead authority figure may be more fully internalized.

The connection between the priest and the pederast in the two stories is drawn carefully through the similarity in their garments, their love of books, and the suggestion that their interiors are rotten. Both men are older and dressed in black with a greenish cast. The boy accounts for the patina of the priest's coat as an effect of snuff: "It may have been these constant showers of snuff which gave his ancient priestly garments their green faded look" (*D*, 13). The pederast, too, is "shabbily dressed in a suit of greenish-black" (*D*, 27). Both are bookworms whose smiles disclose a decayed mouth. As the boy says of the priest, "When he smiled he used to uncover his big discoloured teeth and let his tongue lie upon his lower lip—a habit which had made me feel uneasy in the beginning of our acquaintance" (*D*, 14). Similarly, when the pederast smiles, the boy sees "that he had great gaps in his mouth between his yellow teeth" (*D*, 29). Even when the man makes comments that the boy considers "reasonable," the boy admits that he "disliked the words in his mouth" (*D*, 29). Joyce's focus on the men's decaying mouths provides a visual image of internal corruption;[12] moreover, by making the mouth the site of that corruption, Joyce associates it not only with their own internal state but also with what they are unconsciously communicating to the boy about themselves: their desire for superiority and their fear of inadequacy. There are *two* boys in "An Encounter"—the narrator and Mahony—and they react very differently to the pederast. Mahony gets distracted and runs off after a cat, but the narrator is riveted as well as frightened by the man's monologues. The older man tells the boy narrator that he and the boy are alike—both are bookworms, whereas Mahony "goes in for games" (*D*, 28). By implication, the boy's thirst for knowledge makes him more susceptible to the kind of corruption he associates with the man's rotten mouth. Together, these stories prompt us to wonder whether there is another, more ethical, way of teaching desire than the ones utilized by these two men. They teach simony (in the language of the church, we would call it materialism, the desire to *possess* knowledge, people, and things) and paralysis, which we know better as the hopelessness or apathy that Dante associated with hell.

12. Compare the "Circe" episode of *Ulysses*, where Bloom gets a glimpse of the inside of Zoe's mouth and it appears to him as a graveyard full of gold and rotting bones (fillings and decaying teeth): "*The roses* [her lips] *draw apart, disclose a sepulcher of the gold of kings and their mouldering bones*" (*U*, 15.1340–41).

The teaching methods used by both priest and pederast either require or demonstrate a mechanical form of response: the priest teaches the boy to memorize and to learn by rote; the pederast recites his erotic, perhaps even "literary," fantasies about the pleasures of touching girls and whipping boys as if by heart. But what is the desire that they are simultaneously (and automatically) prohibiting and licensing in such repetitive ways? The underside of this desire is a fear: it is the pleasure/anxiety at seeing both self and others as inescapably inadequate or, to use the language of religion, irredeemably sinful. The priest teaches the boy to give up hope of understanding the mysteries of the Eucharist, and the story implies that as he learns to despair at the possibility of learning *wisdom* (the merciful or caring version of knowledge), he confirms his own sense of inadequacy and at the same time learns to focus on the inadequacies and limitations of others: the poor grammar and shoddy dress of the sisters, to take the most obvious example. Similarly, the pederast is sexually *excited* by the badness of boys and girls, which gives him the license to touch them in ways that are hurtful to them but pleasurable to himself (he imagines whipping bad boys and stroking girls who "were not so good as they seemed to be if one only knew" [*D,* 29]). In different ways, both men practice a punitive pedagogy that perpetuates itself by insisting upon the psychological incapacity rather than the worth of the individual. Here, the main effect of this teaching on the boy is that it diminishes his pleasure: the pleasure of learning (in "The Sisters") and the pleasure of disobeying (in "An Encounter") are both tarnished, and he learns to replace the pleasures of adventure and novelty with a compensatory pleasure in the shortcomings of others. As the example of the pederast shows, the habit of pleasuring oneself at the expense of others is the root of abuse.

In "The Sisters," we can see how the priest has altered the boy's way of thinking and feeling by observing how the boy reacts to others: he looks down on them now, and he does so with impatience, irritation, and sometimes anger. As we mentioned above, he used to regard Old Cotter as "rather interesting," but he has grown "tired of him," dismissing him as a "tiresome old fool" with "little beady black eyes" (*D,* 10). The boy's attitude toward his faith has also changed; he now views its tenets as requiring scrupulous exegesis rather than as simple exhortations to love and to sustain hope (*D,* 14). The boy notes small instances of ignorance and shabbiness in the priest's sisters. Instead of sympathizing with their straitened circumstances ("as poor as we are—we wouldn't see him want anything" [*D*, 17]), he dispassionately reproduces all Eliza's grammatical errors: her references to "them flowers and them two candlesticks" (*D*, 18), her claim that "the duties of the priesthood was too much for him" (*D*, 19).

We might compare the boy's lack of affect when listening to the dead priest's sisters with the evidence of how the priest himself treated them. Although he spent time and effort educating the boy, his sisters' errors show that he made no such effort with them, despite the fact that they fed him and cared for him for years; the boy's aunt refers to all their "kindness to him" (*D*, 18). They seem more like servants than sisters, and one of them is even called "Nannie," as if to underscore her role as nurselike caretaker. The sisters' long and faithful nurturing of their brother is as invisible to the priest and the boy as it is to most first-time readers.[13]

Reasoning backward from these observations, we are able to construct a different story than the one the boy relates. We see a priest who had been acting strangely for an unspecified period of time, who is no longer "of S. Catherine's Church, Meath Street" (*D*, 12), who has been tutoring a young boy in a way that changes the boy's attitude not only toward the "simplest acts" of the church, but also toward other people. The boy has learned to doubt his own ability to fathom the central tenets of his religion, and simultaneously he has learned to be scrupulous and "mean" in his observation of others. Every time he notices something that demeans someone who is in other respects caring or faithful, he fancies that the dead priest is smiling his approval (*D*, 16). In short, the priest has passed on to the boy not only precision but also smallness of mind, which has interfered with the boy's ability to

13. Margot Norris suggests a reading of "The Sisters" as "a naturalistic tale of poverty, ignorance, and sadness that betrays the politics of gender differences. The story of Nannie and Eliza Flynn may well concern two very poor women from the slums of Irishtown . . . who never married and rose to little more than a meager draper's business in Dublin. . . . Meanwhile, their brother managed to receive an education and travel to Rome to attend the Irish college there. . . . Yet instead of transferring the respectability and benefits of this vocation to his sisters, the outcome of their brother's ecclesiastical career was unhappiness, disappointment, and a final dementia that now threatens to further cloud their lives" (2003, 24).

feel grief or compassion. The teacher has infected his pupil with the "original sin" of feeling unworthy and incapable, which makes him quick to note and disdain the ignorance and shoddiness of even the most devoted caretakers. (Compare Gabriel's attitude to two other sisters in "The Dead," whom he mentally refers to as "only two ignorant old women" [D, 238].)

In "An Encounter," the pederast addresses human "sin" in a way that justifies not emotional detachment but invasive physical touch. Instead of alienating the boy from others, from his own emotions, and from the lessons of his own experience, all in the name of "education," the pederast uses an assumption of the children's innate depravity to justify touching them: stroking or whipping them so as to give himself pleasure. The boy narrator responds in different ways to the two modes of intervening in a child's education. The boy *accepts* Father Flynn's interpretations; he might even be said to learn from him a new way of seeing the world, one that has made him newly impatient with Old Cotter and allows him to forget, like his mentor, the diurnal constancy of the sisters' devotion. He has "learned" from the priest to secure a place for himself above others by perceiving them to be less capable of technical precision than he. In the language of Dante, he has learned justice, but forgotten love.

In "An Encounter," the boy learns the same lesson from a less respectable teacher—that if he can establish himself as superior he may claim the right to interpret, judge, and punish others—although the pederast imagines expressing his power in physical terms, as the privilege to stroke and whip. Listening to the pederast enjoy his superiority over bad boys and girls, the boy catches a brief glimpse of a similar tendency in himself of which he was previously unaware: he has always condescended to his friend Mahony as his inferior. At the end of the story, when he is eager to get away from the pederast, he calls for Mahony. Mahony runs as if to bring him aid, and the narrator is conscience pricked, "for in [his] heart [he] had always despised him a little" (D, 32).

If Joyce yokes the priest and the pederast as using a comparable pedagogy, what can we learn from the narrator's apparent approval of (or at least ambivalence toward) that pedagogy when it is presented as a way of thinking (in "The Sisters") instead of a way of touching (in "An Encounter")? Joyce's decision to place "An Encounter" directly after "The Sisters"

allows the fantasy of physical touch to illustrate some of the more disturbing implications of Father Flynn's teaching by making them tangible: not
only is it potentially abusive, but there is also a masturbatory pleasure in
the contemplation of other people's worthlessness. Readers and critics have
historically had trouble understanding the relation between these two stories, interpreting the priest as someone who may have sexually abused the
boy.[14] Such a reading registers the kinship between priest and pederast; however, to understand Father Flynn as a pederast is to overlook the subtlety
of his theology by misreading his social and theological indoctrination as
physical abuse. There is no evidence that the priest has physically abused the
boy—and this point is crucial, because physical abuse is easier to recognize
and deplore than indoctrination in the hallowed guise of education. "The
Sisters" focuses on the abuse of indoctrination, which is notoriously hard to
identify because most socialized individuals—including the priest himself—
have been similarly indoctrinated.[15] "Doctrinal" abuse is not identical with
sexual abuse, but Joyce's stories suggest that—by stressing the unworthiness
of the uninitiated—it may be used to license more physically abusive forms
of punishment and reward.

Indoctrination is powerful precisely because it has been dissociated from
anything we can readily see through and condemn, such as physical abuse.
When the priest insists on teaching the boy the uselessness of trying to interpret sacred mysteries, not only is he seducing the boy to cede his interpretive
authority to him, as priest, but he is also gutting the boy's agency and his spirituality in the process. The priest's corruption is that he knows he is "sinning"
by simultaneously teaching the boy vanity (that the boy is more special than
other people) and dependence upon male authority. In the boy's dream, the
priest's attempted confession to him suggests that the boy is unconsciously
aware that the priest has somehow wronged him, since the priest is asking

14. See ibid., 26, for an account of these readings.

15. Michael A. Williams, in "The Rubrics of Guilt in 'The Sisters,'" presents an utterly
persuasive case that the priest teaches the boy in the way that he himself was trained: scrupulously. He gives examples of that training by quoting from the 1880 *Missale Romanum*. This
paper was presented at the Twenty-Second International James Joyce Symposium in Prague
on June 15, 2010.

him for absolution. The episode in which he is found laughing to himself in the confession box reinforces the suggestion that he has something to confess. Why is this man laughing? What is he laughing at?

The image of an authority figure named James laughing to himself over others' bewilderment at a complex system of ideas exemplifies many people's vision of Joyce himself (Mahaffey 1988, 26–32). Many who read "The Sisters" have approached Joyce as akin to Father Flynn, a dead authority figure whose determination to make an impact on the lives of others grotesquely extends beyond the grave. But in fact "The Sisters" is Joyce's repudiation of that model. Readers who make an a priori assumption that understanding and caring are beyond them will have that assumption confirmed by their experience of reading the story, a confirmation they may find unexpectedly disquieting.

The title of "The Sisters" is a clue not only to the priest's blind spot, but also to a blindness that readers may well share with him. The title identifies what the priest takes for granted: his sisters' steady care and silent support that allowed him to rise above his class, in return for which they received no apparent recognition or reward. The story presents a quite literal microcosm of a patriarchal society or church, complete with a father and the faithful but neglected nuns who minister to him, who can never be ordained themselves. The sisters, like the unexamined assumptions upon which reading is often based, provide a foundation for development, but are too often overlooked as the precondition on which everything else depends. In Joyce's story, the sisters exhibit a very different kind of faith than the faith of their brother: it is simpler, more loving, more tiring, and less rewarding and mysterious. It expresses itself through actions, not words. Which kind of faith is closer to the teachings of the religion that the priest claims to understand and represent?

IF WE APPROACH "The Sisters" in light of these two different but perhaps not incompatible approaches, it may prompt us to take another look at the "gnomon." Perhaps it should be seen not only as an incomplete or damaged figure, but also as it was defined by Hero of Alexandria: "that figure (a number or a geometric figure) which, when added to another figure, results in a figure similar to the original" (Gazalé 1999, xii). As Midhat Gazalé beautifully explains, a gnomon is a unit of growth or reproduction that ensures or demonstrates self-similarity. He is expanding the use of the gnomon, adapting its Euclidian definition and applying it to the more irregular forms of incremental self-similarity found in fractals (snowflakes being one memorable example of the irregular formations of self-similar parts). Fractal geometry postdates Joyce, since it was named by Benoit Mandelbrot in 1975 to designate "monstrous" geometrical figures that eluded Euclidian and Newtonian categories. Mandelbrot defined a fractal as a rough or fragmented geometric shape that can be split into parts, each of which is (approximately or irregularly) a reduced-size copy of the whole (1983, 4). In order to understand how such a conception of the gnomon might work, and how it might illuminate what Joyce is suggesting about the relation between the boy and the priest in "The Sisters," we should briefly retrace the history of the gnomon from its origin in ancient Egypt. Then it becomes clearer how a gnomon can designate the indicator on a sundial, a damaged parallelogram, and also be metaphorically applied to the growth of fractals, in which "each successive increment is said to constitute a *gnomon* to the entire structure" (Gazalé 1999, 4). Ultimately, we will see that the gnomon served Joyce as a metaphor for the relation of "father" to son, showing how knowledge (which comes packaged with damage and incompleteness) is transmitted from one generation to the next, ensuring a "progression" marked by self-similarity. To put it another way, the shadow cast by the sun on the "dial" of time is the shadow of the (dead) father; the father is the "instrument of knowledge" that makes it possible to "know" both time and the heavens, but at a price.

In the eighteenth dynasty of ancient Egypt (1479–1425 BCE), the solar clock that was used to tell time was shaped like an *L,* and that *L* would more than a millennium later be identified with a geometrical gnomon. As Gazalé explains, "An L-shaped object with a short vertical arm and a long graduated horizontal arm . . . was rotated in such a manner that the shadow of the vertical arm fell on the graduations of the horizontal arm. That instrument was called *setchat,* or *merkhet,* literally meaning 'instrument of knowledge'" (1999, 6). Much later, around 575 BCE, the sundial was attributed to the Greek Anaximander (ca. 610 BCE–ca. 546 BCE) and the L-shaped indicator was given the Greek name "gnomon," which literally means "that which allows one to know" (Gazalé 1999, 7). Euclid, who lived around 300 BCE, called the portion of a parallelogram that remains after a smaller parallelogram has been taken away a gnomon, and we can see why if we picture a parallelogram constructed with right angles: the portion that remains after the smaller parallelogram has been removed has an L-shape, like a carpenter's square (Hall and Stevens 1893, 120). When Gazalé uses the gnomon as the principle of self-similar growth, he can do so because every "increment is similar to its predecessor, and the whole, after every spurt of growth, is just like it was before" (1999, 4, citing Thomson 1966). This statement is an apt description of how the priest in "The Sisters" was himself educated, as well as how he educates the next generation: he "reproduces" or "re-creates" the boy in his own image by the way he teaches him to interpret. The shadow of the gnomon, like a priest or an interpreter, can be understood as that which falls between the heavens and the earth, connecting the great and the small: "A gnomon's shadow is the tangible manifestation on earth, nay, literally on the dust, of celestial events of cosmic magnitude" (ibid., 10). It also provides us with a natural image of fractal growth—as in a shell or a galactic nebula or a spider web—that can be used to describe the perpetuation and expansion of social roles across generations. Here, the emphasis is not on subtraction—the parallelogram that has been taken away—but on accretion: the gnomon that when added to two sides of a parallelogram produces a bigger parallelogram. In this sense, it is the boy who is the gnomon and who will, by having been joined to the figure of the priest, create a future that can only be an enlarged version of the past. Joyce's collection of stories is also designed in this way: it grows by increments, in which each story is a gnomon or partial figure that adds new facets while failing to change the shape of the whole.

With the incremental growth of the gnomon (as a fractal unit) in mind, let us return to the first version of "The Sisters" published in the *Irish Homestead*. In that version, the priest was closely associated with mental illness: Old Cotter remarked that the priest's "upper storey" was gone, and the church where he officiated was identified as St. Ita's. In the later version, Joyce changed "St. Ita's" to "St. Catherine's," presumably because he discovered that St. Ita's was not built until 1902 and the priest died in 1895. St. Ita's was in Portrane (Port Reachrainn), and it is the church of a well-known psychiatric hospital.[16] Joyce seemed to be trying to correlate intellectual ability and mental (or emotional) deficiency, especially since he was careful to emphasize that "neither of his [Father Flynn's] sisters were very intelligent" (J. Joyce 2000a, 192).

When Joyce revised the story for publication in the collection, he changed the emphasis on the priest's shortcomings from mental illness to a repression rooted in emotional and material deprivation that produces silence. Instead of being associated with St. Ita's mental hospital, the priest is linked with St. Catherine's Meath Street. St. Catherine's is a Gothic Revival Catholic church designed by J. J. McCarthy in 1852 that in Joyce's time had an unfinished tower (the tower has since been completed). It is located in an area defined not by madness but by poverty: in 1796 more than two thousand people had been found in a starving condition in only three streets of the parish. James Connolly remarked, "Evidently 'prosperity' had not much meaning to the people of St. Catherine's" (1910, 56).

The figure of St. Catherine of Alexandria (fourth century), to whom the chapel is dedicated, stands as the antithesis of both the priest and the sisters. Unlike the sisters Flynn, she was a beautiful, articulate, and confident young woman who was accomplished in philosophy, theology, and oratory. She never married, and she became the patron saint of theologians, preachers, and unmarried women. Preachers would pray to her for eloquence, because she epitomized the expressive potential that could be achieved by learning and openness to inspiration. When she was condemned to death on a breaking wheel (thereafter known as a "Catherine wheel"), the wheel broke when she touched it. This point is significant in view of the fact that "to die by the wheel" has become slang for keeping silent about something, especially in Spanish, where *morir en la rueda* idiomatically means to refuse to speak. Catherine, in contrast, refused to be silent, appearing before Emperor Maximinus at the age of eighteen to challenge his policy of cruelly persecuting Christians. He called all the scholars of the land to trick her into apostasy,

16. Saint Ita herself forms an interesting contrast to Father Flynn the simoniac, because she once told Saint Brendan, who was in her foster care, that the thing that was most displeasing to God is the worship of material things.

and she not only prevailed against them but also converted many of them with her eloquence, including the empress herself (see *The Catholic Encyclopedia*). When the emperor failed to break Catherine, he consigned her to the wheel. It was broken by her touch, whereupon he had her beheaded.

When read against the legend of Saint Catherine, the silence in "The Sisters" takes on a more sinister implication. The boy's growing capacity for silence emerges as part of the legacy of his tutor, who never confessed the doubts or conflicts or even (possibly) the illness that was incapacitating him (the confession box in which he was found contained no auditor). The exercise of silence emerges as a self-discipline, and perhaps also a torture; it is a response to being "crossed" (or obstructed) that turns the observer into an acute recorder of events, but one who is potentially blind to his own repressed feelings. Silence is the self-subtraction that configures a pupil as a gnomon; the boy here takes over the priest's role of valorizing "that which allows us to know," participating in the fractal growth of an attentive and abusive pedagogy. *Fractal,* after all, comes from the same root as *fractured:* growth is produced by incremental breakings. In this silent struggle of fathers to shape and break their sons, women do not figure at all.

"The Sisters," then, is a portal into *Dubliners;* the world into which it beckons us, if not a hell, is nonetheless a Dantean limbo of diametrically opposed possibilities. Like the boy, we are invited into a region that is both "pleasant and vicious" (*D,* 12); that "viciousness" suggests not only "vice" but also the root of *vice, vitium,* which is *fault.* We meet a boy who has grown silent and dispassionately observant (which cost him his former curiosity and enthusiasm) under the tutelage of a man. That man, however, formerly of "S. Catherine's Meath Street," worked in memory of a woman who embodied—and was martyred for—the opposite virtue of speaking out, of refusing to remain silent. "The Sisters" leaves us suspended between these two differently unsatisfactory options. If learning to remain silent promotes increased observational acuity dogged by hopelessness, speaking out may cost the speaker his or her life. One possible response to this double bind is to learn to speak differently, in a kind of code that will be meaningful only to listeners who are actively curious and committed to new modes of understanding. The stories of *Dubliners* are written in such a code: clear but oblique, detailed but apparently pointless.

With the priest's encouragement, the boy of "The Sisters" has become a kind of living gnomon, a damaged figure whose damage replicates the wound of his tutor on a smaller scale. The gnomonic shape of the boy and the priest also describes the condition of the characters we will meet in the rest of the volume, predicting its larger, irregular fractal design. As readers, do we fill the gaps in these gnomons with explanations? If we do so, how can we hope to accurately register the damage to which the gaps testify, to diagnose an endemic paralysis that we may perhaps share, and to "look upon its deadly work" (*D*, 9)? Our joint conclusion is that the task and privilege of interpretation are to imagine ways that this gap may have been produced; if we fill in the gap, we should do so provisionally, with dotted lines, thereby preserving the openness of the figure even while tracing the outlines of the corner that was lost. Our wish is to preserve the holes in the text while actively participating in its imaginative restoration. The "wounds" that damage these characters are also potential portals of discovery, both for them and for the readers they mirror.

2

"An Encounter"

James Joyce's Humiliation Nation

MARGOT GAYLE BACKUS AND JOSEPH VALENTE

Our collaboration, which we honed over several talks and essays, proceeds by way of a combined oral and written dialogue. Beginning with a textual part-object, composed by one of us and then examined by both, we identified our main line of argument over a series of telephone conversations. At that point, we undertook gradually to expand and revise our brief on an alternating basis, sending drafts back and forth for one another to elaborate, until the need for renewed telephone conversations asserted itself. We repeated this process a few times, allocating different chores and sections to one another as the essay grew toward completion. It would be fair to say that we never, or rarely, write together, although in another sense we are doing so throughout.

An Encounter" narrates an encounter with shame: the boy narrator tries to escape the strict routine of school, replacing it with an escapist adventure, and instead he becomes witness to the shameful exhibition of an older man who claims to be his "fellow," a "bookworm" like himself (*D*, 28). His chance meeting with this "queer old josser" precipitates a startling encounter with his own shame, affording a disquieting glimpse of an unexpected association between the ethnic shame of Irish Catholicism, which he and Mahony are perpetually colluding to project elsewhere, and the shame of the quasi-homoerotic emotional bonds through which such projection is accomplished.

48

Shame attaches itself to the interior, socially defined identity of the sufferer. Both because it is hidden and because it results from the necessity of being part of society, shame cannot be verbally expiated or mitigated under the prevailing symbolic order. Speech, too, is a social construct, and hence speech can neither absolve nor amend the humiliation of a subject who is—necessarily—only partly assimilated into society. Shame adheres to the residue of social definition, that which exceeds or defies social norms of legibility and acceptability. Because speech cannot reconcile the shameful with social norms or their enforcing institutions, people habitually endeavor to rid themselves of shame by projecting it onto "Others." The inexpressibility of shame, therefore, is not only a significant psychoanalytic and phenomenological problem, but a pathogenic social and political condition as well. James Joyce made a sustained effort throughout his career to render shame visible and revalue it as a collective good rather than an individual ill, which is therefore a politically salient aspect of his life's work.

We will begin by briefly reviewing how Joyce was positioned—both materially and culturally—in relation to the intellectual establishment of his day. Such an overview will help to show why his strategies for representing shame in an affectively and politically destabilizing manner became central to the stylistic innovation for which he is so celebrated. Joyce occupied an inherently shameful position within existing Irish and British cultural hierarchies. He was an intellectually and formally ambitious Irish Catholic writer educated within the second-tier university system that, as Terry Eagleton argues, served both to disguise and to institutionalize growing cleavages among the Oxbridge elite, a philistine middle class, and an alienated petit bourgeoisie shot through with ethnic and regional grievances. On the one hand, attempts on Joyce's part to emulate the tastefully erudite allusions of his highbrow modernist betters would have left him open to accusations of imperfect mimicry, or, symbolically, of the "plagiarism" of which Bloom, in "Circe," stands accused by his class superior, Philip Beaufoy (*U*, 15.822). On the other hand, the deliberate, overt violations of prevailing decorum for which Joyce increasingly opted inevitably exposed him to charges of ill-bred intellectual ostentation and tastelessness. Owing to his lack of tony university credentials (like Bloom, Joyce could be said to have learned much of his art from the "university of life"), Joyce was vulnerable to accusations that he had simply smeared shit on his pages, a charge he transfers to both Leopold Bloom and Shem the Penman.

In the "Circe" episode, Bloom is hauled into court for disfiguring Beaufoy's prizewinning story, "Matcham's Masterstroke," with "the mark of the beast," while A VOICE FROM THE GALLERY ethnicizes and literalizes the offense complained of by allusion to the outhouse scene in "Calypso": "Moses, Moses, king of the jews / Wiped his arse in the *Daily News*" (*U*, 15.847–48). The entire courtroom fantasy recalls the trials of Oscar Wilde, whose crimes were, like Bloom's, confirmed in court through the sensational evidence of shit-marked "sheets" (Cohen 1993, xx). For his part, Shem is said to live in "the house O'Shea or O'Shame" (*FW*, 182.30), where he "shall produce nichthemerically from his unheavenly body a no uncertain quantity of obscene matter not protected by copriright in the United Stars of Ourania" (*FW*, 185.29–31), otherwise known as "stinksome inkenstink" (*FW*, 183.6). His excremental effusions ("the squidself which he had squirtscreened") are linked to the literary evidence in Wilde's conviction for gross indecency, the text of "doriangrayer" (*FW*, 186.6–8). In either "case," then, the fictionalized shame of Joyce's class and ethnic inferiority merges with the imposed shame of Wilde's sexual and intellectual irregularities, which themselves have taken on a valence of pathologized Irishness.

As Joyce foresaw, charges of shameful shit smearing were indeed leveled at him by the Dublin intelligentsia, most notoriously in the person of Trinity's provost, John Pentland Mahaffy, who called attention to Joyce's shameful class and educational origins by describing his work as exemplifying the ill effects of educating the "island's aborigines" (Ellmann 1982, 58). He associated Joyce's literary efforts with unclean incontinence as well as immaturity when he identified Joyce himself with the "corner boys who spit into the Liffey" (ibid., 58n). Joyce was also, and equally unsurprisingly, reviled for his class, national, and educational deficiencies by British modernists such as H. G. Wells and Virginia Woolf (Brooker 2004, 15–18), who did not, however, scruple to borrow liberally from the "underbred" pages of *Ulysses* and *Finnegans Wake* (Ellmann 1982, 528). Even Joyce's most well-educated and intellectually gifted early critics were unable to resist attacks that dismissed not so much the work as the right of a person of Joyce's pedigree to produce it. Although many Irish, British, and American intellectuals and artists embraced and supported Joyce, the ones who did not typically argued against Joyce by putting him back in his shameful place, as an Irish Catholic guttersnipe with no right to the intellectual, aesthetic, and professional audacity that *Ulysses* so singularly proclaims.

As in Althusser's description of ideology as something that, in order to function, must always anticipate its own arrival, shaming words work only when they are always already in force. James Joyce was, in effect, already interrogating the shameful dimensions of *Ulysses*'s reception in the novel's first chapter. In the "Haunted Inkbottle" of the Martello Tower, Buck Mulligan repeatedly advises Stephen to affiliate himself with the Oxbridge intelligentsia, to ally himself with Matthew Arnold's benignant project to Hellenize the middle classes, and to use his "real Oxford manner" to gain favor and financial backing from Haines, under whose ethnographic gaze Stephen feels himself teetering between rude native informant and intellectual peer. Far from enabling Stephen to dispel the stigma of his declassé origin and a trajectory that separates him from these Oxford men, Stephen's intellectual and artistic bravura serves only to complicate and embitter their relationship, introducing elements of defensiveness, jealousy, and exploitation that presage and preemptively critique the phobic appropriations of Joyce's tour de force.

Encountering Shame

In one of its myriad dimensions, James Joyce's literary career delineated the anatomy of shame, finding in this most isolating of experiences the primary condition for a properly social being. In recognition of this fact, Joyce punningly nominated himself "Shame's Voice," an intriguingly double-sided gesture worth pausing over. On one side, Joyce stakes the marker of his identity on shame's possession of his voice, his expressive capacity (Brivic 2001, 177). In so doing, he locates shame at the level of his being, of which the voice is but an attribute, thereby indicating that shame is indelible, part of the deep structure of identity (unlike guilt, which is a result of behavior and for which an individual is therefore responsible). On the other, he stakes the signifier of his selfhood (his name) on making shame speakable, giving it a voice. Taken together, these interpretive possibilities remind us how extensively Joyce came to infuse or dissolve his identity into the network of signifiers he manipulated, making a name *of* himself, so that the shame variously attaching to his being would not only be reflected but actually reside in his literary voice. James Joyce *is* shame's voice, not as a role but as a "whole self-involving reality" (Lynd 1958, 49). Here we see how constructively Joyce's egoistic pursuit of his aesthetic destiny is related to his radical social significance: Joyce as master and Joyce as signifier. Only such a combination, one suspects, could turn the common isolation of shame into a *communal* isolation, what cartoon character Kim Possible calls "humiliation nation."

Joyce voices shame regularly through race and sexuality, specifically Irishness and queerness, whose nineteenth-century construction as profound sources of shame were intimately and multifariously interconnected. In this essay we will focus on how shame, together with its ethnic and sexual variants in Joyce's ouevre, enable us to amalgamate the queer and the postcolonial readings of the story "An Encounter" into what we might call a queer nationalist approach. Such a detailed explication of the imbrication of national and sexual identity within the broader field of social shame in early-twentieth-century Dublin will, we hope, help to initiate a more general excavation of the strata of shame that underpin Joyce's writings, a recognition that may have its greatest interpretive significance for readings of the much-debated first half of "Nausicaa."

In her compelling queer reading of "An Encounter," Margot Norris discovers "a doubled text that conceals a non-canonical homosocial fantasy, whose desirous homosexual undercurrents affright it and oblige it to mark itself as a canonical cautionary tale of imperiled innocence" (1998, 21). Key to this mission is the discontinuous at-oneness of the boy with his adult self, who narrates the tale. According to Norris, the young protagonist's reaction to the "josser's" seduction betrays the symptoms of an incriminatory if ambiguous sexual knowledge. The adult narrator labors to sanitize that knowledge in his younger self by duplicitously muting his own awareness of the sexual implications of events as they unfold. To take one exemplary narrative strand: the narrative of a "homosocial elopement of the boy and Mahony" (ibid., 27) is clinched only when their eyes meet briefly on the ferry; immediately thereafter, the boy searches for green-eyed sailors because "I had some confused notion . . ." (*D*, 26). In eliding the "likeliest

possibility—that the boy believes sailors with green eyes are homosexuals"
(Norris 1998, 27)—the narrator is claiming innocence (he had only confused notions). Less plausibly, however, the narrator would have us believe
that he is still ignorant—not only of what those notions entailed, but also
of the contemporary Wildean and sexological associations of the color green
with homosexuality (ibid., 28). If the narrator were to recognize the homoerotic overtones gathering over the course of the adventure, he would come
uncomfortably close to admitting that the protagonist was unconsciously
predisposed to meet the josser on his own terms.[1] By assuming his own
"privilege of unknowing," however, the narrator locates the traumatic force
of desire entirely within the josser, who is thereby reduced to a "monstrous
sexual bogey" (ibid., 23). The boy's participation in the erotic scenario is
thus continually denied even as it is being described.

The shame-deflecting power of the narrator's perspective in "An Encounter" is particularly evident if we place the text side by side with "Nausicaa,"
the *Ulysses* chapter to which, as Katherine Mullin has noted, the short story
strikingly corresponds (2003, 29). In both narratives, young people in an
outdoor setting and outside of direct adult supervision encounter a queer,
vaguely foreign older man with sadomasochistic tendencies, whose presence
stirs up conflicted feelings of homosocial competition and protectiveness, and
who ultimately forges a bond with one of the youths that culminates in an
act of public and mutually implicating masturbation. In "Nausicaa," Gerty
MacDowell's thoughts about Bloom and her reactions to his intent interest
are not mediated through the perceptions of a strategically reticent narrator,
and we therefore have no doubt about the mutuality of their interest or the
degree to which this interest is consciously and genitally sexual. A comparison of "An Encounter" to "Nausicaa" suggests, by analogy, the probability
that the boy's affective responses to both Mahony and the josser have been
partly occluded. However, as we will describe in this essay's final section,
such a comparison also helps to elucidate further the frequently debated

---

1. Such a recognition would reveal striking parallels between the wandering of the boys
in "An Encounter" and two better-known patterns of seemingly aimless meandering toward
an anonymous sexual encounter in *A Portrait* and "Nausicaa."

stylistics of "Nausicaa," which forge at the formal level a shame-based alliance between subaltern groups, just as the trope of corporal punishment in "An Encounter" forges a cultural alliance predicated on shared bodily and psychic vulnerability and the potential for corporeal pleasure that inheres within it.

In "An Encounter," the narrative collusion of expressive and repressive energies demands a rigorously symptomatic interpretation. Even the boy's cultural snobbery, frequently construed as the epiphany that concludes the story, represents a displacement for a more fundamental desire for belonging, for being in the know. As Norris contends, the protagonist dons "a disguise of snobbery to mask prurience, like the alias he assumes" ("In case he asks us for our names . . . let you be Murphy and I'll be Smith" [*D*, 30]).

This last comparison reveals a structural limit to Norris's marvelously recuperative analysis. In identifying the narrator's "disguise" with the boy's "alias," Norris strengthens the motivational and strategic unity of the character over time, but only by attenuating the crucial epistemic distance between the boy's *méconnaissance,* his ignorant knowing, and the narrator's conscious duplicity, his knowing ignorance. Since the identity and the discontinuity of the boy and his adult self are positively indispensable to Norris's account, this assertion of one at the expense of the other does not constitute an exegetical error; rather, it identifies the need for a fuller conceptual synthesis. If we assume that the narrator's "unknowing," or denial, is a continuation of the boy's, we have lost a sense of the disjunction between them. We need a way of mediating between the narrator and the boy that operates at both the juvenile and the adult phase. First, we need to grasp what socially mandated defense structure operates to guard the boy from consciously knowing what he knows at the subliminal level. Furthermore, we need to understand what constitutes the breach in that psychosocial bulwark that allows him a sense of self-implication so powerful that his adult memories of the encounter reactivate those defense mechanisms. If we look again at Norris's example of the boy's "alias," we can find the solution to both of these puzzles encapsulated in miniature, but in a form that a purely sexual reading could not accommodate. Here we might integrate a nationalist reading modeled by a Len Platt (1995) or Willard Potts (2000).

Uttered outside the old man's hearing, with no intent of gleaning forbidden knowledge, the aliases constructed by the boy evince not "cultural snobbery masking prurience," but the ostensible fear of prurience masking cultural snobbery. The boy assigns Mahony the lower-caste, presumptively Catholic, name of Murphy, while reserving the upper-caste Anglo-Protestant name of Smith for himself, laying claim, even in private, to a position of social superiority (Potts 2000, 78). This naming serves two socially signifi- cant functions corresponding to our two problems of mediation. First, the use of two different "classes" of name testifies to the homosocial rivalry that binds all the boys emotionally, even erotically, while concealing the nature of these bonds under a counterpane of cordial aggression. This rivalry manifests itself in competition for social cachet variously defined (tests of physical prowess, efforts of cultural acquisition, struggles over the relative importance of bodily versus intellectual accomplishment), and it is the social mechanism whereby the protagonist knows without knowing his own desir- ous longings in advance of the "encounter." Second, as the aliases indicate, this homosocial rivalry obeys the same value hierarchy of cultural hegemony that the Anglo-Protestant settler class exercised over the native Catholic petit bourgeoisie.

This double function of the proposed pseudonym Murphy—which marks Mahony as both an attractive, companionable sparring partner and a deposi- tory of burdensome ethnic shame—is remarkably similar to the function of the possibly pseudonymous D. B. Murphy, the possibly homosexual *"soi-disant* sailor" in the "Eumaeus" episode of *Ulysses* (16.415). *This* pseudonymous Murphy is first described in "Eumaeus" as, like the josser, elaborately divert- ing his gaze from two males.[2] While the josser "glance[s] up . . . quickly" and then passes, circling back "very slowly" and with eyes averted as though "looking for something in the grass" (*D,* 28), the red-bearded Murphy stares at Bloom and Stephen long after the other occupants of the cabman's shelter

2. This reading of more averted eyes extends Margot Norris's brilliant reading of the different scopic reactions of the protagonist and Mahony to the josser and his activities, with the narrator's "rigid ocular control" contrasting pointedly with Mahony's open and direct gaze, a contrast that suggests that the narrator has "internalize[d] the magnet that attaches to the old man's erotic field" (2003, 31), whereas Mahony has not. As Norris points out, the act of looking away registers the looker's awareness of something improper, something compromis- ing, in his scopic motivations.

have turned their eyes away. Then, in a movement rendered suggestive through its deferral, he "transfer[s] his rapt attention to the floor" (*U*, 16.339). As Jennifer Levine has argued, D. B. Murphy conjoins ethnic, sexual, and class otherness in Bloom's imagination, becoming "the locus of Bloom's anxiety" and thereby revealing Bloom's pressing if largely unconscious need to off-load the sexual and ethnic shame that Stephen's proximity arouses (1998, 117). Like the moment in "An Encounter" when the josser's activities supply a pretext for the protagonist to bind himself to Mahony through a symbolic marriage, including a name change, the foreign-seeming sailor "sets off some internal alarm" in Bloom (ibid., 103) when he asks Stephen's name. Through his suspicious cultural, class, and sexual alterity, Murphy supplies an excuse for Bloom to bridge the wide cultural, ethnic, and class chasm that separates Stephen and himself in the name of heteronormative prudence rather than homosexual passion. Like the protagonist of "An Encounter," Bloom lays claim to an otherwise unclaimable male using the purported threat of sexual encroachment by an unfamiliar outsider to justify his own ritual of union, touching Stephen's boot under the table, which Stephen experiences as "warm pressure from an unexpected quarter" (*U*, 16.372–73).

As Colleen Lamos notes, "Joyce's texts . . . manifest the seemingly universal habit of displacing degraded sexual desires onto foreigners and other 'queers'" (1995, 21–22). We would differ with Lamos, however, in noting that in both "An Encounter" and "Eumaeus," the scenes that dramatize this displacement pointedly refuse to treat it as natural. Instead, these episodes call attention to the way such projections of sexual and national or ethnic shame facilitate homosocial bonding. We read these representations of homosexual panic as prerequisite to indispensable rituals of male-male bonding in the context of religious rites, newsrooms, and pubs and in intellectual and artistic processes of exchange. Joyce is not merely uncritically recycling the reflexive association of homosexuality with cultural outsiders, as we can see from the fact that the dangerous, foreign Others in both "An Encounter" and "Eumaeus" bear the physical marks of a clichéd Irishness, in the green eyes of the josser and in Murphy's red beard. Joyce never lets us forget that these characters only appear to be Other, a point that the figure of Bloom himself, onto whom everyone's sexual and ethnic shame is constantly off-loaded, serves to reinforce.

Eibhear Walshe and Susan Cannon Harris both argue for a heightened Irish sensitivity to individual sexual irregularities being treated as systemic ethnical disorders (see Walshe 2005, 38–57; and Harris 2005). Ethnic shame rooted in colonial subjugation is closely related to episodes of Irish homosexual panic, as we see throughout "An Encounter." Such a connection suggests that for Irish Catholic males, vigilant precautions against being seen as sexually deviant like Wilde derive primarily from a reflexive and sustained resistance to being racially shamed. Each of the abundant instances of class and cultural elitism, as well as gendered and sexual normativity in the story, carries an indirectly ethnic valence, marking the structural relationship in Catholic Dublin between social ambition and ethnic passing ("and I'll be Smith"). Published for a primarily English audience, the boys' popular reading material ("the *Union Jack, Puck* and *The Halfpenny Journal*") interpellates them as budding agents of empire, and their more athletic diversions ("pitched battles," sieges, explorer fantasies, with attacks on native tribes) all evince an appetite for imperialist adventures, as does the boy's wistful conviction that "real adventures . . . must be sought abroad" (*D,* 23). Athletic diversions also afford the boys an occasion to affect an upper-class status, the signifiers of which carry distinctly Anglo-Protestant associations (Potts 2000, 78–79). Thus, Mahony sports a "cricket cap," and the boy himself wears "diligently pipeclayed" lawn-tennis shoes, leading the "ragged troop" to peg them for "swaddlers" (*D,* 25). The boys' more intellectual challenges likewise carry the imprint and acknowledge the primacy of Anglicized culture. Not surprisingly, the boys take no offense at the invective "swaddler." To be confused with Anglo-Protestants represents a triumph on a number of counts.

All of this is to suggest the obverse truth, that the negative pole of the gang's homosocial rivalry is their own ethnic status, experienced, however unconsciously, as a source of shame. Being irremediable by direct speech or action, such shame unfolds in just the sort of symptomatic fantasy constructions that the boys' games comprise. To fail in these competitions is to be thrust into the role of the conquered, to be derided as "ineffectual" (Leo) or "stupid" (Mahony); in sum, it is to occupy the colonial reality or the imperial stereotype of the native Irish community to which they belong. It is to suffer the shame of one's ethnic profile as if it were pretend. To "succeed," on the other hand, is to entertain the fantasy of transcending this estate in the direction of the more metropolitan profile to which their various cultural accoutrements—dress, speech, reading, sports—already pretend. To succeed is not to escape ethnic shame, but to safeguard its continued denial and hence to maintain its continued unspeakability. In sum, this enactment of homosocial rivalry conforms precisely to the projective strategy of displacement, which likewise binds each of the couples in the Buck-Stephen-Haines and Bloom-Stephen-Murphy triangles in a shamed and shaming alliance against the "third wheel."

This dynamic of colonial abjection explains why that classic arena of competitive homosocial play, the staged siege or rescue, requires at least three protagonists. The unconscious fantasy aim of this activity is not the transfiguration of individual weakness, but the redistribution of ethnic disability or stigma. Hence, triumph must be experienced on a tribal basis, that is, there must be at least two combatants to share in it, and the shared experience in turn must be consolidated by reference to an object of mastery, who bears the burden of subdominance for the group as a whole. In this respect, the identification with an exoticized, subaltern Other, evinced in Joe Dillon's scrupulously observed victory ritual, the Indian war dance, does nothing to mitigate the supremacist structure of their game, its irreducible debt to the ideology of imperial conquest.

But the boys' efforts to salvage this dimension of their big excursion tell still more heavily. Having attacked a "crowd of ragged girls," but still consumed with playing war games, the protagonist and Mahony attempt to mount a siege by themselves, and, failing, they "reveng[e them]selves upon Leo Dillon [the missing third] by saying what a funk he was and guessing how many he would get at three o'clock from Mr Ryan" (D, 25). In other words, they restore the triangular structure of the homosocial rivalry in absentia. Leo's failure to share the escapade consigns him, in their imagination, to the defeated, the derided, the captive, even the tortured, while at the same time serving to warrant their own mettle as conqueror-adventurers. Not coincidentally, it is in this first reference to corporal punishment that the triangular displacement of shame among the protagonist and his mates shimmers closest to the narrative surface.

The fantasy of corporal punishment provides a site of figurative abjection, where the shame of homosexuality and the shame of Irish Catholicism
can be imaginatively conjoined. Corporal punishment bridges the vast cultural, national, and class cleavages that separate the Irish National school
from the elite British public institution where the josser presumably developed his "good accent" and his taste for the birch. While slightly later the
boy protagonist will reject with hauteur the josser's prurient speculation that
Mahony is subject to frequent beatings at school, here the boys take pleasure
in imagining Leo in precisely the iconic, abject position of the Irish National
schoolboy. Later it is made clear that the boys perceive a significant distinction between pandying, which would likely have been the standard corporal
punishment at their Belvedere-like Catholic school, and the more explicitly
eroticized Etonian use of the birch. Whipping with the birch is associated in
the Irish imaginary with the other end of the class spectrum, as the punishment that paradigmatically confirmed the position of the shamefully powerless. In their fantasies of Leo's punishment, however, the boys obscure the
mode of corporal punishment, thinking and presumably speaking of Leo as
receiving only an unspecified number of disembodied blows, and thus nudg-
ing Leo's imagined pandying closer to the more humiliating "whippings"
that constitute the most dramatic Irish instantiation (short of evictions or
the gallows) of ethnic disempowerment. Significantly, this disposal of the
wretched Leo satisfies the boys' thirst for raids and sorties, permitting them,
with the help of cricket caps and tennis shoes, to assume a place in the mock-
imperialist idyll of the English boys' magazines.

At just this point in the narrative, what Norris calls the boys' "homosocial
elopement" can properly be said to begin: a day of shared treats, shared rides,
and shared glances (1998, 27). To put it another way, the boys' "homosocial elopement" begins with their fantasized transcendence of the ethnically
inflected dishonor that Leo Dillon now embodies. The unacknowledged
"homoerotic undercurrents" of their "buddy" escapade, accordingly, spring
in no small part from their sharing the anticipation of living beyond the
oppressive emotional limits of their ethnocolonial being, much as they are
acting outside the boundaries of family and school regulation. A common
frisson, blended of the truly illicit and "boys will be boys" naughtiness,

infuses, and confuses, all of their diversely transgressive proceedings in a manner that foreshadows Joyce's more extensively ritualized enactments of ethnic, gendered, and sexual humiliation in "Circe." The unspeakability of the ethnic shame they repress passes easily into the convenient unspokenness of whatever attraction they may be developing.

The shape of their adventure suggests that if homosocial rivalry—centered upon colonial shame—is *binding* the boys in affection while *blinding* them to that very fact, it is the shared illusion of having transcended colonial shame that releases those potentially eroticized affections. The covert, intense, and highly pleasurable character of the shame-based bond forged between the boys might give a thoughtful boy pause, in a world where, after the Wilde trials, homosexuality was increasingly visible and thinkable, since in experiencing this imagined shared liberation from colonial shame so intensely, they are veering dangerously close to another kind of stigmatized subjectivity, that of the homosexual. Read in this light, the boy's search for sailors with green eyes owes as much to the color's association with Ireland as with a homosexual subculture. Sailors represent model boundary crossers for the boy, since they live out the fantasy of going to sea that he shares with Mahony. He may be understood as searching the "foreign sailors" for signs of an Irish runaway presence, while at the same time sensing the infection of this national color scheme by its Wildean implications. While the narrator's disposal of this conundrum with the elliptical phrase "I had some confused notion" certainly signals homosexual panic, as Norris proposes (ibid.), it also conveys a genuine confusion between the protagonist's racial and sexual investments.

The josser's narrative function is to increase just this confusion by exposing its operation in the boy's more customary homosocial practices. In this regard, it is important to recognize that the encounter with the josser replicates the triangular structure of the "siege" while shifting its coordinates. In drawing a distinction between the protagonist's bookishness and Mahony's vigor, the josser unwittingly taps a sore point in the gang's workings, introduced at the outset of the tale: the domination of the "studious" by the robust. This internal cleavage among the boys is emphasized from the story's first paragraphs, in which the narrator describes himself as one of the "reluctant Indians who were afraid to seem studious or lacking in

robustness" (*D*, 22). More than snobbery is at stake in the boy's quiet affirmation, at Mahony's expense, of his own cultural attainments. He extends
the homosocial rivalry to the level of its subtending values. When the josser
identifies the boy as "a bookworm like myself," the latter takes the opportunity to drift into allegiance with the josser's Anglicized cultural capital—
his "good accent" and conversance with British literature—and to distance
himself from Mahony, who begins to fill the stereotype of the "Irish savage"
as "stupid," "rough," and "unruly" (*D*, 28, 31). In this way the protagonist,
and, retrospectively, the narrator, exacts revenge on the robust, just as the
boy and Mahony took their revenge on Leo Dillon. If the boy comes to
implicate himself in the josser's erotic field by affecting cultural superiority
to his friend, as most readings of the story agree, he is driven by the same
dialectic of ethnic shame and social ambition that has defined his homosocial
romance with Mahony. The josser's gradual disclosure of his perverse desires
has such power to disturb the boy because of the uncanny way in which
the boy's momentary alliance with the old josser repeats the motives and
rehearses the implications of his daylong partnership with Mahony. He does
not suddenly find himself implicated in a sexual knowledge entirely beyond
his ken; rather, he *suddenly* finds himself to have been *already* implicated, a
Freudian *Nachträglichkeit* that the narrator's imperfect censoring devices
perfectly convey. What the boy recoils from in the perversions of the josser,
with whom he has culturally allied himself, are the perverse possibilities of
the previous homosocial alliance he forged on an analogous basis.

This complicated process of arrested enlightenment culminates with
the josser's discourse on flagellation. When the josser's query as to whether
Mahony received corrective flagellation at school provokes the (suppressed)
response on the part of the narrator, "we were not National School boys to
be whipped" (*D*, 31), the old man immediately embarks on a call for erotic
flagellation, as if to suggest that dignity, in the elitist sense, is nothing to
the point. This brief interchange brings the questions of social status and
sexual perversity into open juxtaposition. The josser's speech itself goes on to
flamboyantly, vertiginously interweave the opposed affective and ideological
components of the lads' homosocial rivalry: shame and desire, abjection and
ambition, aggression and affection, tacitly challenging the very structure of
the homosocial agon. The speech's looping, recursive, incantatory rhythms

reflect its substantive refusal of the rectilinear emotional logic on which the projective dynamics of othering are based.[3] The aggregate effects of these rhetorical operations are *not* to so overcome the defenses of the boy, or the narrator, that he can *see* the connection that he lives every day, precariously poised between the suffering and the discharging of disparaged ethnic and sexual identities. "Peering" into the man's "bottle-green eyes," a pun and an image that conjure up "pierglass" and "looking glass," the boy finds mirrored back at him neither the searched-for green sailor's eyes nor the earlier exchanged gaze with Mahony, but only the opaque reflection that protects him from their interlocking racial and sexual implications. These same rhetorical operations do, however, bring the boy to *feel* these elided connections, feel them in the texture of the language, rather than its sense, in the quality of the man's voice, shame's voice, speaking out of its isolation.

The narrator recalls, in words that resemble the language in which Radclyffe Hall in *The Well of Loneliness* would soon describe Stephen Gordon's encounter with a ravaged homosexual youth in a Parisian gay bar, and Stephen's reluctant acknowledgment of the boy's filial claims, that "his voice . . . grew almost affectionate and seemed to plead with me that I should understand him" (*D*, 31–32). Here, however, in keeping with the more general narrative pattern of disavowal, the boy refuses the josser's plea; indeed, he finally breaks with him at this point and fears to be accosted. He is threatened with a traumatic insight into his own fellowship with abjection, an insight

---

3. The josser's violation of his larger society's prohibition against the too-open homoeroticization of flagellation (Lamos 1995) could be read as a sort of queer baiting of the British aristocracy, a cultural stance from which both Valente and Lamos have shown Joyce was not immune. However, given the intricate parallels that "An Encounter" constructs between the British system of punitive homoerotic desire and shame that has shaped the josser's libido and the Irish National school system of homosocial competition and desire forged through public displays of ritual domination and submission (both in the staged siege and in public displays of schoolroom discipline), it seems unlikely that Joyce is merely unconsciously reiterating the cultural politics of projection. Rather, as we have argued, Joyce seems to be calling attention to not only the homoeroticized domination and submission that circulate within elite British public schools, but also a variant of this economy among Irish Catholic schoolboys.

he cannot accept and continues in this narrative to defend himself against. But his ensuing response to Mahony's return indicates that the josser has not failed entirely in his appeal to their common human *indignity,* and that the boy has not entirely failed to understand it.

Although he abruptly flees back into the fantasy space of the homosocial romance, consigning the old man to unspeakability once again, he looks to meet Mahony not on the wings of illusory transcendence but on the ground of mutual unworthiness. It is here that our reading most decisively deviates from that of Norris, who perceives the boys' relationship as "surviv[ing] its brutal disruption by homosexual panic" (1998, 32). In our reading, the josser subliminally reframes the boys' relationship through his own reflections on the erotic potential of bodily shame, and the result is not a brutal disruption to be survived, but an infusion of alterity to be internalized. In his telling of this story, the narrator contrives both to express and to deflect precisely this (self-)otherness. Like his use of pseudonyms, the boy's "accent of forced bravery" involuntarily reveals too much, even, or rather especially, to himself. The "paltry stratagem" fills him with a sense of embarrassment, rather than the sense of mastery at which the boys' play-adventures customarily aim (*D,* 32). At the same time, the narrator, who is now in control of the narrative deployment of shame, reconfigures the story's earlier shame triangles, constituting himself, as Norris observes, as the helpless damsel and the formerly despised Mahony as protective hero (1998, 32). The beating that is administered now is internal: even as the josser has been (shamefully) used yet again as a pretext for another otherwise proscribed male-bonding ritual, he has also been unconsciously internalized. The protagonist exclaims, "How my heart *beat* as [Mahony] came running across the field to me! He ran as if to bring me aid" (*D,* 32; emphasis added). It is through the narrator's conscious encounter with shame, an alternative to his routine projection of shame onto others in the form of contempt, that he can now "confess" to a "refigured homosocial affection" (Norris 1998, 32) that allows him to see Mahony anew, not with a sense of rivalry contoured by ethnic or erotic shame but with a sense of solidarity and gratitude enhanced by a certain *ethical* shame: "He ran as if to bring me aid. And I was penitent; for in my heart I had always despised him a little" (*D,* 32).

"Something Poetical Like Violets or Roses"

In "James Joyce and the English Vice," Colleen Lamos points to a puzzling feature of the Victorian obsession with flagellation: while the discourse of corrective chastisement was almost exclusively same-sexed, the pornographic discourse of flagellation was exclusively cross-sexed. She offers Joyce's representations of sadomasochism, particularly the sadomasochism surrounding Bloom's famous transformation into Ruby Cohen, as a case in point. But as we have seen, the pornographic ramblings of the josser violate the cordon sanitaire between both corrective and erotic flagellation and between the same- and other-sexed quality of the act.

Of particular interest for our study is Lamos's contention that the schism between homoerotic corrective flagellation and heteroerotic sexual flagellation serves simultaneously to mask and preserve the homoerotic origins of flagellant desire, both within British fin-de-siècle culture and in Joyce's ouevre. Lamos nicely points to the moment of decisive transformation in "Circe" when the now-male Bello penetrates Bloom's body with his fist, so that at the moment of penetration Bloom's anus is nominally transformed into a vagina, thus staving off by the thinnest possible margin the ultimate humiliation of male-male penetration. But the wafer-thin margin by which anal penetration is averted could be read as flagrantly *calling attention to* rather than minimally sustaining fin-de-siècle denial concerning the homoerotic underpinnings of Edwardian sexual transgression. This scene constitutes a virtual parody of the characteristic bait-and-switch tactics by which male-male eroticized violence and humiliation, encoded in fantasies of female dominance, displace the transgressive desire and resentment stirred up by oedipal accommodation to patriarchal authority. Likewise, the transformation of the central scene of initiation in "An Encounter" into Bloom's encounter with Gerty in "Nausicaa" could be read as a queering of heterosexuality rather than as a maintenance of heteronormative denial. Here, however, it is in the conventional and publicly disparaged register of style that shame-based and simultaneously sexually enabling bonds are forged.

Like flagellation, rhetorical tropes such as alliteration, hyperbole, and personification (to name three that recur throughout the first half of "Nausicaa") were applauded or denigrated in Edwardian society, depending on their gendered context. The same rhetorical figures that Gentile schoolboys were studying in their Latin classes in elite educational institutions throughout the UK became, in the pages of the bourgeoning women's magazines of the era, stigmatized symptoms of excess. For Joyce, Oscar Wilde straddled the division between these two opposed spheres, elaborating out of the aesthetic and philosophical theories he learned at Oxford "a name [that] evoked a vague idea of delicate finesse, a life bedecked with flowers," and then forced by poverty "to accept the position of editor in a very trite magazine" (J. Joyce 2000b, 149). Like Wilde's writing, women's commercial writing, such as the works published by the *Woman's World* (which Wilde edited), and Joyce's own writing were liable to public censure for their exorbitance, their lack of tasteful discretion and self-discipline. The public disciplining of Irish and English national schoolboy Oscar Wilde, meanwhile, instilled a liberal dose of homophobia into traditional middle-class contempt for aestheticism. Through Wilde, the "tastelessly over-aestheticized"—conventionally associated with the female, the Oriental, and Arnold's artistic and overly emotive Celt—became simultaneously queer.[4] Having learned, like Caliban, to speak, women and ethnic minorities threatened, in speaking well, to curse the system that had predicated its stability on their unnegotiable and irremediable inferiority.

In reenacting his earlier textual encounter between a queer foreigner, who has violated the unspoken codes of sexual decorum that underpin the social hierarchy of empire, and a youth who more or less hopelessly aspires to an advantaged position within that hierarchy, Joyce offers a second psychoanalytic *tableau vivant* of Edwardian Irish society. "Nausicaa," like "An Encounter," functions both to reveal the psychosexual motivations through which empires are, for a time, maintained and to offer an alternative erotics in which the subject embraces his or her shameful corporeal excessiveness rather than projecting it elsewhere. Sensitive to the shared plight and interests of

---

4. Jews, too, with their Oriental affiliations, could be easily grouped with this amorphous cluster of cultural arrivistes whose increasingly notable mastery of the rhetorical tropes that formed the very basis of British public school education threatened to disrupt the cultural distribution of shame within the British Empire by contesting the intellectual and cultural superiority of English elites on their home turf.

the queer and the colonized subject, Joyce refuses the standard fin-de-siècle strategy of sublimating homoeroticism into heteronormative perversion.

In Joyce's essay on Wilde, he implicitly links Oscar Wilde's transgression of the rules of class, cultural, and ethnic refinement (rules that Gerty strains every nerve to embody) with the stigmatized, evacuating excesses of a feminized consumer capitalism when he describes Wilde as having resolved, like Gerty, to put into practice a theory of beauty, "beginning with himself" (J. Joyce 2000b, 149). Wilde's self-commodification through the "aesthetic reform of his dress and his home," Joyce suggests, made him both famous and suspect, an object of cultural hostility as well as cachet, so that "his fall was greeted with a howl of puritanical joy" (ibid.). In his poetry and love letters, Wilde prettifies the grosser specifics of sexual embodiment with references to flowers, particularly roses. In Lord Henry Wotton's revelation to Dorian Gray of Dorian's own inchoate thoughts and feelings, the moment at which Lord Henry constitutes Dorian as both object and subject of sexual desire is framed in imagery of roses: "You, Mr. Gray, you yourself, with your rose-red youth and your rose-white boyhood, you have had passions that have made you afraid, thoughts that have filled you with terror, day-dreams and sleeping dreams whose mere memory might stain your cheek with shame" (1988, 159). Drawing on the language of flowers, a language that Joyce speaks fluently throughout *Ulysses,* and also on the carpe diem tradition, by which the figurative "flowering" of a young man betrays a conventionally explicit wish to deflower him, Wilde wrote, in a famous letter to Lord Alfred Douglas, "My own boy. Your sonnet is quite lovely, and it is a marvel that those red rose-leaf lips of yours should have been made no less for the music of song than for the madness of kissing. . . . I know Hyacinthus, whom Apollo loved so madly, was you in Greek days" (Cohen 1993, 150).

The mythic transformation of Hyacinthus into a flower in Wilde's notorious letter is reenacted when Gerty leaves Bloom to rejoin her friends. Bloom's last glance "reach[es] her heart, full of a strange shining, [and hangs] enraptured on her sweet flowerlike face," in an image that directly recalls Wilde's saccharine hyperbole, which is always at its sweetest when it is closest to raw sexual desire, a simultanaeity that "Nausicaa" makes plain (*U,* 13.763–64). Gerty similarly expresses an aversion to the grossness of eating and wonders "why you couldn't eat something poetical like violets or roses" (*U,* 13.230).

Like Wilde, and like Joyce himself, Gerty is walking a fine line, reorganizing cultural signifiers so as to distinguish herself as a superior and hence marketable commodity, while at the same time risking our ridicule in calling attention to herself *as* commodity through her efforts at self-invention.

The josser's voyeuristic investment in corrective flagellation points to how its public performance, like the ones that he envisions in a school context, implicates the audience in both sides of the transaction simultaneously, that is, creates both an empowering sense of identification with the infliction of edifying pain and a shaming sense of identification with the receipt or suffering of such pain. (Freud, of course, elaborated a similar dynamic in his landmark essay on sadomasochism, "A Child Is Being Beaten.") The eroticism of this species of flagellation, as Lamos suggests, arises from the onlooker's psychic oscillation between these two positions. We see "Nausicaa" as in some sense replaying the sexualized encounter between a younger naïf and an older and socially marginal stranger (who if he is not the nominated "queer" is the nominated "cuckoo"). We further see the ritualized performance of corrective flagellation before an ambivalent audience in this episode as raised to the level of style, in which women's commercial writing and its stigmatized symptoms of excess constitute Gerty MacDowell as the legitimate object of discipline while at the same time immuring the reader, for the first half of the chapter, within Gerty's consciousness. Thus, the reader, while certainly aware of Gerty's standing as a shamefully "marked down" subject, must simultaneously acknowledge the very real problems and contradictions to which her self-(marriage) marketing provides not implausible answers (Leonard 1998, 120–28). If we are at one level identified with the parodic consciousness that critiques Gerty's mode of being in the world, we are, at another level, inescapably immersed in that Being, and so we experience the shame of her parodic flagellation. What is suggestive about reading "Nausicaa" next to "An Encounter" is that in bringing forward a dimension of discipline and humiliation, it shows us that it is not enough to understand Gerty as a commodity entrapped within a circuit of symbolic exchange; she constitutes a particular kind of commodity, the kitsch object, which has its own conditions of marketability.

Kitsch is a particular commodity form that presents itself as an object of inferior taste in need of correction: in pretending to luxury, it pretends to an excess of exchange value over use value, but in failing in its pretense to luxury, its excessiveness registers as shameful and stigmatizing. Gerty, as an object of kitsch who is simultaneously offered as an object of empathy and desire, embodies the double binds of Oscar Wilde's position relative to cultural self-expression, a position that Joyce emphasizes in his own reinvention of Wilde, as Eibhear Walshe points out (2005, 52), and that figures his inevitable hopes that his literary excesses will ultimately be valued according to their intrinsic merits rather than by his Irish, lower-middle-class subject position.

With her invocation of Dame Fashion, Gerty believes she can rise by dint of her taste for the very same reason we are invited to disparage it: taste is the currency of the negotiation among middle-class fractions, who are determined in their specific fractionality, not by their place in the order of production alone, but more significantly by their place in the order of consumption. That is why the question of taste among the middle classes is always moralized, why Kant holds that aesthetic taste, of which consumer taste is a subdivision, entails always universalized (though not universal) judgment (1951, 45–46). The affective currency of this negotiation is a currency of discipline, correction, and shame. Therefore, it is not surprising that we find Gerty, as lower-middle-class subject, objectified as kitsch, to stand toward the more respectably middle-class, judicious Bloom in roughly the same position that James Joyce, as corner boy spitting in the Liffey, stood toward the more respectable denizens of Bloomsbury.

Lighted Squares

Framing "Araby"

KATHRYN CONRAD AND MARK OSTEEN

Our essay began as two discrete perspectives on the story "Araby." Mark's focus was initially trained on the imagery of light and darkness, and Katie's on the concept of vanity introduced in the final lines. Each writer wrote his or her own draft separately and then read the other writer's contribution. In an early correspondence, Mark suggested that the accounts be integrated as two observers "watching and making notes on the same set of scenes. We could do this by setting them off with actual frames on the page. The idea would be to create a sense of binocular vision, thereby demonstrating the ideas about multiple frames and competing visions discussed in the essay(s)." Mark interspersed Katie's reflections into his essay, and then Katie revised and commented further on Mark's essay.

The framed insertions comprise an array of responses: in some cases, Katie expands upon Mark's interpretation; in others, she qualifies or disagrees with it; in others, she proposes a different vision or focus entirely. The strategy yields a result appropriate for the essay's visual theme: one critic reads the story as a self-reflexive commentary on readerly vision, while a second critic reframes the first critic's commentary in light of her vision of the text. The effect, we hope, is of frames or panes sliding across one another, sometimes converging in a single view, sometimes superimposing two views upon each other, sometimes presenting two different perspectives. Rarely have the critical terms "intervention" and "revision" seemed more apt!

In the last double-framed paragraph, the two sets of eyes finally converge—almost. Indeed, the conclusion argues that such a truly binocular vision never occurs, that critical responses, even responses created in tandem such as ours

were, never display—and should not display—convergence, but instead gener-
ate the kind of superimpositions and multiple visions that we find in the critical
history of "Dubliners" and indeed throughout this volume of essays.

Joyce's *Dubliners* opens with a scene of watching, as the unnamed narrator of "The Sisters" studies a "lighted square of window," seeking a sign
of Father Flynn's condition (*D*, 9). Gazing at the window night by night, he
repeats the word *paralysis* softly to himself, as if the combination of word and
vision produces a paralytic condition in the boy. Similar self-referential visual
episodes—in which a character gazes into or through a mirror or window—
reappear with remarkable frequency in *Dubliners;* in almost every case, the
watcher's vision freezes a dynamic process into a static scene.[1]

Dubliners is filled with frames: windows, mirrors, photos, and portraits.[2]
Mirror scenes often appear—as in "Clay"—when characters' self-satisfaction
veils their self-delusion. Window scenes, in contrast, stage characters' feelings
of longing or imprisonment, producing what film critics call internal frames,
where a figure appears to be trapped in a box. And when characters gaze
through windows at dusk, as they so often do in *Dubliners,* they invariably see
both inwardly and outwardly, looking both backward into the past and forward into the future. Inner and outer visions merge to produce double expo-
sures or superimpositions. It is fitting that most of these double visions occur
at twilight—the time of two lights—when a person looking out a window can,
in fact, see him- or herself superimposed upon the outside world. In *Dubliners*
windows become pictures become mirrors.

These visual phenomena are perhaps most evident in "Araby," which even
a cursory reading reveals to be a tale of watching. The boy narrator's complex

1. Peter de Voogd has recently remarked that the opening scene of "The Sisters" (a
young man looks into a window, envisioning a dead older man), coupled with the final tableau
in "The Dead" (an older man looks out a window, imagining a dead youth), frames the entire
volume (2000, 42).

2. Laurent Milesi has noted the prevalence of mirrors in *Dubliners,* of "windows and
(barred) perspectives, as well as an insistence on gazing," and likewise links the first and last
stories in the collection through motifs of mirrored gazes (1997, 91).

framing of Mangan's sister epitomizes a process that, we propose, occurs repeatedly in the volume: he first *sees* her, then *pictures* her—initially grabbing a sight of her, then freezing her into a portrait, thereby transferring her from his external to his internal vision. Eloise Knowlton's distinction between discursive and figural photographs helps to clarify this process. Discursive photographs, she writes, resemble symbolic paintings arranged to signify something specific through pose, decor, and *mise en scène*. Figural photos, in contrast, are "image first and signif[y] only secondarily" (2005, 140). Spontaneous and unposed, they partake of what John Szarkowski has called a "snapshot aesthetic" (1988, 31). We suggest that the "tension between the artistic and the documentary" that Knowlton discovers in *Dubliners* (2005, 142) manifests itself explicitly in the "Araby" narrator's movement from the figural to the discursive: after taking mental snapshots of Mangan's sister, he turns these passing moments into static portraits of her as ideal woman and of himself as ideal lover.[3]

Just as important as the portrait, however, is the frame. The text itself generates multiple frames, from the boy's literal observations to the narrative observations provided after the fact to our own interpretive frames. The "glass" through which we as readers look is not only potentially reflective, depending on the "light" by which we read, but also (de)limited by the frame around it. And, of course, a frame is not merely a boundary. It forms, fits, fashions the very thing it frames. By superimposing multiple frames, Joyce allows us to ask whether the result is the unification of views that might lead to a clearer binocular vision or merely layer upon layer of obscurity and distortion.

In this binocular essay, we propose to frame "Araby" in a number of ways: first, by tracing the narrator's framing of himself and his idealized female

---

3. Knowlton points out that while Joyce was writing the early *Dubliners* tales, photographic practice was shifting from the discursive to the figural (in part because of the availability of portable cameras). She argues that "Eveline" is the story where "the incidental photographic moment" shifts to "the heavily symbolic, meaning-laden space of painting" (2005, 146), but it seems likely that this movement actually occurs within "Araby" itself.

within his mental theater; second, by juxtaposing it with other stories in which Joyce's characters create framed, static pictures from their experiences in order to glorify or diminish themselves (or both). Finally, through our dual perspectives on the story, we both consider and dramatize how employing multiple frames affects critical reading by transforming the page—which appears to be a window onto a world—into a mirror that reflects readers' own biases and frameworks. Seen this way, *Dubliners* becomes a gallery of self-referential portraits presaging Joyce's first novel and an album of pictures in which readers watch themselves watching.[4] Such self-reflexive framing is fitting, for Joyce aimed these portraits at a specific group of readers—his fellow Dubliners— in order, as he stated to publisher Grant Richards, that they might obtain a "good look at themselves in my nicely polished looking-glass" (*SL*, 90).

THE INSISTENCE ON OBSERVATION in "Araby" begins with its opening description of houses on North Richmond Street gazing "at one another with brown imperturbable faces" (*D*, 33). The young male protagonist seems to imitate these houses when, in the failing light of winter dusk, he watches Mangan's sister "peer up and down the street," apparently looking for him and her brother. He then approaches where she waits, "her figure defined by the light from the half-opened door. . . . Her dress swung as she moved her body and the soft rope of her hair tossed from side to side" (*D*, 34). Attentive readers may recall a scene depicted just a few pages earlier, in "An Encounter," when the "queer old josser" tells that story's young narrator that he likes nothing better than "looking at a nice young girl, at her nice white hands and her beautiful soft hair" (*D*, 29): it is as though the "Araby" narrator, having overheard the old man, is now emulating his habits, just as the young narrator of "The Sisters" emulates *his* mentor, Father Flynn. In succeeding days, the "Araby" boy regards Mangan's sister from behind his nearly closed window blind, which serves as a frame, transforming the living girl into a peepshow "figure" (*D*, 34–35).[5] From this point on, he keeps her

4. That James Joyce imagined his stories in such visual terms is borne out by the series of prose sketches he composed as a teenager under the title *Silhouettes*. See *BK*, 90.

5. Knowlton remarks that the boy is here enacting a specific use of photographic (that is, "figural") realism: pornography, with its unseen "detective" camera (2005, 145).

"brown figure always in [his] eye," so that her "image" accompanies him even to the noisy, unromantic marketplace (*D*, 35).

It is worth noting here that the boy's vision, as seen through the frame of the more mature narrator, inevitably shapes the reader's response to the narrative: his observations, in other words, inevitably frame our own. As Margot Norris points out, for instance, critics have tended to accept the boy's own estimation of the street life of Dublin as "hostile to romance," even though the street life of Dublin and its "indigenous bazaar" (2003, 52) environment may provide a more vibrant possibility than the Araby bazaar, which in the story is, literally and figuratively, closed.

The boy now views Mangan's sister through a kind of twilight—the combined lights of imagination and bodily reality—superimposing his fantasy figure upon the actual girl, to whom he has not yet even spoken.[6] She is forever an "image"—whether chalice or harp player (*D*, 35)—to which he plays a complementary role as celebrant or harp: he pictures himself as her other half.[7] To complete this process of internalization, the boy retreats on a dark, rainy evening to a back drawing room; below, a "distant lamp or lighted window" gleams, creating a chiaroscuro effect appropriate for his imaginary exhibition (*D*, 36).

Then she speaks to him, in an encounter that shapes both the story's later events and our framing of those events. Mangan's sister asks if the boy intends to visit the bazaar and says she would love to go but cannot, meanwhile turning "a silver bracelet round and round her wrist" (*D*, 36). Why does she toy with the bracelet? Is she, as a student of mine once proposed, bored and distracted? Perhaps, rather, she is as anxious about his interest as he is about hers. Or perhaps she is attempting, as Garry Leonard argues, to

6. According to Tanja Vesala-Varttala, a similar superimposition affects the story's narrative voice, which juxtaposes and occasionally fuses the perspectives of the adult narrator and the boy protagonist (1999, 129).

7. Garry Leonard likewise writes that the harp image suggests a "mirror response," in which "every movement of the girl generates a reflective movement in the boy" (1989, 466).

"direct the boy's gaze" (1989, 463), as if to say, "Here's the kind of thing I like." The boy promises to bring her something—as well he might, for the tableau seems designed to entice him: "She held one of the spikes, bowing her head towards me. The light from the lamp opposite our door caught the white curve of her neck, lit up her hair that rested there and, falling, lit up the hand upon the railing. It fell over one side of her dress and caught the white border of a petticoat, just visible as she stood at ease" (*D*, 36). The fortuitous arrangement of light, the hands on the phallic rail, the coyly exposed petticoat—these details not only display the boy's eroticizing vision, but also suggest that she is posing for him.[8] If so, his roving gaze and fetishizing vision merely respond to her self-presented portrait of alluring young womanhood. She is, after all, the one who initiates the conversation. And how better to appeal to the young man who has been spying on her than to exhibit herself as the image he desires to see? She may wish to be part of *his* scene, to project her idealized image upon the boy's external and internal eyes, and thus see herself elevated. The two are, in short, becoming counterparts, each one generating an ideal self through the (imagined) eyes of the other.

Of course, we cannot know what Mangan's sister intends; the narration frames and shapes our vision much as it does our vision of other women in *Dubliners* whose stories are framed by those of other characters: Polly Mooney, for instance, or Gretta Conroy.[9] We cannot help

8. Keith Williams observes that in holding the phallic rail, she simultaneously arouses sexuality and denies it (2004, 158).

9. Leonard claims that "Mangan's sister exists alongside the boy's narration and in fact can be glimpsed through those gaps in the text where the boy's story falters. In fact, her desire *is* the subject of the story because it is the subject of the boy's unconscious where it directs—right alongside but outside his awareness—his conscious intentions which he misrecognizes as a call to destiny" (1989, 464). I would suggest, however, that the version of Mangan's sister who exists "alongside the boy's narration" still remains the Mangan's sister *of* the boy's narration; as tempting as it is to construct her as having some sort of agency, she most certainly exists only through the framed lens or mirror of the narrator.

but see Mangan's sister as a secondary character in our narrator's tale. And she has already become an aestheticized object here, presaging the image of Polly on the landing with the "white instep," which "shone in the opening of her furry slippers" (*D*, 80), or Gretta, whom Gabriel sees at one point standing with "grace and mystery in her attitude as if she were a symbol of something" (*D*, 260), both mental portraits captured in single static poses.

What we see in this scene is itself framed, for our vision of such encounters is never innocent; it is inevitably conditioned by our own experience as well as by other stories we have read, including those in *Dubliners*. How else does Joyce frame the scene within the gallery of Dublin gazers? Let us juxtapose this scene with a similar optical evaluation depicted later in the volume. When, in "Two Gallants," Lenehan runs his eyes over the body of his pal Corley's "slavey," the narrator's language betrays none of the "Araby" narrator's rhap-sodizing. Instead, Lenehan's eyes visually penetrate the woman, first coldly assessing her clothing, then frankly scrutinizing her "fat red cheeks," "blunt" features, "unabashed" blue eyes, "broad nostrils," and leering, "straggling" mouth (*D*, 66). Whereas the "Araby" boy's vision incorporates only tantaliz-ing hints of sexual allure (hand, neck, undergarment), Lenehan crassly sizes up the woman like a slab of meat. The first vision is erotic; the second is, at best, pornographic. Yet Lenehan's optical ravishment prompts us to recon-sider the boy's visual delectation. The earlier encounter may at first appear all the more innocent by contrast. But upon a second glance, we wonder: Is this where such juvenile voyeurism leads? Is the "Araby" narrator's elevated dic-tion merely drapery for prurient gaping? Will his innocent peeping inevitably devolve into Corleyian pimping? And is this unnamed woman merely offering a more direct version of Mangan's sister's ingenuous attractions? Juxtapos-ing "Two Gallants" with "Araby" bathes the first encounter in a spectrum of disturbing lights. Such proleptic reading encourages us to superimpose this story's encounter upon the tale of the boy and Mangan's sister. But should we? In such a twilight reading—where we see what is in front of us in terms of what lies ahead—the page becomes a mirror, a half-lit rectangle revealing readers' multiple frameworks, as well as the frames of the volume as a whole.

I would suggest that the "Araby" narrator's visual and geographical routes through Dublin mirror the paths of Lenehan and Corley in "Two Gallants"; this mirroring provides a glimpse of an alternative to the direct and driven narrative vision of romance that the former idealizes and the latter parodies, albeit unself-consciously. Norris points to Joyce's recognition of the alternatives to high modernist elitism by invoking the possibilities opened up by the marketplace—the very possibilities embraced by Bloom in *Ulysses* and rejected by Stephen Dedalus (who himself is reflected in *Dubliners* by the "Araby" narrator and Gabriel Conroy). The possibilities of the marketplace, offered to the reader here only through the narrator's distorted lenses, stand in opposition to the stasis of aestheticization that takes place both when the boy attempts to fix Mangan's sister as an object of devotion and when the more mature narrator "frames" his experiences, thereby turning them into art. The marketplace, unlike the process of aestheticization, includes circulation *and* exchange and gestures toward the complexities of human interaction that aestheticization can never fully transcend: the kinesis that so bothers Stephen Dedalus in *Portrait,* or, more generally, the give-and-take that troubles the unidirectional subject-object economy of vision, a phrase I employ deliberately, echoing Vicki Mahaffey's construction of the "subject/object economy of privilege" that shapes critical analysis (1991, 667).

Joyce implies that those characters locked into a single vision of romance, whether idealized or denigrated—and by extension, the readers who follow their gaze—are entranced by the power of their own vision, to their own detriment. Corley, for instance, exploits the narrative of romance, offering his "palaver," to quote Lily of "The Dead" (herself a "slavey" of the sort Corley pursues), in exchange for "what they can get out of you"—in his case, the coin on which the story ends (*D,* 219, 72). The boy of "Araby" hopes to exchange money for a gift, and the gift for the affection of Mangan's sister, who is unable to go to the bazaar; these exchanges are predicated on a particular vision, figuratively speaking, of women's roles. In "Araby" vision is more than figurative, operating as a prod to his adolescent desires and framing, literally and figuratively, his notion of Mangan's sister, his quest, and his failure, the latter signaled by the darkened bazaar building and his new and unwelcome view of him-self as "derided by vanity," which is both self-love and futility (*D*, 41). In short, the failures of "Araby" and the failures elsewhere in the collec-tion—the "blind spots" Norris notes in the story (2003, 50)—inhere in the subject-object economy of vision itself.

After the boy makes his promise to Mangan's sister, her "image" insis-tently imposes itself between his eyes and the pages he tries to read (*D*, 37). But he does not yet fully "possess" her as a wrought image of desire. Such possession can occur only in solitude. And so, on the night of the bazaar, he retires to upper rooms, where he leans his forehead against the window and gazes at her house, "seeing nothing but the brown-clad figure cast by my imagination, touched discreetly by the lamplight at the curved neck, at the hand upon the railings and at the border below the dress" (*D*, 38). That is, he superimposes a stored page showing Mangan's sister upon the window pane (K. Williams 2004, 158).[10] She is at once diminished and glorified as the boy frames her body—or, rather, body parts—in a twi- or perhaps trilight vision: looking through the window, he beholds a reified version of Mangan's sister as she once appeared to him, shorn of unnecessary words and accoutrements; only her neck, hand, and petticoat remain. He has thus altered his figural photograph into a framed, discursive portrait of her as romantic icon and himself as her chivalrous lover: the window is a portrait is a mirror of the boy's aesthetic desire.[11]

10. Specific meteorological conditions make this visual effect possible: the scene takes place between eight and nine o'clock, and assuming that "Araby" takes place in May (when the real-life Araby Bazaar did), the dusky light would enable the narrator to see both outside and inside simultaneously.

11. Gerald Doherty likewise finds here a conventionalized "art-image" of Mangan's sis-ter and remarks on how the window functions as a framing device that enables the portrait to move from one site to another and permits the boy to edit the picture (2004, 52). But his claim that the "textual blank" that follows the scene indicates its status as a "mild, non-self-shattering reverie" fails to grasp what the lacuna clearly indicates: a masturbatory fantasy whose outcome could not be depicted, or at least not published, at this point in Joyce's career.

This process recurs numerous times in *Dubliners* when characters gaze through windows. For example, the next story, "Eveline," commences with the protagonist staring out her window at dusk, the twilight again prompting visions of future and past that merge when her eyes light on a (framed) print of the promises to the Blessed Margaret Mary Alacoque—an exemplum of self-sacrificial womanhood she has emulated (*D*, 43). Both window and print become Eveline's mirrors, as do the ship's "illumined portholes," the lights of which, like the eyes of Eveline at story's end, show "no sign" of anything (*D*, 47–48). Likewise, in "A Little Cloud," the old men and children Little Chandler observes from his office window at twilight seem to show him how "useless it [is] to struggle against fortune" and foreshadow night falling on his dreams (*D*, 85). When, near the end of that story, he regards a photograph of his wife "enclosed in a frame of crumpled horn," her "thin tight" lips, undesired expensive blouse, and "cold eyes" seem to signify his entrapment in the "narrow cell" of domesticity (*D*, 102, 100). Similarly, as James Duffy, near the conclusion of "A Painful Case," reads and rereads, by a window in the failing November twilight, the account of Emily Sinico's death, the "cheerless evening landscape" mirrors his own loneliness (*D*, 140). Conjuring up "two images" of Mrs. Sinico (*D*, 142)—inebriated accident victim and yearning, passionate woman—he foresees his own future as an unremembered corpse. In each case, a twilit window inspires the character to superimpose her- or himself upon the outdoor scene, behold future and past, and consider an empty life. These dusky reflections generate static portraits—discursive paintings denoting paralysis—that the characters overlay on events past and future. The internalization of vision renders it symbolic, thereby producing the very paralysis the characters lament. Thus framed, the boy's disappointment at "Araby"'s conclusion seems inevitable—another silhouette in a dark gallery of loss. It becomes, indeed, a crucial snapshot in the volume's chronological arrangement (from youth to adolescence to maturity): the moment when disillusionment becomes destiny.

Still unaware of this destiny, the boy belatedly makes his way to the bazaar, arriving at 9:50—a moment when, as Heyward Ehrlich points out, the two hands of the clock's "lighted dial" (*D*, 39) would be "perfectly superimposed" upon each other (2006, 282), as if time has momentarily stopped. But night falls swiftly upon the nearly closed bazaar, accompanied by the symbolic sound of falling coins, as the boy's desultory examination of "porcelain vases and flowered tea-sets" (*D*, 40), his timid approach to the saleswoman, and her flirtatious conversation with the two men yield the famous final sentence: "Gazing up into the darkness I saw myself as a creature driven and derided by vanity; and my eyes burned with anguish and anger" (*D*, 40). Presumably, he sees himself in the leering men, now realizing that Mangan's sister and his own visual fantasies have enticed him into making a futile trip. Ehrlich, however, argues that the boy's inflated rhetoric merely permits him to "play the Manganian hero one more time, alternately inventing, effacing, and enlarging himself, now in the Araby of his own memory" (2006, 283). As Norris puts it, the narrator turns "an empty space into a dark mirror" (2003, 47). But this mirror is strangely framed: the boy packages his knowledge into a pat sentence, a suspiciously well-polished self-portrait.

Indeed, as Norris comments, this ending offers a "variety of interpretive options" that range from a "straight" acceptance of the boy's self-estimation as a vain figure to "sympathy with the idealist's victimization by vulgar philistinism," to "a critique of the narrator's exploitations of the juvenile experience by turning it into an aestheticized social parable" (ibid., 46). Yet most readers tend to see the ending of "Araby" as an epiphanic moment of illumination and insight—a portrait of the boy in disillusioned apprehension in which he recognizes the foolishness of his behavior after his anticlimactic visit to Araby. This reading hinges on the notion that the boy is driven and derided by his *own* vanity, that is, by his own high opinion of himself, perhaps even his vision of himself as a figure in a romance, which has presumably been deflated by his experience at the bazaar.[12] But what is the nature of the "vanity" that leads his eyes to "burn with anguish and anger"? The answer provides yet another frame for interpretation.

12. See, for instance, Norris 2003, 54, although she suggests that "the narrative urges us to disbelieve" his declaration; Flynn 1983, 242–44; Mandel 1984, 53; and Russell 1966, 171.

The definitions of "vanity" evoke more than its common synonym of "conceit" or solipsism. The *Oxford English Dictionary* (*OED*) offers up definitions of *vanity* that hinge on value: "that which is vain, unprofitable, or worthless," "a vain and unprofitable conduct or employment of time," "a vain, idle, or worthless thing; a thing or action of no value." The vanity that turns on him could thus be the journey itself, which is unprofitable insofar as it yields no gift for Mangan's sister. But does his epiphany extend beyond this narrow interpretation? The ending does nothing to suggest that the boy has challenged the notion of value on which his failure at the bazaar depends. He has fallen from his self-portrait as a noble Grail knight and ends the story envisioning himself as a "creature" "derided" by "anguish and anger"—a response as self-abasing as his previous vision was self-inflating. But the passive voice constructs these visions as entities outside himself: vanity pursues him like a person driving a beast of burden or a hunter pursuing prey. By projecting the image of vanity outside of himself, the boy removes responsibility for his own behavior, taking responsibility instead for the vision—"I saw myself." The boy, in other words, is an agent of the vision, but the final lines do not ensure that the epiphany is more than an aestheticized response to his failed and unprofitable quest.

"Vanity" itself evokes the visual, and more specifically the relationship between artist and object, between the power of spectatorship and the objectification of what is seen. Norris connects the vanity of the end of the story with Vanitas: "The boy has been transformed by his own narrative voice into a figure of fable or parable, of the mirrored emptiness that is Vanitas" (ibid.). This evocation of Vanitas refers us to a specific genre of seventeenth-century Dutch paintings, discursive still-lifes that remind their viewers of life's impermanence through their representation of perishable objects, human skulls, and other images of death and decay. I would argue that this genre also simultaneously undercuts that notion of impermanence, however, through the process of *poesis* that the painters enact. This notion of vanity as Vanitas can be further connected to another meaning of *vanity*, a seventeenth-century usage that refers to a vanity fair: "a place or scene where all is frivolity and empty show; the world or a section of it as a scene of idle amusement and unsubstantial display." These allusions trigger recognition of the particularity of the boy's epiphany: as much as he may be sobered by his experience at the "vanity fair"—and arguably, it is the fair itself, an external rather than internal vanity, that pursues him—nonetheless, by eventually narrating the story, he makes something new out of the experience. In so doing, he provides both a pessimistic reflection about life's impermanence and superficiality (as in *vanitas vanitatum omnia vanitas,* "vanity of vanities, all is vanity," from Ecclesiastes 1:2 of the Vulgate) and a reasonably permanent, aestheticized story that elevates, like the basket in Stephen's aesthetic exercise in *Portrait* (179; earlier in the novel associated with young, attractive women selling their wares, 118), whatever is associated with commerce, desire, women, and the body to the level of art, thereby placing the artist himself "within or behind or beyond or above his handiwork" (*P,* 181). We can thus see the boy's epiphany as his attempt to glorify the "artist" and to transform the objects of his gaze into worthy subjects of art—to transform "vanity" into "epiphany," perhaps. In this sense, the boy's final vision as narrated reinforces the notion that the artist must separate himself from whatever is "hostile to romance"—in this case, by idealizing and thereby transforming it into something worthy of contemplation—rather than questioning the logic and economy of the "romantic" vision that drives him to the bazaar in the first place.

The story, Norris suggests, "offers the beauty of its art as compensation to the frustrations that are thematized in [it]" (2003, 45), but destabilizes its own "compensatory gesture" by emptying its rhetoric to restore it to the "idiomatic, 'marketplace' sense of elaborate but insubstantial speech. 'Araby' the story, the ornate but empty narration, doubles 'Araby,' the ornate but empty bazaar" (ibid., 46). Two elements of the ending encourage this reading. First, the narrative perspective, as Norris notes, is a limited one, containing the very "blind spots and solipsisms" that "mirror the closed psychic system of the boy" (ibid., 50). An obscure usage of *vanity* as "an idle tale or matter; an idea or statement of a worthless or unfounded nature" (*OED*) allows the possibility that the boy recognizes the insufficiency of his own story by depicting it as the entity that hounds him; nonetheless, the past tense

> indicates that the idle tale that pursues him may not be the story he has
> *told* but the "story" he experienced, that is, the events preceding the
> epiphany that lead him to "anguish and anger." Second, the image of
> burning eyes not only suggests that the boy ends up with the blindness
> with which the story begins, but, coupled with the pain of "anguish
> and anger," further points to the failure of his attempt to transcend the
> physical. The more mature narrator attempts to turn the physicality of
> the boy's eye pain into a beautiful phrase, but without a challenge to
> the operations of the boy's (and narrator's) vision, the aesthetic gesture
> merely repeats the cycle of blindness, rather than offering an alternative
> to that vision.

In other words, the boy's visual-linguistic presentation *frames* his recognition: it blows it up, and then freezes it forever. A passing instant again becomes a posed picture, as the boy's conclusion does not correct his vision so much as overcorrect it, as if he has donned an ill-fitting pair of magnifying spectacles.

Other mirror scenes in *Dubliners* shed further light on this one by exposing the characters' distorted vision. For example, Polly Mooney of "The Boarding House" also enjoys and invites the male gaze, and as her mother prepares to confront poor Bob Doran for doing more than gazing at Polly, Mrs. Mooney feels "satisfied" with the "decisive expression" she beholds in her pier-glass (*D*, 78). Polly imitates her mother: making ready to meet Bob, she appraises herself complacently in the mirror, then falls into a reverie of plans and "secret amiable memories" (*D*, 82). Her mother has, in effect, superimposed her face over her daughter's. As for the would-be groom, his misted glasses (perspiration? incipient tears?) reveal one-dimensional portraits of his adversaries (glowering boss, young seductress, harpy mother, bulldog brother) and of himself, the victimized suitor at the center of this gallery, peering meekly around. Yet his vision cannot compete with the empowered eyes of Mrs. Mooney, and, as with the boy in "Araby," this "lover's eyes" (*D*, 82) fail to penetrate the surface.

Nor can our own vision easily be drawn away from the image of Mrs. Mooney and Bob Doran. The narrative that precedes the focus on Polly's thoughts and actions shapes our reading of them to such a degree that it is easy to overlook the fact that her own vision is not contiguous with her mother's. The mirror frame is replaced by the pillows that frame her thoughts. But soon her "hopes and visions" break free of the constraints of mirror and bed and become "so intricate that she no longer saw the white pillows on which her gaze was fixed or remembered that she was waiting for anything" (*D,* 83). The latter is potentially the only moment when Polly might be imagining a future unconstrained by Bob Doran or her mother's machinations. Yet our vision of Polly is so circumscribed by the framing narrative that it is easier to accept Bob Doran's vision of her as manipulative or her mother's view of her as wholly complicit than to imagine her otherwise, even when given the textual opportunity to do so.

Likewise, in "Clay," Maria's self-satisfied tone as she regards her "nice tidy little body" in the mirror fails to compensate for her unconscious diminution of her own importance (*D,* 123). Appropriately, at the story's key moment she wears a blindfold. In retrospect, we must wonder whether the "Araby" boy's eyes are, even at his moment of insight, as misted as Doran's or as blind as Maria's. Does he, like the Mooney women, see only what he wants to see in his self-created mirror? And has Mangan's sister, like Polly Mooney, exhibited herself to manipulate him?

The boy's burning eyes also presage a gallery of male weepers in *Dubliners.*[13] "Clay," for example, concludes with Joe Donnelly's eyes so fogged with tears that he is unable to find a corkscrew. Though his tears seem sentimental, they may also indicate remorse over his estrangement from brother Alphy. More significantly, his blurred vision mirrors that of Maria, whose simplicity masks both vanity and a desperate loneliness that emerges in unconscious acts of "forgetting": like the gift that the boy in "Araby"

---

13. The boy's tears also reenact two songs alluded to in the story. In "The Arab's Farewell to His Steed," the speaker asks what the steed's master will do "When the dim distance cheats mine eye, and, through the gathering tears, / Thy bright form, for a moment, like the false mirage appears?" And in the song "Araby," music is said to "Bring tears, bright tears to their brink, / And rainbow visions rise, And all my soul shall strive to wake, / Sweet wonder in thine eyes . . . To cheat thee of a sigh, / Or charm thee to a tear!" (Norton 2006).

hopes to find at the bazaar, her intended gift—the lost plumcake—never reaches its recipient. Thus, Joe may also be crying *for* her. Similarly, at the conclusion of "A Little Cloud," after Chandler has angrily shouted at his infant son, his eyes meet the "hatred" in his wife's (*D*, 103); as he retreats from the light, he feels "tears of remorse" rise to his eyes (*D*, 103)—remorse for making his son cry and for embarrassing himself with Ignatius Gallaher, but mostly for his lifelong timidity. Derided by vanity—he thought himself a poet!—his eyes burn with anguish and anger. But do those eyes see accurately? Why should Chandler—a man with a solid job, competent, attractive wife, and new baby and, therefore, compared to most of Joyce's Dubliners, lucky indeed—feel such regret? His dissatisfaction derives, like the "Araby" boy's, from his fantasies: of an exciting life in Europe, of the voluptuous "rich Jewesses" whose eyes he superimposes over those in his wife's photo. "Why," he asks, "had he married the eyes in the photograph?" (*D*, 101). But, of course, he has married neither the eyes nor the photograph: like the "Araby" narrator, Chandler transforms a woman into body parts, then assembles them into a static portrait of unfulfilled promise. Her photo becomes a mirror onto which he projects his own dissatisfaction and self-loathing—which, like that of the "Araby" narrator, is as self-glorifying as it is self-mortifying.

These visual motifs culminate, like so much else in *Dubliners*, in "The Dead." Gabriel Conroy, though smarter and more self-aware than Bob Doran, wears similar spectacles, the "bright gilt rims" of which "[screen] his delicate and restless eyes" (*D*, 220). To screen is to protect, but also to block or inhibit. Thus, Gabriel's glasses do not simply correct his impaired vision; they also permit him to hide his real feelings—at least from himself. The glasses also seem to magnify his self-consciousness, as if Gabriel, constantly fiddling with his clothes and fretting over his appearance, carries an internal mirror at every moment. He thus feels the need to escape, and just before supper gazes from the window of his aunts' house, taps its cold pane, and imagines himself outside (*D*, 237). A little later he pictures the people outdoors gazing "up at the lighted windows" (*D*, 251) and wishes he were among them. Once again a window grants to the person looking through it the ability to exist imaginatively in two places and times at once.

"The Dead" also provides another moment that frames the move-ment from self-deprecation to self-aggrandizement—from being "driven by vanity" to becoming an artist of a Vanitas painting. At the end of the party, throughout which Gabriel has been wracked with self-doubt, he encounters Gretta on the stairs, listening to Bartell D'Arcy singing "The Lass of Aughrim," a mournful tune that, in most ver-sions, suggests a sexual relationship that ends in misunderstanding and ultimately the death of its titular character. The tune, we later discover, reminds Gretta of the long-dead Michael Furey's passionate attachment to her. But Gabriel distances himself from the music and its grim con-tent—and from his wife—choosing instead to frame the moment as an artist would and make the figural image into a discursive one: "He asked himself what is a woman standing on the stairs in the shadow, listening to distant music, a symbol of. If he were a painter he would paint her in that attitude. . . . *Distant Music* he would call the picture if he were a painter" (*D*, 261).

Only in the concluding episode in the Gresham Hotel does Gabriel achieve a full superimposition of vision, when he sees himself projected out upon the landscape. As the sobbing Gretta tells him of Michael Furey, Gabriel catches sight of himself in the cheval glass, feeling puzzled by the expression behind his "glimmering gilt-rimmed eyeglasses" (*D*, 271). He sees, that is, not his eyes but his eyeglasses: his screened vision perceives only more frames. A few minutes later, when Gabriel hears of Furey's dark eyes, his mirror becomes metaphorical: "He saw himself as a ludicrous figure . . . a nervous well-meaning sentimentalist, orating to vulgarians and idealising his own clownish lusts, the pitiable fatuous fellow he had caught a glimpse of in the mirror" (*D*, 273). Juxtaposing his image with Furey's, he feels inad-equate. Upon seeing himself as a creature driven and derided by vanity—by the idle matter in his postdinner speech, by the vanity fair of his aunts' party—his forehead burns with anguish and anger (shame "burned upon his forehead" [*D*, 273]). Yet the vanity remains: he feels fatuous for believing that "vulgarians" could possibly understand him and angry at himself for stooping to serve his ignorant aunts. If Gabriel, in some sense, reenacts the "Araby" boy's concluding vision, Michael Furey lived out the boy's romantic fantasy: after gazing at Gretta longingly from outside her window, Furey gave the gift, not of a bracelet, but of his life. "The Dead" thus divorces the "Araby" boy's two self-portraits, in so doing perhaps permitting clearer self-reflections.

> Or perhaps not: after all, Gabriel sees Michael Furey—and his wife's own tears—through a single distorted lens of "romance." We learn, "He had never felt like that himself towards any woman but he knew that such a feeling must be love" (D, 277), but there is little in Gretta's own brief story to suggest that Michael Furey was anything more than infatuated; only his death frames his story for Gabriel as one of ideal romantic love rather than, for instance, naive infatuation or dangerous obsession.

The volume's climactic scene offers another image of tear-misted eyes, as the weeping Gabriel envisions Michael standing in the cold rain, then turns to the window and watches the flakes fall, mentally traveling across the Irish landscape to the young man's grave. The outdoor lamplight shining obliquely into the room creates the now familiar twilight effect: Gabriel sees himself magnified and projected out upon the world. A window again becomes a mirror, as Gabriel, gazing up into the darkness and then out the window, mentally roams from past to present to future; "fading out into a grey impalpable world," he superimposes himself upon the imaginary outdoor scene (D, 225). *Dubliners* ends with Gabriel's self-framing as one of the dead. Yet this vision carries him beyond Joyce's other Dubliners: like Stephen Dedalus's artist-god, he seems to dwell "within or behind or beyond or above" the other dead (P, 181). Watching the snowflakes fall, he projects himself across Ireland—from the Bog of Allen, westward to the central plain, then to the River Shannon, ending at the graveyard where Furey lies (D, 225). Gabriel's frames at first constrain but may ultimately lift him above the limited, self-serving, or self-pitying perceptions of the earlier characters. Although this monumental vision—window-cum-mirror-cum-portrait-cum-montage or swooping aerial shot—may seem to render the "Araby" boy's insight insignificant, in fact Gabriel's vision evolves from the boy's insight, as in a chronological arrangement of silhouettes.

Still, does framing "Araby" this way tell us whether the boy's final recognition evinces clarity or more self-delusion? Not really, for the volume's other portraits offer contradictory visions. Joyce's Dubliners habitually project their desire and despair upon the world around them, seeing neither for what it is, yet their perceived entrapment is real. Indeed, as I have noted, exposing that entrapment was one of Joyce's stated aims—to hold up that "nicely polished looking-glass" so Dubliners might see themselves. His book is thus both a window onto an imaginary world and a mirror that facilitates self-reflection. Such self-reflection may help to remedy the paralysis that the characters' self-framing induces.

I, on the other hand, would argue that the frames provided by the other stories—Little Chandler's story, for instance, or Gabriel Conroy's—offer us alternative reflections of the "Araby" narrator's failure to recognize the limitations of his own vision, the "limits of the diaphane," and indeed the failure of the "ineluctable modality of the visible," to borrow from Stephen in *Ulysses* (3.1–4). I agree that *Dubliners* provides a more open system of circulation of meanings if one can see beyond the single frame of each individual story and combine the lighted squares into a compound lens. Yet "Araby" remains another partial vision, exposing the seduction not only of the monoscopic but also of the narrative of progress and "development" that would lead us to trust the older voice of the boy of the story as somehow more "mature." Each story is a limited frame, but taken as a whole, Joyce's oeuvre offers alternatives for understanding and valuing human activity, interaction, and the production of meaning; the frames he provides indeed exceed the visual model on which the boy in "Araby" relies.

Setting "Araby" in relation to these other portraits of *Dubliners* thus engenders multiple frames, multiple superimpositions—a prism of lighted squares, perhaps, or a compound lens that, with each layer of glass, works to correct the distorted image provided by any single piece.

And as we move forward and backward through the volume, each page offering another piece of framed glass, the pages seem to regard each other, like those "Araby" houses, in a *mise en abyme,* like mirrors within mirrors. Yet they also gaze at us, inviting us to share their twilit visions and behold ourselves. Are we dewy-eyed romantics or hard-eyed realists? How much can we see in the "nicely polished looking-glass" of the pages, and do we recognize what we see? Ultimately, we indict or excuse the "Araby" boy and his fellow Dubliners according to our own frames. We are reminded again that all literary criticism is a kind of superimposition in which the critic overlays his or her story upon the author's.[14] Hence, our reading of "Araby"'s ending, like Gabriel's culminating vision, ultimately encompasses all we have seen: not only the narrator's framing of his experience, but also the frames offered by previous readers and other stories. Perhaps most of all, reading "Araby" tests our capacity to superimpose these visions upon each other. In framing "Araby," then, we really frame ourselves.

14. Robert ApRoberts anticipates this insight as early as 1967 in his heated response to Harry Stone's seminal essay on "Araby": "The palimpsest Professor Stone sees in 'Araby' is not in the story but in Professor Stone's mind, and what he takes for depths shimmering with rich, half-obscured images is a mirror wherein the figures of his own perfervid fancy glimmer and shift" (1967, 488). Of course, he misses the point insofar as he fails to recognize the glimmerings of his own fancy in the eighteen pages of New Critical explication that precede this pithy comment.

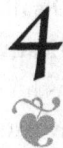

4

"Eveline" at Home

Reflections on Language and Context
DEREK ATTRIDGE AND ANNE FOGARTY

We decided to work independently, to see if our responses to the story complemented or conflicted with one another. The plan was then to write responses to one another's pieces. In the event, our interpretations complemented one another so well that there was very little that needed to be appended.

The Words of "Eveline," *by Derek Attridge*

Best and Worst

S he sat at the window watching the evening invade the avenue. Her head was leaned against the window curtains and in her nostrils was the odour of dusty cretonne. She was tired" (*D,* 42). The opening paragraph of "Eveline" shows Joyce at his characteristic best, achieving immense richness with the utmost economy of means. The second sentence, in particular, seems to me to epitomize his extraordinary skill. Eveline does not lean her head, but her head is leaned; she does not actively smell, but an odor is present in her nostrils. The syntax conveys a draining away of agency, her body parts functioning like independent, mechanical objects as her thoughts pursue a track they have pursued many times before.

Above all, it is "the odour of dusty cretonne" that has the distinctive Joycean signature on it. *Cretonne* is striking in its specificity: it names an eminently practical fabric (the *OED* calls it "stout") that nevertheless suggests an awareness of fashion, indicative of Eveline's experience at "the stores"—the word is not recorded as an English import until 1887, and its evident Frenchness gives it a slightly exotic air. The adjective *dusty*, too, is redolent of a housekeeper's pride, already hinting at a weariness with the daily grind of maintaining cleanliness, while providing the reader, whose consciousness of the sense of smell is already alert thanks to the slightly surprising word *nostrils*, with a vivid sensory image. Whereas the first sentence clearly gives us the words of an observing narrator, and we seem to remain with this narrator for a word like *odour*, the phrase *dusty cretonne* begins to reflect Eveline's thought processes, which will soon take over the narrative.

The play of sound in this second sentence is less marked than in the previous sentence, in which the name of the story and its heroine is echoed in the phrasing—*Eveline, evening, invade, avenue*—but the controlled play of vowels and consonants continues, in, for instance, the chiming of *curtains* and *cretonne* and the redeployment of most of the sounds of *nostrils* in *dusty cretonne*. The last brief sentence—ambiguous as between a narrator's observation and the character's thoughts—is almost unnecessary after this sentence, though nothing explicit has been said about Eveline's tiredness. Its brevity enacts its meaning.

Joyce wrote this paragraph (and the whole story, in something very close to the version he later published in *Dubliners*) in the summer of 1904, aged twenty-two, for the *Irish Homestead*, his second entry into print, following a few weeks after "The Sisters" (see J. Joyce 1993a, 2–3).[1] Only the phrase "window curtains" differs from the first version, which had "window-curtain."[2] The attainment of this peak of stylistic subtlety and assurance at such an early point in a writing career has very few parallels.

---

1. The *Irish Homestead* version of the story is given in the 1993 Vintage edition of *Dubliners*, edited by Gabler with Hettche, 217–21; Gabler's Garland edition gives the variants in footnotes.

2. Perhaps Joyce would have been well advised to delete *window* altogether from the second sentence, as he had already used the word in the first sentence and there is no doubt as to the location. He always liked repetition, however, using it for a number of different purposes.

"No! No! No! It was impossible. Her hands clutched the iron in frenzy. Amid the seas she sent a cry of anguish" (*D*, 48). This short paragraph in the final section of the story, on the other hand, is a rare lapse in the story, as Joyce strives too hard to bring home the drama of his climax. The repeated *no*'s, the slightly excessive *frenzy*, and—especially—the overheated diction of the last sentence fail to register the particularity of the event, giving us instead the diction of a thousand popular fictions. *Amid* is falsely poetic, and although the phrase *the seas* is not as vague as the paragraph taken on its own might suggest, since we have already read, in a far more powerful sentence, at once metaphoric and somatic, "All the seas of the world tumbled about her heart," they remain damagingly unspecific. The *cry of anguish* is a cliché that prevents us from hearing imaginatively the sound a woman in Eveline's situation might have made. In Gabler's text, based on the 1910 late proofs, the story ends with a period; the version printed in the 1914 first edition of *Dubliners* and most editions since then has an exclamation mark after "anguish" that only makes matters worse (*D*, 48).

Paralysis

"Every night as I gazed up at the window I said softly to myself the word paralysis" (*D*, 9). Commentary on *Dubliners* has exploited to the full the hint given by this sentence in the collection's first paragraph, reinforced by Joyce's well-known letter to Grant Richards in 1906, in which he stated that he "chose Dublin for the scene because that city seemed . . . the centre of paralysis" (*Letters II*, 134). In "Eveline" he wrote a story that does not use the word *paralysis* but is, in a sense, all about physical immobility, almost as if to set himself the challenge of treating his theme with literal fidelity. For 135 lines (in Gabler's edition), the eponymous character barely moves other than to look around the room; then at line 136 we encounter a short paragraph beginning "She stood up in a sudden impulse of terror." After a gap in time signaled by a break on the page, the following paragraph also begins with the words "She stood. . . ." She does not move from this position until the end of the story—and her not moving then is, of course, the climax.

Up to now, home has been Eveline's center of gravity, keeping her anchored through the trials of a mother's insanity and death, a father's increasing drunkenness and violence, and the demands of parenting two younger children. (Her sailor lover, by contrast, has taken the world as his domain, leaving Ireland as a deck boy to sail to Canada, traversing the globe by ship, and choosing to settle in Argentina—if we are to believe his own account of his past, that is.) Her immobility in the first part of the story is emblematic of the more general stasis of her life, held in one place by a sense of duty as much as by any positive attachment.

It takes a spasm of terror—induced by memories of her mother's mad behavior—to end Eveline's immobility (which has gone on longer than it ought, as "her time was running out"). But Joyce omits all the actions that we know have followed this sudden movement, until we find her again stationary, being called by Frank to go with him on board the ship. The terror she experiences this time, however, has the opposite effect: she is rooted to the spot, clutching the railing. Between the impossibility of a home that represents unhappiness and physical danger and the impossibility of a leap into the unknown, Eveline has nowhere to go.

How does Joyce make a story out of these twin immobilities? What urges the reader onward, if there is virtually no action to respond to? Elsewhere I have tried to analyze the process whereby Joyce's handling of literary style in "Eveline," with its minute fluctuations and resonances, draws the reader in and on (see Attridge 2004, 4–8). The bulk of the story is presented as free-indirect discourse, or, more accurately free-indirect thought, as Eveline's meditations are presented to us in the third person and past tense.[3] In a practice typical of the stories of *Dubliners* from this point on, however, Joyce surprises us by moving occasionally into different stylistic modes. We have already noted how the first paragraph, although predominantly the narrator's voice, has hints of Eveline's thoughts; the second paragraph continues with what appears to be an objective account of what Eveline sees and hears, but again we are made aware that these sights and sounds are being perceived by a particular character: "Few people passed. The man out of the last house

---

3. It is not interior monologue, as John Wyse Jackson and Bernard McGinley claim (1993, 34), but a quite different technique that retains the tense and syntactic completeness of the narrative context.

passed on his way home; she heard his footsteps clacking along the concrete pavement and afterwards crunching on the cinder path before the new red houses" (*D*, 42). After a sentence that could be a neutral observation but could equally be one made by Eveline, remarking to herself the paucity of passers-by, the phrase "man out of the last house" gives us her recognizable, Irish, diction identifying an individual in terms that relate specifically to her. The repetition of *passed* may seem a stylistic awkwardness, or it may be taken to represent the repetitiveness of Eveline's thoughts. But *clacking* is surely a Joycean narrator's word, unusual and vivid, registering not so much Eveline's mental processes as her unverbalized perception and contrasting with the different sound of *crunching. The new red houses,* however, could well be Eveline's own somewhat condescending phrase, as bare in its expression as the objects being described.

Home

Central to many of the *Dubliners* stories is the question of *home:* how is it constituted, what is its value, what demands does it make?[4] The homes we see are almost all unsatisfactory. The boy narrator in the first three stories is uneasy at home and finds excitement in leaving it. The boarding house in the story of that name is a travesty of a home; Little Chandler and Farrington in "A Little Cloud" and "Counterparts" return to their homes but not to domestic happiness; Maria in "Clay" moves between two establishments, neither of which offers the true comforts of home. Mr. Duffy's home in "A Painful Case" lacks homeyness, and the Kernan residence in "Grace" holds an erring husband and a long-suffering wife. Only "The Dead" celebrates the generosity, tolerance, and hospitality a home can give—and then not without a number of ambiguities.[5]

4. For an illuminating essay on the importance of "home" in *Dubliners,* with particular attention to its significance in post-Famine Ireland, see Gibbons 2000. Law (1987) valuably traces some of the complexities of the notion in *Ulysses.*

5. There is no need to elaborate on the importance of home in *A Portrait of the Artist* (in which *home* is one of the three words that, to Stephen, sound different on the Dean of Studies'

The word *home* occurs ten times in the story. (Interestingly, the first occurrence is in the passage quoted earlier describing the sound of "the man out of the last house" as he passes "on his way home"; another subterranean suggestion in this sentence is that Eveline feels that her house offers a more homey environment than the new houses with their bright red brick and their cinder paths.) Eveline's meditation is largely an exploration of the meaning and the force (mental, emotional, bodily) of home: her thought that she is about to "leave home" prompts her to focus on the word with an internal exclamation, "Home!" (*D*, 43). This impassioned thought is followed by a survey of the room she is sitting in while she examines the significance of home to her. Familiarity is one of its key components, and it is what she first feels the attraction of—yet she is soon pointing out to herself that strangeness is also present, in the photograph of the unknown priest. As she goes on to "weigh each side of the question," the sheer drudgery of her existence is set against the "shelter and food" that home implies (*D*, 43).

Like many of the homes in *Dubliners*, this one is a place of alcoholism and violence; the young woman's desire to leave is in part out of sheer fear: "Even now, though she was over nineteen, she sometimes felt herself in danger of her father's violence. She knew it was that that had given her the palpitations. When they were growing up he had never gone for her, like he used to go for Harry and Ernest, because she was a girl; but latterly he had begun to threaten her and say what he would do to her only for her dead mother's sake" (*D*, 44).[6] The sequence of thoughts begins with the suggestion that her age is some protection from her father's physical attacks—*even now* and *sometimes* signal that in the past, these fears had been more persistent than they are at present. Yet the thought quickly reverses itself, so that it is the very fact of her being grown up that has rendered her a potential victim, no longer protected by her sex. And later she recalls happier times with her father—though their very uncommonness is a silent counterargument. But

---

tongue) or *Ulysses* (where even Plumtree's Potted Meat fails to makes every home complete), and *Finnegans Wake* revolves around a family often glimpsed in a domestic setting.

6. Joyce changed "were it not for her dead mother's sake" (in the *Irish Homestead* version) to the Hiberno-English Irish locution "only for her dead mother's sake."

it is the memory of her mother's descent into madness and the fear that the same fate awaits her that bring about the end of her reflections.

Home as a magnetic force represents not only the familiar, food and shelter, and the pleasures of family relations (however rare), but also obligations.[7] Although the responsibility of keeping house for her father is described in predominantly negative terms, it is clearly a major factor in her deliberations. Added to it is the somewhat mysterious fact that she is caring for two young children. And, to cap it all, there is her promise to her dying mother "to keep the home together as long as she could" (*D*, 46–47)—again the word *home*, here perhaps more forcefully than anywhere else.

It is highly significant, then, that Frank, her sailor lover, has "a home waiting for her" in Buenos Aires (*D*, 45).[8] *Home* here is vague but attractive—one of the many hints that Eveline has been gullible in her acceptance of Frank's tales, perhaps, though it is easy to see why she has fallen for them. She herself thinks of "her new home" (*D*, 44). There is no sign at the end that her paralysis is owing to her mistrust of Frank; it is rather the result of the complexity of her own relation to her home. What she prays for as she clutches the railing is not that God should help her decide what is best for her, what home with Frank will mean in comparison to her home with her father and the two children, but what is her duty. In the balance are her promise to the man who has courted her (not "the man she loves"; the word she uses is *like* [*D*, 45]) and her promise to her mother, a promise that serves to heighten the responsibility that a sole daughter has for her aging father ("Her father was becoming old lately, she noticed") and as a surrogate mother for her two children.

7. The *Irish Homestead* text has Eveline wondering not only whether it is wise to leave home, but whether it would be "honourable"—in revising, perhaps Joyce felt he should not raise the question of duty too early in the story.

8. Margot Norris points out that Hugh Kenner, in an article in the *James Joyce Quarterly* in the fall of 1972, misquotes this sentence as "he had a house waiting for her" (2003, 242). This wording would be a significant alternative, providing greater solidity than the more nebulous but more romantic notion of "a home," but Gabler lists no such variant in his edition.

Decision

Eveline makes two decisions in the story, to go with Frank and not to go. The first, as we have seen, prompts her to stand up; the second prevents her from moving. Neither is a decision in the sense of a thoughtful, considered preference for *a* rather than *b*; both exemplify the conception of decision analyzed by Derrida, following Kierkegaard: a moment of madness in which rationality is left behind (though careful, rational calculation is what brings one to this point).[9] Eveline assembles powerful reasons for going and equally powerful reasons for staying; then the memory of her mother's madness—specifically, the aural memory of her mother's unintelligible, repetitive utterances—produces not a rational affirmation but a physical act and an emotional charge: "She stood up on a sudden impulse of terror." What follows sounds more like rationalization of a decision now taken than a further stage in the process of weighing pros and cons: "Escape! She must escape! Frank would save her. He would give her life, perhaps love too. But she wanted to live. Why should she be unhappy? She had a right to happiness. Frank would take her in his arms, fold her in his arms. He would save her" (*D*, 47). The repetitions here, which would be clumsy in the narrator's discourse, are the reflex of the character's desperation as she clings to the decision she finds she has made.

The second moment of decision is also more physical than it is mental. Eveline is again immobile, again torn between alternatives. This time the painfulness of the dilemma compels her into prayer, as she wrestles with the question of her double, contradictory duties. But at the final moment, when the bell clangs ("upon her heart" [*D*, 48]—another Joycean masterstroke of economic phrasing) and Frank urges her to accompany him, Eveline feels that she is drowning, drawn by her lover into "all the seas of the world," and her paralysis is like that of "a helpless animal." Her face registers no emotion whatsoever. The parallel with the earlier moment of decision is obvious, and we are left with the question: has Eveline descended,

---

9. See, for example, Derrida 1992, 26. The literary exemplification of Derrida's understanding of decision making is fully explored through Henry James's fiction in J. H. Miller 2005.

not gradually like her mother but in one instant of impossible mental and emotional conflict, into madness?

"Dusty Cretonne": Rereading "Eveline," *by Anne Fogarty*

By contrast with Derek Attridge's interpretation that illustrates how an attentive reading of the language and style of Joyce's story can excavate its ambiguities, my analysis will concentrate on several of the social and historical dimensions of "Eveline" in order further to explicate Joyce's peculiar positioning of his seemingly passive protagonist. In this tale we are presented with a protagonist the details of whose life do not cohere. She is, on one level, presented as powerless to save herself from a foreordained fate, whether as unwilling carer for her violent father or as sexual victim of her tale-spinning boyfriend. Yet, on another level, she is seemingly an independent city girl who has a job in one of the quintessential domains of modernity, a shop, and readily pursues her fantasies and desires in seeking out and acting upon the liaison with Frank. As Derek Attridge's analysis has shown, "Eveline" is a slippery tale because it veers between an unstable and artful narrative voice and the unreliable and attenuated consciousness of the heroine. In what follows, I shall consider how an investigation of the ways in which concepts of femininity and domesticity were politicized in early-twentieth-century Ireland allows us further to probe why Eveline is hopelessly trapped between tradition and modernity and why the protofeminist impulses in the story are obliterated and rendered null. Above all, I shall examine the contradictory ideological values with which the activity of housework and the notion of the home were freighted in the pages of the pointedly titled *Irish Homestead*. These buried social and political contexts illuminate why Eveline is faced with an unappealing and self-canceling choice between two forms of domesticity, either in Dublin with her father or in Buenos Aires with her lover. Before undertaking this exploration, I shall first briefly survey the critical reception of "Eveline" that has often falsely condemned the heroine and anachronistically assumed that she possesses an agency that was not a given in the period and the social milieu in which Joyce sets his story.

As previously noted, "Eveline" was first published in the *Irish Homestead,* on September 10, 1904. This newspaper was the organ of the Irish

Agricultural Organisation Society, one of the key bodies that sought to galvanize Irish society and to awaken a spirit of enterprise and self-help in the country that would aid in the achievement of national independence. The circumstances of its first publication and their import, albeit well known, are often glossed over. Instead, even though it shares the cryptic and elusive qualities of the other stories in *Dubliners,* "Eveline" is often seen as definitively encapsulating the pivotal themes and concerns of the collection as a whole, above all the issue of paralysis, and starkly typifying the moral outrage about Dublin life that supposedly fuels the entire volume. In particular, Joyce's polemical and defensive comments in his letters to friends and to hostile publishers have been used as a means of deducing the hidden intentions believed to underlie this story and to shed light on its elusive design.

These authorial pronouncements have become so familiar and have acquired such currency as a basis for analyzing *Dubliners* that they have lost the rhetorical bravado and provisionality with which they were once uttered. The contingency of letter writing is frequently ignored as Joyce's views about his own text are pressed into service to sanction and support interpretations of his stories. Thus, his famous declaration to Grant Richards in 1906 is regularly seen as a summa of *Dubliners* and as voicing an unalterable bass line sounded throughout these tales: "My intention was to write a chapter of the moral history of my country and I chose Dublin for the scene because the city seemed to me the centre of paralysis" (*Letters II,* 134). On closer inspection, it must be recognized that Joyce's confidences to his would-be publisher were tactical, monitory, and deliberately self-aggrandizing. In declaring that he was writing the moral history of his country, he echoed Gustave Flaubert's similar avowal in a letter to Mademoiselle Leroyer de Chantepie in 1864 that his purpose in composing *A Sentimental Education* was to write "the moral history—or rather the sentimental history—of the men of my generation" ("l'histoire morale des hommes de ma génération, «sentimentale» serait plus vrai" [1924, 24]). In suggesting such a strategic alliance with Flaubert's novel, Joyce emphasized the weightiness and timeliness of his own creation. Furthermore, by asserting the existence of a unifying purpose in his text, he strategically deflected attention from its more scandalous aspects. Despite their persuasiveness and their usefulness as props for critical discussion, we need to approach Joyce's piecemeal and polemical epistolary comments on *Dubliners* with caution. The seeming cohesiveness that he invokes to vindicate *Dubliners* is belied by its diverse political objectives and stances and roving historical points of view. Furthermore, any assumption of an easily discernible univocality is vitiated by the structural complexity of these stories and by the opacity of their plots and symbolic scaffolding.

Early criticism of *Dubliners* assumed that the theme of paralysis both was a *clou* to the individual tales and provided a unifying framework for the overall collection. As Derek Attridge has shown, such assumptions have tended above all to color views of "Eveline" and to ground assessments of its heroine. However, often, a concentration on the stagnation of Irish society has been used to castigate the protagonist of this story for her lack of freedom and to hold her to account for the ideological conditions that bind her. Hugh Kenner's commentaries on the centripetal theme of paralysis in *Dublin's Joyce* and *The Pound Era* may be seen to typify such analysis, even though they also constitute a particularly adept elucidation of this grand Joycean preoccupation with Irish social and political stagnation. Kenner dexterously teases out the complexities of "Eveline" while insisting that they are always organized around the central thematic moment of paralysis that he sees the story as staging. In *Dublin's Joyce,* he contends that "Eveline is the book's second thematic image of paralysis" (1956, 54). Further, he argues that she is not a protagonist in the manner of Father Flynn in "The Sisters" but rather a mirror. Hence, her lack of agency is more thoroughgoing than the reduced dynamism of the figures in the other stories. Kenner, however, complicates and revises his view of the story in *The Pound Era* but still insists that the theme of paralysis and, by extension, Eveline's lack of agency are key facets of Joyce's bafflingly compressed fiction. He presents his altered view of the story as a corrective of received accounts of the text:

"The heroine of 'Eveline' longs to escape from her drab Dublin life and she has her chance. But, on the very point of embarking for Buenos Aires with the man who loves her . . ." (Anthony Burgess 1965, *Re Joyce*). So runs a handbook summary, typical of dozens. In missing half Joyce's point they still speak truth. Eveline has rejected that home in South America, though as an act of choice, not of judgment. Her refusal remains refusal whether or not there is any home there for her. We are to imagine the rest of her life ("of commonplace sacrifices," like her mother's) embittered by the remembered panic. She refused, though not from insight. . . . She will never so much as know that Frank may have been less than Frank, but will live out her life in the consciousness of her onetime immobilizing terror. (1972, 38)

Kenner here construes a paradoxical portrait of Eveline as a figure who is castigated for a choice that, in effect, she has never been in a position to make, owing to her lack of autonomy and independent insight. He later contends that Joyce set out to maximize her "ignorance and her pathos" (ibid., 39) and complicates this assessment of her even further by also averring that she lives inside a fiction and that her world is structured around "a febrile unreal story" (ibid.), that is, the romance hinging on Frank. This secondary set of considerations that sees Eveline not simply as an object lesson in cowardice or of myopia but also as an instance of the human capacity for fiction making permits a more nuanced and differentiated take on her plight.

Despite Kenner's attempt to counter the routine and often simplistic moralizing that comes into play in evaluating "Eveline," such approaches to the text remain difficult to circumvent. The crux above all appears to be the uncertainty posed by the ending: "He rushed beyond the barrier and called to her to follow. He was shouted at to go on but he still called to her. She set her white face to him, passive, like a helpless animal. Her eyes gave him no sign of love or farewell or recognition" (*D*, 48). Interpretations frequently attempt to fill out the omissions in this narration and to produce the consequential and well-turned plot that Joyce pointedly withholds from us. The summary of "Eveline" in *The Critical Companion to James Joyce* may serve as a further example of the traps that this text sets for us as readers and the degree to which it lures us into ironing out its ambiguities and substituting faintly self-righteous moral pronouncements for its elisions, puzzles, and subtleties. A. Nicholas Fargnoli and Michael Gillespie (2006), in the synopsis that they provide, comment on the "listless title figure" and conclude that "Frank is forced to leave without Eveline because of her incapacitating fear of change." They also contend that Eveline is "seized with an overwhelming terror that paralyzes her and saps her will to leave." The effort to summarize the tale demonstrates, in fact, how much remains unstated and unexplained.

One could speculate that a condemnatory account of Eveline that takes her to task for her moral dereliction becomes a means of mollifying the reader's unease with a story that refuses to editorialize and appears willfully to call to a halt all the impulses for romance and escape that it had so explicitly toyed with at its opening.

It must be noted, however, that many recent readings of "Eveline" have been at pains to foreground its complexities and to avoid the urge to make the figure of Eveline a scapegoat for the bedeviling social and political circumstances that define her in large part. Margot Norris's (2003) suggestive reexamination of *Dubliners* demonstrates the extent to which these stories abound in silences, omissions, and inexplicable allusions. She advocates that we practice what she has dubbed a method of suspicious reading that allows us at once to accept the ambiguities of *Dubliners* and to question our own assumptions and critical impositions. In a similar vein, Vicki Mahaffey (2007) has contended that the tales of *Dubliners* might be seen as analogous to the detective tales of Arthur Conan Doyle. Just as the latter author encourages his readers to adopt several competing vantage points and to view the world alternatively from the perspective of Sherlock Holmes and of Doctor Watson, so too Joyce urges us in *Dubliners* to see things from the opposing stances of the victim and the perpetrator of a crime and also to adopt the more objective and distantiating position of an investigative reporter (see Mahaffey 2007, 73–123; and Norris 2003, 55–67).

In the interpretation that follows, I would like to consider how this new attentiveness to the cryptic nature and multifacetedness of *Dubliners* might also be extended to the social and historical contexts of "Eveline." Instead of viewing this text as providing a unitary and cohesive view of the political undercurrents of Dublin at the turn of the twentieth century and merely satirizing the abjection and degradation of Irish society, I will track how Joyce alerts us to the moral and political intricacies of the worlds inhabited by his protagonist. To this end, I will consider one of the primary contexts referenced in the story, female labor and the domestic sphere.

Recent Irish feminist historiography has provided fresh insight into the position of women in late-nineteenth-century Ireland. Joanna Burke in *Husbandry to Housewifery* (1993) has demonstrated that there was a large-scale shift in female employment at the end of the nineteenth century that was of a piece with the domestication of women's roles elsewhere in the world. Increasingly, women moved from labor in the fields to full-time housework. The *Irish Homestead,* which was the weekly publication of the Irish Agricultural Organisation Society founded by Sir Horace Plunkett, has generally been seen as focusing on the ethos of a male-centered cooperative movement and concentrating on their economic activities and concerns. However, as Leeann Lane (2004) has shown, it also developed distinct notions of female identity during the period 1896–1912 that track and reflect on the changed responsibilities and status of women in rural Ireland. From the outset, the *Irish Homestead* published columns designed for a specifically female readership. These columns were titled successively "The Fireside," "The Predominant Partner," "Household Hints," and "Pages for Irish Country Women." The early columns that simply relayed society gossip quickly ceded to more practical interventions that were entirely different in tenor and gave advice about daily household chores while also occasionally debating the value of domesticity. The *Irish Homestead* particularly aimed at articulating and translating into action the self-help ideals of Horace Plunkett, who had founded the cooperative movement not only to restore economic vitality to the Irish countryside but also thereby to awaken a new spirit of independence and of national esteem. Central to Plunkett's social revolution were the principles of self-aid, economic enterprise, improved living, and rural regeneration. Above all, the notion of the home was a keystone of his philosophy. An excerpt from one of his speeches reprinted in 1899 makes clear the extent to which he proposed a renovated notion of home as a counter to the negative aspects of modernity and to the deleterious effects of emigration: "We have in Ireland a rare field for hopeful experiment upon the problems of rural life. There, without the rival attractions of great and growing cities, we may try our hands at securing a comfortable and even enjoyable home life among a people anxious to stop at home" (*Irish Homestead,* February 18, 1899, 125). The renegotiation of the roles of women and the formulation of a notion of the domestic sphere were crucial to this project of economic and social renewal.

The cooperative movement furthered not only all manner of agricultural development from beekeeping to dairy farming but also cottage industries. In this way, women who were encouraged to move into the domestic sphere could still play a part in augmenting the economy and also promote the pursuit of self-renewal and self-sufficiency. The inauguration of the "House-hold Hints" column in the spring of 1899 was one of the many ways in which the *Irish Homestead* voiced these new principles of a renovated Ireland. The Irish housewife was seen as a linchpin of this revivified rural life and the new spirit of national self-regard. The contributors to the column were anonymous and variously used the noms de plume "Haus Frau," "Keilam," and "A Working Woman." Jointly, they articulated this ideal of a new Irish social order whose fulcrum was the home, the female domestic sphere. Housewifery and female domestic labor were presented not as drudgery or a form of enslavement but as an active political mission. Haus Frau firmly enunciates this philosophy of an all-sustaining home life: "The home is, or ought to be, the woman's kingdom, and that she may rule it wisely, she must serve it well. . . . The very foundation of a nation's strength is its home life, and the complete fitness of this rests with women. The intellectual life of a family ought to grow on a foundation of comfort, and comfort must come from health, cleanliness and beauty" (ibid., March 4, 1899, 173). The vast preponderance of the "Household Hints" columns was concerned with hygiene and the niceties of domestic management. Such advice chimed with editorial discussions of rural decay and the disorderly nature of Irish peasant life. An intervention on the Irish cottage unfavorably contrasted the condition of local dwellings with the Comte de Ségur's descriptions of villages in the United States at the end of the eighteenth century. The innate integrity of Irish peasant culture was contrasted with the primitivism exhibited by most cottages: "We have got the much desired vote, fixity of tenure and the number of peasant proprietors is gradually increasing. But it must be confessed that our Irish villages and cabins in many districts retain their primitive characteristics of untidiness and dirt. . . . It is amusing, no doubt, to see Biddy's old flannel petticoat or Mickey's trousers—inserted to fill the gap of a broken pane—fluttering in the breeze and otherwise flaunting about, but we ought to cease furnishing 'copy' for the professional humourist" (ibid., April 29, 1899, 311). Here national stereotypes and the specter of an indigenous atavism are brandished as threats. Dirt becomes symbolic of a degraded past that needs to be abandoned.

Consequently, much advice was dispensed in the *Irish Homestead* about how Irish cottages could be transformed and cleaned up. Animals were to be removed from indoors, and manure heaps were to be banished from their traditional location on the doorstep, as Lady Gregory indicates in her analysis of rural slovenliness: "We who live in the West are apt to give in to the sleepy influence of damp and of mists and to give up on the fight against dirt and disorder and dilapidation. . . . Our neighbour's house has an unmended window pane, and a leak in the thatch, and a heap of manure for a doorstep; and our eye grows used to this, and we take it as an excuse for the neglect of our own house" (ibid., May 27, 1899, 368–69). Haus Frau echoes Gregory's sentiments with regard to the necessity for active intervention in her brisk account of dusting: "It should be an imperative duty with Irish housekeepers to do battle with might and main against dust" (ibid., October 6, 1900, 651). Even though the *Irish Homestead* in its weekly installments continued to promote these ideals of national regeneration and of a cleansed and restored rural civilization predicated on the ordering governance and labor of women, it also occasionally permitted dissenting views to emerge. A contributor using the sobriquet of "Queen Bee" demurred against the imposition of these ideals of order and cleanliness and the regime of housework that they entailed: "[Women who obsessively manage their houses] are apt to forget a truth which was this forcibly expressed by a pleasant Mrs Willing-to-Please not long ago: 'Houses are really places to live in, not to be kept clean.'" The writer further complained about a fastidious approach to housecleaning and argued that life should not "simply be a perpetual struggle against dirt, dust, and disorder." She concluded her intervention with the forthright declaration that a single-minded devotion to housecleaning led to "rustiness of heart and mind" (ibid., December 22, 1900, 717).

This survey of the ideological debates in the *Irish Homestead* centering on issues of communal morale, hygiene, female labor, and the strategic role of the home in the process of nation building in the years preceding the publication of "Eveline" in 1904 reveals the degree to which Joyce finessed and cleverly trumped George Russell's invitation to write something "simple, rural? livemaking? pathos? . . . not to shock the readers" (*Letters II*, 43). His story of Eveline with its glancing references at her prolonged battle against dust and the ever-renewing specter of domestic disorder in Dublin suburbia neatly mimics and intervenes in the discussions in the "Household Hints" columns. Further, her quest for independence and her enterprising search for a lover and an alternative life elsewhere are in keeping with the principles of self-help advocated by the *Irish Homestead*. However, they also crucially subvert them by pointing to the gap between personal happiness and social ideals. In showing the struggle that Eveline undergoes in reconciling her clashing roles as a modern urban worker, a keeper and manager of the house and family, a desiring subject, and a self-sacrificing maternal steward of domestic values, Joyce opens up the fissures in the ideological ideals held sacrosanct by the *Irish Homestead* and the cooperative movement. He brings to light contradictions that could be only vaguely gestured at by the female columnists engaged in promulgating and reflecting on the newfound virtues of domesticity in this idealist and partisan publication.

His story reveals the extent to which the aspiration to a sanitized feminine private sphere as a salve to Irish political demoralization and as the grounds for national self-renewal was bound to founder in reality. Eveline, it might be noted, apparently chooses domestic struggle and home life at the end of the story in keeping with the explicit ethos of the *Irish Homestead* and the utopian ideals of national regeneration that motivated so many of the cultural and social movements in late-nineteenth-century Ireland. Yet the tale intimates that the trade-off in such a decision is as much debilitating as empowering for Eveline. She may have escaped the sexual entrapment that Frank represents, but in lieu she succumbs to the violent predation of her father's house. Her actions are ultimately and inevitably nullified by the ongoing and irresolvable clashes between public ideals and private desires in the Irish political arena. Moreover, the description of Eveline's lapse into animal-like passivity at the end of the tale intimates the problems with the Irish campaign to revivify and cleanse the social order in the hopes of holding primitivism at bay: it can produce another kind of devolution. Political activism that demands communal rectitude at the expense of personal happiness, while combating the alleged "laziness" of the disenfranchised classes, can produce paralysis. Eveline is caught between two imperatives: the imperative to keep cleaning her house and taking care of her family and the imperative to explore, to learn, and to pursue her dreams of romantic fulfillment. The result is an impasse. The *Irish Homestead* viewed the activity of housework as part of the larger political project of renewing the country and laying to rest the specter of a savage, primitive, and demoralized Ireland. Cleanliness and domestic efficiency were to become the hallmarks of a renovated and modernized nation. Joyce, in "Eveline," intimates that his heroine is caught in a stalemate produced by the different visions of modernity and tradition that define and underwrite her. On the one hand, she is trapped by the nationalist propaganda that persuasively urges her to stay at home and to assist in the development of a new political order, but, on the other, she is ensnared by the temptations of a commodified modernity and the wish to become a fulfilled subject. Either in perpetuating her mother's role, and thus contributing to a vision of a new national order, or in leaving the country and pursuing her desires, she is faced with a lack of freedom. In sum, because of her gender, she is consigned to servitude by her social environment.

In Conversation: Reconsiderations

DA: Our two approaches to the story, it seems to me, complement one another admirably, and as a result there is not much more to add. Anne's character-istically scrupulous account of the complex demands being made on Irish housewives by the moralists of the *Irish Homestead* gives depth to our under-standing of the plight being dramatized by Joyce. What I have described as the two "decisions" made by Eveline, to go and not to go (or not to stay and to stay), signaled, or perhaps even performed, by action and then by inaction, come as moments of Kierkegaardian madness that cap a deliberative process, part conscious and part unconscious, reflecting a set of complex cultural demands to which there is no "logical" answer. Anne's analysis helps us see that the dilemma Eveline faces is not just a personal predicament but also a deep conflict within metropolitan Irish society in its attitude to married women; or, to put it differently, Joyce is not writing about a single woman's weakness (or lucky escape) but about a cultural aporia. In a way, what Anne gives us is a female counterpart to Joseph Valente's (2000) brilliant account of the "double-bind of Irish manhood" in *Semicolonial Joyce*. The empha-sis on "home" that I stressed is enriched by Anne's reading of the *Irish Homestead*, which in its very title pointed to the growing importance of the domestic scene as a site of ideological investment. Most readers will not have access to this information, but Joyce's achievement is being able to convey to such readers, in the most concrete manner, the irresolvable predicament his heroine finds herself in as she sits at the window.

AF: In fastening on the overdetermined symbolism of the home and on the problem of the seeming choice that Eveline makes and then abandons, Derek's painstaking and nuanced analysis draws out the extent to which Joyce's language encapsulates and is buoyed by the political and social debates in Ireland at the turn of the twentieth century and also indicates how it resolutely commandeers and overwrites them. Even though inquiry into these often remote contexts may seem to take us on prolonged detours, the text appears in some ways to trump any knowledge that we might bring to it by showing that it has already embedded that knowledge and transformed it into artistry. Both our readings, I think, concur in uncovering the psychological intricacies of the story and in underscoring that its unraveling or nonexistent plot evades easy summary. Try as we will, Eveline's predicament cannot fully be circumscribed or explicated. Indeed, the figure of this faltering heroine is an illusion projected by various insinuating and persuasive means. In effect, as Derek's careful teasing out of the narrative stances and points of view has shown, we never quite see her, either from within or from without. She is both withheld and kept at bay. To this extent, I agree that to explain her impasse in terms of a drama of rational choice is to miss many of the dimensions of this endlessly mystifying narrative. Unlike the resourceful heroine in traditional folktales such as "Donkeyskin" by Charles Perrault, "Eveline" nightmarishly throws the fairy-tale plot into reverse as the daughter apparently succumbs to, rather than evading or outwitting, the incestuous father. Joyce succeeds in revealing Eveline to us as a subject in abeyance or a self that falls through the net of narrative. Derek's suggestion that she may well have descended into a vortex of madness in the interval between the two disproportionate halves of the story is very suggestive. Such a denouement, of course, aptly captures Eveline's fate. But it also points to a reluctance at this point in Joyce's career to conjure with female difference other than in archetypal or stereotypical terms. Moreover, there is a sense in which the ending of "Eveline," as intimated in Derek's observant interpretation, is a nicely orchestrated deflection. The devastating plots of sexual abuse, female oppression, and the misery of emigration remain buried deep in the substratum of the artful tale that we have read.

5

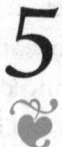

"After the Race"
and the Problem of Belonging

MICHAEL PATRICK GILLESPIE AND DAVID WEIR

Our collaboration proceeded smoothly once we realized how complementary our approaches to the story were. That is to say, we divided our interests between separate examinations of the external history of the story in relation to Joyce's narrative career and an internal analysis of the workings of the story itself. After working individually, we exchanged our essays for comment, made revisions to combine the two essays into one, and submitted it. The whole experience was a wonderful break from the usually solitary pursuit of academic scholarship.

"After the Race" was the third *Dubliners* story in order of the collection's composition, appearing in its earliest version in the December 17, 1904, issue of the *Irish Homestead*. Perhaps because it was one of the first pieces in the volume, written while the unifying thematic principles of the work were still forming, Joyce was uncertain about the place of the story in the collection. At first, in 1905, the order of the "stories of adolescence" was to be "The Boarding House," "After the Race," and "Eveline," the exact reverse of the published order (with "Two Gallants," the fourth "adolescent" story, inserted between "After the Race" and "The Boarding House" [*Letters II,* 111]). Joyce had also pronounced reservations about the story's literary merit. He expressed these views at least twice. In an August 1906 letter written from Rome to his brother Stanislaus in Trieste, he articulates a desire to rewrite the story, and less than three months later, in another letter to Stanislaus, Joyce singled out "After the Race" and "A Painful Case" as "the two worst stories in the collection" (ibid., 151, 189). After that, Joyce provides no further evidence of disquiet over either story, and he included them both in the final version of *Dubliners*.

As is so often the case with extratextual information, Joyce's comments in this correspondence raise vexing interpretive problems even as they make his creative attitude, at least at the time he wrote the letters, more explicit. The most significant question facing the contemporary reader seems relatively straightforward. What difference does any artist's point of view make in terms of our enjoyment of his or her work? If, for example, someone discovered a letter by Mozart decrying "Eine kleine Nachtmusik" as banal, derivative, and repetitious, should that curb audience enthusiasm for the piece? Or suppose researchers learned that Pablo Picasso felt that his approach to painting was fundamentally dishonest. Would that make his *Guernica* any less powerful? While the answer to each question is no, that response does not resolve the issue of what interpretive value the information we have on Joyce's attitudes toward his "worst" stories holds.

Aesthetic reactions are too strong and too personal and the interaction between artist and audience too complex to allow readings to be prescribed by authorial intentionality. At the same time, we do not feel comfortable simply ignoring these views. Certainly, Joyce's attitude toward "After the Race" and "A Painful Case" offers readers useful hints into what he felt his stories should accomplish. The vigor with which he resisted attempts in 1906 by Grant Richards and then five years later by George Roberts to censor other pieces indicates that Joyce was clearly pleased with the remainder of the collection and would not agree to anything that might jeopardize its integrity. As a result, identifying the features that distinguish these two works from the others might also point toward the dominant aims of the collection. Of course, knowing an artist's goals does not preclude readers from interpreting a work in any fashion they wish, but an awareness of the creative standards that Joyce set for himself in his writing offers useful interpretive parameters for readers as they begin to build a reading.

Specifically, in the case of "After the Race" extratextuality functions as a release from prescriptive readings that have grown out of the history of Joyce's collection of short stories. Since Ezra Pound began singing Joyce's praises more than ninety years ago, readers have developed the habit of approaching his work with hushed reverence. In this case, however, knowledge of Joyce's reservations allows us to set aside the accrued prestige of the *Dubliners* collection to enable an independent assessment of "After the Race."

Seeing the story without the expectation that it be accorded immediate legitimacy makes it fresh again. From that reorientation come new insights. Joyce's words free us from what we initially presumed our task to be: justifying a flawed story. Instead, they offer the alternative of constructing a convincing argument that "After the Race" does not live up to the standards set by other stories and, in fact, while technically proficient, is not a very interesting work. Paradoxically, the story is less interesting than the other stories because it tries to do too much. Put another way, we might say that the story is too slight to capture adequately the social and political complexities the narrative implies.

FUNDAMENTAL NARRATIVE FEATURES make "After the Race" strikingly different from every other one in the collection, including "A Painful Case." As we will outline below, the dissimilarities come from broadly divergent approaches. Although these distinctions may not in themselves seem to make the story inherently flawed, the thematic variations that set "After the Race" apart from others in the collection clearly move away from Joyce's creative strengths, and they lead to a series of compositional shortcuts that ultimately undermine the impact of the story.

Perhaps the most striking divergence from the general structure of other *Dubliners* stories is Joyce's deviation from the social and biographical sources upon which he depended in writing the other stories. "After the Race" stands out as the only story in the collection that does not follow a narrative pattern of drawing directly upon the experiences of Joyce or someone in his immediate family. Even in stories seemingly distant from the lives of Joyce and his relations, one can find links. The turning point in "A Mother," the stalemate over whether Kathleen Kearny would perform, draws upon an event in Joyce's own life: "In my first public concert I too was left in the lurch. The pianist, that is the lady pianist, had gone away right in the middle of the concert" (ibid., 340). The other story that displeased Joyce, "A Painful Case," grew out of a fictionalized version of an encounter with an older woman that Stanislaus Joyce had (*BK*, 165–66). And "Counterparts" provides Joyce with a platform for articulating his complex attitudes toward lower-class domestic life: "I am no friend of tyranny, as you know, but if many husbands are brutal the atmosphere in which they live (vide Counterparts) is brutal and few wives and homes can satisfy the desire for happiness" (*Letters II*, 92). In the other stories, references to the Dublin locales where Joyce grew up, to childhood friends, and to momentous family events crop up time and again.

"After the Race" breaks from this self-referential pattern. Instead, it relies upon information gleaned from an April 5, 1903, interview in Paris that Joyce conducted with Henri Fournier, a French race-car driver who was scheduled to compete in the second James Gordon Bennett Cup Race in Dublin that July. Their conversation appeared as an interview in the April 7 edition of the *Irish Times* under the title "The Motor Derby."[1] In this piece, Joyce's questions seem straightforward and a bit predictable, and Fournier's answers, though not quite rude, are perfunctory and not terribly revelatory. Nonetheless, their exchange provided at least an outline of the world that Joyce would incorporate into his story. And it may also have provided the title: when Joyce asks, "Will you remain any time in Ireland?" Fournier replies, "After the race?" (*CW*, 108).

Joyce, of course, felt free to transform details from the interview as it suited his needs: Fournier, the driver whom Joyce interviewed, manages "a motor establishment," whereas the driver based on him in the short story, Charles Ségouin, is an owner. (In "After the Race," Ségouin's cousin, André Rivière, who rides in the front of the car with him, is about to become manager of the establishment.) Like the actual Fournier, the fictional Ségouin does not win the race. Nonetheless, the narrative declares his French group "virtual victors. Their team had finished solidly; they had been placed second and third and the driver of the winning German car was reported a Belgian" (*D*, 49). At the same time, and more to the point, the aura of detachment, present in Joyce's interview and not found in the other stories in the *Dubliners* collection, remains constant throughout the fictional narrative.

1. A reprint of the interview appears in *CW*, 106–8.

The story's setting offers a series of more arresting deviations from Joyce's habits of composition. "After the Race" begins and ends outside the city—opening on the Naas Road southwest of the city and ending in Kingstown (now Dún Laoghaire) Harbor. Only "A Painful Case," the other story in the collection about which Joyce seems to have felt ambivalence, ventures outside Dublin, settling Mr. Duffy in Chapelizod "because he found all the other suburbs of Dublin mean, modern and pretentious" (D, 130). This geographic displacement, though not terribly important in terms of distance, carries a distinct creative significance. It shifts the story's atmosphere from the claustrophobic urban haunts that shape behavior in so many other stories to locations less geographically familiar and less economically constrained.

This displacement in turn sets off a sharp thematic distinction. To a degree absent in any other story in the collection, "After the Race" focuses not simply on the lives of privileged characters but specifically upon individuals whose canny abilities to identify and exploit changing commercial conditions have allowed them to advance socially. Jimmy, the central figure, is the eldest son of a nouveau riche family whose wealth derives from his father's ability to rise from being a butcher in Kingstown to "opening shops in Dublin and in the suburbs. . . . He had also been fortunate enough to secure some of the police contracts and in the end he had become rich enough to be alluded to in the Dublin newspapers as a merchant prince" (D, 50). The source of Ségouin's money is less clear, but he remains so immersed in commerce that he can take unalloyed pleasure from the fact that as a consequence of the race, "he had unexpectedly received some orders [for motor cars] in advance" (D, 50). Farley, the American who owns the yacht upon which the closing card game takes place, has money as well. Though the narrative never specifies how he came to acquire his money, his behavior suggests that he too has come by it recently.

No other story features so prominently this rising commercial class of businessmen. Most of Joyce's characters are either in the lower-middle class or in danger of sinking into outright penury. In "Grace," for example, the central characters may seem at first glance solidly rooted in the middle class, but even their positions are subject to sudden change. Martin Cunningham's wife is "an unpresentable woman who was an incurable drunkard" (D, 193).

And Charlie M'Coy has recently gotten a short-term infusion of cash by borrowing valises from friends only to pawn them (*D*, 197). Acquiring money is in the foreground of a number of stories in *Dubliners* ("Araby," "Two Gallants," and "Ivy Day in the Committee Room" are just three examples), and in most cases it is the lack of financial security—as in "Counterparts"—that haunts the characters no matter what their seeming condition.

Joyce was all too familiar with this kind of stress, and conversely writing outside of immediate experience has a clear effect upon Joyce's prose. The characters in "After the Race" have markedly less development than do figures in any of the other stories. Although the genre itself prevents the elaborate delineation of identity that one finds in novels, Joyce has nonetheless proved to be adept at a suggestiveness that evokes powerful reflections of the individuals he describes. Eveline Hill, for example, though the central figure in a story no longer than "After the Race," projects a rich and complicated character within the constricted environment of her daily life. Likewise, Maria in "Clay," Little Chandler in "A Little Cloud," and Lenehan in "Two Gallants" step off the page as fully formed, if fairly desperate, individuals whose natures Joyce captures in a few deft paragraphs.

Nothing like this economy occurs in the representation of Jimmy (a man, known by a childish diminutive, whose surname, Doyle, barely comes to the reader's attention, since it is mentioned precisely once [*D*, 35]) or in any of the others in the story. Instead, we see types and even stereotypes: the indulgent father, the spoiled rich young man, and the worldly wise friends crowd out any subtler representations.

Perhaps most strikingly, the action of the story falls into a well-worn trajectory that leaves little open to interpretation. From its beginning, the narrative traces the carelessness of a starstruck young man who has always been shielded from his own foolishness by the largess and influence of his father. When, at the end of the story, Jimmy seems to have gone too far and shamed himself through his excessive gambling, the reader can only nod with the sense that, given the facts of the story, it was bound to occur.

Such apparent closure is quite rare in Joyce's other stories. The final scene in the downstairs room in "The Sisters" offers no resolution for the boy or for that matter for any of the other characters. Bob Doran, in "The Boarding House," has clearly accepted the fact that he must marry Polly

Mooney, but it remains quite unclear what that means. And despite the humiliation that Mrs. Kearney faces at the end of "A Mother," the narrative offers no sense of its significance. In these and other stories in the collection, no matter what the outcome of events, Joyce has left it to the reader to find meaning in what has occurred.

Further, this search for meaning goes beyond simply joining the events of the story into a unified impression. Even without closure, throughout the collection, Joyce pushes readers toward a deeper understanding. In many of the other stories in *Dubliners,* including "A Painful Case," at some point in the narrative the central character or the reader (or both) experiences a moment of revelation, an epiphany. At the end of "Araby," the young boy sees himself "as a creature driven and derided by vanity" (*D*, 41). In "Ivy Day in the Committee Room," while the men who have listened to Joe Hynes's poem on Parnell feel deeply sentimental, a clear view of the crippling force of nostalgia confronts the reader. And in the final lines of "The Dead," the most deft representation of identity in the collection, one comes away from the story with a deep sense that a change has come about because of the story of Michael Furey, even if the parameters of that change remain a matter open to vigorous debate.

This kind of insight never comes about, either for readers or for characters, in "After the Race." The epiphanic moment that punctuates the narrative of many other stories remains emphatically absent from this one. Early on, one sees the central character as an indulged and somewhat foolish young man. As one might expect, Jimmy drinks too much and plays cards foolishly. Nonetheless, the consequences of his actions, and more particularly their significance, never really register for him and remain obscure to even the most astute reader. Jimmy has lost more money than he should have and feels a measure of regret, though there is no evidence of any insight. "He knew that he would regret in the morning but at present he was glad of the rest, glad of the dark stupor that would cover up his folly" (*D*, 57). Further, the slipperiness of the word *folly* makes it unclear whether it means a crippling amount or simply a tally that will upset his father. That vagueness in turn makes it difficult to decide how seriously to take the matter, for even if it proves to be an enormous amount, there is little promise of insight coming from his actions.

Taking into consideration all of the points already raised against seeing "After the Race" as on a par with the other stories in the collection, where does that leave one in terms of how to interpret it and its effect upon one's overall impression of *Dubliners*? Certainly, one can find ample similarities between it and other works in the collection. "After the Race" offers a clear view of the lives of a select group of Dubliners. It relies upon the backdrop of the city to inform characterization. It shows the same deft ability to shape narrative as one sees in the other stories. Nonetheless, "After the Race" is somehow different, and the difference from the other stories inheres mainly in the aforementioned nouveau riche social milieu wherein the characters circulate. Moreover, the cast of characters stands out from the characters in the other stories. The young men who populate the social world of "After the Race" are a truly multinational set, in contrast to the mostly Irish figures in the other stories. True, Farrington in "Counterparts" is ignored by a woman with "a London accent" (*D*, 115), Ignatius Gallagher in "A Little Cloud" boasts of his experiences in Paris, and Gabriel Conroy in "The Dead" makes regular trips to the Continent, so the larger world outside of Ireland is acknowledged in the other stories. But "After the Race" is the only story that makes British and Continental characters—not to mention those from the New World—part of the action. As we shall see, the anomalous nature of "After the Race" allows us to tease out some fairly complicated sociopolitical meanings from the story, which only heightens the suspicion that the story has been forced into a collection with which it has no substantial connection.

THE POLITICAL ALLEGORY in "After the Race" is almost too obvious: the Irish lose and the British win, despite the sympathies of the French. In the card game on the yacht that closes the story, the Irishman Jimmy Doyle understands "that the game lay between Routh and Ségouin"—the Englishman and the Frenchman—and that "he would lose, of course" (*D*, 57). The political meaning of the card game is signaled by the narrative parallelism of the late-night supper aboard the yacht where the game is played and the earlier dinner at Ségouin's hotel where the Frenchman "shepherded his party into politics" (*D*, 54). At that dinner, Jimmy feels the "buried zeal" (*D*, 54) of Irish nationalism awaken within him, whereupon he engages the Englishman in a political argument. As the argument escalates to the point of "personal spite," Ségouin calms things down by toasting "to Humanity" and throwing "open a window significantly" (D, 54). Similarly, at the end of the card game, Jimmy's Hungarian friend Villona throws open the door of the ship's cabin where the card game has been played and announces, significantly, "Daybreak, gentlemen!" (D, 57). There can be no doubt that the later scene is meant as a commentary on the earlier one and that the political discussion begun at the hotel continues, and concludes, aboard the yacht, albeit in the allegorical form of the game of cards.

However obvious the political allegory of "After the Race," the interpretation of that allegory is not so obvious. Earlier efforts to interpret the allegory have focused on the role of the French in Irish political history, with the would-be French automaker Ségouin playing the role of liberator to Jimmy Doyle, "who represents Ireland," according to Zack Bowen (1969, 57). In this reading, the commercial overtures that Ségouin and his associates make to Jimmy Doyle correlate with Irish-French relations dating back to "the time of the Stuarts and . . . the days of Wolfe Tone." It follows that "the failure of the French to free the Irish in the 1690's and in the 1790's leads up to the suspicion that still one hundred years later history will again repeat itself in 'After the Race'" (ibid.). This general interpretation has been elaborated by Donald T. Torchiana, who sees the "virtual" (D, 49) victory of the French cars, cheered on by the Irish crowd, and the subsequent defeat of both Ségouin and Doyle by the Englishman Routh as an allusion to the rout of the British by combined French-Irish forces at Castlebar on August 27, 1798, and the crushing defeat of those forces at Ballinamuck less than two weeks later on September 8. Because "the British literally raced from the field" in the battle on August 27, "their singular defeat has never been forgotten in Ireland and has lived on gloriously in the ironic title of the Races of Castlebar" (Torchiana 1986, 81).[2] Even though one may argue about the extent to which such detailed references to earlier Irish history actually operate in the story, there would seem to be no question that Joyce is asking us to think about the political status of Ireland at the time the story is set (1903) and to consider the place of Ireland in relation not only to its colonial master,

2. For an earlier version of Torchiana's essay on "After the Race," see Torchiana 1971.

Great Britain, but also to other nations of the world at the turn of the century—France, Hungary, Canada, the United States. The history of Ireland's prior relations with England and France is necessary to an understanding of the political status of Ireland circa 1903, and the detailed reference to the events of 1798 that Torchiana finds in the story perhaps provides a kind of historical resonance, but in the end the late-eighteenth-century historical background does not provide a sufficient basis for interpreting the political allegory of "After the Race."

That earlier history is still active in 1903, but it omits three of the historical "players" in the story: the Irish American Farley, the French Canadian Rivière, and the Hungarian Villona. Indeed, a fact about the story that has gone largely unnoticed is that Jimmy Doyle is not the only character whose political condition is defined by a relationship to an imperial power. André Rivière, Ségouin's cousin, is French Canadian; Farley, the American, is really Irish-American; and Villona, the Hungarian, while not exactly Austro-Hungarian, reminds us that the nation of Hungary was scarcely one generation removed from the old Hapsburg Empire when the story was written in 1904. The national identities of all three of these characters are hybridized by modern forces of culture and commerce. The basic idea seems to be that capitalism destroys old historical alliances based on culture and forges new alliances based on economic interests. The French Canadian Rivière, for example, has no interest in the kind of cultural identity fostered by French separatist movements in Canada and is merely seeking to forge a relationship with France by commercial means. If the name of his yacht, "*The Belle of Newport*" (*D*, 56), is any indication, the Irish American Farley would seem to have no wish to reconnect to his Irish roots. Jimmy's friend Villona seems to be Hungarian in name only, and, although he does not have the aggressive commercial desires of the entrepreneurial Rivière or the capitalist Farley, he seems motivated by little more than a good meal at someone else's expense (suggesting the false etymology *hungry* > *Hungary,* or some such pun). In any event, the more recent history represented by the three nationally "hyphenated" characters is at least as significant to the story's meaning as the older history embodied by the Englishman Routh, the Frenchman Ségouin, and the Irishman Jimmy Doyle. In fact, the two histories are set in conflict with one another; or, rather, old historical loyalties are compromised by modern historical exigencies.

The nature of this compromise concerns the ideological tension between the idea of a nation based on culture and the concept of a state based on political and economic power. The tension is played out in the career of Jimmy's father, who succeeds in business by compromising his cultural patrimony, leaving his youthful nationalism behind. That career is sketched for us early on in the story in a few highly economical sentences: "His father, who had begun life as an advanced Nationalist, had modified his views early. He had made his money as a butcher in Kingstown and by opening shops in Dublin and in the suburbs he had made his money many times over. He had also been fortunate enough to secure some of the police contracts and in the end he had become rich enough to be alluded to in the Dublin newspapers as a merchant prince" (*D*, 50). Almost certainly, the father's "advanced" nationalism must have included a pronounced cultural component; in fact, specific cultural markers—such as the Gaelic language or the Catholic religion—would have elevated raw ideology into cultural consciousness: culture advances politics; the nation produces the state. The problem with this naive formulation for "advanced" nationalism, of course, is that it is really regressive—preindustrial, in fact. A cultural nation is no match for a capitalist state. Hence, the elder Doyle "modifie[s] his views" by making Irish culture secondary to British capital. And there is no doubt that Jimmy's father is a capitalist: he makes his fortune not because he is a good butcher but because of his "shrewdness in business matters" (*D*, 52). He earns enough money in Kingstown (what's in a name?) to open a chain of butcher shops "in Dublin and in the suburbs" (*D*, 50). Most likely, savings from the Kingstown shop and the shop itself provide collateral for capital financing provided by British banks that allow Mr. Doyle to "[make] his money many times over" (*D*, 50). The "modification" of his advanced nationalism for economic advantage is complete when he becomes "fortunate enough to secure some of the police contracts" (*D*, 50). This final compromise of the Irish nation for the British state makes the man "rich enough to be alluded to in the Dublin newspapers as a merchant prince" (*D*, 50). The epithet nicely captures the conflict of modern economy ("merchant") and traditional politics ("prince") illustrated by Mr. Doyle's career.

The son's career recapitulates the father's, with significant repetitions and reversals. The younger Doyle is hardly the advanced nationalist his father once was, although, in a nod to cultural tradition, Jimmy is "educated in a big

Catholic college," albeit in England, before returning to Ireland for study at "Dublin University" (*D*, 50), the Protestant institution better known as Trinity College. There Jimmy studies law, however briefly, while his father helps feed the police who enforce the law. Encouraged by his father, the younger Doyle looks to invest in a commercial venture under the control of a foreign state, as his father did, though Jimmy's interest in the French automobile industry seems—but only seems—less of a betrayal of Irish nationalism than his father's profiteering from British police contracts. The compromised nature of Jimmy's relationship to Ireland is suggested when Ségouin drops off Jimmy and his Hungarian friend "near the Bank" (*D*, 53). The unnarrated implication of this action is that Jimmy needs to withdraw funds from the bank to invest in the Frenchman's commercial venture. Moreover, the reference to this site in Dublin's cityscape supports the theme of politico-cultural compromise because the building housed the Irish Parliament prior to the Act of Union in 1800 (Gifford 1982, 54). Later, the wealthy American Farley turns up at "the corner of Grafton Street," in the neighborhood of the bank, which is at the intersection of Grafton and Dame Street. This small detail allows us to speculate, at least, that the Irish American character, like Jimmy's father, may have benefited somehow from British capital by investing abroad, as Jimmy plans to do. Farley, however, has made his fortune in America, evidently in the classic turn-of-the-century robber-baron sense. This much is implied by the name of Farley's yacht, "*The Belle of Newport*" (*D*, 56). The yacht, of course, is anchored in the bay just off Kingstown, near the site of the elder Doyle's earliest business success, which is also the site of the son's financial ruin. Indeed, whereas his father takes his profits from the Kingstown shop and makes "his money many times over" (*D*, 36) with the help of British capital, the son appears to lose his money many times over ("the other men had to calculate his I.O.U.'s for him" [*D*, 56]), most of it to the Englishman Routh.

Jimmy's profligate manner with money shows that he is not fully his father's son. Unlike his father, Jimmy does not give himself wholly over to the commercial world: "He divided his time curiously between musical and motoring circles" (*D*, 50). The narrative comment—"curiously"—is ambiguous: either the division itself is curious because unusual, or Jimmy is merely curious—an outsider in both circles, rather than a committed and accepted participant in either. The story sustains both meanings. It is a curious thing for Jimmy to so divide his time, unlike the Hungarian Villona, whose interests are mainly musical, and unlike the Frenchman Rivière, an electrician by trade whose circle is largely limited to motoring. At the same time, Jimmy's role as little more than a curious outsider is certified by his position in the backseat of the race car driven by Ségouin, while his cousin Rivière sits in the front beside him. Jimmy's association with the Hungarian pianist Villona is curious for other reasons. The basis for their friendship is evidently music, but Villona, unlike Jimmy, does not "divide his time." On the contrary, even when he is motoring along Irish roads in the Gordon Bennett Cup Race, the Hungarian maintains his musical identity: "He kept up a deep bass hum of melody for miles of the road" (D, 51). The situation is "not altogether pleasant" (D, 51) for Jimmy because of the conflicting sounds made by the members of the musical and motoring circles who are traveling with him. Jimmy has to strain to hear what the Frenchmen in the front seat are saying, which is made even more difficult by the music hummed by his Hungarian companion in the backseat: "Besides Villona's humming would confuse anybody; the noise of the car, too" (D, 51). Villona does not stray far from the musical circle that circumscribes his existence throughout his day with Jimmy—neither the race, nor the dinner at Ségouin's hotel, nor the card game interferes with his musical interests. He hums melodies in the racing car at the start of the story and improvises "voluntaries" (D, 56) at the piano while the other characters play cards. In the intervening scene, at Ségouin's dinner, Villona talks music with the Englishman Routh while Rivière talks motoring with Jimmy: "Villona, with immense respect, began to discover to the mildly surprised Englishman the beauties of the English madrigal, deploring the loss of old instruments. Rivière, not wholly ingenuously, undertook to explain to Jimmy the triumph of the French mechanicians" (D, 54). No doubt Rivière's explanation is not wholly ingenuous because of concern that the Irishman may harbor second thoughts about investing his money in French manufacturing. In other words, the old French-Irish alliance can no longer be assumed because of modern commercial considerations. At the same time, modern commerce trumps old traditions, so the conclusion of the story should not surprise us, as Jimmy emerges from the disastrous evening just as he began the day—as an outsider, an onlooker, and, probably, a bit of a dupe.

At the very end of the story, the Hungarian Villona occupies a place of greater importance than he has occupied at any prior point in the story. He has the last word—"Daybreak, gentlemen!"—and appears dramatically framed in the open door, his body backlit by the light of the dawn: "The cabin door opened and he saw the Hungarian standing in a shaft of grey light" (*D*, 57). As Bowen and others have noted, Joyce probably decided to make Jimmy Doyle's friend Hungarian because of Arthur Griffith's comparison of Irish and Hungarian political history in *The Resurrection of Hungary*, published early in 1904 (Bowen 1970, 138–39). In addition to spotlighting a Hungarian character, perhaps the end of the story suggests, through its striking, early-morning imagery, a more traditional resurrection scene. That is, the resurrection imagery and the character's nationality combine to make Villona, at story's end, a visual reference to the title of Griffith's political tract. In any case, there would seem to be no doubt that a political meaning of some kind is written into the character of Villona, and, more important, into that character's relationship to the young Irishman Jimmy Doyle. In *The Resurrection of Hungary*, Griffith insists that Hungary's liberation from Austria can serve as a model for the political independence of Ireland: "What the Hungarians did for Hungary Irishmen can do for Ireland" (1904, 96). In Griffith's view, Hungary can serve as a political model for Ireland in several ways. Culturally, the Hungarian movement emphasized use of the Hungarian language in the development of both a national literature and a national press. Economically, Hungarians broke their economic dependence on Austria by developing their own agriculture and industry and by trading directly with other nations ("Today," Griffith claims, Hungary "is the granary of Europe" [ibid.]). Politically, the Hungarians rejected representation and participation in the Austrian parliament as a means of gaining independence. As is well known, Griffith advocated similar cultural, economic, and political strategies for Ireland. Joyce supported the antiparliamentarian and economic aspects of Griffith's nationalist agenda, but parted company with him on cultural grounds, as he indicated in a letter to Stanislaus on November 6, 1906: "If the Irish programme did not insist on the Irish language I suppose I could call myself a nationalist" (*Letters II*, 187). Also, like Griffith, Joyce understood that no Irish state was possible without a firm economic foundation, and in September 1906 he was pleased that Griffith was trying "to inaugurate some commercial life for Ireland" (ibid., 167).

In "After the Race," the only "commercial life" in evidence is British—the source of the elder Doyle's fortune—and Continental; it is, after all, "the Continent" that speeds "its wealth and industry" through the "poverty and inaction" of the Irish countryside at the beginning of the story (*D*, 49). But what of Hungary? The character Villona seems hardly to embody the cultural, economic, and political values that Griffith urged his fellow Irishmen to emulate. Villona even falls short of the political role that the "Hungarian" Bloom plays in *Ulysses*. There, in the "Cyclops" chapter, Bloom's political identity as a Hungarian comes up when Martin Cunningham makes a vague reference to Bloom's drawing up "all the plans according to the Hungarian system" (*U*, 12.1636). In the same chapter John Wyse Nolan claims that "Bloom gave the ideas for Sinn Fein to Griffith" (*U*, 12.1574). Given that Griffith's tract on Hungary was initially published in the *United Irishman* during the first six months of 1904, these wildly improbable assertions about Bloom's foundational role in Irish national politics are most likely owing simply to Cunningham's and Nolan's awareness of Bloom's Hungarian ancestry. Earlier, in *Stephen Hero,* the narrator takes a dim view of those advocates of a certain "patriotic party" who look to other nations for models of the Irish movement: "The analogies they gave out as exact and potent were really analogies built haphazard upon very inexact knowledge" (*SH*, 62). This formulation might be taken as a commentary on Cunningham's and Nolan's claims about Bloom in the later novel, but, more important, the passage argues for Joyce's skepticism about taking other nations as models for Irish independence: "A glowing example was to be found for Ireland in the case of Hungary, for example, as these patriots imagined, of a long-suffering minority, entitled by every right of race and justice to a separate freedom, finally emancipating itself" (*SH*, 62). Hence, it may well be that Villona in "After the Race" is an exemplar in an ironic sense only, a character who provides the pattern, paradoxically, not of Hungarian liberation but of Irish subjugation. Like the Irish sightseers who watch the race cars "careering homeward" through a "channel of poverty" (*D*, 49), Villona is "very poor" (*D*, 51). Villona also shows "immense respect" for the culture of the Englishman Routh when he praises "the beauties of the English madrigal"

(*D*, 54). Villona, in other words, is none of the things that Griffith took the Hungarians to be: he is not a model of economic success, he expresses no interest in the culture of his own nation, and he seems not to involve himself in politics of any kind, just as he declines participation in the game of cards, which, as we have noted, can easily be read as a political allegory.

In the end, "After the Race" seems too slight a story to serve as a framework for the political conflicts suggested in it. Since Joyce thought that "After the Race" was one of the "two worst stories" in *Dubliners* and wanted to rewrite it, we are tempted to imagine that he *did* rewrite the story—as *Ulysses*. One can always argue that in *Ulysses*, Joyce rewrote everything that he had written before, but "After the Race" stands out as particularly suggestive because many of the character relationships and political themes of Joyce's slightest story find fuller expression in his greatest novel. The story features the friendship of a sensuous Hungarian and an anxious Irishman as a possible model for the later relationship of Bloom and Stephen. Likewise, just as Stephen's friendship with Mulligan is compromised and undermined by Mulligan's association with the Englishman Haines, so Jimmy Doyle's friendship with Ségouin is most likely compromised by Ségouin's association with Routh, "whom Jimmy had seen with Ségouin at Cambridge" (*D*, 54). As in *Ulysses*, the route to ruin that the young Irish character takes runs through Westland Row Station (*D*, 55; *U*, 15.636); Jimmy gets drunk and loses his money in Kingstown, Stephen in Nighttown. The card-game scene is hardly as hallucinatory as the "Circe" chapter, but Jimmy does have trouble focusing on reality, "for he frequently mistook his cards" (*D*, 56). Villona, though not a paternal figure, is like Bloom in that he refrains from full participation in the evening's debauch, and, possibly, he is there to sober Jimmy up and see him safely home, just as Bloom takes care of Stephen. Like *Ulysses*, the action of "After the Race" runs through the course of a rather full day and ends at dawn. The larger point here is not that "After the Race" is really a rough draft of *Ulysses*, but that the kinds of large political, economic, and cultural issues that Joyce raises in the short story require fuller treatment. "After the Race," then, is the "worst story" in *Dubliners* mainly because it is just that—a story, not a novel.

FOR ALL OF THESE REASONS, we remain convinced that "After the Race" simply does not fit the plan of the rest of the collection. Its differences have a jarring effect upon expectations that one has for the other stories in *Dubliners,* and in consequence it exerts an anomalous influence upon the way one sees the volume. This point then raises the question of what is to be done. The simple response is to say that it should be dropped from the volume. We realize, of course, that any number of readers will object to the idea of excluding "After the Race" from subsequent editions of *Dubliners,* and we suspect that the Joyce Estate would take a dim view of tampering with the arrangement of the collection. Nonetheless, we see little to be gained by continuing to address a story that at best provokes embarrassed apologies or stuttering bewilderment, even by the story's author himself, who called it one of "the worst stories *in the collection.*" The story's "worst-ness," then, is partly a result of its thematic and formal disparities compared to the rest of *Dubliners.* The story's virtues emerge more fully when it is read on its own, rather than among the collection. The detailed political reading provided above is exemplary in the sense that whatever insights are gained thereby are hardly transferable to the other stories in the collection.

If readers must go on encountering "After the Race" in the collection, there is no reason that they should have to engage. Failing efforts to exclude, we propose simply ignoring it. Its anomalies provide easy justification for that strategy, and the effects achieved by avoiding the need for apology or rationalization will make any interpretation of the collection that much stronger. Indeed, we suspect a number of readers and instructors already follow this practice informally. In fact, the author of a recent critical study of *Dubliners* quite unabashedly excludes the story from consideration. In *"Dubliners"' Dozen: The Games Narrators Play,* Gerald Doherty approaches the stories with a variety of critical "microtheories," but decides to "omit one story—'After the Race'—completely, since [he] can find no microtheory to accommodate it" (2004, 154n14). We merely propose taking this attitude a step further by urging that readers consider "After the Race" in the same way they do the four-act version of *The Importance of Being Earnest* or the Henry James canon prior to the revisions of the New York edition. It stands on the level of draft material, useful in understanding the process of composition, but not necessary for comprehension of the final version of the work under consideration.

En Garde

"Two Gallants"

MARILYN REIZBAUM AND MAUD ELLMANN

The essay that we have contributed to this volume maps the process of our composition in its structure. We began by discussing our general thoughts about the story over distances. We then each wrote a ten-page reflection of those thoughts and based on these reflections determined how we might integrate them. The result coordinates the categories of our mutual assessments: "Heedless Music," "A Crock of Gold," "Triangular Exchange." Our introduction gives some sense of our initial discussion—for example, our concurrence on the nastiness of the story, the dominance of the two senses of sight and sound, the simony of the sexual play. In order to arrive at these categories, we not only discussed strategy, but each wrote a preliminary integrative essay. Then we each took a turn at revising it into the essay we have, first Marilyn, and finally Maud. Overall, it seems that our styles more than our thoughts about the story have been altered.[1]

1. Here is an example of one of the first thoughts we sacrificed in the collaboration:

Maud—
      Waking on a Sunday morning with a mild hangover, after a magnificent dinner cooked by my multitalented friend Peter de Bolla—expert on eighteenth-century cultural history, ace keyboard artist, world-class chef, wine-buff extraordinaire—I intended to get started on the present essay, which was already grossly overdue, but was up to little more than Googling "Two Gallants" on the Internet. The first hit yielded the following anecdote:

"Two Gallants" has always been one of our favorite stories, even though it is arguably the nastiest story in *Dubliners*. What is the source of its appeal? Like adolescence—of which the two gallants are somewhat geriatric specimens—the story is unremittingly mean; like adolescence, it is also scrappy and ingenious. As Jean-Michel Rabaté and others have observed, there is something magnetic about the story's silences that makes us long to be nearer to them and to look upon their deadly work (see Rabaté 1982, 45–72). This effect, however, is largely retroactive, since it is the enigmatic gold coin at the end that casts a veil of mystery over the whole. While the story leads us by the nose to this anticipated conclusion, it is not the silences that mesmerize us but the noise. Sight, always accompanied by blindness, is critical to the action of the story, but sound is crucial to its sense: the vernacular bluster of the two gallants, the musical interlude of the harp, the "palaver" of the narrative itself, and the trumpeted announcement of the gold coin in

---

Rod was sharing his pot with another ski bum, who said, "You should check out Two Gallants."

"The James Joyce short story?" Rod had read *Dubliners* and a few other stories, but, when he thought of Joyce, he was reminded of a whore who called her occasional hook-up "Emo Boy" because, in her words, he cried a lot and his favorite book was *A Portrait of the Artist as a Young Man*.

"No, man. The band. They're a two-piece. Their new album is called *What The Toll Tells*. It's got that punk-fuck-you attitude. . . ."

Emo Boy is the last epithet one would think of applying to either of Joyce's two gallants. Corley is robotically emotionless—his stiff gait and rolling head are reminiscent of a marionette—while Lenehan's emotional repertoire has been reduced to minor fluctuations of self-pity. Indeed, the gallants' emotional bankruptcy goes deeper than the fuck-you attitude of punk, which is a form of blasphemy that reaffirms the sentimental values it repudiates; as T. S. Eliot declares, no one can possibly blaspheme unless he "profoundly believes in that which he profanes." Corley, by contrast, believes in nothing but money and machismo, the shibboleths of Dublin's homosocial pub culture. Equally emotionless is the narrator, with the exception of a couple of set pieces—the lyrical opening paragraph and the evocation of the Irish harp—which advertise themselves as "good writing" and make a striking contrast to the coldness of the reportage. These moments of lyricism con the reader, much as Corley's blandishments con the slavey, by disguising the narrator's machinations. Willing victims of this "gay Lothario" of a narrator, we surrender to his tricks with a contented leer, paying dearly for our own violation.

Corley's noisily outstretched hand. By the end of the story, even Corley's silence is deafening.

The present essay follows these noises in the several directions that they beckon us. First we consider how the noise of the narration implicates the reader in the epistemological condition of the characters, who perform knowingness while owning nothing but their blind, stupefied hearts. Another noise to be considered is the siren song of Irish nationalism, evoked by the street performance of the Irish harp. The lyricism of this scene interrupts the scrupulous meanness of the prose, as if the narrator were busking for our sympathy with eloquence. The harpist's musical performance provides an aural counterpoint to Corley's final dumbshow, when he melodramatically discloses the gold coin in his palm. This coin functions as a blind or decoy, insofar as its exposure reveals nothing of its history or significance. Abstracted from its economic and sexual relations, the coin serves to clinch the nefarious triangulation of the slavey and the two gallants, all of whom are trapped in the circuit of exchange that they are trying to manipulate. The concluding section of our essay homes in on these dynamics of exchange, showing how the erotic geometry of "Two Gallants" prefigures the "French triangles" of Joyce's future.[2]

Heedless Music

The first fall guy to be duped in "Two Gallants" is the reader, insofar as the story's title is doubly misleading: Corley and Lenehan are far from gallant, and their twoness depends on an exploited third. "Two's company but three's a couple," to borrow Adam Phillips's memorable definition of monogamy (1996, 94). In Joyce's story, two depraved companions strike a shady deal: Corley the gigolo wins a bet with Lenehan the leech by cheating a hardworking "slavey" out of a substantial sum of money. Or so we suspect, because the obliquity of the narration makes it impossible to ascertain the facts. It is this obliquity that breeds suspicion, both for the reader and for

2. John Eglinton says of Stephen's theory that sexual jealousy incited Shakespeare's genius: "You have brought us all this way to show us a French triangle" (*U*, 9.1054–56). See also Girard 2000, 256–70.

Lenehan, since both are excluded from the scene of Corley's sexual conquest. Just as Lenehan is forced to "read the result from their walk," and impute the seduction from its signs, so the reader is placed in the position of the looker-on, substituting prurient imaginings for evidence (*D*, 71). Thus, the story confronts us with our own dirty minds, mirrored in Joyce's "nicely polished looking-glass" (*Letters I*, 64). Like Corley, possible pimp and probable police informer, readers are obliged to play the supergrass against themselves, exposing their own desires rather than penetrating Joyce's reticence.

For this reason, readers of "Two Gallants" find themselves in much the same position as the gossips in *Finnegans Wake*, who implicate themselves in the primal father's unknown crime by dreaming up its sordid details. In a letter to his publisher Grant Richards, Joyce speaks of "the special odour of corruption which, I hope, floats over my stories," an image recalling the miasma that descends on ancient Thebes in retribution for Oedipus's crimes (*Letters II*, 123). Like the Theban miasma, the "grey warm evening . . . air" (*D*, 58) that envelops "Two Gallants" seems to emanate from the obscene and the unspeakable. Meanwhile, the maleficent narrator seduces us with "deep energetic gallantries" (*D*, 69) of prose—the aerial view of Dublin in the opening paragraph, where the city is transformed into a living texture, "changing shape and hue unceasingly" (*D*, 58), and the lyrical description of the harp, filling the miasmal air with Ireland's eternal lamentation—only to betray us into the banality of evil. Willing victims of this "gay Lothario" (*D*, 62) of a narrator, we surrender to his tricks with a contented leer, paying dearly for our own violation.

These gallantries about the city and the harp suggest an elegiac attitude to Irishness. Yet any traces of sentimental nationalism are overshadowed by stronger hints that Ireland is enervated, flaccid, out of shape. Lenehan, with his outfit of breeches, white rubber shoes, and jauntily slung waterproof, puts on a performance of youth, but the narrative suggests that he is falling both morally and physically, dragged earthward by his own dead weight. His hair, "scant and grey," is falling off; his figure has fallen "into rotundity at the waist," and his face falls after "waves of expression" have passed over it, giving it "a ravaged look" (*D*, 59). All these falls allude to other falls in *Dubliners*—the fallen chalice in "The Sisters," the falling coins in "Araby," the final snowfall in "The Dead"—as well as looking forward to the fall of

Finnegan. Even the harp in "Two Gallants" is depicted as a fallen woman, "heedless that her coverings had fallen about her knees . . . weary alike of the eyes of strangers and of her master's hands" (*D*, 64). Disheveled and heedless, like the slavey with her "straggling mouth" and "ragged black boa" (*D*, 66), this feminized harp recalls the traditional image of Ireland as the Shan van Vocht, the poor old woman that Padraic Pearse, the leading ideologue of the Easter Rising, attempted to transform into a triumphant image of feminine self-sacrifice. The resilience of this image in Irish martyrology testifies to its ingenious fusion of nationalism and Mariolatry. Stephen Dedalus, however, punctures Pearse's idealization by arraigning Mise Eire as "the old sow that eats her farrow" (*P*, 171; *U*, 15.4581–82).

Ironically, Pearse's attempt to reverse the fortunes of Ireland by reclaiming and revamping its symbolism helped to create a culture of the "triumph of failure."[3] This culture is epitomized by the mournful music of the Irish harp, which has a spellbinding effect on the two gallants, striking them dumb; only when they cross the road at Stephen's Green does "the noise of trams . . . [release] them from their silence" (*D*, 64). In *Dubliners*, idealizations—whether of an object of desire or the nation—are constantly shattered by the noisy materiality of city life. Meanwhile, nationalist balladry tends to operate as an impediment or paralyzing force: in "Araby," for instance, the boy narrator bears his idealized love as a chalice through a throng of foes, including such foes as ballads about "the troubles in our native land" (*D*, 35).

As readers, we also run the risk of being spellbound by the allegorical import of the harp, distracted by its appeal to our interpretative curiosity. The harp therefore functions as a "blind," as Margot Norris has contended, concealing the "unsentimentalized degradations of the story," which pose a gritty resistance to the consolations of allegory (2003, 82). Just as sex is traded in for the gold coin, so the national dirge is traded in for tips; the harpist is busking, and his heedless music prostitutes itself to the winds: "The notes of the air sounded deep and full" (*D*, 64).

"Simony"—one of the three words that fascinate the boy narrator of "The Sisters"—denotes the traffic in sacred things, and the harpist could

---

3. For a discussion of the idea of the "triumph of failure," see Valente 1995, 189–210.

be seen as a simoniac who traffics in the nation's sacred myths, his heedless indifference passing for a gallant act of national pride. "She"—the harp—is also "heedless" but knowing, like the leering slavey with whom the harp is associated by the feminine pronoun and the image of slovenly undress: "heedless that her coverings had fallen about her knees" (D, 64). Indeed, the slavey's abrupt appearance in the wake of the ballad—"There she is!"— suggests that this "fine decent tart" (D, 64) has been conjured up by the mournful music of the harp. The conjunction implies that both the slavey and the harp are stuck in the same old song of exploitation: whereas the harp is "weary alike of the eyes of strangers and of her master's hands," the slavey is triangulated between Corley's hands and Lenehan's eyes.

When Corley and the slavey leave the scene, however, it is Lenehan who imaginatively metamorphoses into a harpist and a harp, an instrument both played upon and playing. Controlled by the movement of the music, his feet trudge to the mournful melody while his fingers strum the railings of the Duke's Lawn: "The air which the harpist had played began to control his movements. His softly padded feet played the melody while his fingers swept a scale of variations idly along the railings after each group of notes" (D, 67). The fact that Lenehan the would-be "player"—playboy, gambler, con man, "toreador"—finds himself the puppet of the music indicates the flimsiness of his delusions of agency. His automatism poses an ironic counterpoint to the young narrator of "Araby," who revels in the sense that his body is a harp vibrating to his idol's fingertips: "My body was like a harp and her words and gestures were like fingers running upon the wires" (D, 35). In "Two Gallants," however, the transformation of the harp strings into railings hints that the Irish are imprisoned by their heartstrings, their susceptibility to the seductive music of national self-pity.

A Crock of Gold

Most of Joyce's stories preserve some distinction between victim and victim-izer, however compromised. But the image of Lenehan played by the music he is playing on the railings indicates that this distinction no longer holds. Even the slavey, the obvious victim of the story, plays along with the familiar tune of seduction and betrayal. Her knowing leer makes it impossible to see her as an ingenue, and even more impossible to see her as an allegory of her downtrodden nation, violated by the British Empire, as some critics have proposed.[4] On the contrary, the story shows how the colonial condition belies any simple opposition of oppressor and oppressed. In Dublin the exploited exploit each other in a world reduced to debt and doubt. Debt generates exchange, while doubt generates suspicion; thus, exchange and suspicion are founded "on the void," on the absence of wealth and information. Yet the mechanics of exchange persist even in the absence of production, just as the mechanics of suspicion thrive on ignorance; no one "makes" money in Dublin, but everyone steals, leeches, inveigles, or extorts it. This parasitical economy resembles Primo Levi's (1996) account of Auschwitz, in which prisoners developed elaborate systems of exchanging almost nothing: a spoon, an egg, a shoe. Similarly, the economy of Dublin is "running on empty," yet its inhabitants still go through the motions of exchange, devising ingenious means of cheating fellow indigents. As Lily puts it in "The Dead," "The men that is now is only all palaver and what they can get out of you" (*D*, 219). And not just men—the slavey's leer suggests that she is trying to get something out of Corley, presumably a husband to release her from wage slavery or prostitution, the career options open to a woman of her class.

But we never glean exactly what the characters are trying to get out of each other. The story poses a riddle that, like Stephen's riddle in the "Nestor" episode of *Ulysses*, has a ready-made solution—the gold coin. Yet this shiny revelation raises more questions than it answers. The coin is the narrative payoff that the reader, like Lenehan, has been "panting" for, yet its significance remains opaque. Why is Lenehan so obsessed with Corley's transaction with the slavey? Does Corley owe him money, as Margot Norris has suggested (2003, 85–91)? How does the slavey acquire the gold coin? Does Corley really extort this trophy from the slavey, or does he pull it out of his long pocket to hoodwink Lenehan? Is it the sidekick or the slavey

4. See T. Williams 1991, 416–39, which argues that Corley's relationship vis-à-vis the slavey is "precisely analogous to the political relation between imperialist power and colonial dependency . . . so that 'Two Gallants' reproduces at a deeply internalized level the relationship between Britain and Ireland" (23).

who is double-crossed? Does Corley con the girl into paying him for sex, or is she "on the turf," with Corley running her? (Remember that Corley's former squeeze has resorted to prostitution, apparently "ruined" by Corley, although this gallant claims "there was others at her before me" [D, 63].) Whether the slavey stole the money from her master or earned it on the game, she is defenseless against Corley, who is likely to inform on her for either misdemeanor; in fact, it is possible that Corley is blackmailing her about her moonlighting.

Does the gold coin therefore represent the price of sex or the price of silence? Joyce mentions this gold coin in a letter to his publisher Grant Richards, protesting at the "one-eyed" printer's objections to his stories. "I am sorry you do not tell me why the printer, who seems to be the barometer of English opinion, refuses to print *Two Gallants* and makes marks in the margin of *Counterparts*. Is it the small gold coin in the former story or the code of honour which the two gallants live by which shocks him?" (*Letters II*, 132–33).[5] Like many of Joyce's protestations to his publisher, this statement has the paradoxical effect of arousing, rather than assuaging, any suspicions the reader might have entertained about the coin.

Gifford points out that the gold coin would be equivalent to six or seven weeks' wages for a slavey, and most critics agree that Corley has charmed the girl into paying him for his caresses, in a reversal of the traditional gender roles of prostitution (1982, 62). Yet although some villainous transaction seems to have occurred, we never see the coin change hands, nor do we ascertain what it is paying for. The exchange value of money disappears,

---

5. Joyce goes on to recommend that the printer read the passage in Gugliamo Ferrero's *Il Militarismo* (1898) that "examines the moral code of the soldier and (incidentally) of the gallant. But it would be useless for I am sure that in his heart of hearts he is a militarist." Giorgio Melchiori translates this passage as follows: "These officers, being short of money to pay for the dissolute lives they were leading, tried, nearly all of them, to become the lovers of rich middle-class ladies, getting money out of them as a recompense for the honour conferred upon those ladies by condescending to make them their mistresses." See Melchiori 1984, 42, where Melchiori also points out the startling physical resemblance between Joyce and Ferrero. In a letter to Stanislaus Joyce of February 11, 1907, Joyce acknowledges that Ferrero "gave" him "Two Gallants" (*Letters II*, 212). See also Spoo 1987; and Manganiello 1980, 43–66.

leaving only its fetishized materiality: "A small gold coin shone in the palm" (*D*, 72). When he opens his palm to reveal this prize to his "disciple," Corley is momentarily transformed into a magician or an alchemist, conjuring gold out of the empty air, rather than a tawdry con man caught up in the strand-entwining debts of Dublin's lowlife. With Lenehan's encouragement, he builds up the dramatic tension through his performance of suspense—the grim stare, the grave gesture, the extended hand, and the smile. His final gesture compares to the so-called money shot in porn photography, in which the ejaculating penis is exposed, coming—but going nowhere. Likewise, the coin displayed in Corley's greasy palm has been abstracted out of circulation, its "shine" blinding all parties to its exchange value. This coin harks back to another round and shiny object described at the beginning of the story, namely, Corley's "large, globular, and oily head," on which his hat sits like "a bulb that had grown out of another." This inimitable description, planted in the sentence like a banana skin to trip up Corley's striding gait, alerts the reader that Corley is not as "hairy" as he boasts. Was the one-eyed printer sufficiently hairy to perceive the double entendre that connects the shiny coin to the oily head with its phallic extension?

By a curious coincidence, "shine" plays a crucial role in Freud's account of fetishism, where his unidentified patient (recognizable from other writings as the Wolf Man) finds himself aroused by a certain "shine on the nose" (*Glanz auf der Nase*). According to Freud, this fetish originated in the patient's childhood, when the little boy "glanced" at his English governess's genitals and discovered that she lacked a penis. The German term *Glanz*, a homonym of the English *glance*, as well as of the Latin *glans*, or *foreskin*, memorializes this traumatic glance, but replaces the absent penis with the child's last-but-one perception, the nose whose shine both marks and masks the revelation of "castration" (Freud 1953–74, 21:149–57). Like the shiny nose, the shiny coin in "Two Gallants" stands in for the absent penis whose surrogates circulate among the characters, Corley having wrested the *Glanz* from the slavey in order to display it to the glance of Lenehan.[6]

6. Here is an example of the collaborative exchange that preceded our synthesis, which can be found in the previous two pages:

This is a glance that fails to see, a shine that blinds. It is telling that Marx and Freud both conceive of fetishism as a form of blindness: in Marx's theory of commodity fetishism, the fetish takes the place of human labor; in Freud's theory of sexual fetishism, the fetish takes the place of gender difference; but in either case, reality is censored out of vision—"scotomised" in order to endow an object with subjective agency. In a revealing analogy Marx associates the fetishism of commodities with the constitutive blindness at the root of vision, whereby "the impression made by a thing on the optic nerve is perceived not as a subjective excitation of that nerve but as the objective form of a thing outside the eye" (1867, 165). This statement implies

---

MR: The slavey, too, seems to be in the know, while needing to perform innocence, as the proper kind of dupe, knowing the score or being up to the dodge, a fine decent tart (your discussion of her leer is terrific). It is Corley only who has no self-consciousness, appearing on a flat plane; he, conversely, performs guile (hairiness) but exhibits none. We have only his word for his "accomplishment." We are told "Corley had not a subtle mind" (it seems as though Lenehan rather than the narrator has observed this [D, 62]), and while his conversation "is mainly about himself," he demonstrates no self-knowledge. The narrator performs these functions of self-referentiality for him, telling us, for example, how he aspirates the first letter of his name, which becomes a kind of linguistic riddle that sets up a secret alliance between the reader and the narrator. The narrator also tips us off, if you'll pardon the pun, on Corley's lack of "hairiness," with the inimitable description of his "large, globular and oily head, which sweated in all weathers; and his large round hat, set upon it sideways, looked like a bulb which had grown out of another" (D, 61). The narrator embarks upon this description as though to trip up Corley's striding gait, as he acknowledges Lenehan's would-be compliment, in this almost conspiratorial chain of moves against him. I have always found this particular description of Corley astoundingly hilarious in its euphemistic adoption of the vernacular, though, again, the reader has to fill in the blank, say the nasty word (Epstein).

(This comes back to your suggestion of "good writing"—the vulgar nicely turned out. I am amazed at how my students rarely perceive the image.) I feel that my relish for this image is somehow unsavory, revealing another way the narration enlists the reader as accomplice, another gallant, as Norris would argue (or as you say, Maud, "implicate us in the characters' depravity." I guess, though, I would depart from your reading of Corley as cunning. He performs it without having it.). Norris's term for the affect of blindness in the story is *pantomime,* as in her characterization of the opening of the story as miming conversation, a "paradigm announcing the strange sign-system of the story as a whole," which requires that readers actively interpret a series of ambiguous and unexplained gestures (2003, 83).

that sight depends on the seer's blindness to the act of seeing; to see is to substitute the object for the subject, the shine for the look, the *Glanz* for the glance. A similar substitution takes place in "Two Gallants," in that showing takes the place of seeing, the gold coin standing in for the sexual transaction occluded in the narrative. Fetishization also operates within the narrative itself, in which the coldness of the reportage is interrupted by two shining epiphanies—the lyrical opening paragraph and the evocation of the Irish harp—which advertise themselves as "good writing," yet stand as fetishes to the romantic sensibility they elegize, a sensibility excoriated by the ruthless naturalism of the prose. Like Corley's gold coin, these showy set-pieces seem extorted from another story, the shiny fragments of a foreclosed scene.

"Then with a grave gesture [Corley] extended a hand towards the light and, smiling, opened it slowly to the gaze of his disciple. A small gold coin shone in the palm" (*D*, 72). Postponing the revelation like a wily flasher, Corley eventually shows the coin—but what does the coin show? Its shine is set against the darkness as the Freudian fetish is set against the void, providing a dam against the terror of castration. What speaks in fetishism, according to Jean Baudrillard, is not the desire for substances but "the passion for the code" (1981, 91). In Joyce's story, the code encrypted in the coin consists of neither the exchange value of the money nor the labor power that the money represents, but "the code of honour which the two gallants live by," a code that prides itself on circumventing legitimated circuits of exchange. If the coin had been designated as a "sovereign," its implications would be very different: not only would it signify a monetary value, but it would also invoke the colonial predicament of Ireland, whose feeble economy is shackled to an alien sovereign. In the epithet "a small gold coin," however, these political and economic codes are "paralyzed," trumped by a code of honor whereby promises to men are kept by breaking promises to women. This code of honor substitutes legerdemain—Corley's Midas touch—for capital and sovereignty, powers to which the gallants have no hope of aspiring. Instead, they prey upon the lumpen slaveys of the "sovereign," flaunting "hairiness" as a superior machismo.

Note that the narrator indulges in an act of simony, trafficking in the language of sacred things, in the mock apocalypse in which the gold coin is revealed. The words *disciple* and *gold coin*, presented in tandem, allude to the parable in Luke 19, where Jesus tells the story of the rich man who entrusts his ten servants with ten gold coins. Those servants who invest their respective coins for interest are rewarded, but the servant who kept his coin "laid up in a napkin" is forced to relinquish it to "him that hath ten pounds." In this parable, prudence is presented as sinful because the cautious servant is sticking to the status quo (that is, the Pharisees), resisting the new religion that will take possession through dissemination. Instead, the prophet and the profit motive must be served by multiplying the gold coins that represent the word or gospel. In Corley's case, as in the cagey servant's, it is clear that the gold coin will have no issue—the buck stops here.

We have been prepared for this mercenary climax from the beginning, when Corley boasts about the slavey's paying his expenses in tram fares and cigars, and later when Lenehan imagines how "some good simple-minded girl with a little of the ready" (D, 69) might redeem him from his weary life of "shifts and intrigues." "A little of the ready" conflates sexual availability with financial solvency, in a kind of simoniac transference between economies. A similar transference takes place in the gallants' discussion of the slavey, in which such terms as *close, ticklish job,* and *bring it off* refer to either financial or sexual extortion: "But tell me, said Lenehan again, are you sure you can bring it off all right. You know it's a ticklish job. They're damn close on that point. Eh? . . . What?" (D, 63). Corley's answer is to swing his shiny head. "I'll pull it off, he said. Leave it to me, can't you?" (D, 64). Far from leaving it to him, Lenehan's anxiety about the "outcome" intensifies throughout the story like the buildup to an orgasm. If Lenehan and Corley are miming conversation at the beginning of the story, they seem to be miming the sex act at the end: Lenehan "start[s] with delight" (D, 71) when he lays eyes on the returning Corley, yet crumples a split second later, and even the language stops and starts, roller-coastering between the hope of success and the fear of failure.

Earlier, Lenehan attempts to soothe himself by thinking about Corley's bulbous head rolling in its pantomime of speech: "The memory of Corley's slowly revolving head calmed him somewhat; he was sure Corley would pull it off all right" (D, 70–71). If Corley's spectral talking head is reassuring, his silence has the opposite effect, plunging Lenehan into despair as the returning lovers loom into his field of vision: "They did not seem to be speaking.

An intimation of the result pricked him like the point of a sharp instrument. He knew Corley would fail; he knew it was no go" (*D,* 71). Thick with innuendo, such phrases as *slowly revolving head, pull it off,* and *pricked him like the point of a sharp instrument,* along with the words *fail* and *no go,* signal the occluded sex scene, while making Lenehan the metaphorical recipient of the "sharp instrument." Thus, Lenehan is placed in the same position as the slavey, metaphorically "pricked" by Corley. In this erotic triangle, it is difficult to tell the prick from the prickee; Lenehan's homosocial alliance with Corley is undercut by the homoerotic desire encoded in the double entendres and frictional rhythms of the prose. Furthermore, the fact that the slavey tips her seducer, reversing the conventional roles of prostitution, leaves us unclear about the grammar of the story: who is the gallant, the prostitute, the base betrayer?

Triangular Exchange

Joyce told Grant Richards that "Two Gallants" was so important to *Dubliners* that he would sooner sacrifice five other stories than allow this masterpiece to be amputated. He also said that "Two Gallants," along with "Ivy Day in the Committee Room," was the story that pleased him most (*Letters I,* 62). Why was this disturbing story so pleasing to its author? For one thing, "Two Gallants" prefigures the theme of circulation and exchange that resurfaces in Joyce's later works: the exchange of sex and gallantries for money, in Corley's case, or wit for drink, in Lenehan's. No one knows how Lenehan achieves "the stern task of living" (*D,* 59), but we learn that his tongue is "tired" from entertaining fellow drunkards in the hope of being treated to their rounds. If talk can be exchanged for drink, so food can be exchanged for sex: when fantasizing about Corley's "dongiovannism" (*U,* 9.458), Lenehan consumes a meager meal of peas, the food serving as a surrogate for offstage lovemaking.

Throughout "Two Gallants," as in many other stories in *Dubliners,* sexuality is displaced into other economies, and these displacements could be understood as simony in reverse, the spiritual trafficking of worldly matters. In the case of "Araby," sexual longing is displaced into religious devotions, or at least the gestures of such ("I pressed the palms of my hands together until they trembled, murmuring: *O love! O love!* many times" [*D,* 36]). In "Two Gallants," sex is exchanged for money, the gold coin standing in for the absent but supposedly triumphant phallus. Meanwhile, food, sex, words, and money become "symbolic equivalents" for one another, in much the same way that florins, rats, and excrement become equivalents for one another in the phantasmagoria of Freud's Rat Man (1953–74, 10:213–16). Later these equivalences provide the basis for the economies of *Ulysses* and *Finnegans Wake,* in which language, money, and bodily processes are presented as interpenetrating systems of exchange and circulation. In the "Aeolus" episode of *Ulysses,* for instance, set in the offices of the *Freeman's Journal,* the newspaper is announced as the "GREAT DAILY ORGAN" at the "HEART OF THE HIBERNIAN METROPOLIS," which pumps misinformation into the collective bloodstream (*U,* 7.84, 1–2). Meanwhile, the transportation system circulates the characters, like corpuscles, on odysseys around the city's arteries. At the stylistic level, Joyce recirculates the literary tradition in the form of citation, allusion, pastiche, and parody. By doing so, he leeches off the dead in much the same way that he leeched off handouts from his put-upon admirers, who might have said of Joyce that "no one knew how he achieved the stern task of living." In this sense, Joyce's literary borrowings could be seen as a vindication of his spendthrift habits, flaunting a Lenehanian economy of freeloading and waste in defiance of the bourgeois ideology of thrift.

Like Lenehan, Joyce paid his way with words, "armed with a vast stock of stories, limericks and riddles" (*D,* 59). In this regard, both Lenehan and Joyce resemble the disgraced Oscar Wilde, who spent a few months in Naples in 1898, where he cadged a drink from Graham Greene's father and another schoolmaster on holiday. Hearing them speak English, Wilde asked if he might join them. Although he looked vaguely familiar, they failed to recognize him during the hour he spent with them, delighting them with his humor and charm. He left them to pay for his drink, and later, when they realized who he was, Greene's father used to say, "Think how lonely Wilde must have been to spend so much time and wit on a couple of schoolmasters on holiday." But as Graham Greene observes, "Wilde was paying for his drink with the only currency he had" (Ellmann 1988, 558). Likewise, wit was the only currency that Joyce could not exhaust, no matter how determined his extravagance.

Lenehanian, too, was Joyce's voyeuristic interest in the sexual exploits of other men, particularly when those exploits involved his wife. René Girard, in *Deceit, Desire, and the Novel* (1961), has demonstrated how the European novel is dominated by erotic triangles, in which the bond that draws the rival men to one another is often stronger than the bond that draws them both to the female object of desire. The most famous "French triangle" in Joyce's work arises from Stephen Dedalus's disquisition on Shakespeare as "bawd and cuckold" to Ann Hathaway. Speculating that the young Will Shakespeare was "overborne" by Ann in a cornfield or a rye field—"If others have their will Ann hath a way"—Stephen proposes that Ann later committed adultery with her husband's brothers, Richard and Edmund, which provided Shakespeare with the names of two of the worst villains in his plays (*U*, 9.256–57). Meanwhile, Mr. W. H., commissioned to play go-between for Shakespeare with the Dark Lady of the Sonnets, stole her heart. It was these betrayals by his mistress and his wife, as well as by his brothers and his closest friend, that produced the fury of Shakespeare's tragedies. At the same time, Shakespeare secretly wished to be betrayed, and even pandered to the lovers, for reasons both voyeuristic and artistic: jealousy, suspicion, and doubt were the energies that fueled his creativity.

Stephen admits that he doubts his own theory, and evidently it was Joyce himself, more perhaps than Shakespeare, who needed doubt to spur him into creativity. Nora told Frank Budgen in 1918, "Jim wants me to go with other men so that he will have something to write about" (Ellmann 1983, 475). Some years earlier, in 1909, Joyce belatedly discovered that his friend Vincent Cosgrave had been pursuing Nora while Joyce was courting her in 1904. This discovery plunged Joyce into jealous torments, and even when Nora managed to assuage his doubts, Joyce insisted on picking at the wound. This picking persists in his writing, which repeatedly invokes erotic triangles, consisting of a passive husband (for example, Bloom), competing and colluding with a virile rival (Boylan) for the favors of a passionate woman (Molly).

In Joyce's play *Exiles* (1918), Richard Rowan urges his wife, Bertha, to embark on an affair with his best friend (and her former lover), Robert Hand, Rowan hoping that jealousy will galvanize his genius, inspiring Shakespearean tours de force. In addition to the wish for inspiration, however, Rowan entertains the "icky" wish to be humiliated and betrayed.[7] Like Bloom in the "Circe" episode of *Ulysses,* Rowan wants to play voyeur, peering through the keyhole while his friend "goes through" his wife. "In the very core of my ignoble heart," Rowan confesses to Hand, "I longed to be betrayed by you and by her—in the dark, in the night—secretly, meanly, craftily. By you, my best friend, and by her. I longed for that passionately and ignobly, to be dishonoured for ever in love and in lust" (*E,* 200).

"Two Gallants" prefigures these erotic triangles in pared-down form. First of all, the slavey takes the role of the third person who makes a couple of the two gallants and consolidates their homosocial bond: "Two's company but three's a couple." From another angle, Lenehan assumes the role of the third person whose spectatorship emboldens Corley to exploit the slavey. Meanwhile, as Nathaniel Small (2006) has pointed out in a brilliant essay on erotic triangles in Joyce, Corley "shows Lenehan what and how to desire," so that Lenehan's desire is "mimetic": he wants what Corley wants; he wants to desire his desires.[8] Here it is worth remembering that Gabriel Conroy in "The Dead" suffers torments not so much because his wife, Gretta, has loved another man, but because Michael Furey loved her with a greater passion than Gabriel can muster. It is Furey's fury that Gabriel envies, rather than its object.

In "Two Gallants," Lenehan finds himself in the position of Joyce's jealous husbands, Shakespeare, Bloom, Rowan, and Conroy, except that Lenehan has no prior stake in the affections of the nameless slavey. As he tells Corley, he merely wants to have "a squint at her" (the 1916 edition says "look" [*D,* 65]). When Corley snaps back, "Are you trying to get inside me?" Lenehan insists that his intentions are purely scopophilic: "All I want is to have a look at her. I'm not going to eat her." He eats peas instead, while Corley gets inside her. At the same time, Corley's seduction of the slavey is performed for Lenehan's voyeuristic appreciation, although Lenehan actually

---

7. The term *icky* is aptly chosen by Nathaniel Small (2006).

8. See also Borch-Jacobsen 1982, which argues that there is no "essential bond between desire and its object," and that "the desire for an object is a desire-effect; it is *induced,* or at least secondary, with respect to the imitation—the mimesis—of the desire of others. In other words, desire is mimetic before it is anything else" (26 and passim).

witnesses nothing of the sexual, financial, and verbal intercourse between the pair; he merely imagines these transactions, just as Corley presumably imagines Lenehan's spectatorship. What is clear is that the slavey serves as an object of exchange between the men, who are using her to get inside each other. Note that Corley asks, "Are you trying to get inside *me*?"—not *her*. Apart from its homoerotic implications, Corley's question raises the possibility that Lenehan is trying to assess the market value of the slavey, with the intention of ousting Corley as her pimp. In any case, it is clear that the woman functions as erotic currency between these men and that the force that binds the rivals to each other is stronger than the lechery that draws them both to the "fine decent tart" (*D,* 64).

This erotic triangle resembles Freud's account of dirty jokes, in which the woman functions as the pretext rather than the partner of the "smut" exchanged between two men. Smut, Freud argues, originates in sexual aggression directed at a woman, but the presence of a male third person diverts this impulse into the detour of a dirty joke. In polite society, men "save up" their jokes for times when they can be "alone together," excluding women from their smutty talk. Thus, the woman, originally the addressee, latterly the butt, and finally the sacrificial victim of the joke, vanishes from the scene of masculine pleasure, reduced to the ghost of a deflected rape.[9]

Freud's analysis of dirty jokes provides a clue to the sexual geometry of Joyce's fiction, in which two men, ostensibly competing for a woman, actually use her as an object of exchange to establish a bond between each other. A particularly disconcerting example may be found in the "Eumaeus" episode of *Ulysses,* when Bloom passes Molly's photograph to Stephen, inviting the young man to share her bosomy charms. The rudiments of this triangular relationship are sketched in "Two Gallants," but in the course of Joyce's evolution as an artist, the woman increasingly asserts her independence, refusing to be effaced by in-jokes between men. Limited as she is, Bertha has more to say for herself than Corley's slavey, whose mouth seems too twisted in its leer to adapt itself to speech. It is in Molly Bloom's soliloquy that the slavey finally talks back; here it is worth remembering that Nora Barnacle

9. For this discussion of "smut," see Freud 1953–74, 7:97–102.

was working as a slavey or (more politely) a chambermaid in Finn's Hotel when Joyce first fell for her. The relation between Lenehan, Corley, and the slavey uncannily prefigures the triangle between Joyce, Cosgrave, and Nora, suggesting that Joyce "found in the world without as actual what was in his world within as possible" (*U*, 9.1041–42).

For the most part, women are sidelined in the first seventeen episodes of *Ulysses,* figuring at best as incentives for male repartee. But Molly Bloom has the last word and the last laugh in the novel; her blithe autoeroticism exposes the French triangle as a masculine defense against the fear of female *jouissance.* Could the slavey's "contented leer" also betoken a secret *jouissance,* incalculable to her male manipulators? Although it would be foolish to imagine that the slavey has outsmarted Corley—it is clear she is more sinned against than sinning—her leer could be seen as the dangerous supplement to her slavish position in the triangle. Her "straggling mouth," lying "open in a contented leer," reminds us of what Molly calls the "hole in the middle" of the female body, the genital and ontological abyss that threatens to engulf the disappointed bridges between men (*U*, 18.151).

Garry Leonard, in his Lacanian study of *Dubliners,* proposes that the bunch of red flowers, pinned stem upward on the slavey's bosom, provides "the tiniest suggestion that a real woman ex-ists behind the masquerade," since it is a detail spotted only by the narrator, not by the two gallants for whom she functions merely as a object of exchange (1993, 130). Leonard misses a Lacanian trick, however, by overlooking the resemblance between these flowers and Lacan's famous schema of the inverted bouquet, in which a complex play of mirrors produces the illusion that a vase of flowers is hanging upside down. The schema implies that the subject's vision is constituted by an unseen other. Similarly, the slavey's upside-down corsage subverts the gallants' visual command over the scene, since they fail to register its presence; as a detail that sticks out, the sloppy flowers correspond to her straggling leer, at once conspicuous and abyssal. Lying open, her leer resembles the gaping mouth in Munch's painting *The Scream* (1893), a vacuum that seems to be engulfing its surroundings; as Mladen Dolar comments on this painting, "We see the void, the orifice, the abyss, but with no fetish to protect us or to hold on to" (2006, 69). The slavey's open mouth is equally vertiginous, since we never learn the meaning of the leer, and it is from this vacuum that every inference unravels, leaving all the questions of the story lying open. Furthermore, the leer makes it impossible to sentimentalize the slavey as a victim, or by analogy to sentimentalize her nation, to indulge in the mawkish lamentation of the Irish harp. The leer implies that the slavey is something other than the currency of patriarchy; the slavey has something up her sleeve. Has she somehow outwitted her gallant, or fobbed him off with a shiny substitute for a gold coin? We never know, since we are forced like Lenehan to squint, rather than to gaze directly at the scene.

"The Instinct of the Celibate"

Boarding and Borderlines in "The Boarding House"

RICHARD BROWN AND GREGORY CASTLE

Both Gregory and Richard were new to the idea of this kind of collaboration, with no preconceptions about how to proceed with it. We wrote brief statements and then exchanged longer, independently conceived pieces of around two thousand words—Richard on boards, boarding, and boarders and Joyce's references to the popular press and song, Gregory on the culture of confession as it impinges upon Bob's masculinity. Since we found much to agree with in each other's starting positions, we merged the independent approaches rather than staging a dialogue or debate between them. As this eminently Hegelian process of dialectical synthesis developed, it became apparent that we both shared an interest in the cultural politics of Bob Doran's situation, and Foucault as well as Žižek emerged as vital points of reference. We both found that the independent sections reflected on each other in unanticipated ways, allowing new insights and associations to come about. The collaborative aspect of the essay might therefore be characterized as being a "laboratory" as well as a "shop window," to borrow two terms of reference offered by Jonathan Arac in a 1997 essay on collaborative work in the humanities. But neither term would completely define the process or the essay that resulted from it, which is in its own way a "third thing," one that has been produced from our two separate contributions but would hardly have come into its present final form if it had been written by either one of us without the other.

Collaborative writing is a fascinating exercise, and it has produced some extraordinary results that call many apparently unshakable, established ideas

144

about writing and selfhood into question. One of the best known of all recent collaborations was between Gilles Deleuze and Félix Guattari, coauthors of "Anti-Oedipus" and "A Thousand Plateaus." At the start of "A Thousand Plateaus" they write, "The two of us wrote Anti-Oedipus together. Since each of us was several, there was already quite a crowd. . . . We have been aided, inspired, multiplied" (1987). That passage gets to the heart of the matter—that the ideal collaboration can emerge as more than the sum of its parts.

B oarding," which Joyce's title announces as being prominent among the concerns of the story, is a widespread condition of habitation in modern urban societies, which, we propose, governs the relation of the characters in Joyce's story to sexual pleasure, economic power, and ideology, pointing up those ambiguities of meaning that Joyce's narrative scrupulously preserves. The boarder or lodger, in the primary sense of the word used here, is some-one who "has his . . . food and lodging, at the house of another for com-pensation"; the *OED* traces this usage back to the early sixteenth century. Through the analyses of modernity in Freud and Marx, we might see board-ers, like Bob Doran in the story, as being located in a liminal condition, on the uncanny "borders" of the domestic economies in which they lodge. On the one hand, they lack the empowerment implied in the full rights of domestic property ownership that are important in bourgeois societies. On the other hand, they are yet to be constrained by its obligations and responsibilities. In modern societies, residence in owned domestic property is closely connected to the legitimation of heterosexuality through marriage. The sex life of the boardinghouse becomes an object of fascination, illicit and unstable, excluded from legitimation but potentially open to a certain wildness or freedom from constraint. No wonder that the term *boarding house* gets so tangled up with connected terms like *bawdry* (prostitution) and *bawdy* (sexual innuendo or licentiousness) in the boozy pub culture of Dublin to which Joyce exposes us in returning to the story of Bob Doran in the "Cyclops" episode of *Ulysses* or in references to the "boardelhouse" in *Finnegans Wake* (186.31). Here the erotic and the economic are entangled in problematic ways. No less a figure than Shakespeare, as Joyce knew, lived in a boardinghouse in London and uses the word *boarding* in ambiguous sexual and nautical senses in, for example, the Falstaffian comedy *The Merry Wives of Windsor* (II.i.79–80). Doran best exemplifies the boardinghouse condition of single men in Dublin: cloistered but not celibate, the new urban dweller with just enough resources to survive, but only "at the board" with others at his stage of social development. This condition signals not so much a liminal space, where one is challenged and changed, as a borderline zone, hemmed in by implicit or explicit legislation, where one may have to wait for permission to go on.

One of the most important borders depicted in the story is that which separates Bob Doran's sense of what it means to be an Irishman (or, better, what it means to be a man in Catholic Ireland) from that sense of him derived from Mrs. Mooney's and Polly's limited experience with men and masculinity. Doran's attempt to reason out his predicament takes on the character of a confession. He confesses himself in a way no less calculated than does the priest who had heard his confession the night before, and his deliberation over his own sin has all the earmarks of Father Purdon's brand of "practical" Christianity designed for "those whose lot it was to lead the life of the world and who yet wished to lead that life not in the manner of worldlings" (*D*, 214).

But is it a sin to be overtaken by the sins of others? To be engulfed in hostile waters (in hostile discourse), to be accosted, seized, taken over? Doran may have moved into Mrs. Mooney's establishment, but in the end, it is he, his life, that is irrevocably *boarded*. It is this sense of the word (related, by the way, to the sense of providing with meals and lodging) that colors Doran's long wait in his room, "sitting helplessly on the side of the bed" (*D*, 80). There is some potential freedom in the boardinghouse but also the danger of exploitation, and his awareness of this fact places him on the ideological borders of a society where compulsory theology, celibacy, and marriage are intertwined and where a kind of confessional despair opens up: a desire to speak, to disburden, *a desire to confess desire* that is overwhelmed by an authority that curtails desire and brings shame and guilt in the wake of curtailment. To be sure, in this sense, Mrs. Mooney functions as the phallic mother, whose conference with Doran clearly awakens in him castration anxiety and does so to such a degree that he capitulates to the rule of Law, to the cruel drama of a boardinghouse economy in which desire—both his and Polly's—is "cleaved," in which the very blow that separates desire from a hoped-for object prompts the unhappy lovers to "cleave" together in mutual disappointment and moral befuddlement.[1]

In Joyce, the shifting terrain of language—principally along semantic and etymological axes—inevitably invites the reader to focus on wordplay as an entrée to the text. The word *boardinghouse* would have invoked in a late-Victorian or Edwardian reader a fairly wide range of images and meanings, many of them modeled by figures in "The Boarding House." *Boarding* in one sense derives from traditional ship construction, specifically the creation of decks from wooden boards; another, perhaps more relevant sense, derives from the nautical practice of lodging "on board" for long sea journeys. Going, or taking people, things and by extension eventually also ideas "on board" implies the acceptance (or relinquishing) of obligation and commitment. Consider, for example, the reluctance of Joyce's character Eveline, in the story of that name, to undertake the act of embarkation. However, for a reader born since the 1980s at least, the word *boarding* may be just as likely to refer to the libidinal activities of contemporary leisure culture— "skateboarding," "snowboarding," and even "wakeboarding," all with their basis in the sport and lifestyle of surfing—that have also held a certain position in global branded leisure-wear retailing for a number of years in brand names from *Free Spirit* and *O'Neill* to the frankly libidinal *Porn Star*. Such a reader, struck with vertigo at the commodification of desire, confronted with a seemingly endless array of choices for cathexis, cannot help but be struck by the obstacles put into the path of Doran and Polly and the ease with which Mrs. Mooney orchestrates what for Doran must seem like grim fate. It is no wonder that Doran wishes to escape, to perform the inverse of that aggressive "piratical" boarding he now awaits with such anxiety, that is to say, to board *life*, to take off from present circumstances into an arena that would effectively be without board (the table of the law), and borderless, an arena in which desire can be expended without fear of the cleaver, in which confessional despair (or the kind of blithe unknowingness—or is it boredom?—that

1. There is something of Paolo and Francesca in these two, Dublin style. They are not quite so bad as the Bradford millionaire and his consort, with her automatic hand, in *The Waste Land*.

has Polly in her thrall at the end of the story) can give way to self-knowledge (*Bildung*) or to Foucauldian pleasure and care of the self.

To follow this series of associations might risk our being accused of "surfboarding" associatively through the polysemantics of Joyce's text rather than grounding our readings in the demonstrable evidence of histori-cal and cultural contexts. But such an accusation fails to take into account how etymological stratification indexes historical and cultural conditions of language production. The linguistic richness of *boardinghouse—board, boarder, border, borderline, boarding, boredom*—corresponds in many ways to an underlying ambiguity, contingency, and open-endedness, one that is frequently attributed to Doran's moral or even physical cowardice. The socioeconomic habitus in which his desire for Polly plays out is disturbingly *public*. There is something of Kafka's K. in Doran, who has found him-self saddled for good with a docile, forgetful Leni. The point is that Joyce, like Kafka, presents an erotics of social difference in which contemporary class struggle is exemplified in the daily attractions and interactions within the *boardinghouse* constellation. Joyce astutely locates Mrs. Mooney's turn-of-the-century boardinghouse in Dublin's Hardwicke Street, which would have a "resident population" of "clerks from the city" as well as a "floating population" of tourists and "*artistes* from the music halls" (*D*, 74). Theatri-cal performers who take to the stage, we might recall, are also said to "tread the boards."

The boardinghouse was for many young men a way station on the road to marriage and family, to a home of one's own. The ideal of marriage, the amorphous possibility of which is signified to Polly in her "hopes and visions of the future" (*D*, 83), might well be summed up in Gerty MacDowell's phantasmatic life with the darkly mysterious Leopold Bloom: "a nice snug and cosy little homely house" (*U*, 13.239). The "homely house," overdeter-mined ideologically, is the habitation of desire under the delusion of an ideal. The boardinghouse presents, more starkly, the social structure behind the ideal. It is nothing if not a model of capitalist family formation; nor should the absence of the father fail to remind us that the position of Father struc-tures relations among all the inhabitants. For many lodgers, this relation is not translated out of its paternalistic, mercantile frame, but for Doran, and who knows how many other "resident young men" (*D*, 74), the mercantile frame falls away. In one sense, Mrs. Mooney occupies the position of Father, but the position had already been carved out by Mr. Mooney, ineffectual though he may now be ("a shabby stooped little drunkard" [*D*, 73]). His surrogates, especially Polly's brother, keep alive within the boardinghouse the tables of the law. Polly and Doran behave much as any young couple might, given the furtive intimacy that characterizes their contretemps: they are trapped within a confessional culture in which their desire and, more to the point, the consequences of desire are *proscribed*, but it is a culture too in which the confession of desire is desire *reinscribed*.[2] It is the guilty pleasure enjoyed again and again. Indeed, as Foucault and others have shown, confession, in modern times at least, is precisely the repetition of desire in a ritualized speech act; the discursive pleasures of atonement put into play, as part of this speech activity, the very desire, or substitutes for it, that has been proscribed (Foucault 1988, 61ff). Doran understands this fact, since what he does as he waits patiently, anxiously, is go over in his mind the very thing he has already confessed. Self-confession thus becomes a form of repetition compulsion, a form of ritualistic memory associated with the *affect* of anxiety: a way of feeling the complex core of which is the "repetition of some particular significant previous experience"—part of a "prehistory not of the individual but of the species." Memory and prehistory cohere in this "heritage" form of anxiety, which yields not the substance of a memory but the "precipitate of a reminiscence" (Freud 1989, 191–92). Doran's anxiety is focused not on what may or may not have happened, which is vague enough anyway, but rather on a purely formal memory, not his exactly but born in his unconscious, of trauma. What he turns to in his lonely room is this "empty" memory of himself.

2. *Confessional culture* used in this sense refers to a country or territory dominated by the church and the sacrament of penance, of which confession is a chief element (*confessional identity* would thus refer to self-formation under conditions of a specific "confession"). On the sacrament of penance, see the *New Catholic Encyclopedia*, http://www.newadvent.org/cathen/11618c.htm. Another sense of these terms, derived in part from Michel Foucault's work, refers to a more generic phenomenon, in which the world becomes one's confidant: we thus see the emergence of secularized and highly mediated (and mediatized) forms of the traditional confessional culture.

In Joyce's fiction, confession flows into channels governed by the imperatives of juridical disclosure: "to judge, punish, forgive, console, and reconcile" (Foucault 1988, 62). It is a masculine discourse in the service of patriarchal authority, quite different in form and content from the discursive styles we find in Gerty MacDowell's portion of "Nausicaa" or Molly's soliloquy. Stephen Dedalus voices a desire for freedom and wholeness, but he does so in the language of confession, of disburdenment and, at least residually, clings to the promise of absolution—though the end of *A Portrait* strongly suggests that absolution will be sought outside the confines of the confessional dialectic. When he "confesses himself," he *reveals* himself, even *betrays* himself, in the face of cultural imperatives that would otherwise forbid such revelations and betrayals.[3] This space of discursive freedom provides an opportunity to try on, to amend, to subvert, to exaggerate the protocols of masculinity and masculine sexual identities. In this profane space, he is able to overcome the consciousness of sin precisely because the *confession* of sin enables the *profession* of the self. In *Dubliners,* a text that might well be regarded as a proving ground for attitudes that are brought to a greater maturity in *A Portrait,* the power to overcome the consciousness of sin is not yet developed; the subversive force of a secularized confession is, to borrow a phrase from Stephen, "almosting it" (*U,* 3.366–67). From the young boy in "The Sisters" to Gabriel Conroy in "The Dead," Joyce's protagonists pit themselves against themselves in a confessional discourse that retains much of the moral authority that the church and contemporary theorists like Foucault ascribe to it.

Bob Doran best exemplifies the cloistered quality of confessionalism, the closed circuit of sin and absolution that becomes internalized and thus operates with greater force and subtlety than it does in the confession box. These are the conditions for a failure not only to achieve *Bildung* but even to aspire toward it. Trapped in a bare boardinghouse room, Doran falls upon his own sinfulness with the skill of a surgeon. He is the type of the Joycean penitent, suffering and sinning outside the boundaries of the church, yet committed, almost unconsciously, to the forms and a good deal of the substance of the

3. On Stephen's "confessional identity," see Castle 2006, chap. 3.

sacrament of penance.[4] He possesses, perhaps more than any other character in Joyce's canon, the "instinct of the celibate," an instinct characterized by both a "curious patient memory" (*D,* 80) and a consciousness of sin that cannot be overcome.[5] The structures of feeling that govern Doran's life make it impossible for him ever to forget. He does not repudiate confession as Stephen does; he has instead fearful memories of "acute pain" in which "the priest had drawn out every ridiculous detail of the affair" (*D,* 78). There is no breaching this closed circuit, except by way of a "reparation" (ad)ministered by a priest substitute, who holds out, as a last resort, the possibility of marriage, a simoniacal arrangement cut to order with a cleaver. Doran surrenders to a phallic mother-wife who places him in the position of embattled, subordinate partner in an arranged marriage. Yet in another sense, he is a victim of an arrangement that his own behavior has put into play, but only if we accept that he did indeed seduce Polly in her "combing-jacket" (*D,* 80) and that there was at least some element of deception in that seduction.

Because his memories of Polly are mixed up with anxiety that is rooted in losses he has not yet learned to recognize, Doran's entire situation becomes vulnerable to even slight misinterpretations. His self-consciousness lends even his genuine feelings an air of theatricality, as if he were reading for a part in his own life. This is especially true of the story he tells himself of his own desire. He seems to accept the arrangements being made in his name, not because he is forced into it (though one easily gets the sense of a deal that Doran could not refuse); rather, he recognizes it as a socially sanctioned choice, perfect for an "incomplete" man like himself. Unable to live up to other ideals of masculinity, he falls into the passive role of husband to the offended Polly. Her mother's intervention subverts a masculinist system of sexual relationships by doubling the deception: Doran may have deceived Polly into sex, but not into marriage; her mother arranges for the marriage by a more open deception, one that traps him more decisively.

4. Confession is a principal element of the sacrament of penance, another being absolution. See the *New Catholic Encyclopedia,* http://www.newadvent.org/cathen/11618c.htm.

5. Stephen, by comparison, is able to overcome the consciousness of sin in the deliberate fusion of priest and artist: the priesthood of the imagination and a eucharistic aesthetics make of sin a luscious kind of deviance in language and thought.

Joyce undermines both nationalist and continental ideals of masculinity by dramatizing—with this sad little vignette of a man beaten down by his own social mistakes with women, unmanned by his own "manliness"—the gap between gender ideals and stereotypes and the heterogeneity of men's lives, between Mrs. Mooney's and his own sense of himself. Every unpleasant element in his life repeats itself in his confessional reminiscences.

In the social space of the boardinghouse, monkish single men sit in their rooms, their stark confessionals, chewing the cud of their transgressions, suffering the shame of their lost aspirations, unaware any longer of when the downward slide began. In colonial Dublin in the late nineteenth century, men like Doran were not scarce on the ground. The cast of characters in "The Boarding House"—the mother and brother, the artistes, the other lodgers, Doran's boss, and so on—constitute something like a cross-section, making Mrs. Mooney's house a model not only of the family but of a certain parvenu element of the rising Catholic middle classes. Thus, the activities of "boarding" and all those "boarders" and "borders" sketch social relations in their materiality. To speak of Mrs. Mooney "piratically" boarding young Doran is only to put an "apt" image to a particular form of coercive social control, from *within* the local community.

Mrs. Mooney's boardinghouse, then, ought to be seen as modeling what actual boardinghouses at the time more than probably were: halfway houses for a population moving from the countryside to the city; way stations for the established members of the "clerking class," as they moved up and down the ladders in the city's colonial and commercial bureaucracies; and hotels for traveling performers and artistes, whose professions limited them to short-term and humble habitation. The denizens of such places would be largely Catholic and mostly male, though women would have their role to play on the fringes of boardinghouse life. Doran, it must be remembered, was presented with a rare opportunity: a young, flirtatious woman *on the premises,* in a "loose open combing-jacket of printed flannel" (*D*, 80).[6] Surely, this

6. An affectation, perhaps, for a girl with Polly's social profile. The combing jacket was commonly worn by Victorian ladies to protect their clothing while combing or brushing their hair. They are short and flimsy, meant to be worn in the privacy of one's boudoir.

circumstance would overpower any young Catholic Irishman of little experience, especially one like Doran who, while not afraid of priests, certainly fears the wrath of a social world dominated by the church and Catholic morality. He "remembered well, with the curious memory of the celibate, the first casual caresses her dress, her breath, her fingers had given him" (*D*, 80); he remembered how "she had tapped at his door" and stood there in her combing jacket, and he "remember[s] well" their kisses and "her eyes, the touch of her hand and his delirium" (*D*, 80–81). Now, the delirium having passed, he fears what lies beyond the fantasy environment he has made of Mrs. Mooney's establishment. He fears the greater powers at work in the world, represented by his employer, "Mr Leonard," who, in the young man's "excited imagination," "call[s] out in his rasping voice: 'Send Mr Doran here, please'" (*D*, 79). This summons anticipates, in his memory, the one he will shortly receive from Mrs. Mooney. Everything he does adumbrates this summons, for on the proffered "reparation" of marriage hangs every other aspect of his future life. It serves proleptically the function of traumatic "kernel" that has been jettisoned from his knowledge of the past.[7]

But is it primarily spiritual punishments and loss of spiritual rewards that underwrite Doran's despair as he anxiously and patiently waits for the other shoe to drop? Indeed, what sort of despair results in both anxiety and patience, if not the despair of the Catholic Dubliner at the turn of the century, whose social ambitions and attitudes have an increasingly wider arena for their growth and development, but whose self-image and sense of self-formation are still powerfully shaped and driven by sacramental and, more specifically, confessional demands? That punishment for which Doran waits

---

7. For Freud, the dream-work constructs a "new and transitory concept" out of disparate and heterogeneous images, all of which have a common element, the unknown and unknowable nucleus (1989, 211). Joan Riviere uses the term *kernel* in her translation, rather than *nucleus*, and speaks of a "new and *fugitive* concept" (1963, 180). Žižek is clearly drawing on Freud as well as Lacan when he refers to the "kernel" as a fundamental *antagonism*, a point of resistance against the Symbolic, an "original trauma," an "impossible kernel which resists symbolization, totalization, symbolic integration" (1989, 6). The "real, impossible kernel" lies outside what we can know (ibid., 45). But it is also the symptom of our enjoy-meant (our *jouissance*) of the Real.

anxiously can result only in forgiveness—so long as he pays his penance, makes his reparation "for the loss of [Polly's] honour: marriage" (*D*, 77)—but it is not really God's forgiveness he seeks. Reparation is, for him, a social obligation that issues in a social bond. Certainly, Mrs. Mooney works out her advantage by considering precisely Doran's social and economic vulnerability *as a Catholic*: "He had been employed for thirteen years in a great Catholic wine-merchant's office and publicity would mean for him, perhaps, the loss of his job. Whereas if he agreed all might be well. She knew he had a good screw for one thing and she suspected he had a bit of stuff put by" (*D*, 78). This demand for reparation incontestably links marriage and money, libidinal and monetary economies, and it neatly echoes Doran's own feelings on the matter, for the priest to whom he had confessed the night before "had so magnified his sin that he was almost thankful at being afforded a loophole of reparation" (*D*, 79). Doran and Mrs. Mooney misrecognize the nature of expiation, the atonement demanded of the sacrament of penance; they see it in the pragmatic way of the men in "Grace," for whom Christ is a "spiritual accountant" (*D*, 215). They see in expiation not the disburdenment of confession and the atonement through penance for sinful action and knowledge, but rather a reparation in which the sacrament of marriage all too easily slides into a form of economic stabilization. To make reparation is to repair, to make amends, to offer expiation, to give satisfaction for a wrong or injury.[8] The reparation the mother demands is what Doran sought in confession, which was "a cause of acute pain to him" (*D*, 78). It is, of course, significant that Doran invokes the language of contracts to describe reparation as a "loophole," a legal or permissible reneging on the terms of an obligation. For Doran, this loophole means avoiding the social humiliation of putting the madam's daughter in the "family way" and the economic devastation of offending his Catholic boss.

The sexual politics of the story that center on the "affair" of Doran the boarder and Polly the landlady's daughter are forcibly underlined by the logic of pleasure as a desired commodity that must be enjoyed but that incurs a debt requiring repayment: an economics of consumerism that, as

---

8. *Webster's New Collegiate Dictionary*, s.v. "reparation."

Jean Baudrillard's early analyses demonstrated, emphatically re-reinforce the commodification of the body (1970, 129–50). Doran's sad memorial, his "curious patient" accounting of pleasures, and his rush to "reparation" are driven by the intimidating voice of Mrs. Mooney. His moral conformity, his assumed guilt, and the threat of physical violence are all strongly present in his memories of a recent past with Polly. To be fair, Doran recognizes, in a way that Mrs. Mooney does not, the spiritual gravity of his situation, but any victory he might claim withers in the heat of his awareness that she will force a resolution of the only situation that matters to her. The strong "instinct of the celibate," an instinct of self-mystification rather than of self-preservation, prevents him from seeing his options sooner and more clearly, but he does at least recognize that he has sinned (unlike James Duffy in "A Painful Case," he cannot quite achieve the level of self-abstraction that would make his sins seem airy nothings). And he is quick to work out that the "option" of reparation—a shotgun wedding to Polly—can "compensate" for sin: "Even his sense of honour told him that reparation must be made for such a sin" (*D*, 81). The use of *even* here suggests that "honour" compels him toward reparation (understood as spiritual atonement or expiation) but only after a more fundamental kind of reparation (understood as compensation or marriage) has revealed itself as an option. He could marry Polly, and will have done the honorable thing, but more important, he will have saved his job, "all his long years of service," all his "industry and diligence" (*D*, 79). The fear his employer inspires is palpable, while the fear inspired by almighty God is barely discernible, save in his references to himself as a celibate, but in these fears we detect a diffidence, a sense of discomfort with himself that precludes intimacy of any kind ("Once you are married you are done for," his instinct urges him [*D*, 80]) rather than a sense of renunciation for the sake of God. In this situation, he resembles Duffy, who also has the "instinct of the celibate" and who also feels a crushing blow to his self-image upon the "intrusion" of a woman whose sexuality is loosened from its restraints.

Doran cannot escape the requirement of disburdening and reparation. Nor can he escape a conception of manhood in which confession forms an essential component. This "devotional manliness" requires fortitude in the face of sin and a willingness to commit oneself to "nurturing, domestic values," which Joanna Bourke links to the "devotional revolution" led by

Archbishop Cullen in the years following the Famine (1999, xxx). Doran quakes at the prospect of this manliness, in part because his instinctual celibacy urges him to "hold back" from the very matrimonial intimacy into which he now sees himself about to be forced. Joyce's critique of confessionalism in "The Boarding House," as elsewhere, is an indictment of the Irish manliness authorized and delimited within "a devoted, family-centered environment" (ibid.). Of course, as *Ulysses* demonstrates with cruel brevity, Doran is a mockery of the family man envisioned by the ideologues of the devotional revolution, a mockery of the idea that he and Polly ever had a shot at a wholesome family life. He does not measure up to Irish Catholic "devotional" masculinity or to other native models—for example, Irish republican masculinity—that could offer an ideal of virtuous manhood grounded in mythic heroism.[9] His failure (if we want to call it a failure) to attain an ideal of masculinity becomes part of the overall critical design in *Dubliners*. It draws our attention to the gap between the *system* of hegemonic gender formations, where "social ideals" are generated, and the lives of individuals whose behavior is in some way determined by these ideals. Doran contemplates a future domestic life for which he feels no bonds of affection and remains perennially torn among the limited options available to him to "be a man," all of which will, effectively, unman him. This castrating duplicity can be found in a wide spectrum of Irish modernist literature, but most preeminently in W. B. Yeats's *Cathleen ni Houlihan*, in which the young Michael Gillane refuses the comforts of wife and family to follow, and die for, the very spirit of Ireland, an old hag who is transformed into "a young woman with the walk of a queen." If we take Joyce at full parodic measure, Mrs. Mooney (like Mrs. Kearney, in "A Mother"), does double duty: she is a powerful woman who upsets the masculinist economy of Irish life, but she is also the icon of a debased idealism. No Mother Ireland here. Nor does she (or Polly) walk like a queen.

Polly is, in some ways, a "seaside girl," a "New Woman," who joins the artistes in the sexually suggestive performance of her song *"I'm a . . . naughty girl"* (D, 74). The ellipsis in the line shows Joyce reinforcing her

---

9. On "Irish republican masculinity," see Curtin 1999.

flirtatiousness, one of several examples of the overlapping of eroticism and commodification that should have served as a warning to Doran, who in any case never had a chance. He is mired in an ethical quagmire the danger of which he realizes only when he has been drawn in beyond rescue. Mrs. Mooney's deft handling of the whole affair leaves Doran a single option: the charade of marriage and the grim reality of watching what little social capital he has accrued being transferred to the new women in his life. But, as we have suggested already, a man like Doran is not trapped by Mrs. Mooney or Polly alone; the trapping mechanism is primed in advance by his own feckless, half-conscious investments in a particular vision of Irish manhood that fails him. On Bourke's terms, Doran cannot get it right. Meeting Polly on her "bath night" (*D*, 80) and the new familiarity such a meeting entails: are these not the consequences of subtle shifts in the way domestic space accommodates men? The fluid public space of the boardinghouse subjects young men like Doran to the intimacies of others' lives at close quarters and leaves open the possibility of illicit encounters in the evening. But the very fluidity of the boardinghouse and the limited, public channels in which desire flows tend also to increase vigilance on the part of those individuals who disapprove or who see opportunities to enrich their own enjoyment. To seduce Polly in these circumstances would be churlish and unmanly; but more to the point, it would be dangerous.

Though they have offered several different approaches to and implicit or explicit judgments upon the rights and wrongs of Doran's situation, most careful readers are likely to be quite shocked by the stark juxtaposition of the economic and the erotic in the story and by the extent to which it stresses the entrapment and paralysis of the characters, especially Doran, in a world of conformity and constraint that cripples their sense of freedom and self-esteem and leaves confession the only viable outlet for the expression of disappointment or regret. Fresh from the freedom and warmth of his recent elopement with Nora to Trieste, Joyce comments on the story's "frigidities," writing that he was "uncommonly well pleased" with it and sending readers in search of a "neat phrase of five words" (*SL*, 86). Those words, "like a little perverse madonna" (*D*, 75), simply and powerfully indict the complicity between Polly's flirtatiousness and Roman Catholic morality. Joyce in fact expressed surprise in his letters to Grant Richards that the "theme" of the story (along with the theme of "An Encounter") was not more shocking to the printer than it was. Subsequent readers, though, have since been rather more alert to a reading in which (as John Wyse Jackson and Bernard McGinley put it) "two women conspire to take advantage of a convention-bound man" (1993, 60). The story clearly "reflects badly on the venality of women"; however, if we follow Margot Norris (2003), the curious narrative "breadpudding" that brings disparate strands together—both recycled and clichéd attitudes toward desire and sin and a sustained critique of the "weight of social opinion"—actually works to reflect just as badly on the narrative voice that would appear to be passing judgment on Mrs. Mooney and her lovely daughter.[10]

Despite his desire to offer up a critique of Dublin paralysis, whether of the characters or of the narrative voice of opinion, Joyce writes in an oblique style that leaves much open to interpretation. There are, it might be observed, considerable hints that, with her "casual caresses," her "white instep [that] shone in the opening of her furry slippers and the blood [that] glowed warmly behind her perfumed skin," not to mention her capacity for "thoughtfulness," Polly and Doran (again vividly communicated by the use of three dots for an ellipsis) "could be happy together . . ." (D, 81). Polly's parallel train of thought at the close of the story—her "secret amiable memories" at the sight of his pillows, the "nape of her neck against the cool iron bed-rail" (D, 82)—confirms the exciting sexual potential of their marriage as something that may underpin her final recollection of "what she had been waiting for" (D, 83).

A key feature of this sexual promise is that their memories remain private to the couple. But everyone seems to assume a knowledge about their "affair." For Mrs. Mooney, "things were as she had suspected" (D, 76), and the priest, as we have seen, has "drawn out every ridiculous detail" (D, 78). Doran might want to condemn Polly for "what she had done," but "he had done it too" (D, 79). "It had happened," we are told, though the more

10. See also the classic discussion of "The Fear of Marriage" in Cixous 1972, 51–87; and Kershner, who argues that Doran is "caught at the point of intersection of two conflicting ideologies, that of gallantry and that of bourgeois Christianity" (1989, 89–93).

the rumors and assumptions are confirmed by such pronouns, the more we might be entitled to ask what the "it" that has happened actually is. (Joyce never tells us what "it" is; as in Hemingway's "Hills Like White Elephants," the unsaid is clamorous.) "All the lodgers in the house knew something of the affair," we are told, though "details had been invented by some" (*D*, 78). The word *affair* suggests sexual intercourse to a modern reader but not necessarily to one of the time, and we might note too the use of the phrases *a good screw* (apparently meaning a good salary) and *a bit of stuff* (meaning some savings) where the modern meaning is emergent in the way these phrases are used by Mrs. Mooney. In one rather revealing classic early debate on the inexplicit discourse of the story, Florence Walzl claims that Polly was pregnant, while Fritz Senn maintains that there is no evidence that they had even had full sex (see Senn 1986).[11] It is not always clear that Polly herself is aware of what has happened to her. Is it not a painful, almost punishing irony that Polly, that "perverse madonna," at the moment Doran accepts the terms of his reparation, "no longer . . . remembered that she was waiting for anything" (*D*, 83)?

Social and clerical attitudes conspire to produce guilt and remorse even if Polly and Doran have not had sex. The mechanism by which these attitudes are conjoined and by which they determine Doran's reactions to Mrs. Mooney's demand for reparation, is, as we have noted, the profane practice of "confessing oneself." Like so many of Joyce's protagonists, Doran doubles as his own antagonist, framing his self-doubt and self-awareness within the context of a confessional discourse that has become privatized while retaining all of the force of its institutional, sacramental form: unlike Stephen Dedalus, for whom profane confession becomes the instrument of artistic self-knowledge, Doran experiences in confession a profound melancholy caused by a lack of self-knowledge. His desire to "fly away to another country" (*D*, 81), again unlike Stephen's, is frustrated by the sheer weight of a mysterious force that urges him to accept reparation cloaked as absolution rather than a risky and lonely escape. This force, associated with "the

11. A further discussion of the silences of the story can be found in Leonard 1993, 132–48.

implacable faces of his employer and of the Madam" (D, 81), is an attribute of a confessional culture that expresses itself in every aspect of Doran's life and propels him toward a fate he has courted without knowing it. In "The Boarding House," as in other *Dubliners* stories, it is this lack of self-knowledge, which the artist Stephen possesses, that hobbles the free and satisfying formation of character.

In fact, we might say that any chance for self-knowledge is canceled in the face of the violence offered by nearly everyone in the social habitus Doran occupies—Mr. Leonard, Mrs. Mooney, Polly's brother—and canceled chance emblematizes his position, in large part because it is the primary cause of despair, even though he may never realize it. As with self-knowledge, so with any instinct for self-preservation or self-interest (his instincts are the same as the celibate's, we must recall): Doran simply succumbs to an environment in which desire and economics, sex and money, are tied in ways he cannot (or refuses to) understand. Contemporary readers of this story and others in *Dubliners* will recognize the combination of seductive sexiness and meticulous economics, for Doran's and Polly's response to the all too human moral dilemma they find themselves confronting might well serve as a prototype for our contemporary libidinally driven consumer societies with their heavy reliance on desire, consumer debt, and the promise of reparation.[12] Whereas late capitalism is sometimes said to thrive (however precariously) on the ultimate deferment of the promise to "pay the bearer" of its promissory notes, Dublin society at the time depicted in the story seems to depend upon the frequent threat and actual deployment of the intimidating physical violence of the "sheriff's man" (D, 75) or, presumably, bullying "clerk," roles that Mr. Mooney and Jack Mooney take on. No doubt we should not miss how close the name *Mooney* is to the word *money,* as the Mooney family increasingly and with increasing violence comes to be identified with and to do the bidding of the "money" system in its raw ideological form. We may recall that, as Slavoj Žižek points out in a rare discussion of Joyce, hegemonic ideologies pretend to operate by pleasurable consensus,

12. On the link between debt and moral obligation, between debt and guilt, see Nietzsche 1998, second treatise.

but when their rules are transgressed, then they may reveal the true nature of their power (1997, 12–35). Elsewhere, Žižek writes that the bureaucracy in Kafka's work signifies "obedience to the Command in so far as it is 'incomprehensible,'" adding that "brutish" Law, the Law understood as violent force, is repressed under the cover of the idea of the Law as Truth (1989, 38–39). Ironically, the "enjoyment" (*jouissance*) of ideology is tied precisely to "the non-integrated surplus of senseless traumatism" at the heart of the Law, which confers on it "its unconditional authority" (ibid., 43). Perhaps Doran submits so willingly to Mrs. Mooney because he perversely enjoys the very force that is otherwise well hidden. In this case, enjoyment displaces pleasure in the "full submission" to the Law as the call of the big Other.

However we read this point, the relations in "The Boarding House" between crime and punishment, error and its redress, psychosocial debt and reparation, are disturbing. Along with the all-important "weight of social opinion," there seems to be more self-incriminating guilty feeling than actual guilt on Doran's and Polly's parts, especially on Doran's. Indeed, Doran may at times resemble another famous "boarder" from European literature, Dostoyevsky's Raskolnikov, who also suffers from an acquisitive and "imposing" landlady. Doran is hardly identical with Dostoyevsky's murderer. In Joyce, it is Mrs. Mooney's husband who "went for his wife with the cleaver" (*D*, 73), and it is she who comes to control the epistemic violence of the "cleaver" of moralistic opinion. There is one other thing, though, that the two texts have in common. Dostoyevsky, in playing with the meaning of his characters' names, reminds us of the prerevolutionary alienation of Raskolnikov, his dissent from the social norm, in the echo of the word *raskol*, or split. Similarly, Doran (or *Deoradhain*) in Irish Gaelic means "exile" or "wanderer." So in this respect—having significant names and names whose significance points to a kind of social alienation—they may be similar.

That Joyce also wants to show up his Doran as a figure who is to some extent self-conscious in his apparent ideological detachment is evident in the typically suggestive detail that Doran is a onetime reader of a contemporary weekly paper called *Reynolds's Newspaper*. Set up by the Chartist George Reynolds in the 1850s, *Reynolds's Newspaper* declared itself in favor of "Government of the People, by the People, for the People," and it enjoyed a wide circulation throughout the next half century, especially in northern and provincial England, becoming the more or less official voice of political liberalism in the 1890s and socialism in the new century. Even by today's standards, it was quite an advanced and politically explicit radical socialistic paper, full of critical examinations of society; indeed, toward the turn of the century, it began to respond to discussions of the New Woman movement and the marriage system from a radical materialist point of view. Making Doran a reader of it might suggest that Joyce wishes to present him as a self-confident radical intellectual with a well-developed and -articulated critical perspective on the entrapping bourgeois norms of his society, including those standards that governed marriage and sexual relations—or at least a man who longed for the freedom such radicalism so tantalizingly suggests.

However, rather than depicting Doran as a revolutionary hero empowered by the liberatory potential of this critical perspective to reject the hegemonic Catholic, capitalistic, marital system of Dublin society, Joyce shows him in retreat from it, however reluctantly returning to a "regular life," and perhaps permanently unable to free himself by using the very intellectual tools that have enabled him to see that he is entrapped. Only the reader gains the liberating self-consciousness provided by this level of dramatic irony.

On the other hand, we may argue that the implicitness of the story's manner fails to provide us with a clear view of whether Doran and Polly will ultimately be happy together. There is a tendency to argue that they will suffer the unhappy fate of their parents' generation or that to which Joyce consigns them in *Ulysses*. The few brief details Joyce gives us of their sexual intimacies hint that they may be able to continue their boarding lifestyle into the future with the full endorsement of marital legitimacy to back them up and with every prospect of becoming the owners of the boardinghouse in due course.

In this respect, the critical picture of society that Joyce presents in "The Boarding House" may be one that is prescient of more recent consumer societies, where power over the subject is confirmed and defined by a pleasurable excess that works to resist its being questioned or opposed or undermined or "confessed." Whatever fate that it holds in store for its characters, Joyce's story exposes the "borders" in the boardinghouse, as well as the "boardings" that have violently changed the lives and futures of those persons within it. The weblike structure of the bordering house indexes an ideology that governs social actions through the hidden menace of complicity, which guarantees that only a critical self-awareness can mount an effective resistance against co-optation and despair. The very structure of the story, as of *Dubliners* generally, requires that it is the reader who supplies this guarantee, coming "to the board" or "treading the boards" in the performance of his or her own act of reading, providing a borderline for Joyce's meanings to cross.

8

The Small Light in "A Little Cloud"

MARIAN EIDE AND VICKI MAHAFFEY

This essay was inspired initially by a stimulating paper delivered at the Modern Language Association in 2006 by Nicholas Miller that encouraged us to think about the issues of reproduction and creativity in "A Little Cloud." From that rich point of departure, we each pursued our own research tendencies from the theoretical to the etymological, from the literary to the sociological. Our process was for one author to compose an initial very rough draft that the other revised. We wrote on top of each other's prose very freely. Too little comment is made about disagreement in collaboration, but one of the most productive aspects of the experience we had in writing together was finding at an early stage that we disagreed about Little Chandler's poetic voice: Vicki saw it as derivative and "little," whereas Marian emphasized Little Chandler's sensitivity, which she viewed as the sensibility of a potential poet. Eventually, we were able to regard our differences as both illuminating and productive; by simply labeling our diverging perspectives, we were able to view them side by side without anxiety. We also found that by emphasizing our differences, we came to see each other's points of view with more clarity and to appreciate the extent to which our readings were more compatible than they originally seemed.

I n "A Little Cloud," Little Chandler, a clerk whose routine duties in the King's Inns in Dublin undoubtedly include some copying, expresses his desire to write poetry with an urgency warmed by the unaccustomed whiskeys he drank with his friend earlier in the evening.[1] The tension between the routine of work and the hope of novelty runs throughout the story, raising a question: what is reproduction? Can reproduction be a source of change, a *modified* repetition that disrupts the tedium of mechanical duplication? "A Little Cloud" is thematically concerned with copies, duplications, and reproductions; it spurs the reader to wonder whether duplication is necessarily the opposite of originality, prompting her to question the assumption that copying bars the path to newness, unique expression, or even authentic experience. Various forms of literary indebtedness—such as allusion, influence, parody, and revision—call into question the usefulness and even the accuracy of sharp differentiations between "original" and "copy." In "A Little Cloud," Joyce depicts Little Chandler as a sensitive yet conformist clerk burdened by the paid labor of reproduction and longing to be a romantic rebel freed for the meaningful work of creativity. The two of us have different views about what Little Chandler signifies as a man and aspiring artist. Marian would argue that although he longs to imitate the "literary" success of others (most notably Gallaher, Byron, and the Celtic school), Little Chandler's private idiom is not simply derivative. Vicki agrees that his private idiom is sometimes poetic, but she has doubts about Little Chandler's ability to do anything with that poetic ability. Moreover, Little Chandler has "reproduced" in the biological sense, as well, and although we understand that biological reproduction is a problematic model for poetic achievement, it may well be the case that Joyce is using one mode of reproduction to comment on another. If so, what is that comment?

At the end of the story, as Little Chandler reads Byron's poetry in the hope of rekindling his poetic inspiration by imitation or literary reproduction, his concentration is broken by his sobbing child. The problem of the story centers on the child: Does the child represent an obstacle, an unobserved opportunity, or both? Does the moment of resistance to domestic routine signal the imminent production of something "new," or is it only a brief, fitful rebellion against a life dominated by responsibility for small

---

1. The narrator refers to Little Chandler's "tiresome writing" when he is sitting at his desk in the King's Inns (*D*, 85).

things? What is the significance of Little Chandler's sudden storm of anger at his son, followed by his tears—the rain—of remorse?

This essay will reflect two possible responses to the problems of originality and doubling in this story about the writing process: Vicki Mahaffey situates creative interruptions of repetition in relation to images of the violence of conception and birth, which allows her to consider Chandler's poetic aspirations in ironic relation to the fatherhood he seems to discount, while Marian Eide emphasizes reproduction and representation as processes that require the writer to re-view what is already written, a review that can inspire original revision. The doubling of these two options in the story is repeated in the doubling of our own conversation. Throughout, our two responses are playing off the title of the story, which can be understood to designate a nascent *possibility* (through its echo of the book of Kings in the Hebrew scriptures, which we will discuss in greater detail later), or a little obstacle, or both. Marian is more interested in the creative possibilities she discerns in Little Chandler, whereas Vicki is intrigued by the obstacles that seem to block his progress. We have written the rest of the essay in the form of a dialogue, so as to keep these two emphases provisionally separate (and introduced by our initials), but it should be noted that each position is also written through by the other person's response.

The Title

VM: Let us begin with the title of the story, which helps us understand the complexity of Joyce's notion of home and the irony of Little Chandler's charged—perhaps petulant—reaction against it. After a little research and much reflection, it becomes apparent that the phrase *a little cloud* designates a small obstacle that is also a modest opportunity, and that obstacle or opportunity is identified both with Little Chandler's home, wife, and child and with his deferred desire to write poetry. We know the title designates an obstacle both from the overtones of the phrase *a little cloud,* which suggests a slight darkening, and also from the etymology of the word *cloud,* which paradoxically derives from the Old English *clud,* a mass of rock. Presumably, this derivation is indebted to the visual similarity between cloud formations and rock formations, but Joyce, who was exceptionally attentive to etymology, certainly was aware of the irony in rooting a word for vapor in something as obdurate and solid as rock. The association of a little cloud with a suggestion of darkness perfectly counterbalances Chandler's surname, which designates the maker of a small light.[2] The idea that "a little cloud" can be a double image portending both darkness and hope, vapor and rock, is reinforced in the way it appears in the Hebrew scriptures: During the contest on Mount Carmel, when Elijah is showing the Israelites the difference between Yahweh and the false gods of Baal, he defeats the opposing prophets by proposing a contest to see whose offering to their god will burst into flame, signifying that it was accepted—his offering is burned, and theirs is not. Elijah's last act is to ask the Lord to end a three-year drought that has ravaged Samaria. He bows down to the earth on the top of Carmel and sends his servant to look toward the sea seven times. The seventh time, the servant reports that "a little cloud no bigger than a person's hand is rising out of the sea" (1 Kings 18:44; echoed in the Ithaca episode of *Ulysses*, 17.42). This little cloud is the sign of the Lord, who brings both trouble (to the prophets of Baal, whom Elijah has killed) and salvation (through the end of the drought), and who works through human hands.

Critics have also argued that the title echoes Dante, which highlights other aspects of the story's meaning (see Reynolds 1981).[3] Mary Reynolds points out the allusion to Dante's *Inferno*, and specifically the phrase *si come nuvoletta*. Dante uses the phrase in an epic simile designed to describe the flames that obscure the souls of the false counselors in the eighth ditch of hell (canto 26). Dante's simile recalls Elisha's effort to watch the ascension of Elijah's chariot in 2 Kings: Elisha "could not follow it with his eyes so as to see anything but the flame alone like a little cloud mounting up." (Dante seems to have identified the little cloud that Elijah's servant saw in 1 Kings with the "whirlwind" that enveloped Elijah's fiery chariot in 2 Kings 2:11.)

2. A little chandler is a small candle maker. Joyce draws attention to the name—particularly its Englishness—when Little Chandler thinks, "It was a pity his name was not more Irish-looking" (*D*, 69). John Wyse Jackson and Bernard McGinley draw attention to the story's emphasis on darkness and light, arguing that "Gallaher is 'a brilliant figure,' at home in the 'light and noise' of bars," whereas "Little Chandler is a creature of the dark" (1993, 75).

3. Werner alludes to her reading of the title (1988, 113).

One of the flames Dante sees in Hell is cloven, and Virgil tells him that two souls dwell together in it: Ulysses and Diomedes, condemned for their gift-trick of the wooden horse to the city of Troy.[4]

What is initially intriguing about Dante's association of lost souls in infernal flames with the fire and cloud-whirlwind that enveloped Elijah is the unexpected comparison of hell with heaven: in both places, a soul is perceived as simultaneously luminous and obscured. The fire that contains both Ulysses and Elijah is a visualization of their rhetorical power, but Ulysses is eternally consumed by that fire, whereas Elijah is assumed into the sun: the whirlwind that removes him from sight protects human eyes against the unbearable sight of divinity. By implication, Dante has presented Ulysses as the anti-Elijah, a deceptive trickster, who lacks the God-given power to perform miracles.[5] In

4. In contrast, Robert Spoo argues that the phrase came from Ferrero's *L'Europa giovane* (Young Europe [1897]), and that it refers to the smallness of even the largest human conceptions, arguing that they are like a "little cloud against the unbounded expanse of the sky; a breath disperses it and no human eye will see it more" (1987, 32). Interestingly, the Ferraro source suggests that the story is about perspective, and especially about the smallness of human ideas and endeavors, a smallness that leads us to see the littleness of Little Chandler in a different, less demeaning light.

5. Dante's Ulysses, unlike Homer's, is a mis-leader who calls his men toward death, not life. By connecting (and implicitly contrasting) Elijah with Ulysses, Dante explains his reservations about Ulysses: Dante sees the Christian God as having condemned the very cunning for which Athena loved Ulysses in the *Odyssey*. The tongue of fire in which he is encased (and from which he speaks in *Inferno*) signifies a dangerous inspiration, one that derives from impatience with domestic stability and love of the unknown, an inspiration that is *not* guided by God. (At the beginning of the twenty-sixth canto, the Dante pilgrim reminds himself of the importance of being guided by virtue: "e più lo 'ngegno affreno ch' I' non soglio / perché non corra che virtue nol guidi" [more than I am wont I curb my powers, lest they run where virtue does not guide them] [Sinclair trans., 321].) When Ulysses speaks through his tonguelike flame, he confesses that when he left Circe, neither "fondness for a son, nor duty to an aged father, nor the love I owed Penelope which should have gladdened her, could conquer within me the passion I had to gain experience of the world and of the vices and the worth of men" (ibid., 325). He recalls exhorting his men "not to deny experience, in the sun's track" (Bloom echoes this phrase almost verbatim in the "Calypso" episode of *Ulysses:* "in the track of the sun" [*U*, 4.99–100]) "of the unpeopled world," and they are so excited by his call to discover the world that he could not have held them back. Then he relates how a fatal storm wrecked and killed them all.

contrast, Dante's apprehension of Beatrice as an admirable representative of divine inspiration is signaled by his description of her as a little white cloud, or *nuvoletta,* in the *Vita Nuova.* Dante's "little cloud," then, represents divine power: the power to torture and obscure Ulysses in the fire of his own inspirational speech; the power to assume Beatrice into the heavens with the angelic host. An understanding of how Dante uses a *little cloud* in the Ulysses canto also helps us see why Joyce may have chosen to call his epic *Ulysses,* instead of *Odysseus:* "Ulysses" is what Dante called the ancient hero in the *Inferno.* Dante seems to have understood Ulysses not as a domestic hero who endured years of tribulations in an effort to return home, but as a deceptive leader whose main faults can be traced to an allergy to domesticity.

For experienced readers of Joyce, the phrase *a little cloud* proleptically evokes *Ulysses:* specifically, it seems akin to the matutinal cloud that the narrator of "Ithaca" recalls as having been perceived by both Stephen and Bloom earlier that morning: a sign of trouble that was "at first no bigger than a woman's hand" (*U,* 17.42, a slight emendation of 1 Kings 18:44). For Stephen, the cloud darkened his thoughts with images of his dying and subsequently dead mother (*U,* 1.248–83); for Bloom, the cloud brings black thoughts of Molly as barren, the promised land a mask for the Dead Sea, the womb a tomb (*U,* 3.228–40). And finally, the Italian word for *little cloud, nuvoletta,* brings us to *Finnegans Wake,* where Nuvoletta is one of the guises of Issy, the daughter, whose fall from the heavens (as rain) brings moisture and fertility to the earth and marks her transition from young girl to woman as she becomes part of the river Liffey (and the river of life).[6]

In order to understand what Joyce is doing with a little cloud in relation to its opposite, a little flame, it is helpful to think of Dante and the Bible in relation to one another. Moses, when he was leading his people out of slavery in Egypt to the promised land, followed a pillar of cloud by day and a pillar of

---

6. Dante also uses *nuvoletta* to describe a young woman, although in the *Vita Nuova,* it signifies the soul of Beatrice after death. See canzone 23, in which Dante relates, "I imagined that I looked toward heaven, and it seemed to me that I saw a multitude of angels, who were returning upwards, and had before them a little cloud of exceeding whiteness." It is then that he realizes that Beatrice must be dead.

fire by night, as Joyce notes several times in *Ulysses*.[7] In the book of Exodus, Yahweh leads his people to freedom by taking the form of a heavenly opposite, providing darkness in the day and light at night: "The Lord went in front of them in a pillar of cloud by day, to lead them along the way, and in a pillar of fire by night, to give them light, so that they might travel by day and by night" (13:21).[8] Later, God appears to Moses as a luminous cloud: "and the glory of the Lord appeared in the cloud" (16:10). Because humans cannot see divinity, the power of divine light must, like the sun, be veiled by a cloud, but it nonetheless signifies the source—or origin—of life and inspiration.

ME and VM: How does this background help to illuminate Joyce's story "A Little Cloud"? It directs us to realize that this story about an apparently failed poet is as much concerned with access to the source of inspiration as it is with the more realist and even mundane concerns of originality versus imitation. Divine inspiration, above and beyond the poet or writer, signifies an opportunity, but it also highlights the obstacles that must be laboriously overcome to realize that opportunity.

VM: I would argue that the "little cloud" in the story is the "littlest" Chandler, the infant son of the candle maker, Little Chandler, whose little light is temporarily obscured by the cloud that eventually brings tears to his father's eyes. Little Chandler's son is a living realization of poetic inspiration: as Chandler thinks about the poetic thought that touched him, "A light began to tremble on the horizon of his mind" (*D*, 88), and he feels that his

---

7. The first mention is in John F. Taylor's speech in "Aeolus," when Taylor is describing Moses bringing "the chosen people out of their house of bondage" and following "the pillar of the cloud by day" (*U*, 7.864–66). The second mention is by Stephen in "Scylla and Charybdis," in response to a question about the celestial phenomena that he says marked Shakespeare's birth, which he describes as "a star by night" and "a pillar of the cloud by day" (*U*, 9.944). Finally, the phrase is used in "Ithaca" to describe Bloom's fantasy departure inspirationally guided by the polestar at sea and a woman's posterior on land: a "bispherical moon," "revealed in imperfect varying phases of lunation through the posterior interstice of the imperfectly occluded skirt of a carnose negligent perambulating female, a pillar of the cloud by day" (*U*, 17.1996–99).

8. The *New Oxford Annotated Bible* notes that "cloud and fire have become traditional ways of expressing God's presence and guidance" (86, 13:21–22n).

every step thereafter brings him "farther from his own sober inartistic life" (*D*, 88).

ME: Here we should pause a moment and try to disentangle two things that are happening in Little Chandler's mind. On the one hand, he experiences the promise of new life, a life that is associated with a light trembling on the edge of his mind and also with his infant, his son, whom Little Chandler believes to have trapped him and condemned him to an inartistic and "mean" domesticity; when the child's wailing pierces "the drum of his ear" (*D*, 102) as the word of God once pierced Mary's during the Annunciation, he reacts not with joy but with resentful anger: "It was useless, useless! He was a prisoner for life. His arms trembled with anger and suddenly bending to the child's face he shouted: —Stop!" (*D*, 102). And the child stops wailing and begins to scream.

ME and VM: The "little cloud" of the title seems to refer to this incident with his son, as the tears precipitated by the event show. Little Chandler sees his child as raining on his poetic parade, extinguishing—with the help of Annie and the rented furniture—his hope for realizing his poetic dream.

VM: However, Joyce's allusions prod us to see that his son/sun, who also acts as a little cloud, has some of the characteristics of a divine being, offering exactly the kind of inspiration that Little Chandler despairs of being able to nurture.

Gallaher has awakened in Little Chandler some of the characteristics of Dante's Ulysses, prompting him to turn away from his domestic duties with a potentially abusive impatience, but the reader may recognize the extent to which procreative labor preserves his sense of himself as potentially and ideally creative, since with the help of his wife he produced his son.

VM and ME: Instead of making a little light like a real chandler, Little Chandler temporarily loses touch with his core, his heart. Corless's, the name of the place where he meets Gallaher, suggests "coreless," and the word *core* is etymologically akin to the French *coeur*, or "heart." When Little Chandler remembers walking by it at night, he recalls images of "richly dressed ladies, escorted by cavaliers" (when used as an adjective, *cavalier* means "disdainful"). "Their faces were powdered and they caught up their dresses, when they touched earth, like alarmed Atalantas" (*D*, 86). Like Gallaher, Atalanta did not want to marry, so she challenged her suitors to a footrace, and she

outran them all (the losers were killed by her father). Ultimately, she suc-
cumbed to matrimony when Hippomenes distracted her during the race by
rolling three golden apples (given to him by Aphrodite) by her at strategic
moments, and she lost the race.[9] Although Atalanta and Hippomenes were
married, they showed no gratitude to the goddess of love, who in turn pun-
ished them by tricking them into having sexual intercourse in a sacred temple,
a defilement that prompted the mother of the gods to turn them into lions.
Atalanta is "coreless" in that her attraction for gold superseded her initial aims
and bound her in a loveless marriage to her cavalier. In this respect, she anticipates Gallaher's equally heartless position: "I mean to marry money" (D, 98).

VM: We can best appreciate what Joyce is doing when he reunites Little
Chandler and Gallaher by looking more carefully at their names. A little
chandler is, as noted earlier, a maker of a little light, whereas "Ignatius"
(Gallaher's first name) means "fiery" (it is related to the Latin *ignis*, "fire").
Gallaher is not only a bigger flame than Little Chandler, but also a kind
of supportive invader, as his surname implies: it comes from the Irish *gall*,
meaning "strange" or "foreign," and *cabhair*, "help" or "support." The fiery
foreigner helps to produce an emotional distance that alienates Little Chandler from his home and makes him regard his own light as a small flame in
contrast to the light of his friend. But the opposition between Gallaher and
Little Chandler serves to show the *reader* that artistic originality is a kind of
reproduction or procreation that comes from embracing incompatible realities (such as the ones represented by Gallaher and Little Chandler together).
Together, they create a richer worldview than either does individually.

ME: The paradoxical idea that reproduction might in some cases be a
source of originality is made most explicit in Ignatius Gallaher's complaint
about the routine demands of journalism. "It pulls you down," he said.
"Press life. Always hurry and scurry, looking for copy and sometimes not
finding it: and then, always to have something new in your stuff" (D, 90). In

---

9. In Ovid's *Metamorphoses*, Aphrodite describes Atalanta as "a girl who used to race against
men and defeat even the fastest runners." When she asked Apollo about a husband, he replied,
"You have no need of a husband, Atalanta. You should avoid any experience of one. But assur-
edly, you will not escape marriage and then, though still alive, yet you will lose your own self."
That is why Atalanta sets up the harsh terms of the footrace. See Ovid 1955, 240–44.

the newspaper business, there is no "copy" without originality; the journalist submits copy to report news. But the pressure for newness is what makes the reporter's life pressed. In contrast, Little Chandler finds creativity from copying other writers and from a stereotypically poetic reverie. Gallaher and Little Chandler, then, are disagreeing not only about home—Ireland and domesticity—but also about modes of artistic reproduction: one pressured and mechanical, associated with mechanical presses and even a windmill (through the literal meaning of the phrase *moulin rouge*), the other alive and caring, albeit burdened with the labors of reproduction, with the daily, repetitive concerns of birth and growth. The challenge to the poet is to balance imitation and novelty, pressure and reverie, repetition and invention, acknowledgment and innovation.

Hemiplegia

ME: In the final section of the story, Little Chandler is at home, having forgotten to bring his wife the parcel of coffee he had promised to pick up on his way home. His wife decides to go get it herself and leaves their sleeping young son in Chandler's arms. What we see as Chandler looks around him, tries to read a Byron poem, and ultimately shouts at his crying child is the psychological equivalent of hemiplegia; it offers us a metaphor for how Chandler's inability to triumph over Gallaher in their contest for manhood results in an involuntary (and unconscious) heartlessness at home.

In July 1904, Joyce had described *Dubliners* to Constantine Curran as his effort "to betray the soul of that hemiplegia or paralysis which many consider a city" (*Letters I*, 55). Whereas the second term of the description (*paralysis*) has driven a rich tradition of reception, the first has been less often explored: hemiplegia is a paralysis of one side of the body caused by a lesion on the opposite side of the brain. It is what we might call a reflective paralysis: the expression of injury is displaced elsewhere on the body, almost like the phenomenon of referred pain.[10]

---

10. Readers might readily supply examples of hemiplegia as displaced injury in *Dubliners* (Farrington's injured pride at work results in abuse of his son at home; Gabriel rebuts Molly

Gallaher's effect on Little Chandler is arguably hemiplegic, in that their encounter turned Little Chandler helplessly (and we hope temporarily) against his home and family, causing him to demean them (he finds something "mean" in his wife's pretty face and in the pretty furniture [*D,* 100]). He longs to "escape from his little house, . . . to live bravely like Gallaher" (*D,* 101), and this desire leads him to open the volume of Byron's poems and to dream of producing such writing. Little Chandler feels trapped, and the "dark anger" of Byron's idealistic melancholy turns into actual anger against his child.

VM: His wife rushes in and snatches the boy, comforting him and calling him "Lambabaun" (lamb child) and "Mamma's little lamb of the world" (*D,* 103). Through Annie's words, we hear echoes suggesting that the child has played the role of a sacrificial lamb, but the sacrificial lamb of Christianity is also an incarnation of the divine word. One of the forms of the word *lamb* is also, interestingly, *lamp,* which associates Little Chandler's child with the "little lamp" shining on the table at the beginning of this scene, as well as with the "little flame" that Little Chandler as candle maker made. And finally, as John Wyse Jackson and Bernard McGinley point out, there is a rarely used Irish word, *lampa,* that normally means "lamp" but can also (rarely) mean "cloud" (1993, 75).[11] When Annie calls her son a lamb in Irish, she triggers a linguistic set of associations that can lead us to see the child as a "lamp" who is also "a little cloud," the twin (and opposed) representatives of divinity and inspiration in the Hebrew scriptures, and the lamb and incarnate word of the Christian gospel.

Ivors's criticism only in the guise of a toast to his aunts). In "A Little Cloud," Little Chandler's disappointed expectations in his old friend Gallaher are expressed in a paralytic flaccidity at home. He is ineffectual at soothing his son and unable to defend himself against his wife's anger, and he concentrates poorly on his poetry selection.

11. In *Ulysses,* Joyce uses a similar double image to represent Stephen's dead mother (an oxymoron in itself) in the "Circe" episode when he has Stephen attack her in the form of a chandelier. As a chandelier she is both fire and "shade," and we discover when Bella Cohen tries to make Stephen pay for a new chandelier that he only crushed the shade, thereby spreading more light over the world.

Melancholy and the Stalling of Writing

VM: Let us go back to the crucial words that conclude the story: "tears of remorse started to his eyes" (*D*, 103). Little Chandler's remorse is appropriate; it represents a moral correction against his bullying reflex to blame another for "his own sober inartistic life" and a compassionate response to a helpless child's pain (*D*, 88).[12] Does his remorse signal anything more than the moment when he turns the anger he had directed at his child against himself? Such a reading would position remorse not as a mechanism of ethical responsibility, but as the root of melancholy.[13] When we think of Little Chandler as the feminized, romantic, poetic counterpart of the frustrated, angry Farrington of "Counterparts," the story that immediately follows, that connection suggests that Joyce may be presenting the dreamy indulgence of melancholy as potentially productive of verbal abuse. Little Chandler's verbal abuse of his infant son is parallel to (as well as different from) the physical abuse to which Farrington subjects his son.[14]

Ingrown, helpless anger is Little Chandler's usual state of mind, and the story suggests it is in fact a mode of self-imprisonment in the sense that the

12. The etymology of *remorse*, however, emphasizes the metaphor of "biting"; the word stems from the Latin *remordere*, "to bite again," or "to bite back," and it is related to the Latin *remorsus conscientiae*, which was translated into Middle English as "agenbite of inwit," a phrase that expresses Stephen Dedalus's discomfort with his behavior toward his dying mother in *Ulysses*.

13. *Melancholy* can be translated etymologically as "dark" choler (literally dark, *mela-*, and bile, *choler*), and more figuratively as "anger against the self." It is interesting to pause a moment on anger and to probe its proximity to fear (Little Chandler bewails his unfortunate "timidity"). *Anger* stems from the Latin *ango*, "to press tight" or "to throttle," and it is related both to the German *angst*, "fear," and the Dutch *eng*, which means both "narrow" and "eerie, uncanny." This linguistic net of associations implies that anger (and its self-reflexive cousin, melancholy) is claustrophobic, narrow, and strange, like a prison cell, or even the grave Chandler reads about in Byron's "On the Death of a Young Lady."

14. To put it slightly differently, Little Chandler is the "Henry Flower" of *Dubliners*; if *Dubliners* were *Ulysses*, "A Little Cloud" would be the "Sirens" episode, permeated by lyricism and sadness. What that point implies, of course, is that Little Chandler—like the "Henry Flower" side of Bloom—is a thoughtful, sensitive embodiment of one part of Joyce himself.

mood "owns" the person: "A gentle melancholy took possession of him. He felt how useless it was to struggle against fortune, this being the burden of wisdom which the ages had bequeathed to him" (*D*, 85). Little Chandler's historical sense of his condition is a legacy of melancholic paralysis. The narrator reinforces the point: "Melancholy was the dominant note of his temperament" (*D*, 88). Unlike the dominant Gallaher, who strikes a note of gaiety but whose trustworthiness is suspect, Little Chandler thinks that melancholy is his gift.

ME: Little Chandler's melancholy is indeed a gift—if of a difficult kind— a gift of creation and creativity. Joyce's account of melancholy in this story precedes Sigmund Freud's more familiar 1917 account of the emotion as a failure in the process of mourning. For Joyce, however, melancholy is not necessarily a failure or even a limitation. Unlike Freud, he associates melancholy with anticipation of an idealized, perpetually delayed future and not with a failure to relinquish the past.

In this approach, Joyce's view is allied with more recent theories of melancholy. Giorgio Agamben argues that "melancholy offers the paradox of an intention to mourn that precedes and anticipates the loss of the object" (1993, 20). Slavoj Žižek has described melancholia as a sleight of hand (or imagination) in which the experience of loss "obfuscates" the fact that "the object is lacking from the very beginning, that its emergence coincides with its lack, that this object is *nothing* but the positivization of a void or lack." Žižek notes the paradox through which the experience of actual lack as imagined loss "enables us to assert our possession of the object; what we never possessed can also never be lost." If the melancholic maintains the sense of loss, he or she can *possess* the lost object through the fact of absence: "The melancholic displays the metaphysical yearning for another absolute reality beyond our ordinary reality subjected to temporal decay and corruption; the only way out of this predicament is thus to thank an ordinary sensual material object (say, the beloved woman) and elevate it into the absolute" (2000, 660). Žižek provides as a particularly effective example the love between Newland Archer and the Countess Ellen Olenska in *The Age of Innocence:* the romance between these two lovers is predicated on its impossibility; they own their love by forsaking it from the beginning and thus maintaining its pristine and ideal condition.

For Joyce, melancholy has qualities similar to the anticipation and desire described by Agamben and Žižek, but has no distinct object: it is a generalized condition of being in the face of loss, of anticipating the potential for disappointment, the belief in a future that is both better than the present and never to be realized. Little Chandler "felt how useless it was to struggle against fortune, this being the burden of wisdom which the ages had bequeathed to him." He imagines reading aloud to his wife from the poetry books collected during his "bachelor days," but is held back from this anticipated pleasure by "shyness" (*D*, 85). In both anticipating reading to his wife and refraining from doing so, Chandler preserves for himself a melancholic pleasure in a future he constantly defers. By retaining the exchange of poetry in his imagination and never acting on it, he insulates his anticipated pleasure from disappointment. He tests neither his marriage nor his wife's sensitivities; he never exposes his favorite verses to the possibility of her inattention, incomprehension, or even scorn. Like Olenska and Archer, Chandler can retain this fantasized moment in his marriage as a pleasurable anticipation for the future by never testing it in the harsh light of a reality he has learned to find disappointing. Some readers may be frustrated by this cramped mode of relation, but others might see in Chandler's pleasurable fantasy the nascent articulation of fiction, the imagining of an idealized scene from an idealized marriage.

vm. I see why you say that there is something creative about the production of what is essentially a melancholic fantasy, because that fantasy is an imaginative conceit infused with poetic power (like the fantasy of the grimy houses as tramps who will "move on" after sunset). But the effect of this fantasy is very different from the effect of Joyce's art: Chandler's productions substitute fantasy for the actual poetic production he desires, which relieves him from the responsibility of actually writing anything down. Chandler's art, which takes place solely in his imagination, can never be challenged or evaluated.

me: With no particular loss to mourn, Chandler's melancholy seems itself a creation, the emotional means whereby he glamorizes the apparently mundane routines of his life (a life that *lacks* romance and excitement) by idealizing it as the product of loss. The loss possesses its mourner and becomes him, laying the grounds on which he imagines his creativity may be practiced. Through this production of melancholy, Little Chandler, while not having himself yet composed a verse, can remain the ideal poet much like the ideal beloved, never tested, always slightly out of reach, and thereby pristine and perfect. He attributes to himself the potential or "light" that makes ordinary existence both possible and promising.

VM: Joyce paints Little Chandler as torn between light and darkness, between the "little light" that he would like to bring into the world and the "little cloud" of melancholy that both paralyzes and soothes him, a melancholy that is his embryonic poetry. If we take the poetic aspect of Little Chandler's nature seriously, acknowledging that like all things associated with him, it is diminutive but nonetheless real, it is easier to appreciate (if also to belittle) the subtle beauty of his perceptions and the language in which he clothes them (see Ruoff 1957, 256–71, cited in Torchiana 1986, 125, 139).

To access Little Chandler's delicate perceptions, we should first clarify the relation between the narrator's language and the language of the protagonist. The third-person narrator's idiom throughout the story is an imitation (or reproduction) of Little Chandler's. This free-indirect discourse is immediately apparent in the first paragraph, when the narrator apes Little Chandler's appreciation for Gallaher's success with a string of clichés: "Few fellows had talents like his and fewer still could remain unspoiled by such success. Gallaher's heart was in the right place and he had deserved to win" (D, 84). Sportsmanlike jingoism is not Little Chandler's most characteristic idiom, however, and may represent a stylistic interruption, an anticipation of how Gallaher would like to hear himself described; what distinguishes Little Chandler most vividly is his propensity to transform the world around him by embedding it in another highly visual story that expresses his own feeling: melancholy projection.

ME: Thus, two modes of narration come into conflict in the story's first section: the narrator's mode is a mean realism, while Little Chandler's is self-consciously influenced by the romanticism and Celticism he wishes to emulate.[15] The narrator suggests that Little Chandler's mode of perception disallows him from seeing the reality around him, which the narrator

---

15. Margot Norris (2003) makes a similar observation about the narrative style.

indicates metonymically by drawing attention to the children Little Chandler passes by. "A horde of grimy children populated the street. They stood or ran in the roadway or crawled up the steps before the gaping doors or squatted like mice upon the thresholds. Little Chandler gave them no thought. He picked his way deftly through all that minute vermin-like life and under the shadow of the gaunt spectral mansions in which the old nobility of Dublin had roystered" (*D*, 85–86).[16] While the narrator indicts Little Chandler for ignoring the impoverished children and avoiding them as he walks past, the narrator's moral superiority is undermined by the comparison of the children to vermin.

VM: Are you saying it is the *narrator* who compares the children to vermin? I would argue that although this passage is written in the third person, it represents Little Chandler's own idiom and way of thinking. I think it is Little Chandler who regards the children as vermin and that this opinion foreshadows his later burst of anger at his own son.

ME: I don't think it is possible *both* for Little Chandler to give the children no thought *and* to denigrate them as vermin.

VM: This is a place where we will have to disagree. A voice is telling us that Little Chandler gives the children no thought *because* he regards them as too "small," even verminlike, living in a poverty that he regards as squalid.

ME: Look at Little Chandler's own language about the poverty of his city, produced in preparation for the poem he anticipates writing, in which

16. The description of Capel Street contains a compressed history of Ireland over the past century. Once Dublin housed the great wealth produced by the Union, and in the Georgian period, British colonial administrators, government officials, and plantation settlers had grand homes in Dublin. During this period, Dublin was a boisterous, festive boom city, as indicated by the image of the "old nobility" as they "roystered." With the Famine of the 1840s, much of the wealth left Ireland, and rural populations gravitated to the major cities in search of relief work. The former grand houses were marginally converted by owners to house families in large numbers. The children Little Chandler passes are of the next generation whose conditions of life are scarcely improved from the circumstances of their Famine-era parents. While the narrator seems to indict Little Chandler for his insensitivity to the plight of poor children, this scene of poverty is decades old and a daily encounter in the clerk's life. Like so many of his class, Little Chandler is a few paychecks away from these perilous conditions and, with his limited means, helpless to make much difference in their lives.

he compares the architectural style of the decaying houses he sees along the river and their occupants' conditions of poverty and transience. "As he crossed Grattan Bridge he looked down the river toward the lower quays and pitied the poor stunted houses. They seemed to him a band of tramps, huddled together along the river-banks, their old coats covered with dust and soot, stupefied by the panorama of sunset and waiting for the first chill of night to bid them arise, shake themselves and begone. He wondered whether he could write a poem to express his idea" (D, 87–88). Little Chandler's description might be idealizing, but it also indicates an awareness of his fellow Dubliners' struggles, financial conditions he is not that far from himself with his mortgaged furniture and rented flat. In contrast, when the narrator insistently draws the reader's attention to the plight of the children, his language betrays a sense of superiority ("vermin-like," "squatted like mice"). Little Chandler, unlike the narrator, uses a poetic vision to alter his perceptions, to see his surroundings differently: "For the first time in his life he felt himself superior to the people he passed. For the first time his soul revolted against the dull inelegance of Capel Street" (D, 87). Joyce's prose indicates not that Little Chandler is a snob, but rather that he is trying out a new way of seeing surroundings (possibly imagining their appearance through his returning friend's more privileged eyes) and that this mode of perception is how he comes to understand himself as a poet. Additionally, his Celticism, while potentially sentimental, may also represent the kind of work of retrieval W. B. Yeats pursued in rural Ireland; Chandler's desire to describe Irish city dwellers with the dignity of a poetry produced in the light of an indigenous tradition emerges as a project very similar to Joyce's own fictions of the urban and the working class. Imagining the houses as transient, poor, and dirty, like a Dublin tramp, Chandler also imagines them, and by extension their inhabitants, as worthy of exactly the aesthetic sense idealized in the tradition of poetry he wished to emulate, a tradition in which the poet might also be being "stupefied by the panorama of sunset."

VM: Here we have another disagreement. I see the sense of superiority you are attributing to the narrator as Little Chandler's, and the fact that he is described as feeling himself "superior to the people he passed" simply reinforces our awareness that he is momentarily experiencing an inflated sense of self-importance.

I would argue that Joyce's portrait of Little Chandler is drawn partly as a self-caricature, a picture of how he himself might have been had he stayed in Dublin and obtained a respectable clerkship. Look at the poetic way the narrator (imitating the voice of Little Chandler) describes the late evening light as Little Chandler gazes out his office window: "The glow of a late autumn sunset covered the grass plots and walks. It cast a shower of kindly golden dust on the untidy nurses and decrepit old men who drowsed on the benches; it flickered upon all the moving figures" (*D*, 85). This melancholy, lyrical description of the sunset recalls aspects of Joyce's own poetic technique in *Chamber Music*. Both Little Chandler and Joyce (at least in his early poetry) have a fondness "for elegant and antique phrase" (*CM*, xxvii; *CP*, 35) and for animating the inanimate: Little Chandler anthropomorphizes houses when he sees them as resting tramps; Joyce brings the ocean to life, hearing its roar as "an army charging upon the land" in "black armour," "horses plunging," crying "their battle-name" into the night (*CM*, xxxvi; *CP*, 44).

I would claim that "A Little Cloud" offers a caricature of a "small" but musical would-be poet based partly on a fanciful vision of Joyce himself had he stayed in Ireland, and partly on Thomas Moore, Ireland's national bard, musical performer, and author of the plangent *Irish Melodies* (1807–35). Joyce's decision to call Little Chandler "Tommy" and "Little" may well be more than a glancing allusion to Moore, whose first book was called *The Poetical Works of Thomas Little* (1801) in reference to his own diminutive stature.[17] Both Moore and Little Chandler share a fondness for Byron: Moore was Byron's friend, biographer, and literary executor. Also like Moore (but unlike Joyce), Little Chandler plays up his Irishness: he contemplates inserting his mother's Irish name before his English surname so he could publish under the name of Thomas or T. Malone Chandler (*D*, 89).[18] Moore

17. Tom Moore was only five feet tall. See L. Kelly 2006, 15.

18. Little Chandler's identification with Catholic Ireland (in contrast to the vulgar and libertine unionism of his friend in the orange tie) continues in Corless's, which Joyce marks as hosting a confrontation between Ireland and England by taking special note of the "red and green wineglasses" that confuse Little Chandler's sight when he enters the bar (*D*, 69). As in the Christmas dinner scene in *A Portrait of the Artist as a Young Man*, the prominence of

saw himself as "little" not so much in height as in talent; he knew that his poetry—musical and pleasing as it was—lacked the rich complexity of his contemporaries Byron and Shelley. Joyce may well have sympathized as a poet who knew his verse could not compare to the poetry of Yeats. Finally, Joyce threads Moore's songs throughout *Dubliners,* using their melodies to give emotional resonance to the "scrupulous meanness" of the spare style: the harpist's performance of Moore's "Silent, O Moyle" is crucial to the complex effect of "Two Gallants," and Stanislaus claimed that "The Dead" was heavily indebted to Moore's song "O Ye Dead!" that Joyce urged his son, Giorgio, to perform (*Letters III,* 339–40, 348).[19]

Tommy Chandler, unlike Little Tom Moore but like Joyce the poet, knew "he would never be popular. . . . He could not sway the crowd but he might appeal to a little circle of kindred minds" (*D,* 88). When Little Chandler thinks of himself as a writer, it is through others' eyes: through the anticipated reviews of an English critic or reader. Little Chandler's invented phrases from press notices of the book he has not yet written are reminiscent of Joyce's own early reviews: where Little Chandler's invented reviewers recognize his *"gift of easy and graceful verse'* . . . *'A wistful sadness pervades these poems.'* . . . *The Celtic note'"* (*D,* 88), Joyce's friend Thomas Kettle wrote of *Chamber Music,*

---

red and green underscores the conflict of national allegiance that will develop between Little Chandler and Gallaher as they mark themselves as moral and cosmopolitan, Irish and internationalist, respectively.

19. Another of Moore's songs that is important in *Ulysses* is "The Last Rose of Summer." Joyce's awareness of a poetic and musical kinship with Thomas Moore may well have been reflected in his final title for his volume of poems, which according to Arthur Symons was originally called *A Book of Thirty Songs for Lovers* (*CH,* 36). By changing the title to *Chamber Music,* Joyce was able to stress the musicality of the verse and its suitability for a small audience while also subtly denigrating it as the tinkle of urination in a chamber pot. Joyce's poetic "chamber music," then, is similar to Moore's, whose statue at Trinity was erected over a urinal, perhaps as a commentary on his song "The Meeting of the Waters." Bloom notes the ironic appropriateness of associating Moore with urination in *Ulysses:* "He crossed under Tommy Moore's roguish finger. They did right to put him up over a urinal: meeting of the waters" (*U,* 8.414–15). Finally, one of the titles for ALP's Mamafesta in *Finnegans Wake* (rival titles for the *Wake* itself) acknowledges Joyce's sense of kinship with Tommy Moore, whose name he changes to "too many more": *"Inglo-Andean Medoleys from Tommany Moohr"* (*FW,* 106.8).

"His work, never very voluminous, had from the first a rare and exquisite accent." He calls Joyce's poems "light and frail," referring to them as "delicate verses" with "the bright beauty of a crystal," a "distinguished playing with harps."[20] Joyce himself extracted phrases from the notices of *Chamber Music* and had them printed so they could be inserted in press copies of *Dubliners* when it appeared in 1914. From the *Scotsman,* Joyce chose the phrase "A volume of graceful verse" (Deming 1970, 42), which comes very close to Little Chandler's description of his own "graceful verse." The *Leader* piece appreciates "lines of such apparent ease" (*"Mr Chandler has the gift of easy and graceful verse"*). The *Glasgow Herald* asks, "Verse such as this has its own charm but where will it find its audience?" (ibid.).

ME: If we take Little Chandler's poetic potential seriously, the proleptic reviews of his poetry that he composes gauge the effects he would like to produce in his work, the impression he would like to make on a reader. On the one hand, Little Chandler is blurbing his book before he writes it.[21] On the other hand, he is independently acquiring practical tools for composing: he identifies his voice, seeks models, and performs audience analysis. It is only when he imagines himself as a poet that he is briefly released from the diminutive descriptor that haunts him: *Little* Chandler becomes "Thomas Malone Chandler," or better still, "T. Malone Chandler." Even his artificial plan to "put in allusions" can be something we respect if we see his description of the women outside Corless's as Atalantas as an example.

Little Chandler Versus Gallaher

ME: Little Chandler is himself a kind of allusion: to Joyce himself and to Thomas Moore. He even anticipates aspects of Farrington in "Counterparts," the next story, despite the fact that on the surface they are completely different (in assertiveness, gentility, and size). Hemiplegia may also be a way

20. Kettle's review appeared in the *Freeman's Journal* on June 1, 1907. See Deming 1970, 37.

21. Hugh Kenner notes that the phrases with which Little Chandler describes his planned poetry are "reviewers' jargon" and argues that "quotation is as close to reality as he gets" (1956, 9).

to understand the contrasting forms of masculinity Joyce presents in Little Chandler's encounter with Gallaher, who is his antithesis. Gallaher seems to reflect and reverse all of Little Chandler's delicate, abstemious, even feminine attributes.

VM: I agree that the narrator emphasizes the contrast between the temperaments of Little Chandler and Gallaher: the former is melancholy and timid, the latter lively and brave (if somewhat vulgar). Their values are also sharply opposed: Chandler champions morality, whereas Gallaher advocates a salacious freedom. One wants to be a poet, and the other is a successful journalist, and their attitudes toward marriage and childbearing differ significantly as well.[22] Chandler is a homebody; Gallaher poses as a world traveler. Chandler prefers a romantic style; Gallaher is a gritty realist. Chandler does his wife's bidding; Gallaher presents himself as almost contemptuous of women: he sees women as instruments for the gratification of his sexual appetite and eventually for economic security; he means "to marry money" (D, 98).[23]

ME: The meeting between the two friends exaggerates the differences between them; each man becomes almost grotesque in the fun-house mirror of the other's perceptions. By contrast with Gallaher, Chandler's refinements appear mincing and fastidious; next to Chandler's cultured ways, Gallaher's brash enthusiasms look vulgar and seedy. When Little Chandler mentions his domestic comfort, Gallaher hints at his own sexual conquests, both potential and actual. Gallaher proposes a gender principle in which domesticity is effeminate; in contrast, his independence, metropolitan exposure, and mobility secure his masculinity. Little Chandler undercuts that principle

22. Brandon Kershner comments that the story is built on "a framework of massive oppositions" and that the two men "seem to exist only in order to complement one another" (1989, 96).

23. Joyce stresses Gallaher's view of women as food for his consumption through the last recorded moment of his meeting with Little Chandler when he has him pretend to taste something with "a wry face" when he contemplates being tied to one woman, commenting that it "must get a bit stale" (D, 77). Kershner notes of this passage that while "Chandler eats nothing," his counterpart "eats the world, and thus both dominates it and becomes it" (1989, 99).

by suggesting that unattached irresponsibility is actually a case of arrested development; he infantilizes or belittles Gallaher's freedom, suggesting that commitment and responsibility are the markers of mature masculinity. Gallaher counters with an advantageous marital plan in which a rich wife could ensure his continued freedom. Little Chandler hardly needs to respond; if his friend chooses to be a kept man, he will have to struggle against the common link between breadwinning and masculinity.

However, the struggle produces its own forms of hemiplegic injury: damage done by seeing a copy of the self in the other's vision. In his domestic life, Little Chandler appears established, whereas Gallaher is transient, insecure. Little Chandler has ambitions to be a poet; Gallaher writes hard news.[24] Gallaher indulges in the pleasures of a successful return by describing himself in his best light to someone who knows he left Ireland under a little cloud of scandal, asserting success after the fall from grace that precipitated his departure. But in the presence of Little Chandler, Gallaher is made to see his success as brash and even tawdry. Conversely, Gallaher also affects Little Chandler: his vaunted freedom from responsibility temporarily damages Little Chandler's attachment to home. Little Chandler's brief but intense reaction against the provincialism of his country and also against domesticity itself—specifically his wife and child—is a hemiplegic aftereffect of his encounter with Gallaher.

vm: What Joyce suggests through his careful depiction of Little Chandler's burst of rebellion against a home that he momentarily experiences as a cell, prison, or even tomb is that "originality" is possible only through an engagement with origin—an origin embodied in one of its guises by Little Chandler's infant son. Little Chandler's desire to emulate Gallaher, the Celtic school, or even Byron deflects him from another potential source of inspiration: the poetic moment that the narrator compares to an "infant hope" coming to life inside him as a fetus begins to grow in a woman, a hope that could give birth to a poem, just as his wife gave birth to his son. "Could

24. In *Ulysses,* Gallaher is identified as working for Alfred C. Harmsworth, "a publisher of two London papers and distributor of sensational popular literature." See Kershner 2008.

he write something original? He was not sure what idea he wished to express but the thought that a poetic moment had touched him took life within him like an infant hope" (*D*, 88). Here, Little Chandler is inspired with life, like a woman at the outset of her pregnancy: his inspired and inspiring thought begins to live and grow inside him.

ME: Little Chandler is both inspired and frustrated by the life of his own infant: the child represents hope and futurity and parallels his inspired and inspiring thoughts. But the child's needs also take the place of that specific futurity with the demands of sustained life. While the word *original* denotes a "beginning, source, birth," Little Chandler's own originality may be possible only through—not despite—the embrace of these opposite claims for reproduction and production, imagination and labor, parenting and publishing.

A Little Conclusion

What do we learn from this encounter between two men interested in writing: between a poet and a journalist, a homebody and a wanderer? Strangely, we discover that despite their stylistic differences, both rely on imitation or "copy" and both want something new in their writing. One—Ignatius—is, as his name suggests, a big flame, like Dante's Ulysses in the eighth circle of the *Inferno*. He is a trickster who misleads others and is impatient with domesticity. The other has made a small flame—he is a little chandler—but he does not understand how or why his child represents his "little lamp," the candle he has made, and we catch him reacting angrily against the very principle of originality or origin that could provide him with a model for poetic productivity. Little Chandler is not quite a Homeric Odysseus, because he lacks Odysseus's determination, cunning, and endurance, nor is he an Elijah who can cause his sacred offering to burst into flame, as Elijah did in the contest on Mount Carmel. Instead, he is a miniature, timid version of both, attached to his wife and home (like Odysseus) and capable of making only a small light (in contrast to Elijah's dramatic fire). He and Gallaher together constitute an early version of Leopold Bloom, a journalist of sorts who would be both attracted to and repelled by home as a place of origin and the condition of originality.[25] "A Little Cloud" is a story about "artistic gestation and reproduction"[26] and their relation to sexual reproduction. Real inspiration comes from a "little light" that is also "a little cloud," a smaller version of the divinity that led the Israelites to the promised land, and that the prophet Elijah wielded to help his people recognize the origin of all things. No wonder Joyce wrote, "A page of *A Little Cloud* gives me more pleasure than all my verses" (*Letters II*, October 18, 1906, 182).

25. "A Little Cloud" helps us see that Bloom is both a Ulysses (in Dante's sense) and an Odysseus (in Homer's), someone who knows that the struggle to embrace opposite extremes at the point of origination is a heroic task.

26. See *A Portrait of the Artist as a Young Man,* chap. 5.

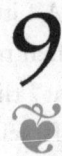

9

"Counterparts"

JAMES HANSEN AND JEAN-MICHEL RABATÉ

Jean-Michel: Our collaboration went like this: thinking I was very late for the deadline, I wrote my piece first, fast, furiously. I sent it to Jim, who then wrote his as a response, and sent it to me. We both liked the way the two parts seemed to complement each other. Did I say compliment?

Parts, *by Jean-Michel Rabaté*

A Man Is Being Beaten: "Counterparts" and the Phenomenology of Anger

> Every act of becoming conscious
> (it says here in this book)
> is an unnatural act
> —Adrienne Rich,
>   "The Phenomenology of Anger" (1972)

Now the virtues and vices are not emotions because we are not pronounced good or bad according to our emotions, but we are according to our virtues and vices; nor are we either praised or blamed for our emotions—a man is not praised for being frightened or angry, nor is he blamed for being angry merely, but for being angry in a certain way . . . we are not angry or afraid from choice, but the virtues are certain modes of choice, or at all events involve choice. . . . it is not easy to define in what manner and with what people and on what sort of grounds and how long one ought to be angry;

188

and in fact we sometimes praise men who err on the side of defect in that matter and call them gentle, sometimes those who are quick to anger and style them manly.

—Aristotle, *Nicomachean Ethics* (1934)

In Bk. II: iv. 6, is correct view, //
v. 3 on not getting angry enough, is good.

—Ezra Pound, *Guide to Kulchur* (1970)

For a long time, whenever I had to teach "Counterparts," I would resort to an old ploy, an inviting comparison—following a hint provided by Morris Beja whom I had heard give a wonderful talk on "Farrington the Scrivener" at the Copenhagen Symposium in 1986. This groundbreaking reading of "Bartleby the Scrivener" next to "Counterparts" listed all the possible parallels between the two stories; the construction of Farrington's character was illuminated by such a comparison, since it allows us to become more sympathetic to this "fierce and ill-natured man with a wasted life" (1989, 121). Considering that we, as readers, can become Farrington's "counterparts," Beja concluded with a Melvillean pastiche: "Ah, Farrington! Ah, humanity!" Interestingly, Beja also pointed out that Joyce's text was less ambiguous and undecidable than Melville's opaque allegory: "There are ambiguities enough in Joyce's story, but for once another writer seems even more indeterminate than he. Yet however uncertain we remain about the true sources of Bartleby's behavior and his plight, we must—given the comparisons I have pointed out—feel that at least some may well be shared with Farrington: and among those their frustration and alienation and social plight are surely central" (ibid.). However, I will try to show that there is an irreducible ambiguity in Joyce's text, and it has to do with the direction of anger.

More than once, I have followed the tip, and verified that the contrast between Farrington and Bartleby would trigger heated discussions among students. The productive parallel provided an opportunity to refer to Deleuze's wonderful essay on "Bartleby." There, Deleuze presents Bartleby as a comic figure and not as pure allegory. He sees him as a Kafkaesque "bachelor" who is moreover the incomparable author of a radical "formula" ("I would prefer not to") with which this paradoxical "medicine-man" would attempt to cure a sick America (1993, 89–114). In a distant echo, the increasingly frustrated and humiliated Farrington is the author of a witty retort ("I don't think, sir, that that's a fair question to put to me," as an answer to: "Do you think me an utter fool?"), a perfect sentence that condenses an instant of verbal glory while being the cause of his impending downfall. More recently, Margot Norris has "revisited" the comparison and extended it in the direction of Russian models of scriveners found in Gogol's stories (2003, 122–39). Norris also makes good use of David Lloyd's productive analysis of the legal language ("counterparts" refer to a copy that authenticates the original) and of the economics of Irish pub dynamics (Lloyd 2000, 128–49).

More recently, though, I have abandoned my usual reference to Melville, since I found a more forceful and direct connection—Richard Wright's *Lawd Today,* his famous last novel that was posthumously published in 1963. Under the direct influence of Joyce, Wright started writing it at the outset of his career in the thirties, and the novel is replete with topical allusions to Roosevelt, Hitler, and Mussolini. Wright himself pointed out Joyce's pervasive influence on his work, and his novel can be described as a cross between "Counterparts" and *Ulysses.* The narrative technique of *Lawd Today* is definitively modernistic and often stylized to an extreme, but if we sum up the plots of the two texts, they appear very similar: in "Counterparts," Farrington, a scrivener in a Dublin law office, is called by his boss, who complains that he has forgotten to copy a contract. Instead of hurrying, Farrington rushes to a pub, where he has a quick drink and comes back to his desk. But his mind wanders, and he realizes that he cannot finish on time. He is called again, insulted in front of a woman, and then the felicitous retort comes to his lips. However, he has to apologize abjectly. After work, he pawns his watch, as he cannot borrow from the chief clerk. His triumph comes during a protracted pub crawl with his friends, during which he repeats his witticism and is feted, but more often than not at his own expense, and he spends a considerable amount of money on drink. The group includes Weathers, a British acrobat, who seems to know several actresses, one of whom excites Farrington's sexual interest. A more fit Weathers twice beats Farrington in a trial of strength. Defeated, bitter, broke, not even drunk, he catches a tram back home. When he reaches his house, his wife has gone to church, no dinner is ready for him, the fire is out and the children asleep. Finally, he unleashes his anger at one of his sons, whom he viciously beats with a cane, while the boy cries and futilely offers prayers to buy his father's mercy.

Lawd Today was completed in 1937; no publisher accepted it in Wright's lifetime because of its brutal description of a black man's day (February 12, Lincoln's birthday) in Chicago. The "hero" is Jake Jackson, a postal worker who appears as unsympathetic as Farrington: he drinks, gambles, cheats on his wife, whom he taunts and beats up as early as breakfast time. He has a grudge against her (she is regularly called "that bitch" in his interior mono-logue), but anyway he seems unhappy about everything, while blaming the others for his mishaps. Sometime before, he had used a ruse to force his young wife to have an abortion, and as a consequence she needs an expensive operation for which he is reluctant to pay. He visits a barber and a gambling house, then goes to work at the post office. In a scene full of echoes of "Counterparts," he is severely berated by a white overseer. He learns that his wife has come to complain about him and that he is in danger of losing his job. Ironically, he is saved at the last minute by the doctor who wants to make some money—thus, under the pretext of paying for his wife's opera-tion, he receives a loan of a hundred dollars, which he plans to use to enter-tain himself with prostitutes. Later that day, he and his friends from the post office visit a nightclub and meet several prostitutes, whom they invite for a copious dinner that he pays for.

Dancing wildly, they almost reach a sexual paroxysm, and as Jake is about to go up with his partner, he realizes that his money has been stolen by the prostitute's pimp. He makes a scene, but is soon overpowered by the pimp's friends and the bouncer. His friends drag him, bleeding and uncon-scious, to the street. Broke, bitter, and drunk, he staggers home, only to find his wife asleep on the bed, still in the position of prayer. He wakes her up and proceeds to beat her up savagely as a revenge for the denunciation. Bleeding from a wound to her face, she stabs him with a sliver of broken windowpane, and Jake collapses into a drunken torpor. The novel ends on a bleak note: "'Lawd, I wish I was dead,' she sobbed softly. Outside an icy wind swept around the corner of the building, whining and moaning like an idiot in a deep black pit" (Wright 1963, 189).

The main common feature is that these stories are about frustration and anger, about alienation and anger, about dispossession and anger: these stories are angry texts aimed at making their readers as angry as their main characters are. In both narratives, anger comes both from within and without. In the breakfast scene, Jake expects his wife to be silent and respect him and evinces a paranoid jealousy when he catches her chatting with the milkman. Later in the day, when he is caught daydreaming instead of sorting the mail properly, the dispute with a white inspector quickly escalates into a verbal match and a racist climax:

> "How do you account for these eight missing letters?"
>
> "I don't see how in the world it happened," said Jake. "I was working pretty careful . . ."
>
> "Yeah," sneered the inspector. "You were working carefully, all right! You've been running your mouth like a bluestreak for half an hour! Why don't you quit playing around and do your work!"
>
> Jake's neck grew hot. The inspector had spoken in a loud, harsh voice. . . . "I'm going to give you a write-up."
>
> "Do it and quit yelling at me!" Jake snapped.
>
> "Don't give me none of your lip!"
>
> "Don't give me none of *yours*!"
>
> "Who do you think you're talking to!"
>
> "You didn't have to yell at me!"
>
> "I'll talk to you like I damn please!"
>
> "Naw, you wouldn't if you wasn't in here!"
>
> "You *threatening* me!"
>
> "Give me my writeup and quit talking to me!"
>
> "I'm not taking orders from you!" (ibid., 123)

As in the verbal confrontation between Mr. Alleyne and Farrington, the whole group of coworkers is watching, and the whole workplace turns into a panopticon in which it is essential not to lose face. In Dublin as in Chicago, men are expected to behave as docile cogs in the machine. The sounds betray the industrialized and dehumanized nature of the work: in "Counterparts," we hear a bell ringing furiously, voices calling furiously, and the hurried clicking of a typist's typewriter. Jake's day begins when he is woken up from anguished dreams by the vociferous voices coming from his wife's radio, and his workplace is defined by the clatter of machines and by "rusty steel grating on rusty steel." The post office assumes mythical dimensions as it turns into a kind of hell: "The clatter of canceling machines rose like the rumble of an underground volcano" (ibid., 102). After he has brought upon him the reprimand and the feared but deserved "demerits," Jake once more dreams of violence, although he has interiorized a bitter awareness of absolute powerlessness: "He felt that something vast and implacable was crushing him; and he felt angry with himself because he had to stand it. He had an impulse to whirl and sweep his arm in a wide swift arc and brush away everything. But there was nothing he could solve by doing that; he would only get into more trouble. And the feeling that he could do nothing doubled back upon him, fanning the ashes of other dead feelings of not being able to do anything, and he was consumed in a fever of bitterness" (ibid., 124). The only thing that he can do is imagine a fully fledged fantasy of mayhem and mass war, with "millions o black soldiers marching in black armies," black ships shooting at the Statue of Liberty until it explodes and tumbles into the sea (ibid., 125). But it is only an elaborate daydream, nothing more. "He sighed, blinking, pushing a letter for Mississippi through the twelve-inch guns of the black battleship. He was sleepy. And thirsty" (ibid., 125).

A similar impulse threatens to engulf Farrington after the first reprimand: "Mr Alleyne bent his head again upon his pile of papers. The man stared fixedly at the polished skull which directed the affairs of Crosbie & Alleyne, gauging its fragility. A spasm of rage gripped his throat for a few moments and then passed, leaving after it a sharp sensation of thirst" (D, 105). What adds to their indignities in both cases is the gaze of female onlookers. The visit of Miss Delacour triggers the second outburst of Mr. Alleyne, and her body leaves a "moist pungent perfume" in the office. Farrington is quite conscious of her amused smile after he has uttered the felicitous rejoinder. In Jake's case, what rankles even more than the steady stare of the inspector after their verbal duel is the visit of six young white women: "He heard murmurs of laughter, light, silvery. Through lowered eyes he glimpsed the flash of a flesh-colored ankle. *They're looking at us like we was monkeys in a zoo!* A phrase he had heard an old Negro preacher say down South in his youth welled up in his consciousness, ringing in his ears like a bell. *Lawd, if I*

had my way I'd tear this building down! If only there was something he could
do to pay the white folks back for all they had ever done! Even if he lost his
own life in doing it! But what could he do? He felt the loneliness of his black
skin" (Wright 1963, 125).

The anger of the two protagonists remains sterile: Jake is depicted throughout the novel as ignorant, xenophobic, racist, sexist, and a protofascist, who
dreams that a "Mussellinni" (ibid., 157) would come and wipe out all that
has been erected by the white people, and he despises the black colleagues
who play the game (he thinks of Howard: "*Gawddam nigger licking white
folks' boots*!" [ibid., 111]). At the end of the day, Farrington appears "full of
smouldering anger and revengefulness," also "humiliated and discontented,"
but when remembering the woman who brushed against him, "his fury nearly
choked him" (*D*, 117). In both cases, this rage will be turned to those persons
who are closest to them, wife or child. Symptomatically, both wives have palin-
dromic names, Ada and Lil. Lil gets her second revenge during the night when
she stabs Jake, and we know that Ada can bully her overbearing husband: "His
wife was a little sharp-faced woman who bullied her husband when he was
sober and was bullied by him when he was drunk" (*D*, 118).

Why can't Farrington and Jake turn their anger into a more positive
outcome? It is the central question about anger, a question that Aristotle
posed well in his ethics. For Aristotle, one should not condemn anger, and
there are situations when it would be a mistake or a sign of weakness not to
get angry. Anger is often a political emotion, and it makes us react strongly
to injustice. "Those who do not get angry at things at which it is right to
be angry are considered foolish, and so are those who do not get angry in
the right manner, at the right time, and with the right people. It is thought
that they do not feel or resent an injury, and that if a man is never angry he
will not stand up for himself; and it is considered servile to put up with an
insult to oneself or suffer one's friends to be insulted" (Aristotle 1934, 231).
If anger can be described as a political passion, the issue is to be angry at the
right people or source.

In Farrington's case, Joyce seems to have hesitated, and such hesitation
is crucial if we are to feel, as Beja argued, that we can become the main
character's counterparts. The biographical source of the story is well known:
as often, Joyce found it in his brother Stanislaus's diary, who deplored the

violence unleashed by their uncle Willie, who would beat up his children when drunk; once the young Bertie begged his father not to hit him, promising that he would say a Hail Mary if he was spared. Typically, Stanislaus reacts as a moralist who condemns without any nuance the horrible behavior of his uncle facing his defenseless little cousins. Joyce had planned to use such a scene for an aborted attempt entitled "Silhouette" in which the drunk father was first seen threatening a nagging woman with his fists, then the profile of the woman appears next to two children just awakened by the noise of the fight, and she says, "Don't waken papa" (Ellmann 1983, 50).

This tends to prove that such a scene had imprinted itself in Joyce's psyche. Yet when he later discussed his story with his brother Stanislaus, Joyce was cautious and refused to condemn the "man" without giving him a chance to understand the rationale of his brutality: "I am no friend of tyranny, as you know, but if many husbands are brutal the atmosphere in which they live (vide Counterparts) is brutal and few wives and homes can satisfy the desire for happiness" (*SL*, 130). Immediately after this general remark, he adds a personal sign of his own unrest: "In fact, it is useless to talk about this any further. I am going to lunch." It is as if the acknowledgment that anger exists and has social causes had suddenly been converted not into thirst, as with Farrington, but into hunger, and the exchange is abruptly terminated. This point suggests that even in the biographical sources, something like a brotherly dialogism underpins the depiction of anger. Stanislaus is angry at his uncle's anger, and James Joyce seems angry at the very possibility of his own anger.

The explanation offered by Joyce is of course sociological: there is a vicious circle linking the two opposed worlds of the pub, where one gets drunk with one's male friends so as to be granted a short moment of triumph and fraternity, and the bleak family life in which the nagging wife and the hungry children bring back the breadwinner to a more somber appreciation of the realities of life. The circularity of the mechanism is condensed in the story's title: "Counterparts" refers less to our possibilities of imaginative empathy with a destitute and alienated man than to the social mechanism in which the family economy (*oikos*) and political economy buttress each other. Such a circular mechanism defuses the ethical spark contained in anger and perverts it. Thus, one might even assert that "Counterparts" contains its own Dantean parallels: what is hinted, behind the obvious exchange of blows, is

Dante's system of retribution beyond death, the famous "Contrapasso" or the law of punishments that somehow repeat the sins accomplished in the world of the living. As Farrington surmises, Mr. Alleyne is going to make his life in the office a living hell: "He felt savage and thirsty and revengeful, annoyed with himself and with everyone else. Mr Alleyne would never give him an hour's rest; his life would be a hell to him" (D, 111). Indeed, part of the diffuse anger felt by Farrington stems from his awareness that he is already in a living hell.

Dante himself would quote Aristotle's *Nicomachean Ethics* in canto 11 of *Inferno* to characterize as the three sources of sin "incontinence, malice and mad bestiality" (1980, 99). Dante's *contrapasso* often entails, as has often been noted, a curious contagion, at times real and at times only metaphorical, between the torments described and Dante's own emotions. Thus, when he discovers the fifth circle of hell where the Wrathful are, he himself become furious and violently insults Filippo Argenti. What interests Joyce in fact is the imaginative leap made again and again by Dante so as to understand from within the ethical logic of damnation. This reaching out to characters, however mean or unpleasant they may be, entails elaborating a whole phenomenology of anger and of its perversion.

As Sartre had noted in the early essay "The Emotions: A Sketch of a Theory" (1939), it is often my body that tells me that I am undergoing a strong emotion: if a wild animal comes toward me, I get pale, my legs tremble, and only then do I know that I have experienced fear. If this situation is the case in *Lawd Today* and "Counterparts," the body will have to carry most of the weight of the text. This point can be easily demonstrated and would take too long to do in detail, but one can observe in both texts a similar strategy that consists in splicing the mechanical and the organic themes: men become machines, as we have already seen, but all these machines speak of aggression and alienation. Given the principle of machinic circularity, anger is just the first mover in a series of equivalents that follow an unconscious logic of supplementarity or fictionality. This logic of substitutions and displacements has been analyzed by Lacan about Joyce.

It was Joyce's management of anger that seemed to interest Lacan in the yearlong seminar that he devoted to Joyce. In the last meeting of Le Sinthome, Lacan focused on what he saw as a peculiar structure of the Joycean ego. He took his cue from a passage of *A Portrait of the Artist as a Young Man,* when Stephen muses and calls up a painful incident. Earlier, a few friends from school had tormented him because he had claimed that Byron was the greatest poet of all. The others viciously lashed at him until he was overcome by anger. Sobbing and clenching his fists, he chased them. Suddenly, he felt his anger recede, literally fall from him in a curious moment of subjective dispossession. The analysis acquires more validity from the fact that Stephen only remembers a scene and does not experience it in the present, but what he remembers most precisely concerns the fading of his anger: "He had not forgotten a whit of their cowardice and cruelty but the memory of it called forth no anger from him. All the descriptions of fierce love and hatred which he had met in books had seemed to him therefore unreal. Even that night as he stumbled homewards along Jones's road he had felt that some power was divesting him of that suddenwoven anger as easily as a fruit is divested of its soft ripe peel" (*P,* 69).[1] Lacan comments on this scene by insisting that such transformation of anger into indifference or disgust is suspect for a psychoanalyst. He sees in this short scene the model of the Joycean body: a body that can fall from one's self as a mere envelope that cannot really hold the subject. Joyce's ego would constitute a "peel," a mere rim that is loosely captured by the Imaginary. It is labile, porous, artificial, and can be dropped just like that. For Joyce, then, as a consequence, the Real is not knotted to the Unconscious but emerges in symptoms.

The knot performed by a writing that supplements a paternal defect will therefore assume an essential function. "What I am suggesting is that, for Joyce, the ego intervenes to correct a missing link. Through this artifice in writing, I say that the Borromean knot can be reconstituted" (Lacan 1977, 152). The concept of the ego that is proposed is not therefore a "natural" one: on the contrary, it is even more artificial than before, but it cannot be reduced to the register of the Imaginary. One should not be worried too much by the fact that Lacan speaks of Stephen as if he were Joyce himself— what interests him is a structure of the body, a Joycean body that is evidently shared by the character and the author.

---

1. Lacan's close reading of this passage can be found in Lacan 2005, 149–50.

Thus, Joyce's ego ends up replacing the Sigma of the Symptom. Joyce's ego would be an effect of his writing, as such identified with his Symptom. The reasoning is as follows: originally, there had been a mistake in the knotting of the three registers of the Real, the Imaginary, and the Symbolic. In order to compensate the error, the ego—in Lacan's drawing it is represented by double square brackets—plays the role of a clamp that keeps the circles together. "What I am suggesting is that with Joyce, the ego comes to correct the missing relation. By such an artifice of writing, the Borromean knot is reconstituted" (ibid., 8). Joyce's ego as symptom is a creative artifice, a beautiful "supplement" by which all of Joyce's riddles turn into writing while reattaching the main structure of subjectivity.

This structure has affinities with the behavior of the saint or of whoever will identify strongly with Christ as the Savior. We see this tendency in Stephen's evolution depicted in *A Portrait of the Artist as a Young Man*, when the young man believes that he has "amended" his life and has rejected mortal sin altogether by countless spiritual exercises: "His prayers and fasts availed him little for the suppression of anger at hearing his mother sneeze or at being disturbed in his devotions. It needed an immense effort of his will to master the impulse which urged him to give outlet to such irritation. Images of the outbursts of trivial anger which he had often noted among his masters, their twitching mouths, closeshut lips and flushed cheeks, recurred to his memory, discouraging him, for all his practice of humility, by the comparison" (*P*, 127–28). This passage confirms Lacan's reading, since here Stephen's management of anger uses two weapons: first a negative identification, which works via imaginary representations of other people caught in flushed or contorted expressions, and then the distance afforded by memory as it immediately introduces a mediation between the subject and the outburst of an irrepressible emotion.

Such a management of anger would underpin Bloom's surprising equanimity in "Ithaca." Instead of being swept away by justified anger at the discovery of traces that all attest to Molly's recent infidelity, he muses instead on the law of series and mathematical probabilities. We know that, caught in a similar situation, James Joyce gave full vent to his anger and slapped his alleged "rival" Prezioso in the full light of a Trieste street. In the autobiographical reconstitution provided by the *Portrait*, memory and identifications function as a double projection of fantasy. Which does not mean that Farrington was Joyce's projection, or Jake Wright's later ego. They are the bearers of an almost anonymous fantasy of violence enacted upon a defenseless child or woman, a fantasy that, like Freud's famous example, can revolve around the central image of "a child is being beaten." The question is not, "Whose fantasy is it?" but, "What grammar of fantasy can these texts allow us to elaborate?"

The lack of any redemption at the ending of both texts shows that we cannot fully identify either with Jake or with Farrington. We cannot identify any more with the beaten ones like Lil or Tom. The reader, like Tom, may well feel that he or she has been wounded or "cut" by the sadistic "cane" wielded by the text. The "cut" of castration, foregrounded by the silent ending of the text and marking a certain material limit, expels the male subject from a female world in which empty religious consolation still dominates. Finally, the assertion Joyce and Wright probe is, "I do not need to be angry at my anger, if I can learn from my anger and find in it some lever to change the conditions of my hellish life." What Tom will be forcibly taught will be either to follow in the steps of his father and become a bully for his own children later or to renounce the pious world of devotion that passed as a refuge from universal violence and learn to cope with it productively. Will he then join the violent strikes of 1913 before entering into armed struggle against the British? At least, "Counterparts" provides a very sobering critical appraisal that permits a deeper understanding of the roots of Easter 1916, of doomed violence aiming at converting its self-destructive aspect into a more positive political future.

"Counter," *by Jim Hansen*

What Does Farrington Want? The Machine
of Missed Pleasure in "Counterparts"

It should be noted that a clue may be found in the clear alienation that leaves to the subject the favor of stumbling upon the question of its essence, in that he cannot fail to recognize that what he desires presents itself to him as what he does not want, the form assumed by the negation in which the misrecognition [*méconnaissance*] of which he himself is unaware is inserted in a very strange way—a misrecognition by which he

transfers the permanence of his desire to an ego that is nevertheless inter-
mittent, and, inversely, protects himself from his desire by attributing to it
these very intermittences.
—Jacques Lacan, "The Subversion of the Subject
and the Dialectic of Desire in the Freudian Unconscious"

When I teach Joyce's "Counterparts," I begin by asking my students the
question that constitutes the first half of the title of this essay. What
precisely does Farrington, the hypermasculine, intensely aggressive, overly
embodied, hard-drinking copy clerk from the ninth story of *Dubliners*, really
want? Where is his pleasure located? In response, the students quickly come
up with a list of Farrington's desires. Inevitably, some of the items on the
list are activities, and some are states of mind. Farrington wants to strike
his boss, Mr. Alleyne. He wants to be seen as heroic by his coworkers and
friends. He wants to drink enough alcohol to escape reality. He wants to
get away from work as quickly as possible. He wants to win a physical confrontation with the Englishman Weathers. He wants an evening of homosocial bonding. Farrington clearly experiences some form of pleasure when
he fantasizes about hitting Mr. Alleyne, about getting drunk, about beating
Weathers, and about being the hero of an evening of male conviviality, but
he never actually realizes even one of these desires in material form. He does
not strike Mr. Alleyne. He does not achieve intoxication. He does not beat
Weathers. In fact, despite paying for many rounds of drinks, he does not
even end up as the hero of the evening with his friends. These desires always
remain at the level of fantasy for Farrington. What he wants he does not get,
and it seems that what he gets he does not want. For the few pages that we
know him, Farrington seems to be a man devoid of pleasure. Following Jean-
Michel Rabaté's suggestion in the first part of this essay, we might say that
what Farrington wants most is to be angry and that, reflexively, Joyce wants
to make the readers as angry as Farrington. Farrington certainly experiences
impotent rage, and the readers of the story are likely to be angry with him
when he mercilessly beats his innocent son at the story's conclusion. As I
have argued elsewhere, a strange kind of cyclical, self-fulfilling, self-defeating *ressentiment* seems built into the anger that drives Irish masculinity (see

Hansen 2009). As Rabaté rightly indicates, the outrage that we encounter in most of the texts that we read every day, texts ranging from newspaper articles to serious pieces of fiction, nearly always longs to present itself as a justifiable form of anger. Does Farrington also experience some form of pleasure in the very impotence of his rage? Do we? Eventually, amid all of this speculation, one of the students in the class will come up with the idea that what Farrington wants is to be in control of his own life.

Of course, the question "What does Farrington want?" is something of a ruse, a trap that I have drawn from Jacques Lacan's famous rethinking of desire in "The Subversion of the Subject and the Dialectic of Desire in the Freudian Unconscious." In the essay, Lacan uses the question "Che vuoi?" roughly translated into English as "What do you want?" to indicate that one's fantasy-desire is never one's own but actually always the desire of the Other (1977, 312). In Lacan's version of desire, fantasy is always a staging of the Other's desire. Fantasy involves a subject attempting to imagine what precisely the Other desires. So the question that we must ask ourselves, as Lacan and as one of his more Marxian interpreters, Slavoj Žižek, present it, is never really "What do I want?" but rather "What does the Other want from me?" From both the Lacanian and the Žižekian perspectives, this question exposes the subject's psychic insufficiency. To put it another way, I want to believe that I, as a subject, determine the objects that I desire. When I ask "What do others want from me?" in order to calculate how I should behave and what type of individual I should be, I also, unwittingly, admit that my private, internal desires are always tailored to fit a psychosocial schema or to please a symbolic big Other. In a sense, then, my desires are neither private nor internal. Hence, by asking the question "What do others want from me?" I witness that central myth of modern consciousness, the one that allows me to believe that I choose what I desire, melt into air.

Whenever a student in my class makes the very astute claim that Farrington wants nothing so much as control over his own life, over his own identity, then the trap that I have set for the class (and the one that Joyce has set for all of us) has been sprung, and we can go on to talk of the ideological problem of Farrington's desires and of why his desires can never really link up with what Lacan refers to in "Aggressivity and Psychoanalysis" as the subject's "experienced identity" (ibid., 20). That is, we can go on to discuss why Farrington is not in control of his own life, and, simultaneously, we can discuss why his desires, determined by a psychosocial schema and by the stylistic maneuvers of the text itself, actually militate against his ever being autonomous or "in control."

When Is Your Desire Not Your Desire?

"Counterparts" observes the interconnected psychic and ideological structure of Farrington's lack of control over—or his misrecognition of—his own desire. One of the more remarkable things about the text is that it stages this drama both at the level of content, where we witness Farrington struggling with himself and with the consumer capitalism of modern Dublin, and at the level of form, where we watch as the stylistic techniques of Joyce's story challenge the idea of the subject's autonomy at the same time that they articulate, precisely, the subject's insistent demand for that autonomy. The following passage from the story may be taken as a case in point:

> The chief clerk began to hurry Miss Parker, saying she would never have the letters typed in time for post. The man listened to the clicking of the machine for a few minutes and then set to work to finish his copy. But his head was not clear and his mind wandered away to the glare and rattle of the public-house. It was a night for hot punches. He struggled on with his copy, but when the clock struck five he had still fourteen pages to write. Blast it! He couldn't finish it in time. He longed to execrate aloud, to bring his fist down on something violently. . . . He felt strong enough to clear out the whole office single-handed. His body ached to do something, to rush out and revel in violence. All the indignities of his life enraged him. . . . Could he ask the cashier privately for an advance? No, the cashier was no good, no damn good: he wouldn't give an advance. . . . He knew where he would meet the boys: Leonard and O'Halloran and Nosey Flynn. The barometer of his emotional nature was set for a spell of riot. (*D,* 109)

At the level of content, we see Farrington, referred to here with the anonymous title "the man," both listening to a typing machine as it clicks away and setting to work making a counterpart, a document that constitutes a facsimile of an original document (see Lloyd 2000, 128–49, especially

145–46). He is a copier copying out copies. He may even constitute a coun-terpart of some original notion of masculinity, but his desires also appear to orient the passage. He wants to be at the public house. He wants a "night of hot punches." He wants enough money to allow him and his circle of male companions a long evening of drinking. But even as those desires become more and more apparent, we also see him, almost unconsciously, comparing himself both to the machine that clicks away in order to reproduce a let-ter, and to Miss Parker, who, like Farrington, appears under the sway of an employer who fears that a copied letter will not be finished on time. Though Farrington is at once the man whose perspective guides the story and the figure for masculinity in it, he develops as both a desiring ego and a cog in the capitalist machine. In other words, he seems like a textbook case of alien-ation, a man whose labor quite simply does not get him what he desires. But he also clearly struggles with the fact that he is at once an anonymous object, a veritable machine-man, and a male individual who, at least on the surface, desires autonomy and control.

Moreover, he also recognizes his similitude with Miss Parker, a woman secretary at the office. Not only are his desires apparently on hold because of his job as a machinelike copier, but his identity also elicits comparison with a woman, and Farrington, "the man," clearly seems to put a good deal of stock in his own masculinity and in his capacity for physical force. His status as feminized object in the passage militates against his desire for control. In fact, the primary tension of the story measures out Farrington's struggle to sublimate his feminized, objectified identity and to realize his abiding desire to be an admired male subject. He can never quite separate these identities, either, and, as we will go on to see, even his concept of masculinity is a thor-oughly objectified one.

At the level of form, the text reinforces this dynamic. By using the Flau-bertian style of free-indirect discourse, Joyce sets us within Farrington's perspective without allowing the character himself to have any real agency or control. Though we certainly experience Farrington's thoughts in a shad-owy way when the narrative voice exclaims "Blast" or "No, the cashier was no good," Farrington himself is never a first-person narrator. In addition, we cannot readily attribute these explosive interjections to the narrator, either. They exist in a borderland between narrator and character. No one assumes full control of either the world of the story or Farrington's reactions to that world. This technique works throughout the narrative—and throughout the entirety of *Dubliners*—to position us close to subjects who can never really speak directly to us, subjects who want to say "I," but rarely ever can. In fact, the stylistic effect of free-indirect discourse in general has led Martin Jay to refer to the method as presenting us with "experience without a subject" (1998). We get to experience action, plot, and development, but the notion of agency itself is withdrawn by the technique of free-indirect discourse. Via this technique, then, the story itself appears to lack a controlling, orienting consciousness.

To underscore this technique in "Counterparts," Joyce often reduces Farrington, like the clicking typewriting machine, to a collection of nonautonomous, bodily reactions. We see that "his head was not clear and his mind wandered away," that his "body ached to do something, to rush out and revel in violence," and, in perhaps the most dehumanizing terms deployed thus far, that the "barometer of his emotional nature was set for a spell of riot." In these sentences we witness bodily actions removed from the fiction of an originating or authorizing subjective consciousness. Farrington emerges as a nonautonomous object, continually referred to as a "heavy," "great body," and he cannot even seem to "keep his tongue" under control (*D*, 118, 111). By slowly reducing Farrington to a body, an object that appears devoid of coherent consciousness, a body that remains at the whim of competing, conflicting, unfocused "wants," the stylistic technique of "Counterparts" presents us with a limited perspective that desires, a perspective that can never realize those desires, and a perspective that forcefully misrecognizes those desires as singular, as issuing from a coherent ego, as realizable, and as consistent with each other. On the surface, it appears as though Farrington believes merely—though quite forcefully—that his desires are constantly frustrated by the vicissitudes of his world. In fact, the story's balancing of his perspective with free-indirect discourse also allows us to see, and to some extent to share, his impotent rage at a world that always frustrates desire. From the point of view of the psychoanalytic ideological critique offered to us by Žižek's various reinterpretations of Lacan, however, we might say that Farrington's pleasure is located elsewhere and that, in some perverse way, something about this state of impotent rage—his object status—must appeal to him, must meet some need for him. In fact, if we take the Lacanian view of desire seriously, we might even go so far as to say that Farrington's desires are not really "his." In modern capitalist societies, after all, ideology is the condition of possibility for the subject and its fantasies.

What Farrington Wants

Žižek's essay "'Che Vuoi?'" builds an excursus on ideology into the Lacanian question of desire, the "What do you want?" that orients desire toward the Other.[2] To some extent, Žižek's ideological reading of desire is staked on a notion of identity. That is to say, in any given ideological field, we identify ourselves via our answer to the question, *"Che vuoi?"* Of course, you can identify with the perspective that regards you—with the so-called symbolic order or "big Other"—or with the imaginary and the object that you believe the big Other to find desirable. In the first case, the subject overidentifies with the Other and, so desires what he or she imagines the Other would desire. For Žižek's version of psychoanalytic ideology critique, this identification with the symbolic order is called the "ego-ideal" (1989, 105). In the second case, the subject identifies with—and as—an object of desire and, so, models the self on a conception of that object. In the Žižekian language, this identification with the imaginary is referred to as the "ideal-ego" (ibid.). In either event, the subject does not choose the object of desire directly because that object is, in effect, determined by an ideological and psychosocial field. The field itself might be arbitrary, but something makes it appear as fixed and certain. As Žižek explains, in this dynamic the subject is represented for a signifier, or, in other words, the ostensibly free-floating signifier "assumes concrete, recognizable shape in a name or in a mandate that the subject takes upon himself and/or that is bestowed on him" (ibid., 104). Even in order to achieve identification, the subject must necessarily alienate him- or herself and imagine that the desire of the big Other is, in some fashion, his or her own. This experience, as Žižek tells us, is the subject's way to "misrecognize his radical dependence on the big Other, on the symbolic order as his decentered cause" (ibid.).

2. See in particular "Identification" (Žižek 1989, 100–110).

When we apply Žižek's psychoanalytic theory of ideology to Farrington, we run up against a problem, a kind of tension between the ego-ideal and ideal-ego. If the ego-ideal is an overidentification with the big Other and the ideal-ego is an identification with an object that the big Other might find desirable, then where does Farrington fit into this schema? On first glance he might appear to prefer the ego-ideal. As an intensely masculine subject who seeks control over his life and revels in violence, Farrington certainly appears to have identified with the big Other, with the system of power that makes subjects and holds them in place. He wants to identify himself with masculinity and with the power of physical force. But, if we think back to most of his desires—his desire to imagine himself as a hero, his desire to have a reputation as "a strong man," his desire to be thought witty, his desire to be seen as the champion of the evening—we observe in Farrington a penchant for identifying as an object of desire, as a man who is liked and admired by his cohort. Does he want what he perceives the big Other to want? Does he want to run the office? Does he want to tell everyone what to do? Though he appears to long for autonomy, he does not really want to be in charge of anything, least of all his own life, hence his desire to escape from it via drink. So his ego-ideal remains in tension with his ideal-ego. He longs for autonomy, but he seeks it precisely by imagining himself as an object that is physically and socially—and, of course, in a deeply masculine way—homosocially desirable. His pleasure comes from imagining himself as a version of "man." He desperately wants to be admired, and this desire takes precedence over and, in fact, takes the place of his desire for autonomy. In effect, he wants his ideal-ego to make him into an ego-ideal. He wants to imagine that he controls the big Other by becoming the object of desire. He performs a certain masculinity in order to be liked and admired, and his pleasure comes from being an admired object. He is firmly an ideal-ego who has misrecognized himself as an ego-ideal, and this tension seems to pull him apart at the same time that it allows him to have an identity in the first place.

We see this tension played out in an overtly ideological way in the encounter with the young Englishman Weathers. By this late point in his evening Farrington has already been embarrassed by Mr. Alleyne, he has already been forced to admit this embarrassment to his friends, and he has already pawned his watch to pay for several rounds of drinks. At the pub, Farrington temporarily loses the attention of his fellows when they are all joined by Weathers, an acrobat and performer who shows off his biceps and talks to the company about "feats of strength" (*D*, 116). The Englishman refers to the hospitality at the pub, and particularly to Farrington's purchasing of rounds of drinks, as "too Irish" (*D*, 114). In "Counterparts: *Dubliners*, Masculinity, and Temperance Nationalism," David Lloyd indicates that the reference to a hospitality that is "too Irish" underscores the problem of alcoholism in Ireland and of how "drinking practices remain a critical site for the performance of Irish masculinity" (2000, 133). When Farrington, the resident strongman, is called upon to "uphold the national honour" (*D*, 116), the colonial implications of this particular ideological encounter become quite clear. At the same time that he symbolizes a controlled exhibition of imperial identity and power, the much-admired Weathers also competes with—and eventually usurps—Farrington's role as the admired male, as the object of homosocial desire. Within the story, the Englishman Weathers emerges as both an object of desire and a subject controlling others. Moreover, as he defeats Farrington in two consecutive arm-wrestling matches, Weathers also demonstrates, however briefly, the capacity to control and manipulate Farrington's own body, a feat that even Farrington himself struggles with. At this point in the text, Farrington's fury mounts as he recognizes that his friends at the pub seem to admire Weathers even more than they admire him.

As we have explored it thus far, the tension for Farrington has been between his misrecognized ego-ideal and his ideal-ego. He hopes to gain control over his life and environment by becoming the desired hypermasculine object. When Weathers intervenes, Farrington observes a man who appears to constitute both an object of desire and a subject controlling others. The young Englishman seems to have achieved precisely the balance that Farrington lacks. At least in Farrington's eyes, Weathers becomes the sublime subject/object of colonial ideology, and in the Englishman's shadow, Farrington feels, as we are told, "humiliated and discontented" (*D*, 117). From this perspective, Weathers gives the impression of having realized an identification with the big Other and with the object desired by the Other. He is both a controlling masculine subject and the male object that all the others desire. The apparent tension between ego-ideal and ideal-ego does not pull Weathers apart as it does Farrington. We are limited here precisely by the free-indirect discourse of Joyce's text. We are caught between Farrington's perspective and the psychosocial truth of his situation, and without either a secure first-person perspective or a secure third-person narrator, we cannot see Weathers with any real clarity. Colonial interpellation is written into the story at the level of form, in other words. Of course, as we know from both Lacan and Žižek, there is always a lack in the Other. The Other would make no demand on us if it did not lack something. As Žižek explains in "'Che Vuoi?'" even the Other has not gotten the object of desire; even the Other has not achieved self-identity (1989, 122).

In "Counterparts," however, Farrington believes that Weathers has achieved precisely the balance that he himself lacks. If Farrington imagines a "man" as someone who revels in violence, as someone who is a hero to his fellows, and as someone who is a physical marvel, controlling the bodies of others, then he cannot achieve identity—and so pleasure—when he faces Weathers at the bar. He cannot become the object of desire and hence imagine himself as a subject. That is, he cannot even be an ideal-ego who has misrecognized himself as an ego-ideal. So, as the text explains, "he was full of smouldering anger and revengefulness. . . . He cursed everything. He had done for himself in the office, pawned his watch, spent all his money; and he had not even got drunk. He began to feel thirsty again and he longed to be back again in the hot reeking public-house. He had lost his reputation as a strong man, having been defeated twice by a mere boy. His heart swelled with fury (D, 117).

It is tempting to interpret this incident as leading to a potentially life-changing decision for Farrington. But as Farrington struggles to steer "his great body" home, the text reminds us that this drama is not really such a singular event in Farrington's life (D, 118). The narrative explains that Mrs. Farrington "was a little sharp-faced woman who bullied her husband when he was sober and was bullied by him when he was drunk," so it appears that the drama of returning home from the pub and abusing a family member is a regular occurrence here (D, 118). In fact, Farrington must have played out this little drama time and again. Having failed to be admired on the public stage—or the stage of the public house—having failed to receive pleasure as a male object of desire, he bullies the members of his family in private. When he discovers that his wife is not home, Farrington turns his rage on his son, Tom, another "mere boy." In beating this particular "mere boy," Farrington is finally able to imagine himself as a powerful man who can be feared and can control the body of another, but the trick of the whole scene is that in abusing his son, Farrington cannot be admired. Tom may act as a stand-in for Weathers, but beating Tom in the darkness of his home allows Farrington no pleasure. Finally, he does not make himself likable to others—or to the big Other—and he does not uphold the "national honour."

As the story draws to a close, Farrington transforms into a machine that perpetually misses out on the pleasure it seeks, and the fact that this drama of domestic abuse seems to play out again and again in the Farrington household implies that he will remain just such a machine, continually reproducing this structure of missed pleasure, continually failing to be the admired man. From another perspective, one more conducive to Rabaté's argument, we might say that Farrington finally takes a certain kind of perverse pleasure in the cyclical and impotent structure of his own outrage. Of course, this kind of pleasure always plays directly into the hands of whatever big Other we have imagined for ourselves. But whatever point we choose to argue, it seems clear that rather than balancing an ideal-ego with an ego-ideal, as Weathers appears to do, Farrington fails to be either. So, the psychic problem of the text is not merely that Farrington's desires are inconstant or that he merely fails to achieve them. It is just that they are not really his at all. Instead, they constitute an objectified notion of masculinity, an ideological concept of the masculine that is undercut by Farrington's position as laborer, as copier, and as a feminized, colonized object. At the conclusion of the story, Farrington's explosive rage actually represents both his inability to control his life and his desires and his persistent alienation from his own identity. Of course, through the use of the free-indirect discourse that divests the subject in the story and the subject reading the story of autonomy, Joyce has made us all into Farrington's counterparts, as well. We experience the alienation of not quite being able to realize our desires—or even to realize that they are not quite our own.

10

Working with Clay

GABRIELLE CAREY AND BARBARA LONNQUIST

Our title, "Working with Clay," which conjures the image of an artist with his or her materials gradually giving shape to a whole, is an apt representation of the collaboration between a fiction writer, Gabrielle Carey, who creates with words, and an academic, Barbara Lonnquist, whose creative pursuit lies in trying to plumb their often secret life. The process of reading this story in a dialogue, which occurred in various stages, with some long breaks, and across continents and time zones, seems a fitting response to Joyce's project in "Dubliners" of inspiring reading as a cycle of interrogation and rereading. Gabrielle's "celebration of the naive reading" pointed to the timelessness of "Dubliners," which, although culturally specific and grounded in the historical context of turn-of-the-last-century Ireland, had the power to speak to a young woman in Australia many decades later. With the eye of a creative writer, she was quick to catch the luminous detail or quirk of character that gave the story its human appeal. The academic reader, drawn in by Joyce's verbal play, which opens up multiple possible readings, found liberation in the doubling of "Dubliners." The process of balancing these two approaches has led to a mutual interrogation of not only Maria's story within "Clay" but our own preconceptions about her plight.

In Celebration of the Naive Reading, *by Gabrielle Carey*

I first read *Dubliners* at the age of twenty-two, seven years after I had dropped out of high school, and a year after the publication of my first book. I knew immediately that I had come across something extraordinary. But why and how did a collection of stories about Dublin at the turn of the century have such an impact on a young Australian so many decades after its publication? What meaning could it have for a reader who had never been to Ireland, who was raised in an atheist family, and from a country where there is no tradition of Halloween?

"Clay" has been critiqued much in terms of its symbolism, clay itself being a symbol of death as well as the earth that surrounds a corpse upon burial. Clay also reflects the nature of the main character, Maria, dun-colored and malleable. But can we read this story without the symbols? As I read it all those years ago?

On reading "Clay" for the first time, I found the experience of the Catholic mass utterly foreign. I therefore had no way of interpreting the symbolism of the barmbrack as the host, or the tea among the laundry ladies as communion. Neither did I understand the significance of a Catholic woman working in a Protestant laundry; only recently did I become aware of the history of the Dublin laundries as a despository for fallen women and spinsters. And I completely missed the symbolism of "Dublin by Lamplight," failing to apprehend the withholding of light as a metaphor for the withholding of life, arguably the theme of the entire collection. Yet even though I was blind to all these cultural, historical, and religious references, the story was stubbornly poignant and powerful.

I suspect I am not alone in my first ignorant reading of "Clay." If I were to teach this story to Australian undergraduates now, they too would find the symbolism difficult to read. But the beauty of Joyce is that even an ignorant reading can be rewarding. Indeed, I wonder if we free ourselves of symbolism whether we can experience the story in a less abstract, far more concrete, and therefore more human way. What happens, for example, if we just consider the narrative in terms of character and nothing else? What sort of person is Maria?

If I asked my eighteen-year-old daughter to describe the character of Maria, she would offer one word: *loser*. Maria is a middle-aged, unmarried menial worker with few friends outside the laundry. Nervous, fearful, and unadventurous, she is clearly not much *craic*. But neither is she unlikable.

"Everyone was so fond of Maria" (*D*, 120). This statement comes early in the story and could be interpreted as a kind of establishing shot. But like so many of the statements in *Dubliners,* the reader is uncertain as to its source and veracity. Is everyone so fond of Maria really? Or is it how Maria herself wants to be thought of? Not passionately, not erotically; not as intriguing or cunning, or mysterious, but fondly.

Fond is the word one uses to describe a relationship that is friendly but not intimate, affectionate but not passionate. We are fond of great aunts and small dogs. There is a stability to the word that implies a constant and respectable distance, a relationship that has no risk of falling into either intimacy or adversity. It is, above all, a *safe* emotion.

The word *fond* has its roots in the word *foolish,* and it is hard to imagine that Joyce was not aware of this derivation. Were people fond of Maria in the way one might be fond of a fool? Maria certainly goes on in the story to make a fool of herself various times—while dithering indecisively in the cake shop, when getting flushed by the merest conversational exchange with a man, and then later in the evening, when she unconsciously omits a stanza from her song.

What else do we know of Maria's character? We are told that her role in the laundry is that of "peace-maker" (*D,* 120). Maria does not add heat or tension to a room; rather, she cools down quarrels by pouring soothing, cool counseling onto overheated washerwomen with "steaming hands" and "red steaming arms" (*D,* 122). But as she lowers the temperature by draining the situation of conflict, there is a sense that Maria also drains it of excitement. Her ability lies in *repressing* rather than expressing, and it is indicative of her entire life. Maria has repressed her attraction to men, repressed her sexuality, repressed her anger. It is the other washerwomen who fight, not she; she is not given to passion or rage. Ultimately, she has repressed all her deepest desires—emotional, physical, and spiritual—and she has done so, presumably, because she is modeling herself on her namesake, Mary, mother of Jesus.

At church every Sunday morning, which Maria attends unfailingly, Mary is portrayed without any individual, personal desires—certainly without sexual desires; she is merely a vessel through which the spirit enacts God's intentions. Mary is passive, the one who brings consolation, just as Maria does in the laundry when she speaks so "soothingly" to her agitated washerwomen.

Maria likes order. She also likes ordering. She enjoys her perfectly ordered barmbrack, so neatly cut that they "seemed uncut" (*D,* 120). She also likes overseeing the perfect distribution of the barmbrack, divided evenly among the laundry women. She even enjoys the orderliness of her own flesh, finding it "a nice tidy little body" (*D*, 123). Maria orders her own life, down to the smallest detail: "She arranged in her mind all she was going to do" (*D*, 123). Here is a woman who likes predictability, and when the unpredicted, unrehearsed meeting with a gentleman in the tram ruptures her well-laid plans, Maria is so flustered that she forgets the special gift for her hosts. If only the unruliness of life did not have to intrude on her well-ordered arrangements!

Maria's sense of self is negligible. Above all, she does not want to impose or be a bother. She particularly does not want to display any desires or tastes that might lead to such sins as lust or gluttony. When the nutcracker cannot be found, Maria immediately claims she does not like nuts, although we know from earlier in the story that when she is considering buying something "really nice" for the party, the idea of nuts crosses her mind and is then discounted because "They would be sure to have plenty of apples and nuts" (*D*, 124). "Something nice" therefore is associated with nuts; we might even assume she was quietly looking forward to nuts. But rather than express an appetite for something tasty, sensual, and nourishing, she instructs her host "that they weren't to bother about her" (*D*, 126), as though, because she is so small and insignificant, she is barely there at all.

Maria does not want anyone bothering about her because this might imply she has *needs*. Maria is proud of the fact that she has no needs—either financial (she has her "own money" [*D*, 123] in her pocket) or emotional (people go to *her* for consolation; she does not need to seek consolation in anyone else) or physical (she does not want nuts, and "she would rather they didn't ask her to take anything" [*D*, 126] in the way of liquor). The only point in the story where there is a semblance of human desire is when we learn that Joe had "often" "wanted her to go and live with them" (*D*, 121). And we strongly get the impression that Maria wants this too. Yet for some reason she cannot admit or perhaps permit herself such a desire. Is it because wanting, at least in a woman, is the equivalent to sin?

Maria cannot entertain going to live with Joe and his family because her fear in life, which is so much greater than her desire, is the thought that she might get "in the way" (*D*, 121). Getting in the way would be contrary to her self-image as independent, ordered, and self-sufficient. Her lack of self-knowledge and repression of desire are most poignantly demonstrated when she "forgets" the verse of the song that most expresses desire.

Maria is joined by Joe in her idealization of the past, particularly of the period when she played mother to Joe and Alphy. She and Joe sit "by the fire talking over old times" (*D*, 126). And Joe states that "there was no time like the long ago" (*D*, 129), which is, in a sense, literally true. The "long ago" that Joe remembers is indeed "no time" because it never existed. Rather, the long ago that he looks back to so affectionately is a fiction that he has imaginatively and selectively constructed.

Joe

Although Maria wants to think well of Joe—at the party she thinks she "had never seen Joe so nice to her as he was that night" (*D*, 128)—it seems that, in reality, Joe's behavior ranges from boastful to cantankerous. The first anecdote he tells Maria is how he got one over on the manager in his workplace. This story can have very little interest or amusement for Maria, who presumably does not know the manager or the office. Indeed, it seems that Joe is not telling the story for her sake but rather for his. In his public life, Joe evidently feels oppressed by his superior, which means that in his private life he needs to bolster himself, even to someone as unimportant as Maria. But when Maria sympathizes with him for having to work under such an "overbearing person" (*D*, 126), Joe wants to impress on her that he is, in fact, managing his manager, and he can do so because he "knew how to take him" and understood how to avoid "rub[bing] him the wrong way." In other words, Joe wants to assure Maria (and himself) that he is *in control*.

Joe's need to feel in control results in his being quickly irritated when the world behaves in a way that is clearly not under his control. Even his immediate family surroundings are disordered and beyond his control, as evidenced by the many things that go missing. When the nutcracker cannot be found, it is reported that "Joe was nearly getting cross over it" (*D*, 126), but then that "he would not lose his temper on account of the night it was" (*D*, 127). However, it is clear that the special night does not prevent him from losing his temper because when the name Alphy is mentioned, it is reported that "Joe cried that God might strike him stone dead if ever he spoke a word to his brother again" (*D*, 127). At this point in the party the spirit of celebration and goodwill turns to a moment of raw bitterness and resentment. We also learn that Joe and his wife argue when she criticizes him for speaking "that way of his own flesh and blood" (*D*, 127). Again, the account of what happened tells us that there was "nearly a row" (*D*, 127) when the evidence seems to suggest that there definitely *was* a row.

The exclamatory claim at the beginning of the story that Maria is "a veritable peace-maker" (*D*, 120) is unhappily contradicted at the party when she "thought she would put in a good word for Alphy" (*D*, 126). This decisive opinion offering from Maria is one of the very few moments when she acts rather than reacts and is almost out of character. (Was she slightly inebriated by the drink that Joe insisted she imbibe—port, wine, or stout? Again, we don't know for certain.) Maria is poorly recompensed for her well-meaning intervention. Instead of promoting peace between the brothers, she inspires violent curses.

Joe is clearly deeply disturbed by the thought of his brother, and the anger that is so easily aroused is obviously still warm. The fight between Joe and Alphy, which has led to the loss of his only sibling, must be a source of terrible grief. And the brother's absence at a family gathering like Halloween, particularly with Maria present, must be palpable. Maria may represent happier times when the brothers played together. One cannot help suspecting that Joe uses the sentimentality of the song as a cover up, yet another blindfold, to conceal the real cause of his tears. The apparent irreconcilable nature of the division is yet another unknown story, a story so repressed and unspeakable that when Maria invokes Alphy's name, Joe cries out to God to strike him down. The "long ago" that Joe yearns for is a censored time; some memories are to be remembered, others erased.

Which brings us to the question of *who* exactly is giving this account. Whose version of the evening are we hearing? Who is the narrator? And to whom is she or he narrating? It is tempting to think, at least at this point of the story, that we are being encouraged to see events from Maria's point of view. She is so sympathetic with her surrogate son and so keen to maintain her prearranged vision of her much-anticipated evening that she does not want to admit to herself or her audience—perhaps the women back at the laundry who must be keen to hear the story of her night out?—that Joe lost his temper, maybe even more than once, and possibly ruined the entire evening. If the story's narrator is indeed Maria, it is a narrator who is unaware of her tendency to retell the story in a way that conforms more with her ideal than the actual reality. (Events as retold by witnesses resulting in many different versions of the same event remind us of the many different tales about HCE's crime in *Finnegans Wake*.) Although it is reported that Joe is "full of pleasant talk and reminiscences" (*D*, 128), it is clear that he is also guilty of much unpleasant talk, not only about his brother but also about his manager, as well as a few cross words with his wife. Indeed, Joe's general manner appears to be quite irritable; he is irritated by the missing nutcracker and by his wife's comments, and the irritation then spreads to Mrs. Donnelly when she is annoyed by one of the girls from next door and says "something very cross" (*D*, 128).

All in all, despite the attempt to stage a happy Halloween evening, there have been disappointments, losses, fights, irritation, and, in the end, tears. Despite Joe's blustering and his need for control, it is he who, under the influence of alcohol, music, and melancholy, truly loses control. Blinded by sentiment as a result of Maria's rendition of "I Dreamt That I Dwelt in Marble Halls," Joe cannot find what he is looking for. What he is looking for is much more than the corkscrew. Joe is looking for a happy family and an amiable reunion with his nanny. Instead, the evening has been marked by uneasiness, and Joe perhaps realizes that the place in which he really wants to dwell is not his home at all but some other, imagined, dreamed-up dwelling—a dwelling of desires realized, of riches and servants, of hope and status, and, most of all, love reciprocated.

Although the narrator may be attempting to give an honest account— why else include the embarrassing incident about losing the cake?—it is clear that the story is being told without Maria's genuine apprehension of the meaning of the events. Maria is blind, just as she is blindfolded, to the desperate sadness of her unrealized life, just as Joe is blinded by his own tears.

The true or higher consciousness of the story is, of course, Joyce's. He is painfully aware, just as he makes his readers aware, of both Maria's and Joe's stultified lives. But he has channeled that awareness through his character *despite* her lack of awareness.

In "Clay" Joyce has achieved his ambition of being the God-like, nail-paring artist. Yet this achievement does not equate with the total effacement of the narrator. Rather, the narrator has entirely assimilated Maria's voice and point of view—and life—into his own. The commanding or controlling hand of the author is gone; instead, the author and the narrator are one. Critics might call this "free-indirect discourse"; a better word might be *transubstantiation*.

Joyce's achievement is that while allowing himself to be subsumed into Maria's consciousness, into Maria's interior world, and while allowing the reader to see her repressions, her naïveté, and her self-conceit, he is simultaneously allowing us to see *through* them. The miracle is that we end up loving the character—not in spite of these failings, but because of them.

Reading Hints and Secrets, *by Barbara Lonnquist*

If reading *Dubliners* is, as Vicki Mahaffey and Michael Groden have suggested, a journey into a "grief-wracked city" (see "Silence and Fractals in 'The Sisters'"), it seems that not only hope but feeling itself is an endangered commodity. Nowhere, perhaps, as Gabrielle has demonstrated above, does the sense of repressed emotion strike us more poignantly than in "Clay." As we move from initial impressions of what the narrative tells us to questioning the elements elided by this "narration under a blindfold," as Margot Norris has named it, we begin to appreciate the unspoken and seemingly unspeakable emotions repressed not only by a character all too easily dismissed as one of Dublin's insignificant inhabitants who stand outside of history but by readers as well. Rereading "Clay," we become more than simply curious about the enigmatic Maria: we are struck by the sense of namelessness pervading her narrative, from the clay that is never actually named in the story proper to the unsung second stanza of Maria's song at the climax of the story. Such textual repressions hint at some larger emotion haunting the laughter that "nearly shook [Maria's minute body] asunder" (*D*, 122), threatening the order with which she has, for years, regulated her life. Gabrielle saw in Maria's need for order, from her skilled cutting of the barmbrack so that it seemed uncut to her careful planning of the minute details of the evening, a parallel to her need to regulate her own flesh. Mutual consideration of the things that cannot be deciphered with certainty in this narrative, even with the arsenal of critical approaches now available to a reader, challenges us to reckon with what is ultimately the unknowable story beneath this "deceptively simple" Halloween tale (Norris 2003, 140).

From the start, Maria's lack of a surname distinguishes her from the other adults in the collection. If it underscores the absence of a male protector (father or husband) and consequent lack of social significance in patriarchal, Catholic Ireland, it also portrays her as a ghostly figure, lacking the particularity of a personal history—which has provoked allegorical readings of Maria as a Celtic crone, Mother Ireland, or Virgin Mary. The narrative introduces us to Maria in the aftermath of a past life, the full contours of which we can never discern. She is an aging spinster who was formerly "a nurse" for an allegedly middle-class Dublin family. The term *nurse,* presumably indicating she was a "nanny," recalls, not insignificantly perhaps, the name of one of Father Flynn's similarly sepulchral sisters, "Nannie," in the opening story of *Dubliners.* We meet Maria in her employment as a scullery maid in the "Dublin by Lamplight laundry," a Protestant establishment for fallen women that was part of the Magdalen movement for the reform of prostitutes in Victorian England and Ireland.

As the account of one evening opens, Maria anticipates her escape from her cloister, because "the matron had given her leave" (*D,* 120), a privilege that distinguishes her from the laundresses, actual "inmates" in such institutions, to journey across Dublin for the Hallows' Eve festivities at the home of Joe Donnelly, one of her former charges, where she modestly imagines a "nice evening" with "all the children singing" (*D,* 121). The childlike, almost storybook quality of the narration, much of which is delivered in free-indirect discourse, miming Maria's perspective, is at odds with Maria's intimations of pride in her independence, her value to the Donnellys, and her esteemed position in the laundry, where she has been pronounced by the matron to be a "veritable peace-maker" (*D,* 120). The matron's allusion to the gospel beatitude "Blessed are the peacemakers" provides the first ellipsis in the text: its unspoken response, "For they shall be called the children of God," ironically underscores Maria's status as one of Dublin's "unchosen" and hints at an arrested emotional development, not unlike that of her "nice tidy little body" (*D,* 123).

The trope of littleness that acts as a verbal motif throughout the story (Maria is first described as a "very, very small person" [*D*, 120]) correlates with her social insignificance as an unmarried and thus surplus woman in Ireland, where women outnumbered men in the wake of the Famine and subsequent emigration. Margot Norris's reading of "Clay" in "Narration under a Blindfold" focuses on Maria's repeated attempts in the narrative to compensate for her feeling of invisibility and insignificance. Maria's self-flattering belief "Everyone was so fond of Maria" (*D*, 120) seems overstated at best, planting seeds of doubt in the reliability of her testimony.

Gabrielle interrogated the irony in the word *fond* as signaling Maria's desire to draw an emotional boundary of "respectable distance" around herself that precludes her from being viewed as passionate or erotic. The original meaning of *fond* as "foolish" could not only foreshadow the errors she will make in the story—but perhaps also imply an error she has made in the past. Such gaps in the text both invite the reader to delve beneath the veneer of respectability Maria works so hard to maintain and beg the very questions they tempt us to ask—as if the narrative were asking us to abstain from abject curiosity in order to comprehend the existential emptiness of the socially marginalized adult masked beneath her childlike discourse. The setting of All Hallows' Eve (a revision of Joyce's first draft set on Christmas Eve) mirrors Maria's potential emptiness; as she ventures into the city outside her walls, she seems a hollowed rather than a hallowed Eve.

Maria's childlike anticipation of the festivities, however, only barely masks the adult "note of sadness" that emerges from beneath her laughter throughout the evening. When, before leaving for the party, the laundry inmates tease her about "getting the ring," a symbol of marriage in the divination games traditionally played on Halloween, "Maria had to laugh and say she didn't want a ring or any man either; and when she laughed her eyes sparkled with *disappointed* shyness and the tip of her nose nearly met the tip of her chin" (*D*, 127; emphasis added). Readers find themselves in a position similar to the situation of the young boy in "The Sisters" as he listens for coded meanings behind the ellipses in the adult conversations about a priest who we later discover was, like Maria, afflicted by disappointment (you could tell he was a "disappointed man" [*D*, 19]) and whose laughter, like hers, is the symptom that ultimately gave him away.

Gabrielle's first impression as a young woman in Australia encountering *Dubliners* chimes with my own "unannotated" introduction to *Dubliners* at about the same age, except that, prepared by a Catholic education, I was aware of the religious and liturgical codes operating in the text and particularly of Joyce's appropriation of the term *epiphany* for literary use; I thus approached the collection anticipating signature moments of realization even if they were fleeting or aborted, as in Eveline's recognition of her mother's "life of commonplace sacrifice ending in final craziness" (*D*, 31) or Mr. Duffy's rueful admission in "A Painful Case" that he had "withheld life" from Mrs. Sinico (*D*, 142). "Clay," however, stubbornly resisted the desire for revelation in a way that other narratives did not. It raised for me even then the possibility that the cover at work in the narrative (shielding character and reader alike) could be an unwonted form of authorial clemency on Joyce's part in an otherwise relentless exposure of Dublin's self-deluded. Was this "bandage" (as the blindfold is called in "Clay") shielding Maria from a realization, which, unaccompanied by the opportunity for change, could only prove devastating? And if so, why is the reader kept in the dark as well? In contrast with "Eveline," where, although the character is blinded by fear at the end, the narrative registers a perceivable verdict, "Clay" seems to collude with the silence of the other characters in the text who are reluctant to show Maria her mistakes.

Despite the valuable work of historicist criticism in recuperating the conditions in which Maria lives (the irony of a proper Catholic woman residing in a Protestant Magdalen house, for example, as an embarrassment that helps explain Maria's need for dignity) and of readings that deconstruct Maria's narrative strategies, the question of why this narrative perhaps more than others keeps the reader in the dark about the "real" Maria becomes an instructive one. The name of the laundry, "Dublin by Lamplight," based on historical reality, which Gabrielle reads as a metaphor for "the withholding of light" thematized throughout *Dubliners,* underscores the inscrutability at work within the narrative. If Joyce treats Maria as more than simply an allegorical figure, Gabrielle's reading asks precisely the right question: can we, by setting aside the symbolism that seems to "frame" her, recuperate a Maria who is less abstract, more complex, and thus more human?

Without ignoring the rich critical history of *Dubliners,* our reading investigates the possibilities raised by the "gnomonic" gaps in the text, which both "invite speculation and resist definite conclusions" (Bulson 2006, 37). We attempt to "work with" the narrative's insistence on Maria's right to privacy in "Clay" in a way that allows Maria's "otherness to remain other," as Derek Attridge has movingly advocated in "Touching Clay" (2000, 51).

Like many readers puzzled by the enigmatic Maria, Gabrielle asked if she is the boring spinster who evokes our pity, or is she *not* as dun-colored as she first appears in her "old brown raincloak" (*D,* 123)? (The raincloak is one of the many prophylactic images in *Dubliners* that shield its characters from life, as Zack Bowen has demonstrated.)[1] If Maria does in fact have something to hide, the narrative seems stubbornly resistant to exposing it, unlike other *Dubliners* stories, which gesture more noticeably toward their characters' troubled or even scandalous pasts, even if those warning signals come from dubious sources: Old Cotter ruminates on the "queerness" of the priest as a "peculiar case" in "The Sisters" (*D,* 10); Mahoney in "An Encounter" reacts instinctively to the threat of sexual perversion in the "queer old josser" (*D,* 30). Although "Clay," as Attridge notes, "demands more insistently than most stories, intense interpretive activity" (2000, 51), the narrative makes us complicit not only in its process of signification, but in its repressions as well. Attributing to Maria, an oddly jejune, older woman, an innocence at odds with her years perhaps perpetuates the idea that her lack of a significant history is her greatest problem.

The narrative consistently identifies Maria through what she lacks: her physical lack of stature, as an adult whose "toes barely touch the floor" in the tram, the plumcakes she loses en route to the party, and ultimately her omission of the second stanza of the aria she sings at the end of the night recalling suitors on bended knee. The general assumption of Maria's celibacy or her "sexually unmarked life," as Margot Norris has discreetly put it

---

1. Zack Bowen (1982) discusses a range of prophylactic images—raincoats, boots, umbrellas, and so on—that not only protect characters from the elements in Dublin but shield them from a more direct (and vital) contact with life as well.

(2003, 143), derives logically enough from numerous signals throughout the narrative: her spinster status and shy demeanor, her confusion when chatted up by the "colonel-looking gentleman" on the tram, the image of the Virgin Mary invoked by her name. Even the species of plants she tends with pride in the conservatory carry a suggestion of asexuality: ferns, nonflowering plants that reproduce by the formation of asexual spores, and wax plants, whose cuttings she shares in another form of asexual reproduction (*D*, 121). The scientific names of these plants, however, caution against a monolithic read-ing. The fern, classified as a "vascular cryptogam," a name derived from the Latin *cryptos* (hidden) and *gamia* (marriage), points to some kind of sexual secret. Similarly, the wax plant, a member of the *milk*weed family, bears the name *Hoya carnosa*, derived from the Latin root for *flesh* (*carn*) (Storn-month 1885).² And although the church maintains Mary's virginity after giving birth, much of Joyce's wordplay related to the dogma of the Virgin Mother (or heresies that deny it) undermines the notion of Maria's carrying unequivocal significance.

In fact, student responses to the story over the past several years reflect a particular shift toward questioning Maria's virginity; students almost routinely ask if Maria was Joe's "wet nurse." Their interrogation derives partly from the affectionate tone of Maria's expression: "Joe was a good fellow. She had *nursed* him and Alphy too" (*D*, 121; emphasis added), as opposed to a more objec-tive formulation, for example, had she been identified in the third person as the boys' nanny or even in noun form as "their nurse." The word *nursed* gains emotional nuance by its immediate juxtaposition with Maria's memory: "Joe used often to say: Mamma is mamma but Maria is my proper mother" (*D*, 121). One student, in fact, questioned what seemed a special bond between Maria and Joe, indicated by his use of the singular pronoun *my* (as opposed to *our*) followed by his later denial of Alphy as his brother. Joe's distancing of Alphy echoes Maria's way of mentioning Alphy almost as an afterthought when she recalls how she "nursed [Joe], and Alphy too" (*D*, 121).

2. The "hidden marriage" suggested by the classification "cryptogam" stems literally from the fern's hidden sexual parts (spores). I am indebted to my student Jessica Fisher for first pointing out the significance of the plant species in "Clay."

Joe's phrase *proper mother*, standard in British or Irish parlance in which *proper* signifies the real or actual, could suggest the depth of Joe's affection toward his surrogate mother or—if it is rendered in free-indirect discourse—Maria's need to see herself within a female economy of production, as indicated by her satisfaction with her indoor garden. In class, I have argued for leaving the door open on the question, while nonetheless acknowledging its sexual implications for our reading of Maria's "story" if she did literally nurse Joe, or Alphy.

The term *proper mother*, which occurs within a political discourse regarding wet nursing in European history, heightens its presence as a charged term in Joyce's narrative. The English Renaissance poet Edmund Spenser, for example, expressed fears that the milk of Irish wet nurses would contaminate British babies with "Irishness." According to Julie Kipp, "The Irish wet nurse has long been the victim of British prejudice." Spenser suggested that "fostered children might be corrupted by the love they received from the nurse" (quoted in Kipp 2003, 107).[3] The French philosopher Rousseau duplicated this abhorrence of the hiring of wet nurses and waged, as Rebecca Kukla has demonstrated, "a vitriolic attack" against the practice. Kukla notes that in postrevolutionary France, "the image of the nursing mother was the *proper mother* of the Republic" (2005, 50; emphasis added). Revolutionary France, in fact, employed the iconography of bare-breasted women as allegorical representations of the Republic in paintings and statues of the time (ibid.).[4]

Related readings of Maria within the frame of political allegory as the "Poor Old Woman or Kathleen ni Houlihan," as noted by Terence Brown (1992, xxiv), do so, however, at the peril of privileging allegory over fact in Joyce's realistic depiction of Maria as one of many "wronged women"

3. Kipp's discussion of British anxieties about the Irish foster system and particularly Spenser's fear of the corruption of the child who would internalize the language and the nature of the Irish foster mother seems prescient of the odd similarity between Maria and Joe, mentioned also by Bulson (2003, 41).

4. In Kukla's overall argument, this turn away from the wet nurse is the beginning of the movement toward mothering as a "private" as opposed to a "public" economic function (as it was with the wet nurse). Her emphasis on a private versus public opposition has relevance for "Clay."

in *Dubliners*. Gabrielle's interrogation of my more "suspicious" reading of Maria's secret life provides caution and ballast against a tendency to overread what she calls "the unknowable story within the story" of "Clay." The important convergence in our dialogue on this point lies in a mutual awareness—of the narrative's power to "seduce" us not only with its "storybook" quality but also with its hint of the covert. The narrative's childlike tone reminds us that stories involving children are often notorious for mistaken impressions and elliptical truths, as the opening three stories of *Dubliners* demonstrate.

Belief in Maria's absolute purity or untouched past, however, is complicated by her own ambiguous point of view, as when standing before the mirror she recalled "how she used to dress for Mass on Sunday morning" and "looked with quaint affection at the diminutive body which she had so often *adorned*" (*D*, 123; emphasis added). Given the fact that for Irish Catholic girls, Sunday mass was the one place they could legitimately exhibit their physical charms, one wonders what memories lie beneath Maria's barely suppressed pride in her "nice tidy little body" (*D*, 123). Her obvious pleasure at the sight of her own body in the mirror, furthermore, seems extraordinary for a woman conditioned by Irish Catholic denial of the body.

We are not reading "Clay" as if it might be a "shilling shocker" or a piece of investigative journalism, the goal of which is to expose or "dig up the dirt"—the "clay," if you will—on its subject. Rather, our reading is an effort to consider the wider possible arc traced by Joyce's narrative about an obscure character whom we are challenged to *realize* with critical attention as well as with imaginative sympathy in order to appreciate the "clay" of Maria's humanity. The central, if equivocal, image of clay in the narration (evoked only by associating the "soft wet substance" in the story with the title, as Attridge and others have demonstrated) serves not only as an element within a "divination" game foretelling death, but also as a reminder of Maria's existential human condition, with its potential for both innocence and a fall. Read in this context, the "clay" becomes an extension of the image of "dust" in "Eveline" that also functions doubly as an archetypal image of "death in life" and as a trope for the stifling culture of domesticity regulating the lives of women in turn-of-the-century Dublin.

One of Derek Attridge's subheadings in his essay on "Clay," "A Woman of No Importance," an allusion to an Oscar Wilde play, is an ironic reminder of the cost of reading Maria as a nonsignifier both socially and sexually. Wilde's play, produced in 1893, is about a woman who has a sexual secret in her own past that returns to haunt her. The potential shadow of Wilde as an intertext in Joyce's story of a spinster, one whom we hardly imagine walking on the wild side (or "crossing" the rails, as Mrs. Sinico does in her nocturnal perambulations in the following story), complicates our impression of Maria's innocence. Her denial of sexual desire when she brushes off the teasing of the laundresses about her prospects of "getting the ring" that evening invites some disbelief, undercut as it is by her laughing gray-green eyes that "sparkled with disappointed shyness" and, more emphatically, by her second, somewhat hysterical laugh that "nearly shook [her minute body] asunder" (*D*, 122). This mark of violence registering almost seismically through her small frame further arouses our suspicions about Maria's contentedness with her "nice," tidy life. The verbal motif created by the repetition of the word *nice,* ostensibly by Maria, twelve times throughout the narrative also plays against the Irish usage of the word, as seen in the ending of "A Mother" when Mr. Holohan remarks with biting irony of Mrs. Kearney, "That's a nice lady. . . . O, she's a nice lady" (*D*, 183).

If we do not immediately doubt Maria's verbal claims to respectability, her appropriation of social autonomy linked with the New Woman of the 1890s clearly arouses some suspicion. When preparing for the evening out, she thinks "how much better it was to be independent and have your own money in your pocket" (*D*, 123). The "two half-crowns and some coppers" (*D*, 121) amounting to five shillings and some pennies in her purse hardly support this inflated sense of independence. The image of Maria's alleged freedom is metonymically represented by her purse with the silver clasps that reads "A Present from Belfast," bought for her five years ago by Joe when he and his now estranged brother, Alphy, had gone on a "Whit-Monday trip" (*D*, 121). The image of the purse links her again with Eveline, a younger version of Maria in *Dubliners,* whose narrative, when read as a counterpart to "Clay," amplifies their shared sense of economic dependence and even servitude. Eveline, a young working woman who lives at home with her widowed father, hands over her entire salary to him and then has to wait until his generally inebriated return on a Saturday market night for him to grudgingly hand over the money (or what is left of it) so she can run out to buy provisions for the house. In the story she recalls going out, not unlike Maria, "holding her black leather purse tightly in her hands as she elbowed her way through the crowds" (*D*, 45–46). The female inversion of the heroic self-construction of the narrator in "Araby" who imagines bearing "his chalice" bravely through the noisy market crowds (*D*, 35) in Eveline's defensive guarding of her purse in the marketplace foreshadows Maria's social timidity on alighting from the tram at Nelson's Pillar, as she "*ferreted* her way quickly through the crowds" to buy treats for the Donnellys (*D*, 123; emphasis added). The mark of naturalism implied in the animalistic verb is hard to miss; unlike Chandler in "A Little Cloud," who combats his disabling sense of smallness by deeming himself above the "vermin-like" life of Dublin (*D*, 87), Maria's bent posture expresses her feeling of inferiority and, perhaps more ominously, her fear of being hunted or found out.

The shopping interlude between the two trams heightens the sense of Maria's vulnerability in public, and particularly in mixed company, as her inability to win respect from the young men on the tram suggests. This point is reinforced when the stylish young clerk in the shop on Henry Street, impatient with Maria's dithering over her purchase of the plumcake, rudely asks "is it a wedding cake she wants to buy" (*D*, 124), which evokes from Maria another telltale blush. It is this same plumcake that Maria later "loses," and her recollection upon that discovery of "how confused the gentleman with the gray moustache had made her," at which she again "*coloured* with shame and vexation and disappointment" (*D*, 126), a physical reaction that silently approximates an epiphany in the narrative. The emphasis produced by the elongated grammatical arrangement of "shame *and* vexation *and* disappointment" reaches its climax in the uncharacteristic eruption of pain in the next sentence: "At the thought of the failure of her little surprise and of the two and fourpence she had thrown away for nothing she nearly cried outright" (*D*, 126), signaling the deflation of her mood as well as her purse. Maria's loss of the plumcake seems more than simply an economic or imaginative failure. The role of the plumcake in traditional Christmas divination games where guests vie for the piece of cake with the plum or in some cases for a coin or a ring hidden in the cake, auguring wealth or a marriage in the new year, deepens the sexual significance of the plumcake and helps explain the piqued shopgirl's reference to a wedding cake. The sexual overtone suggested by Maria's losing her "plum" cake because she was "confused" by a dubious gentleman seems obvious even without recourse to folklore or cultural tradition.

The presence of the "purse" as a sartorial accessory robbed of any economic power in both "Eveline" and "Clay" points to the thematic linking of these characters as politically and sexually colonized women. The Belfast source of Maria's purse recalls Eveline's evocation of the businessman from Belfast who bought the field outside her house. Both narratives associate Belfast with an economy of change. The "bright brick houses" that now dominate the field that used to stand outside Eveline's house advertise the entrepreneurial spirit of the prosperous northern Anglo-Irish and recall the traditional metaphor of Britain's stealing Ireland's "green fields." Joe and Alphy's trip on "Whit-Monday," which is a "bank" holiday in England and Ireland, heightens the association.

The female purse, as Freud would later demonstrate, can also be read as an object "containing erotic information," an idea developed at length in *The Interpretation of Dreams* (see chapter 6). Freud saw the purse, like other objects that act as receptacles, as symbolic of female genitalia. Although Joyce's composition of "Clay" predates Freud's clothing analysis, the sexual symbolism of the purse was a common trope in Victorian iconography. Coins and purses functioned within a discourse of female sexuality in much Victorian literature and recur especially in the Pre-Raphaelite treatment of the fallen woman. Imagery of coins and the purse recurs throughout Dante Gabriel Rossetti's dramatic monologue "Jenny" about a prostitute. Wilde's play *The Importance of Being Earnest* ends with the secret of Jack's birth (and rightful name, Ernest) being revealed when his former nanny identifies her lost purse in which she had mistakenly left the baby. ("Joe and Alphy" in "Clay" bear a phonetic, even parodic resemblance to Jack and Algy in *The Importance of Being Earnest*. The nickname Alphy, suggesting the Catholic saint Alphonsus Liguori, known for his *scrupulousness,* is in direct opposition to Algy, an evocation of Wilde's fellow aesthete and decadent poet Algernon Swinburne.) The musical reworking of Wilde's comedy as *Ernest in Love* (1960), furthermore, features a hit comic song titled "A Handbag Is Not a Proper Mother," which combines the sexual innuendo implied in the purse and Joe's epithet for Maria as his "proper mother" in "Clay."

One Freudian reading of the sexual significance of the purse in contemporary consumer behavior theory provides a fitting gloss on Maria, who regards with pride the "silver clasps" of her purse: "A lightly snapped, zipped and buckled purse suggests a woman who guards her physical and emotional privacy closely, one whom it will be difficult to get to know, in either the common or the biblical sense. An open topped tote bag suggests an open trusting nature: someone who is emotionally and sexually accessible" (Lurie, quoted in Webb 1999, 140).[5] The recovered purse in *The Importance of Being Earnest* furthermore points to the theme of the changeling that is inscribed in Balfe's opera *The Bohemian Girl*, another intertextual presence that directly links "Clay" and "Eveline." The opera, about a young girl stolen by the Gypsies, to which Frank takes Eveline, is also the source of the aria that Maria sings at the end of "Clay" about a heroine's dream or memory of a happier past. It has not been uncommon for readers who perceive the dialogic relation between "Eveline" and "Clay" to view Maria's fate as a retrospective warning of the emptiness that could face Eveline after refusing the invitation to follow "her lover" to Buenos Aires. This reading of Maria as a future version of Eveline is also supported by the biblical linkage between their names—the Hebrew Eve is replaced in Christian typology by Mary. Joyce's deconstruction of the binary opposition between virgin and whore in other works points to the potential irony of Joyce's cautionary tales in "Eveline" and "Clay," ones that subvert, however, Victorian warnings to young women against following Eve's desire.

"Clay" might be more properly understood as warning against Eveline's failure to claim her freedom, dramatized by her inability to follow "Frank," who despite his potential as a rake in disguise bears a name that signifies honesty and freedom. The questions her story raises cast an important light on Maria's failure to sing the second stanza of the aria from *The Bohemian Girl*, "I Dreamt That I Dwelt."

Maria's repression of the second stanza is consistent with her repressions, denials, and euphemisms—especially with regard to men—throughout the

---

5. Lurie's reading of the clasped purse versus the open tote replicates the distinction between Maria's protected purse and her more exposed and ultimately vulnerable parcel.

narrative. Maria's euphemistic description of the "colonel-looking gentle-man" who "had a drop taken" (reminiscent of Eveline's description of her father as "fairly bad of a Saturday night" [*D*, 44]) and Maria's denial of Joe's anger when she mentions Alphy—the most she can admit is that he "was *nearly* getting cross" (*D*, 126)—emerge within a pattern of submission and denial regarding men. By contrast, she does hear Mrs. Donnelly say "something very cross" to the next-door girls who planted the clay in the saucer (*D*, 128). Maria's defensive strategy with men invites the reader to question what she fears—is it the expression of strong or violent emotion or the memory of having been "crossed" by men in the past?[6] Her equivocations are followed by Maria's acquiescence when Joe "insists that she take a drink"; the narration tells us she "let him have his way" (*D*, 126), a phrasing suggestive of sexual surrender. Again the text reports Joe "made Maria take a glass of wine," after which he prevails upon her to sing: "and so Maria had to get up and stand beside the piano" (*D*, 128).

As Francine Masiello reveals in "Joyce in Buenos Aires: Talking Sexuality Through Translation," being "obliged to sing" is, in that city, "a trope for sexual favors demanded of women" (2004, 65). Masiello offers this point within an explication of Joyce's Latinate pun "Buellas Arias" in *Finnegans Wake* (435.01).[7] And although Masiello does not address Maria's being made to sing in "Clay," she does link the trope with the expression "going to Buenos Aires" as taking up a life of prostitution that Katherine Mullin and others have identified as a potential allusion to the white slave trade in "Eveline" (Masiello 2004, 65; Mullin 2000).

6. Vicki Mahaffey and Michael Groden explicate the word *crossed* in "Silence and Fractals" in this collection.

7. The pun "Buellas Arias" in *Finnegans Wake*, furthermore, not only evokes singing an aria within the context of a sexual favor but is also situated in a passage that assembles a constellation of images relevant to my discussion. The passage gathers Wilde's Algy and Joyce's Eveline and Maria. "Autist Algy" (decadent artist), known to the "vice crusaders," takes a young woman (echoes Eveline) "to the playguehouse" (theater and brothel, house of disease) to see *The Smirching of Venus*, where he asks her "with a *nice tiny little* manner and in a *very nice little tony way*" (Maria's diction and nasal intonation in "Clay"; emphasis added), "Won't you be an artist's moral and pose in your nudies" (artist's moral as model exposed in the nude) (*FW*, 434.35–435.5).

Joe's overwrought response is also part of an alcoholic bipolarity seen throughout *Dubliners.* Joe's emotional overdrive makes one suspect, with Eric Bulson, that "even though Joe attributes his tears to the nostalgic song and 'the long ago' we might also venture a guess that he is hiding something," that he "like Maria is repressing something that bothers him" (2006, 41).

Masiello's provocative claim for the role of the secret in modernist writing has relevance for "Clay": "High modernism works through the secret. . . . [I]t is part of the strategy of difficult writing that elevates the value of the puzzle and perpetuates its claims on institutional power." This strategy, she argues, divides readers into "those in the know" and those "who remain on the margins" (2004, 55). Furthermore, she adds, "The private flow of information is not without purposeful leaks" (ibid.). The questions raised by hints and silences in "Clay" regarding Maria's sexual or nonsexual past are prompted by language both within ("leaked by") and beyond the text (for example, the unsung second stanza of the aria); at the same time, they remain unanswered and seemingly unanswerable—as if the text itself crosses our own desire to have truth exposed.

If Joyce's narrative suggests that interpretation has ethical limits, it does not necessarily follow, however, that we cannot or should not consider the implications of why Joyce might have chosen the path of inscrutability. It is possible to perform such an interrogation without violating Maria's or the narrative's right to remain "other"; moreover, can we do so in a way that holds our own voyeuristic impulses in check and tries instead to elucidate the social or ethical foundations of Joyce's determined secrecy? Asking why Joyce might have chosen "gnomonic" silence in "Clay" may not answer the questions projected by our natural curiosity as readers, but it can help to contextualize them within a framework of empathy.

Joyce's identified technique of "scrupulous meanness" in *Dubliners* developed in the opening years of the twentieth century concurs with an invitation by George Russell in 1904 to write a story for the *Irish Homestead* that "would not shock" the readers of the agricultural paper. After submitting three stories, "The Sisters," "Eveline," and "After the Race," Joyce was asked by the editor "not to submit any more because of complaints from shocked readers" (Manganiello 1980, 38). "Clay," the fourth story in order of composition (appendix 1, J. Joyce 1992, 227), and thus the first to be written after Joyce's disappointing tangle with Russell, obeys the editorial injunction not to shock—but with a vengeance.

Joyce's interest in preserving the unknowable story in "Clay" could also stem from his personal experience of living through two sex scandals that dominated his youth: Charles Stewart Parnell's affair with Kitty O'Shea and the homosexual scandal of Oscar Wilde. Critical attention to the presence of Wilde in *Dubliners* has focused largely on the issue of homosexual panic at the turn of the last century, and thus concentrated on stories with sexually ambiguous male figures such as the priest in "The Sisters," the "queer old josser" in "An Encounter," and the celibate Duffy in "A Painful Case." In these narratives, Joyce has mined both his own biography and his memory of the Parnell and Wilde cases. In "Clay," however, Joyce avoids any overt reference to the Wilde of public scandal and taps instead, even if obliquely, Wilde the playwright. Wilde's literary presence, which haunts "Clay" (and possibly "Eveline"),[8] may help to illuminate the aesthetic strategies Joyce entertained as he imagined his own "woman of no importance," who finds herself, by sheer economic necessity, living in a house for fallen women, whom she views as "a cut" below her, as we see by her response when Ginger Mooney teases her: Maria "knew that Mooney meant well, though of course, she had the notions of a common woman" (*D*, 122).

Joyce's potential nod to *The Importance of Being Earnest* (its theater run aborted in 1895, in reaction to the Oscar Wilde trial) occurs, as noted above, in Joyce's evocation of the purse in relation to a "proper mother." It can also be seen in Maria's far from comic echo of Miss Prism's misplaced parcels (Prism puts, as many will recall, the baby in the handbag and her manuscript in the perambulator). The reunion of the brothers Jack and Algy, effected in Wilde's play by the discovery of the nanny's missing purse, is also tragically inverted in the fractured relationship of the brothers

---

8. In *A Woman of No Importance*, the "savage" Patagonians serve as an example of "modern" topics of conversation between the sexes in upper-class society. Thus, Wilde could be one source for Frank's entertaining Maria with "stories of the terrible Patagonians" in "Eveline" (2000, 32).

Joe and Alphy in "Clay." The more allusive, and perhaps more significant, presence of Wilde's play *A Woman of No Importance* in "Clay" underscores Maria's status as a woman who, if not morally ruined, seems at least to have been tragically left behind. The play's central theme of a sexual secret also seems to haunt Joyce's representation of Maria in "Clay" and perhaps helps to explain Joyce's aesthetics of silence about her past.

Although Joyce never identifies Maria as a fallen woman, his situating of her in the "Dublin by Lamplight laundry," a name hinting at the potential exposure of dirty laundry, suggests the possibility that Maria may have a sexual history. Wilde's experience of having his dirty laundry aired was painfully enacted at his trial in the "Savoy hotel evidence" when soiled bedsheets were displayed by a chambermaid of the hotel. Margot Gayle Backus uses this event as an illustration of a "scandal fragment" that was a mainstay of the "new journalism" or "scandal journalism" circulating in London at the turn of the last century. Backus defines a scandal fragment as "a reference to or evidence of some private act that, owing to its reconstitution as evidence in a trial or other empirical investigation, becomes superlatively public" (2008, 107).

Backus's argument that the Savoy incident provided the background for the excremental imagery in *Ulysses* (ibid.) perhaps offers some context for Margot Norris's impression that the purpose of the children's trick in "Clay" may have been "to make prim, 'genteel' Maria recoil in shock and disgust at the mistaken sensation of touching excrement" (2003, 152). Norris's reading of the "clay incident" may be consoling to those readers who imagined something similar on their first reading but banished or censored the impression as somehow unworthy. The two extremes—exposing dirty laundry in a narrative and fearing to face the sexual or potentially debased content of a story or event—are rehearsed in "Clay," which simultaneously displaces the possibility of Maria's sexual past onto her residence in a Magdalen laundry and offers resistance to the questions this image invites. In Wilde's play *A Woman of No Importance,* an aristocratic Lady Hunstanton dismisses the emotional pain of the ruined woman with an unfeeling response that similarly tries to place Mrs. Arbuthnot in the seemingly progressive shelter of a Magdalen house: "Ah those things are very sad no doubt, but I believe there are admirable homes where people of that kind are looked after and reformed." Lord Illingworth, the secret father of the ruined woman's son, similarly dismisses her as "a woman of no importance"; Illingworth depends throughout the play on the snappy turn of phrase to displace true emotion and undermine middle-class (and by extension Irish) notions of morality. Not until the creation of Leopold Bloom in *Ulysses* would Joyce find a more humanly calibrated comedy that includes sympathy for the fallen woman. In "Eumaeus," Bloom, seeing the prostitute through the window, is nervous regarding his own complicity in underwriting her profession: "Unfortunate creature!" Bloom thinks. "Of course I suppose some man is ultimately responsible for her condition" (*U,* 16.731–32). Still distancing himself, as the phrase *some man* suggests, Bloom's sympathy nevertheless exceeds the sympathy of Stephen Dedalus, whose ironic detachment in defining the prostitute as a "bad merchant"—"one who buys dear and sells cheap" (*U,* 16.738)—retains the mordant wit of fin-de-siècle Wilde.

Wilde's aestheticism, it should be noted, evolves not only from Pater's celebrated dictum of "art for art's sake" but from Keatsian and Pre-Raphaelite aesthetic practice as well. Stephen's image of the merchant calls to mind the Pre-Raphaelite fallen-woman poem "Goblin Market," by Christina Rossetti, the sister of Dante Gabriel, who was forced by her gender to disguise the adult theme of her tale in a children's allegory. Rossetti's awareness of the reality of prostitution is demonstrated by her social work among fallen women in London's Magdalen houses. Her poem's relevance to "Clay" is suggested by Joyce's adoption of a storybook tone. "Goblin Market" is a retelling of the sin in the Garden of Eden. Joyce subverts, however, its formulaic Victorian opposition between the good sister and the bad sister (Laura who buys the fruit of the Goblin Men is the Eve and must be redeemed by the virtuous Lizzie, a type of Christ or the Virgin Mary, who resists their offer).

Joyce's awareness of the aesthetic trajectory in nineteenth-century Britain from Keats through the Pre-Raphaelites to Wilde becomes apparent from images deployed in *Dubliners:* "Eveline" mirrors Keats's "The Eve of St. Agnes" except that Keats's "Madeline" (a name cognate with Magdalen) trusts the suitor who promises (like Frank) that "over the southern moors I / have a home for thee" (lines 351–52). In Dante Gabriel Rossetti's "Jenny," the sleeping prostitute in the poem, robbed of a voice, anticipates Eveline and Maria who are effectually silenced in their narratives. Beside her inarticulate, "demure nods and hems" to the gentleman on the tram (*D*, 125), and her submissions to Joe, Maria's discourse of domestic contentment within the prison of a "nice" life in a "nice" Magdalen house suggests that she has learned to ventriloquize a conditioned set of responses expected of a woman dependent upon the kindness of society. "Discontent," as Wilde's Illingworth quips, "is the first step in the progress of a man or a nation"; such discontent is the unspeakable truth that Maria cannot utter.

To probe too insistently into Maria's silence with the intention of catching Maria out risks violating her privacy. (Wilde once criticized a biographer of Keats for exactly that transgression, asserting that the biographer showed "neither tact in the selection [of facts] nor sympathy in the use to which they are put" [quoted in Stokes 1999, 75].) The line between public and private that Joyce negotiates in "Clay," complicated by free-indirect discourse, parallels possible narrative options Joyce confronted in writing "Clay": oppositions between unfeeling irony satirized by Wilde and Irish sentimentality embodied in Joe, between romantic mythologizing of the Celtic past and a naturalist critique of his city, between the censoring silence of the *Irish Homestead* and the fascination with scandal in modern "new journalism," among others.

What Joyce chose was an empathetic as opposed to a censoring silence, challenging the reader to a Keatsian sense of "negative capability" that can live with uncertainty and doubt without overreaching for fact. Keats's "The Eve of St. Agnes" demonstrates this aesthetics of silence. Ironically, it is the "nurse" in the poem who acts as the agent for the young lovers, who "hides [Porphyro] in a closet of . . . secrecy" (line 165), a stratagem that enables the lovers (modeled on Romeo and Juliet) to escape scrutiny and overcome the social obstacles to their love.

Like Keats, Joyce frustrates the voyeuristic desires of his readers. Instead, he uses a gnomonic silence to create a space of narrative empathy around Maria's unknowable story, whether it be of the utter lack of a sexual drama in her past or of a secret trauma too painful to be resurrected. The presence of Keats and Wilde in "Clay" suggests the motif of "peeping through keyholes," to quote Wilde himself (Stokes 1999, 75). Perhaps Wilde's Mrs. Arbuthnot, the "woman of no importance," foreshadows Maria's own need for privacy as a way to avoid the verdict of insignificance or the rush to judgment by a scandalmongering readership when she pleads, "Leave me the little vineyard of my life; leave me the walled-in garden and the well of water; the ewe lamb God sent me in pity or in wrath." The lesson of Wilde's trial may well stand behind Joyce's unusual reticence in "Clay." If no one in Joyce's story "tried to show [Maria] her mistakes," perhaps it is a sign to the readers that we should refrain from exposing her as well.

"Working with Clay," *by Gabrielle Carey*
in Response to Barbara Lonnquist

When I read Barbara's essay on "Clay," my responses were immediate and definite. First, the last line was so brilliant I could not possibly add anything; she had summed up the sense of the story. Second, I felt overwhelmingly inadequate, underread, and uneducated (readers would know *immediately* that I was not a *real* academic). Then third, I felt, perhaps as self-consolation, that Barbara's analysis, in a way, proved the point I set out to make in the first place: that "Clay," along with all the other stories in *Dubliners*, can be read, enjoyed, marveled at by everyone, from the mildly dyslexic dropout to the insightful, learned scholar.

Even amid Barbara's precise mining of "Clay," as she manages to bring to the surface all sorts of treasures I had not previously noticed, Barbara is humble enough to remind us of Attridge's comment about the virtue in not interpreting. In other words, my first rather blind and naive reading of "Clay" at the age of twenty-two might still have value, in much the same way that the first draft of a writer's story is valuable. It may be rough and without the layers of meaning, texture, and subtext required for the final draft, but it *is* the first layer, and, therefore, fundamental.

Finally, one last point about Maria's character, specifically about sexuality. There has been a suggestion that when she is blindfolded and touches the clay, the sensation on her fingers could be likened to a person touching human feces. But if she had thought that, surely she would have recoiled. My response to this part of the story was completely different. I imagined that the feel of wet clay might well have suggested moist human flesh, in particular, perhaps, female labia. I wonder if the key difference between my Australian response to that scene in "Clay" and a European reader's response is that, for me, clay is *warm* and wet, like aroused genitalia, rather than cold and wet.

In the Northern Hemisphere clay is nearly always cold, often freezing. In the Southern Hemisphere, especially in my part of it, clay is warm. As a child, I spent much of my summer holidays playing on a beach that was lined with clay deposits. When I got tired of making sand castles, I scooped handfuls of warm, damp, squidgy clay from the eroded earth along the shoreline. Wet and malleable, it was ideal for sculpting, and many tiny sculptures molded by tiny hands were left to dry on the rocks that jutted out of the shallows. So whereas for people growing up in Europe, clay might represent cold and death and burial, for me it represents warmth and play and creativity. I grew up with a love for the feeling of clay in my hands, for its potential to be so many things—pots, bowls, figurines. At home we even had a potter's wheel where my father threw lumps of brown poo-like substance onto a spinning surface and then shaped them into vases or plates that would later be fired in a kiln. I remember watching how the clay was miraculously shaped under his hands: broadening, flattening, smoothing, rising, and falling, as the wheel spun 'round and 'round.

Another important difference between a Southern and a Northern Hemispheric reading might be the fact that, in Australia, the driest continent in the world, being wet is a *good* thing. In a country of deserts that is permanently in a crisis of droughts, even the smallest source of water means life. On the other hand, in Europe, particularly in Ireland, and even more particularly in Joyce's time, water, rain, and wet mean Frank McCourt–style ill health—bronchitis and damp, infant mortality and tuberculosis. In the opening to McCourt's famous memoir, he sets the dismal scene of poverty-stricken Limerick, ending the passage with the line, "Most of all it was wet." Wet in Ireland at the turn of the twentieth century meant danger and impending death. Wet in Australia means survival.

How does this background relate to Maria's blindfolded response to a lump of clay? (Or, should I say, my response to Maria's blindfolded response to a lump of clay?) Simply, that I imagine she touches something pleasant and inviting, rather than repellent. And the fact that she does not recoil suggests that the experience (and the enjoyment possibly) of touching the wet, warm, and fleshy is not foreign to her, confirmed perhaps by the fact that she admires, rather than recoils at, the sight of her own body. Yes, her story is still inscrutable and there is no proof or even real suggestion that she has any kind of sexual history, but my bet is that she is not a virgin. Surely, Joyce would not be so blatant and unsubtle as to name a virgin Maria?

But in the end, such a line of inquiry is not to be explored too far. It is too probing and too private, a bit like asking your own mother about her sexual habits. So I can only reiterate Barbara's beautiful conclusion—which should really be an adage that we all take through life when dealing with people: "If no one in Joyce's story 'tried to show [Maria] her mistakes,' perhaps it is a sign to the readers that we should refrain from exposing her as well." After all, why should we insist on correcting people we consider to be making errors? Why can't we, instead, marvel in their fallenness? In the felix culpa of all beings and existence? Why not, rather than showing our fellows' mistakes, refrain from exposing their faults and frailties? If there is one thing that I have learned after all these years of reading Joyce, it is that his principal subject is love. Perhaps this aspect of human love—the willingness to accept the "mistakes" in others, not to mention the mistakes in ourselves—is the most difficult of all. Because what Joyce is asking of us is not just to accept the mistakes and the errors, but to see them as beautiful and meaningful, even lovable.

11

Reopening "A Painful Case"

PAUL K. SAINT-AMOUR AND KAREN R. LAWRENCE

*We think of our essay as an intergenerational pas de deux. Its analytical moves
and steps lead back over several decades, places, institutions, scenes of instruction, and discrete moments in both Joyce scholarship and literary studies more
generally. As an undergraduate in Mark Wollaeger's "Ulysses" seminar, Paul
Saint-Amour read Karen Lawrence's 1990 essay "Joyce and Feminism," just
published in "The Cambridge Companion to James Joyce," with the result that
his hitherto Bloomian reading of Joyce was critically checked by Karen's poststructuralist feminist approach. A dozen years later, a "Confessions of Xenos"
panel Karen chaired at the 2002 International Joyce Symposium in Trieste
engaged Derrida's recent turn toward Levinasian ethics as a way of exploring
questions of hospitality and foreignness raised by Joyce's work. By then we had
become friends and begun to talk together about Joyce and hospitality, not least
about how an ethics of hospitality in Joyce's work might have helped foster the
nonhierarchical sense of welcome that characterizes the Joyce community, making friendships among scholars of different generations—friendships like our
own—remarkably common. The following year both of us gave papers on hospitality at the University of Tulsa's "Post-Industrial Joyce" conference, whose title
pronounced the death of the so-called Joyce industry while holding that Joyce
scholarship was, nevertheless, alive and well. Paul's talk explored Joyce's interest in uninvited guests and the communities they both threatened and consolidated, linking that dynamic to the relationship between Joyce's grandson and
literary beneficiary, Stephen James Joyce, and the scholarly community that was
galvanized by his antagonism. Karen's keynote address, subsequently published*

238

in the "James Joyce Quarterly," considered hospitality and literary form in several of Joyce's works, including "The Dead," and helped spark, in turn, Paul's tandem reading of that story and Dickens's novella "A Christmas Carol" in the "Counterfactuals" special forum of the journal "Representations."[1]

We drafted "Reopening 'A Painful Case'" much as we have written elsewhere of Joyce and hospitality: in a serial, antiphonal manner, with one writer pushing the argument dialectically ahead by responding to what the other had just written. If the finished essay contains only vestiges of this way of writing, it is because we met several times in person to agree on the general argumentative direction of the piece and to revise it with an ear toward vocal consistency. Already well acquainted with the alternating sounds of our exchange, we were curious to write in some less familiar compound voice. Our meetings about the essay took place over taco salads in an Irvine mall, so that the wintry hard precincts of Joyce's story are now softened in memory, for us, by the light and contours of Southern California, a place we have both since left. We are grateful for the chance this volume has given us to let years' worth of conversations—with Joyce's work, with other readers, and with each other—leave this collaborative trace.

How stands the case with the eleventh story in *Dubliners*? Is it a case for a detective, a judge, a physician, a psychoanalyst, or a social worker? What exactly is the case the title names as painful? And is that case open or closed? On the face of things, "A Painful Case" seems to be as decisively sealed as the inquest into Emily Sinico's death, with its diagnosis of "shock and sudden failure of the heart's action" and its verdict, "No blame attached to anyone" (*D*, 140). James Duffy's journey from isolation to entanglement back to isolation ends with a paragraph of decelerating repetitions—eight sentences beginning with "He," each sentence a hammer blow on a coffin nail—the last of which is the most unlyrically terminal of *Dubliners*' last lines: "He felt that he was alone" (*D*, 143). But already the cases have multiplied: Are we talking about the case of Duffy's entanglement or that of his isolation?

1. Published work referred to in this headnote: Lawrence 1990, 2003–4; and Saint-Amour 2007. On copyright and the Estate of James Joyce, see Saint-Amour et al. 2007.

About the medicolegal case made necessary by Mrs. Sinico's death, taking shape as an inquest that also reveals her case of alcoholism? Or are we talking about the text itself, a story that appears to be signed, sealed, and delivered?

In the tradition of the most generative scholarship on "A Painful Case," our essay insistently reopens the extravagantly closed case—or rather cases—of Joyce's story. We understand Joyce's story as itself revisiting a case—as reactivating a series of past conditions and events in order to learn or exhibit something. We ask: Why is this case worth reopening? What kinds of attention does it ask us to pay to someone else's predicament? And how have previous readings of the story replicated its vexed status as a case? Our responses to these questions challenge Joyce's own dismissal of the story as one of the two weakest in *Dubliners* (*SL,* 127); "A Painful Case," we suggest, is indispensable, and not only in its role as an etude for "The Dead," whose more explicit engagement with problems of hospitality, politics, and ethics it anticipates. Insofar as it dramatizes a risk run by all the *Dubliners* stories—the risk of diagnosing or sentencing their subjects as if they were cases—"A Painful Case" is the most formally and ethically self-reflexive story in a sequence known for its self-reflexivity. As a snare that anatomizes its own lures and springs, "A Painful Case" may be the paradigmatic story in *Dubliners.*

Let's begin, then, with the word *case* itself.[2] Joyce's original title for the story was "A Painful Incident," and his decision to alter it suggests a more than casual investment in the word that prevailed in the final title. *Case* in its many senses of an example or circumstance or action derives from the Latin *cadere,* "to fall," and suggests some condition or event that has befallen. (*Incident,* though less multiple in its definitions, descends from the same verb.) *Case* means "a state of matters pertaining to a particular person or thing," that is, a specific rather than a general set of conditions or circum-

2. The two numbers of *Critical Inquiry* dedicated to the case as genre appeared after this essay was completed. Rather than revise our piece into a direct engagement with these already influential numbers, we have let the points of contact remain serendipitous. The present essay might be read, then, as a kind of inadvertent supplement to those eighteen essays. See *Critical Inquiry* 33 (Summer 2007) and 34 (Autumn 2007), particularly special-issue editor Lauren Berlant's introductory essays to each number. We also missed the chance to benefit from Cóilín Owens's *James Joyce's "Painful Case"* (2008), a book-length study of the story.

stances. In law, a "case" pertains to "the state of facts juridically considered" as well as "the case as presented or 'put' to the court by one of the parties in a suit; hence the sum of the grounds on which he rests his claim." The word squints both at the content of the matter at hand—its facts, exhibits, and testimonies—and at the rhetorically charged staging of that content in the theater of the courtroom. In considering the cases put to us by Joyce's story, we will need ask where propositional content ends and staging begins, as well as what happens when these dimensions in the story fuse together.

In contrast to this first semantic cluster, the word *case* in the sense of a container or receptacle comes from the Latin *capsa,* "box," from the verb *capere,* "to hold." Thus, when we speak of opening or closing a case, we are, in a sense, conflating two etymologies, imagining an instance or situation or set of arguments as if it were an enclosed space. This imagined closure, we might add, is one of the ideological functions of a "case" in the medical, forensic, legal, and bureaucratic senses. The production of imaginary closure is also among the aesthetic functions of a work of fiction. But if Joyce's story foregrounds the notion of a "case," it may be in order to question the continence and the ethical viability of that very notion. One presumptively closed case encloses another: Mrs. Sinico's death, adjudicated at inquest and encased in cold print, is embedded in Mr. Duffy's case history, which is in turn enclosed within a short story written by James Joyce. What if these embedded cases were all prematurely closed? What work would be accomplished by their foreclosure? What violence? And what would it mean to reopen, and to hold open, these cases? In order to address these questions, we begin by tracking the language and logic of case through the story, attending to how the text narrates its several cases while also exhibiting tendencies to close, foreclose, diagnose, fix, and adjudicate. We also pay close attention to what interrupts or troubles these tendencies—namely, *invitation, voice,* and *touch.* These terms, we suggest, converge in a thematics of hospitality that is not only ethically and politically charged but also historically inflected by Dublin's status as an occupied city. In our closing discussion of the story's critical reception, we argue that the theme of hospitality has implications for Joyce's readers: the story's prospect of radical hospitality and its litany of failed invitations ask us to read and to encounter the Other with a fuller welcome.

"A Painful Case" putatively takes its title from that of the *Dublin Evening Mail* account of Mrs. Sinico's death, "DEATH OF A LADY AT SYDNEY PARADE: A PAINFUL CASE" (*D*, 138). But this subtitle is itself a reference to a bit of indirect speech in the body of the article: "The Deputy Coroner said it was a most painful case" (*D*, 140). The identity of the speaker here is significant: a coroner is a public official charged with investigating the deaths of those persons who have died by nonnatural causes such as an accident or violence. Such a person's duties straddle the boundary between medicine and law, combining the work of diagnosis with the work of legal adjudication. The coroner's title comes from the phrase *custos placitorum coronae*, or "guardian of the crown's pleas"—a phrase attached to the medieval origins of the coroner as an "officer of the royal household responsible for safeguarding the property of the Crown." It is a reminder of the intimate connections between colonialism and bureaucracy in turn-of-the-century Dublin. But whereas colonialism seems to be only an element of the story's background, urban infrastructure is, in a sense, a shadow protagonist of "A Painful Case." While composing the story, Joyce wrote to his brother Stanislaus with the following questions: "*A Painful Case*—Are the police at Sydney Parade of the *D* division? Would the city ambulance be called out to Sydney Parade for an accident? Would an accident at Sydney Parade be treated at Vincent's Hospital?" (*SL*, 75). Although Joyce made similar sorts of informational queries about other *Dubliners* stories, none of them is as densely populated with urban officialdom and other infrastructural figures as "A Painful Case." These figures congregate most thickly in the newspaper account of the inquest—a fully quoted article that takes up a fifth of the story's length—in which an assistant house surgeon of the City of Dublin Hospital, a sergeant and constable of the police, two railway employees, and a representative of the railway company appear alongside the Deputy Coroner and the husband and daughter of the deceased in establishing the cause of Mrs. Sinico's death. As if to confirm the link between governmentality and the varieties of "case" in play here, the story's title phrase recurs in *Ulysses*'s "Cyclops" episode in a hangman's letter to the high sheriff of Dublin: "*Honoured sir i beg to offer my services in the abovementioned painful case i hanged Joe Gann in Bootle jail on the 12 of Febuary 1900 and i hanged . . .*" (*U*, 12.419–20; original emphasis and spelling).

If the title of "A Painful Case" is a third-order quotation—a title quot-ing a subtitle quoting an article quoting a witness—it seems to have ema-nated from the mind of its protagonist, who, we are told, has pasted the headline of a patent medicine ad onto the first page of his collection of epi-grams (*D*, 130). But in many respects, Mr. Duffy is less the origin than the object of the narration, which provides the reader with a record of his exis-tence. That "A Painful Case" begins with the words *Mr James Duffy* iden-tifies the story itself as a case file bearing the name of its subject as if on a folder's protruding tab; it is, notably, the only *Dubliners* story that begins in this manner, with the title and full name of a protagonist who thus appears to be the sum of his file. An aphorist, bibliophile, and would-be translator who lives "at a little distance from his body" and "read[s] the evening paper for dessert," Mr. Duffy is a testament to the victory of word over flesh (*D*, 131, 137); he is, as R. B. Kershner puts it, "a man made of words" (1989, 111). The opening paragraph, whose catalog of Mr. Duffy's things seems to mimic the purple-inked stage directions he has written in his translation of Hauptmann's *Michael Kramer*, threatens to set a stage on which no actor will appear: the paragraph's last nine sentences avoid mentioning Mr. Duffy in name or pronoun, replacing the man with a roster of objects. Thanks to a series of passive verbs, even his writing seems to proliferate without him: we are told that "stage directions . . . were written," "a sentence was inscribed," "a headline . . . had been pasted" (*D*, 131), but we are never told explicitly *by whom*.[3] Eerily, this subtraction of agency extends beyond Mr. Duffy to the reader. Just as we become aware that the narrative has enlisted us in conducting a warrantless search of the protagonist's room—that we have been casing the joint—the syntax of the paragraph's final sentence describes a trespass *with no agent:* "On lifting the lid of the desk a faint fragrance escaped—the fragrance of new cedarwood pencils or of a bottle of gum or of an over-ripe apple which might have been left there and forgotten" (*D*,

---

3. Kershner also observes Duffy's elision from these sentences and links it to the character's spectrality: "We cannot fail to notice that in the description of his most intimate activity Duffy is not present. He haunts the syntax of the sentences like a passive ghost, never appearing even as pronoun. Like a déclassé Deity, he is the absent cause of his own creation" (1992, 112).

131).[4] By starting with a misplaced modifier (surely, "a faint fragrance" is not what lifts the lid of the desk), this sentence revolves around an absent figure—an investigator dissolved in the details of the case. The uncanny implication: that cases are not built by invasive agents but are self-made, self-compiling. We are not casing the joint after all; the joint is self-casing. What is more, we learn a paragraph later that the suspect, with his habits of dispassionate self-description, has understood himself as a case from the start: "He had an odd autobiographical habit which led him to compose in his mind from time to time a short sentence about himself containing a subject in the third person and a predicate in the past tense" (D, 131).

When the narration finally turns from the room back to its inhabitant, it does so in a diagnostic rather than a forensic manner, as if the foregoing inventory of his personal effects were a document in his medical file: "Mr Duffy abhorred anything which betokened physical or mental disorder. A mediæval doctor would have called him saturnine" (D, 131). The whiff of archaism in the prose accords with Mr. Duffy's habit of living "at a little distance from his own body, regarding his own acts with doubtful side-glances" (D, 131). By enumerating his distinguishing features, his habits, his movements, and his associates, the ensuing paragraphs continue to build the case of Duffy, although it is difficult to know whether we are reading a brief for the prosecution or for the defense. Even where they describe Mr. Duffy's isolation and rage for order, the aphorisms in the prose also radiate something of his self-satisfaction, as if they shared Duffy's pleasure in neatly

4. The apple that "might have been left" and forgotten in Duffy's desk has been much remarked on. R. B. Kershner connects it to an anecdote about the German dramatist Schiller, whose wife told Goethe that her husband could not write without the odor produced by a drawer full of rotting apples (1992, 406). Roberta Jackson reads Joyce's allusion to the Schiller anecdote as signaling Duffy's homosexuality on the grounds that German culture functioned at the time *Dubliners* was written as both a terminological source and a shibboleth for same-sex desire (1999–2000, 93). For Colleen Lamos, the rotting apple "testifies to Duffy's constrained appetite in general" (2001, 62). It is also worth noting, apropos of the weird elision of agency in the sentence, that the narrator's uncertainties as to the exact source of the "faint fragrance" and to the very existence of a rotting apple that "might have been left" depart from the omniscient point of view that otherwise characterizes the narrative.

dismissing the company and predicaments of other people: "He never gave alms to beggars and walked firmly, carrying a stout hazel"; "He had neither companions nor friends, church nor creed" (*D*, 131, 132). These epitomes of Duffy's likes and dislikes defend and insulate him, allowing his life to unfold without incident, painful or otherwise. His one early dalliance with thoughts of transgression ("He allowed himself to think that in certain circumstances he would rob his bank but, as these circumstances never arose, his life rolled out evenly—an adventureless tale" [*D*, 132]) is carefully controlled, a moment of mental permissiveness. In "A Painful Case," sentences *sentence*—they judge the case summarily—but they collude with Duffy too, providing a stay against eventfulness and singularity.

The "adventureless tale" of Mr. Duffy's routine becomes a narratable "adventure" (*D*, 132) with the introduction of Mrs. Sinico, whose voice breaks the protective spell of iteration and aphorism. Having sat down in a sparsely attended concert hall, Mr. Duffy is addressed by the woman sitting next to him: "—What a pity there is such a poor house to-night! It's so hard on people to have to sing to empty benches" (*D*, 133). Her remark, the only line of direct discourse in the main narrative, is the first event in a story that has so far described only conditions. Even more remarkably, it is the first intersubjective act that suggests a reciprocity not born of duty; prior to it, Mr. Duffy has "lived his spiritual life without any communion with others, visiting his relatives at Christmas and escorting them to the cemetery when they died" (*D*, 132). The neat symmetry of the sentence levels the holiday and funeral accompaniments, both of which Mr. Duffy regards as "social duties [performed] for old dignity'[s] sake" (*D*, 132): living and dead relatives, before his friend's arrival, were indistinguishable repositories of social principle.

Even direct discourse in a text is mediated, but Mrs. Sinico's comment departs multiply from what precedes it—as speech rather than narration, as exclamation rather than description, as an address to a particular listener (Duffy) rather than to an implied general one (the reader). Duffy takes her utterance as an "invitation to talk," and his acceptance of that invitation seems to shunt the story away from its opening profile, or profiling, of Mr. Duffy onto a narrative track that promises that something will happen. Nonetheless, his eventual withdrawal from Emily's life—his final refusal of her invitation—is already legible in this first exchange: the conversation her speech opens gets entirely drowned out in the narrative by a description of Mr. Duffy's scrutinizing her for future recollection's sake: "While they talked he tried to fix her permanently in his memory." He learns that the young lady who accompanies her is her daughter, he judges the mother's age accordingly, and then he studies her face: "Her face, which must have been handsome, had remained intelligent. It was an oval face with strongly marked features. The eyes were very dark blue and steady. Their gaze began with a defiant note but was confused by what seemed a deliberate swoon of the pupil into the iris, revealing for an instant a temperament of great sensibility. The pupil reasserted itself quickly, this half-disclosed nature fell again under the reign of prudence" (D, 133). So detailed a description might suggest a deep attentiveness on Mr. Duffy's part to his interlocutor, an attentiveness that takes in her facial features, her eyes, the temporality of her gaze, and what that gaze appears to reveal about her conflicted temperament. Yet Mr. Duffy's scrutiny, we should remember, is driven by a desire to "fix her permanently in his memory"—to immobilize, master, and possess rather than to listen, understand, or respond. He no sooner hears the first strains of Mrs. Sinico's call—her appeal as a fellow being—than he begins transforming that appeal into an inventory; Mr. Duffy cannot shut down his writing machine.[5] As philosopher Emmanuel Levinas has argued, the stakes of face-to-face encounters, and of their failure, are by no means trivial. For Levinas, such encounters are the fundamental scenes of ethics, scenes that bid us respond to the Other not as an object but as a subject, however unlike ourselves. Levinas comments:

> Access to the face is straightaway ethical. You turn yourself toward the Other as toward an object when you see a nose, eyes, a forehead, a chin, and you can describe them. The best way of encountering the Other is not even to notice the color of his eyes! When one observes the color of the eyes one is not in social relationship with the Other. . . . [T]he face is meaning all by

---

5. In this way, the ethics of the writer, as instrumentalist and master, are implicitly introduced. Joyce always boasted of the use he could make of the cases he discovered around him, and it is a commonplace of Joyce lore that his friends worried what he would make of them in his fiction.

itself. You are you. In this sense one can say that the face is not "seen." It is what cannot become a content, which your thought would embrace; it is uncontainable, it leads you beyond. (1985, 85–87)

In stark contrast to Levinas's ethical encounter with the uncontainable face of the Other, Mr. Duffy's gaze reduces Mrs. Sinico's face to a list of appurtenances and a story about their owner's divided temperament—in other words, to a content, another closed case study. This encasement begins to look like the story's master gesture: every opening is foreclosed, every "invitation" refused, every swoon recovered from. With each reassertion of the "fixing" logic of case, the possibility of an ethically vital relationship—of a radical attentiveness, of a listening without limit—withers away.

We will return in a moment to the case of Mr. Duffy and Mrs. Sinico, but here it is worth glancing at the politics that this story (about a failure of face-to-face ethics) keeps in its peripheral vision. As Levinas points out, one cannot extrapolate in any simple way from the ethical relation to the political, from the second person to the third person; even if the Other can demand an infinite attentiveness of me, how do I square that potentially limitless demand with the presence of *other* others—with their aggregate demand upon me or with my responsibility to relations of solidarity or justice with individual third parties? Yet "A Painful Case" attempts to describe one hinge between the ethical and the political. As Mrs. Sinico becomes his "confessor," Mr. Duffy tells her about his past association with the Irish Socialist Party. "The workmen's discussions, he said, were too timorous; the interest they took in the question of wages was inordinate. He felt that they were hard-featured realists and that they resented an exactitude which was the product of a leisure not within their reach. No social revolution, he told her, would be likely to strike Dublin for some centuries" (*D*, 135). Four years later, as he sits in the public house at Chapelizod Bridge thinking over her death (he has learned of it in the Tory, antinationalist *Mail*), five or six workingmen nearby discuss the value of a gentleman's estate in County Kildare. Sipping his punch, "Mr Duffy sat on his stool and gazed at them, without seeing or hearing them." Although his gazing without apprehension presumably results from the "shock which . . . was now attacking his nerves" (*D*, 141), the moment is symptomatic of Mr. Duffy's more general incomprehension of the working classes, and it brings his relinquished political life within the radius of the ethical question of attending to the Other. If such an attention is insufficient to account for the political, it is nonetheless indispensable to the formation of solidarity with other political subjects, particularly with members of another social class. Mr. Duffy's observation that "no social revolution . . . would be likely to strike Dublin for some centuries" is rhetorically self-serving, casting him in the role of a radical intellectual who is disappointed by the unrigorous pragmatism of the working classes and therefore qualified to prophecy the failure of their movements. But whereas Mr. Duffy's prophecy is offered as a detached observation about someone else's revolutionary ambitions, it indicts the prophet more than it glorifies him. By connecting Mr. Duffy's failure to listen in his face-to-face encounters with Emily and his failure to see or hear the working classes, the story implies that his inability to attend to the Other makes him partly responsible for the very political conditions that disgust him. If an educated and politically sympathetic member of the clerkly class cannot attend to the workers deeply enough to see why they might be apprehensive, concerned with the question of wages, or resentful of his "exactitude" when it is underwritten by his leisure, it is no wonder that the prospects for social revolution seem so remote.[6]

The story of Mr. Duffy's aborted political involvement surfaces as a testament to the power of Mrs. Sinico's invitation to talk. Unlike Mr. Duffy, Mrs. Sinico has the capacity to hear the Other, and it is this capacity—her role as his confessor—that momentarily invades the defenses Mr. Duffy has erected against face-to-face encounters. Before the glimmer of "adventure" is extinguished by routine, the pair's thoughts become entangled through conversation indirectly reported. Phrases like *for many years* and *every morning* give way to adverbial markers such as *little by little* and *sometimes* that

---

6. In "Having to Answer," an unpublished essay on the law of the "second person" in "A Painful Case," James McMichael says, "For me, Duffy has to be touched by Mrs. Sinico's insistently particular need before he can as much as begin to identify the political oppressions operating within himself. . . . [I]t is my view that on the way toward all third persons who are collectively the stuff of any first person's political world, there can be no detour around the second person."

hasten toward the singularity of scene. "Little by little, as their thoughts entangled, they spoke of subjects less remote" (*D*, 135). The vibrating music unites them as they experience the sensation of hearing together. "Sometimes he caught himself listening to the sound of his own voice. He thought that in her eyes he would ascend to an angelical stature; and, as he attached the fervent nature of his companion more and more closely to him, he heard the strange impersonal voice which he recognised as his own, insisting on the soul's incurable loneliness. We cannot give ourselves, it said. We are our own" (*D*, 135). Although this voice calls to mind Mr. Duffy's "odd autobiographical habit" of alienated self-description, we might also read it as a kind of empathy through hearing, as if he heard his own voice with her ears instead of his own. This momentary opening, this accelerating pace of intimacy, however, leads to a singular encounter that ruptures the relationship: "One night . . . Mrs Sinico caught up his hand passionately and pressed it to her cheek" (*D*, 136). Mr. Duffy reacts with surprise. "Her interpretation of his words disillusioned him. He did not visit her for a week." The steel trap of aphorism swallows the moment: "They agreed to break off their intercourse: every bond, he said, is a bond to sorrow" (*D*, 136).

Along with Mr. Duffy's life, the narrative returns to the comfort of habit and summary, reporting events with so little affect or emphasis that they are barely distinguishable from routine: "His father died; the junior partner of the bank retired. And still every morning he went into the city" (*D*, 137). We learn that two months after his last meeting with Mrs. Sinico, Mr. Duffy sentences their relationship once again: "Love between man and man is impossible because there must not be sexual intercourse and friendship between man and woman is impossible because there must be sexual intercourse" (*D*, 136). The aphoristic law according to Mr. Duffy obliterates the face-to-face encounter. The second person, like Mr. Duffy's "I," disappears into the third persons of man and man or man and woman.

The drive to "fix" the Other permanently in a summary judgment finds its correlate in the newspaper account of an event—the inquest—that reduces the circumstances of a life and death to the question of blame for the latter. This fixation happens partly through the name's relationship to the case. Whereas we have previously known only the last name of the deceased, the *Mail* names her fully as "Mrs Emily Sinico," as if the native climate of the name were the juridical setting in which its bearer becomes a case or file. (The full name of "Mr James Duffy," remember, was duly stated for the record at the story's outset; "A Painful Case" has been a mock inquest from the start.) Given the constraints of social codes and of his own nature, Mr. Duffy was, during their "intercourse," no more able to address Emily by her Christian name than to invite her back to his room, and the narrative has observed the same distance. But although her full name never explicitly reappears in the story, it is invoked toward the end, when Mr. Duffy hears it in the noise of a goods train: "It passed slowly out of sight; but still he heard in his ears the laborious drone of the engine reiterating the syllables of her name" (D, 143). The manuscript of "A Painful Case" spelled out those chugging syllables: "Emily Sinico. Emily Sinico" (see Giles 1997, 209).[7] By invoking her name—sans title, significantly—without putting it on the page, Joyce's revisions gesture toward the unutterable nature of a male-female intimacy that was neither polite friendship nor publicly acknowledged marriage. In its ghostliness, the deceased friend's intimate name, heard but not written, also resembles the spectral "touch of her hand" Mr. Duffy is shocked to feel while he is alone in his rooms; it resembles, too, the kinesthetic "touch" of the dead woman's voice on his ear (D, 142). As he retraces the steps of their last extended walk together, he again experiences her annunciation: "She seemed to be near him in the darkness. At moments he seemed to feel her voice touch his ear, her hand touch his. He stood still to listen" (D, 142). Still, as shocked as he is by her voice and touch, their mutual disappearance in the story's final paragraph proves even more terrible. Haunting is at least a form of accompaniment, the touch and voice of even some ghostly Other testifying to the presence of a second person, of a "you." The end of such a haunting marks the final death of that "you" and the arrival of a world in which the self is truly alone. Fittingly, it seems to be the locomotive's incantatory repetition of Emily's full name, linked as her name is to the closed case of her inquest, that drives away the impression and the ethical appeal of her presence; the legalities and generalities of the *case* banish *voice* and *touch*, the experience of the second person.

7. See also *James Joyce Archive*, 4:133.

Before we turn to the story's final paragraph, we need to attend to what enters the text alongside the sense of Emily's nearness. Her visitation, while it lasts, suffuses the narrative with the language of hospitality, a language— and with it, an ethic—that until now has been repeatedly warped or warded off. Early on in an intercourse initiated by his friend's "invitation to talk," Mr. Duffy hastened to deform the scene of invitation into one of coercion: having "a distaste for underhand ways and, finding that they were compelled to meet stealthily, he forced her to ask him to her house" (*D*, 134). No one in "A Painful Case" is both unconditionally welcomed (think of the warrant-less search in which the story's opening paragraph enlists the reader) and able to accept such a welcome—to come in. As if in recognition of this impasse, nearly all of "A Painful Case" is set on peripheries: Duffy lives "as far as pos-sible from the city of which he [is] a citizen," spends his evenings "roaming the outskirts of the city," later visits the Sinico cottage "outside Dublin," and at long last, walking in Phoenix Park to the west of the city proper, "turn[s] his eyes to the grey, gleaming river, winding along towards Dublin" (*D*, 130, 132, 125, 143). But by the time Mr. Duffy gazes for the last time from the outskirts to the center, that gaze has altered: whereas the story's first sen-tence records his contempt for the city from which he has distanced himself, now, with Emily's voice and touch drawn near, Dublin's lights "burned redly and hospitably in the cold night" (*D*, 142). The sight of those lights, and of lovers entwined at the base of the park's wall, prompts Mr. Duffy's realiza-tion that he is "outcast from life's feast," a phrase that chimes twice (*D*, 143). The feast he has refused is partly the feast of eros and partly, as a scriptural reverberation reminds us, what the narrator earlier called "any communion with others" in his spiritual life (*D*, 132).[8] But the story's social geography also identifies the foregone feast as that of the civic—of that scorned city center and the "civic life" (*D*, 132) to whose conventions Duffy made only grudging concessions. Duffy's double refusal of hospitality and of the civic

8. The passage, commonly associated with the Eucharist, is from 1 Corinthians 5:7–8: "For even Christ our Passover is sacrificed for us: therefore let us keep the feast, not with old leaven, neither with the leaven of malice and wickedness; but with the unleavened bread of sincerity and truth." We are grateful to Vicki Mahaffey for hearing this echo and drawing it to our attention.

might make us hear even the inert institutional name "City of Dublin Hospital" a little differently: this setting of the inquest into Mrs. Sinico's death is haunted by an alternate narrative path in which the city of Dublin had been a site of hospitality rather than a swarming ground of "case"—of investigation, judgment, and reportage.

In its opening profile of Mr. Duffy, the narrative voice caught its subject's scorn for "the conventions which regulate the civic life," but we should remember that his occasional nods to those conventions—"visiting his relatives at Christmas and escorting them to the cemetery when they died"— were the only moments prior to his "adventure" with Mrs. Sinico when he veered from his righteous solitude. Thus, the "civic" was set up early on as a matrix of social reciprocity, and thus as a foil to those institutional structures (court, hospital, press, police) that would later preside over the painful case of Mrs. Sinico's death. By then figuring the city as the locus of hospitality and of the vital feast from which Mr. Duffy is outcast, the story's penultimate paragraph suggests that the civic might be more than a bourgeois social code: it might be that which welcomes the outcast. Mr. Duffy is a disaffected citizen of Dublin rather than its outcast, but his figurative self-description invites us to imagine a literal counterpart: the true outcast, the asylum seeker, the noncitizen who wants to come in. Such a figure haunts the story's last page alongside Mrs. Sinico and briefly recasts Dublin, its lights burning hospitably in the cold night, as a city of refuge.

The hospitality granted the outcast by such a city would be radical, unbounded by pact or by the expectation that the city would benefit economically or politically from the welcome it proffers; it would be the very kind of unconditional hospitality that Mr. Duffy can neither accept from Mrs. Sinico nor extend to her.[9] That these two varieties of hospitality—the intimate and the civic—can be thought in tandem here points up, again, the story's interest in considering the political stakes of the face-to-face relation. But we should note that this consideration does not lead to an easy cosmo-

9. The constellation of city-hospitality-outcast in "A Painful Case" makes Sophocles' *Oedipus at Colonus* one of its unrecognized intertexts. See Jacques Derrida's discussion of the play and on cities of refuge (2000, 2001, respectively).

politanism, as an echo of contemporary political oratory in the story attests. On the day of Edward VII's coronation in 1902, John Edward Redmond, then head of Ireland's Nationalist Party, gave a speech on the steps of Dublin City Hall, protesting the festivities taking place in London. Addressing England, Redmond said, "You cannot hide from your guests the skeleton at your feast." That skeleton was the fact that Ireland "lies at your very heart oppressed, impoverished, manacled, and disloyal, a reproach to your civilization, and a disgrace to your name" (1910). Joyce's echo of Redmond's words situates the problem of hospitality in respect to the history of British colonialism. It insists that acts and failures of hospitality, both individual and civic, might have an altogether different meaning and being in an occupied colonial capital; that Mr. Duffy's rejections of solidarity and intimacy might allegorize the colony's stunted political powers of initiative, welcome, accord, and reciprocity in domestic and international registers; that the skeleton at one feast might understandably fail to preside as host over another. For all that the lights of Dublin burn hospitably toward the story's end, a certain historical skepticism keeps them distant: the city of refuge is a prospect, not yet a present space of asylum.

The final paragraph of "A Painful Case" performs a feat of subtraction: the train with its dactylic cargo ("Emily Sinico. Emily Sinico") has passed out of sight, its rhythm ebbing from Mr. Duffy's ears and with it the sound of Emily's name and his sense of her nearness—his short-lived impression of her voice and her touch. Element by element the once-detailed world of the story is pared away, leaving a nullity in which Mr. Duffy's listening is a call that elicits no response but perfect silence. "He turned back the way he had come, the rhythm of the engine pounding in his ears. He began to doubt the reality of what memory told him. He halted under a tree and allowed the rhythm to die away. He could not feel her near him in the darkness nor her voice touch his ear. He waited for some minutes listening. He could hear nothing: the night was perfectly silent. He listened again: perfectly silent. He felt that he was alone" (*D*, 113–14). The lines are Joyce's prose at its most elemental or skeletal, as shorn of ornament as Mr. Duffy's room. If Duffy's habit has been "to compose in his mind from time to time a short sentence about himself containing a subject in the third person and a predicate in the past tense," then the paragraph marks that habit's reassertion, suggesting that Mr. Duffy has "turned back the way he had come" in mental routine as well as in space. The language describing his self-portraiture—technicalities about sentence parts, person, and tense—should draw our attention to the grammar of this final paragraph, which is the crowning instance of his "autobiographical habit." Here, alongside the dwindling of Mr. Duffy's world, the resources of language seem to have narrowed to a lone kind of declarative sentence. The proper nouns whose specificities of place, name, title, institution, and season are so important both to the rest of "A Painful Case" and to the logic of "case" in general have all been deducted, leaving a spare archipelago of pronouns. Looking more closely at these, one discovers that the story's final closing down of "case" is grammatical. In the first half of the paragraph, the masculine pronoun that stands in for Mr. Duffy appears in the subjective, objective, and possessive cases—*he, him,* and *his,* respectively—as if the possibility were still open that he could enter into reciprocal relations with others, be the object to another's subject, be claimed, or claim another as his own. In the fourth sentence the masculine and feminine pronouns are still found entangled, if only to declare "her" vanishing: "*He* could not feel *her* near *him* in the darkness nor *her* voice touch *his* ear" (emphasis added). But if an intimacy lingers in those pronouns even as they describe the withdrawal of Emily's ghost, the elimination of *her* in the last four sentences closes the masculine pronoun down to the subjective case alone, to the *he* that tolls five times before the full stop. No longer haunted by her, he seems to lose even the solace of his own self-division. The benches are empty: Duffy is a listener in a vacant hall.

How do we understand the subtractions of this final paragraph—its repetitions, its loss or renunciation of variety and specificity, its listening without response? Do these moves signal Mr. Duffy's entrapment in a solitude from which no one will rescue him? Or his willful retreat to a solitude on which no one, thankfully, will impinge? Are they the culmination of the logic of "case" as general law rather than case as particular instance? Or do they enact the supersession of that logic, with its love of specifics, by something else? Do they make us want to convict and sentence Mr. Duffy? To exonerate him? To damn or absolve him? To diagnose and treat him? And if they strand the reader in a space of radical undecidability, to what end do they do so?

One thing is clear: the story's final paragraph tends to function as a decision space for its readers. The paragraph practically impels us to take an interpretive stand about it and, by extension, about its protagonist's final status. Many of those scholars who have written on "A Painful Case" have found a kind of tragic epiphany in its final lines, where the blows of the previous paragraphs land fully: Mr. Duffy realizes that he has missed his chance at intimacy, that he has brought about the death of the one person who offered it to him, that he will be unremembered when he dies, that he is absolutely alone. This way of reading sees Mr. Duffy as a figure of pity and terror and his readers as experiencing both instruction and relief at the hands of Duffy's chastening example. By contrast, several recent commentators have viewed "A Painful Case" as ending *happily* insofar as its protagonist gets what he wants—what he has, in fact, engineered: a life so sealed off from desire, vulnerability, and responsibility that what would be self-incriminating utterances for less walled-off people ("He had sentenced her to ignominy, a death of shame. . . . No one wanted him; he was outcast from life's feast" [*D*, 143]) are self-congratulatory ones for Mr. Duffy. Such a reading is advanced by Garry Leonard, who traces Duffy's rage for isolation to a condition of primary narcissism, one that compels him to uphold the fiction that he has an integrated ego and to do so without even minimal recourse to others (1993, 210–27).[10] Seamus Deane makes a similar diagnosis, although with an emphasis on ethics rather than the psyche: "The closed, repetitive structure of Mr Duffy's inhuman life has resumed. There is no other in his world, no responsibility for the other. This is a style that excludes ethics, by the intensification of repetitive rhythms that betoken morbid self-obsession. It is the opposite of an ethical condition, the fleeting prospect of which disappears as the serried ranks of final sentences close up in their neat, neurotic repetitions" (2000, 25). Deane goes further than Leonard in claiming that the style of Joyce's story is complicit in its protagonist's inhumanity, neurosis, and ethical nullity, its repetitions ratifying Mr. Duffy's choice of routine over Mrs. Sinico's posthumous appeal to him.

10. The descriptor *self-congratulatory* in relation to Duffy's realizations is Leonard's (1993, 227).

For Deane, the text itself plays silent partner to its protagonist, doubling his ethically closed self-regard.

These readings vary from one another in obvious ways, but they also have something crucial in common: a moment at which Mr. Duffy's psycho-sexual or ethical state (or both) is decisively adjudicated. In this common-ality, they are strangely faithful to "A Painful Case," most obedient to its immanent logic precisely where they are most critical of that logic's outcome (as in Deane's reading). The story's self-presentation as a "case"—as the case of Mrs. Emily Sinico nested within the case of Mr. James Duffy—has repro-duced itself, that is, in a tendency among its commentators either to diagnose Mr. Duffy or to certify his moral condition as if for sentencing. As we have seen, the text invites such critical gestures by staging diagnoses, verdicts, and sentencings of its own ("A medieval doctor would have called him sat-urnine"; "Death . . . had been due to sudden failure of the heart's action"; "No blame attached to anyone"; "he had sentenced her to ignominy"; "he was outcast from life's feast"). Not all of the critical verdicts are as unsparing as Leonard's judgment of Mr. Duffy or Deane's of the text itself, but even those readings that plead Duffy's case remain within the narrow thumbs-up-or-thumbs-down option embedded within the story's medicolegal settings and architecture. If "A Painful Case" invites such judgments, however, its theme of hospitality issues a counterinvitation to its readers—an invitation to extend a hospitality of our own, one that does not (as no truly radical hospi-tality does) depend on the health, innocence, normality, or ethical receptiv-ity of the guest. This interpretation would be to chart a third way through the story, neither condemning nor recuperating Mr. Duffy but instead offer-ing him precisely the kind of welcome he refuses Mrs. Sinico, the "hobbling wretches" and other "wrecks on which civilisation has been reared," the working classes, and finally all humankind (D, 141). It would also be the kind of welcome that no one, in the wake of Mrs. Sinico's death, will extend to him in the world of the story—again, a welcome beyond diagnosis or verdict, a hospitality that takes neither his wellness nor his illness, neither his culpability nor his pitiableness, as its precondition.

Such a hospitality would knit closely with the queer readings that have lately quickened the story's critical reception; it might also draw us past the binarisms that have at moments characterized these readings. Roberta

Jackson criticizes the medicalization of same-sex desire by turn-of-the-century criminal and sexological discourses, adding that this process led to unacceptably confining and essentialist models of homosexuality. Yet she concludes, with a certainty the text simply cannot sustain, that the story's "accumulated allusions leave no doubt as to Duffy's sexuality" (1999–2000, 95). Margot Norris, by contrast, marks the queer reading of "A Painful Case" as an "indeterminate and unverifiable" possibility whose power to "abash the reader in ethically productive ways" lies in the undecidability of Mr. Duffy's sexuality. Norris argues that the story arouses readerly expectations of an adultery narrative in order, by frustrating those expectations, to expose the heterosexism of both the adultery narrative and the reader who defaults to it. Such a reader has either missed or declined textual invitations to queer reading and thereby enforced a "compulsory heterosexuality," in Adrienne Rich's (1980) phrase; in subsequently reconsidering a queer reading, says Norris, the reader must "take ethical responsibility for now imagining the thoughts, feelings, and anxieties of the possibly homosexual man. . . . The heterosexual reader experiences a thickening of identity and a doubling of vision as different questions pose themselves in an effort to enter a gay subjectivity" (2003, 169, 170, 168).[11] The imperative of taking responsibility for the Other is compelling here, but it is pinned to the kind of inflexible, identitarian coordinates Norris otherwise rejects. This argument not only explicitly posits a heterosexual reader, but also assumes the absolute otherness of queer reading and queer subjectivity for such a reader. These assumptions produce several outcomes: first, radical alterity is made to seem a function of sexuality alone. Second, subjectivity (for example, "gay subjectivity") is conflated with sexuality, ruling out the possibility of a more mobile, multiple, or performative model of sexuality that corresponds only imperfectly with subjectivity. Finally, Norris's reading sets up the straight reader as the lone enforcer of compulsory heterosexuality—an odd result given the story's demonstration

11. Heterosexuality in Rich's (1980) discussion is "compulsory" in the sense of being conceptually and ideologically presumptive—that is, beyond question, taken for granted—and not in the sense of being compelled through the use of brute force, although Rich touches on situations in which the latter is also true.

of how its possibly homosexual protagonist accedes to compulsory hetero-sexuality in his actions, confining his dissent to dire and private epigrams.

To Norris's construction of an "abashed" heterosexual reader, one might respond that "A Painful Case" imagines a broader bandwidth of both readers and ethical effects. Norris's reader, in hot pursuit of the adultery narrative, first ignores and only later is ethically chastened by the story's oblique and encrypted references to homosexuality. But those same refer-ences would function very differently for the closeted reader, providing the secret password's consolation under a repressive regime, establishing Mr. Duffy as a fellow sufferer with whom to feel solidarity or, alternately, as a warning example of the tragic potentials of the closet. One also imagines a reader—Mrs. Sinico herself might well have been one—who is alive to the ties between compulsory heterosexuality and patriarchy. However unavail-able Mr. Duffy's subjectivity-as-gay appears, Mrs. Sinico's subjectivity tout court is even less accessible, lacking even his moments of unpublished semi-candor. The question of what she wants, thinks, and feels is simply inad-missible to the narrator, and the reader—male or female—who notices this silence or interdiction, instead of being abashed, will begin to consider the political anatomy of a story that consigns both its main female character and its possibly gay male protagonist to similar fictional closets.

Still another kind of reader seems to be addressed by Mr. Duffy's last aphorism; for this reader, the unsettled question of Mr. Duffy's sexuality is not just a sign of repression or self-censorship but also an invitation. The aphorism again: "Love between man and man is impossible because there must not be sexual intercourse and friendship between man and woman is impossible because there must be sexual intercourse" (D, 136). This for-mulation, which tends to function as the epicenter of queer readings of the story, describes a double bind—what Colleen Lamos calls "the *proscrip*-tion of homosexuality, side by side with the *prescription* of heterosexuality." Readings of Duffy as affirmatively homosexual take the epigram to map mutually exclusive modes of desire and subjectivation, concluding that he *is* homosexual—and by the same token *is not* heterosexual—but simply cannot enact his homosexuality. But as Lamos points out, *both* heterosexuality and homosexuality are closed to Duffy, who is stranded between the two: "Nei-ther does the disavowal of homosexuality . . . produce a homosexual subject, nor does the disavowal of homosexuality produce a heterosexual subject" (2001, 66; emphasis in original). One kind of readerly hospitality would attempt to join Duffy in a place of suspended adjudication; it would extend a welcome to him without relying on the mutually exclusive relationship between queer and not queer, closeted and out, symptomatic and asymptomatic. In a sense, such a hospitality would underwrite the more generatively "queered" reading of the story insofar as it understood the interpretive gesture of "queering" a text not as a onetime conversion or correction of the text to the fixed status of queer but as a perpetual opening and reopening of the case: as a vexing of the very concept of a case.

Let us return to Deane's discussion of the story's final sentences, and particularly to his claim that their repetitive style "excludes ethics, by the intensification of repetitive rhythms that betoken morbid self-obsession." Deane's criticism, we should note, is directed less at Duffy than at Joyce; moreover, "A Painful Case" becomes, for Deane, the pattern of Joyce's subsequent fictions, whose incantatory endings betray the critical and political potentials of the texts by aestheticizing them "into a form of writing that has the ambition to be entirely autonomous," self-referential, and therefore exempt from "History" (2000, 34–35). Deane's conclusive dismissal of Joyce's lyrical finales on the model of "A Painful Case" demonstrates how powerfully that story seems to prescribe, in its last paragraph, some act of readerly adjudication in the image of Mr. Duffy's decisive aphorisms. But Deane also rather surprisingly dissevers the story's ending from earlier passages that might prepare us to read it more equivocally or multiply. As we have attempted to show, much of what precedes the final lines—the aphoristic profiling, the face-to-face encounter and its relation to politics, the theme of hospitality, the play of name and case—opens the very questions that are, for Deane, so extravagantly foreclosed by the ending. These openings equip us to read the final paragraph as enacting rather than endorsing the closing down of a world. They help us to read that closure as a symptom of Mr. Duffy's condition even as they challenge us not to leap from symptom to diagnosis—to a state in which, having drawn conclusions about the Other's pitiable state, we may dispatch his closed case to cold storage. This would be the prospect of radical hospitality opened by the story, for all that its protagonist fails in it: to respond without diagnosis to the symptom of the

Other. None of this is to deny "A Painful Case" its profoundly self-regarding energies. They remind us of the way writing—and Joyce's writing in particular—can fix, immobilize, finish off. Joyce's claim that *Dubliners* was meant to "betray the soul of that hemiplegia or paralysis which many consider a city" (*SL*, 22) is worthy of Mr. Duffy in the way it subjects a whole city full of painful cases to a terse and scornful diagnosis. But "A Painful Case" does nothing if not recognize and critique this very tendency; it stages the crisis produced by such habits of mind, taking them to the end of the line as if to exhaust them and perhaps to glimpse what lies beyond their terminus. That "beyond" would include "The Dead," whose central theme of hospitality arose, Joyce claimed, from the realization that he had been "unnecessarily harsh" about Ireland in the other *Dubliners* stories (*SL*, 109–10); "A Painful Case," which variously inflicts and flinches at Joycean harshness, may well be the record of that realization. The story asks us to listen, amid its sentencings and arid epigrams, for moments of voice, touch, welcome, and annunciation; in narrating a failed appeal to the ear of the Other, it invites its readers to receive that appeal.

12

"Ivy Day in the Committee Room"

JENNIFER LEVINE AND ANDREW GIBSON

I have used imaginary characters and didactic dialogue primarily because
this venerable literary form is suited to expounding inquiry and developing
argument, but also because the form implicitly invites a reader to join the
characters and enter the argument too.

—Jane Jacobs, *The Nature of Economies* (2001)

*We liked the impetus for this collection of essays and have taken seriously its
invitation to do a different kind of literary criticism. In writing our essay (if
that is what it is), we did not either proceed from a reconciliation of different
positions and practices or seek to work toward one. We wanted rather to use our
pairing, not only to develop and explore differences but also to multiply them,
to make differences proliferate. To say this does not mean that the essay was bred
of irreconcilable conflict. Quite the reverse: we knew what we wanted to do from
the start and were agreed on it. We simply took a specific view of what we were
doing. We were not inclined even to start to try to work toward a consensus,
but rather to foster differences, to let them thrive. No doubt there was a kind of
statement at stake in doing so, a philosophical commitment that, though we did
not articulate it to ourselves as such, more or less immediately took us over. In
other words, there was a decision: there always is. But it was a decision in favor
of a final and, we like to think, quite radical indecisiveness. It was a decision
made in favor of gaps, breaks, lacunae, aporias, all of which condition what follow. In effect, we rejected all thought of a (Habermasian or Arendtian) consensus, choosing rather a (Lyotardian) production, if not of dissensus, then at least
of conscious multiplicity, of a kind not dissimilar to what is found in his own*

text "The Differend" (though we would not flatter ourselves that it is so expertly achieved) (see Lyotard 1988).

The experimental character of what we have attempted, however, will not be evident at once. The piece begins with an original contribution to recent historical research on "Ivy Day" that both draws quite substantially on materials not exploited before and joins in a debate apparent in earlier and recent instances of such research on the story, particularly the work of James Fairhall and Anne Fogarty. This section relies on the kind of scholarship that Andrew Gibson likes to practice. The research is as painstaking and thorough as he can make it, and the discourse is forensic, single toned, and orthodox. He comes to his task as an archaeologist, sifting through texts that have been rearranged by time (fiction in one place, political writing or government reports somewhere else) to put them back into relationship with each other. By contrast, Jennifer Levine in the second half of the essay is confident that without knowing what Joyce knew, it is possible to read "Ivy Day" and find it meaningful (keeping in mind always that "meaningful" is an elastic term—though not so elastic as to be merely self-indulgent). Criticism can be an extension of teaching: she wants to model here how, in dialogue, we stretch our understanding. She thus invents three characters, each one interested in "Ivy Day" for his or her own reasons. Ultimately, their three voices are intended to sound out her own response to this story of performance and judgment.

The essay is therefore deliberately structured as a movement from monologue, not only to dialogue, but to dialogues within a dialogue, though a dialogue and dialogues that incorporate responses to the original monologue. In a closing double reversal, however, we complicate this structure: while Jennifer Levine's monologue finally emerges from the dialogue she has staged, in its closing section, Andrew Gibson's voice emerges from its monologic self-enclosure into dialogue. Jennifer Levine meets him there. We like to think that the result is, at least, intriguing and, if not Joycean—how could we possibly claim that it is?—appropriate to Joyce, analogous to certain aspects of his work, in a way that criticism is only seldom. This is the case in at least two important different ways. First, we aimed to create a quite blatantly multivoiced text, a text that is a tissue or tessellation of voices. Jennifer Levine speaks in at least four voices in the essay, and there are two or three Andrew Gibsons, too. There are the voices of the three students, of course, and the voice of Jane Jacobs makes a significant,

distinctive, and special if brief appearance. All of it, of course, merely makes
explicit the principle of heteroglossia latent in any critical text, however con-
servative its views or their expression. Louisa, Jock, Selwyn, and Jane Jacobs are
merely "marked" and function on the surface of the text, whereas, say, Anne
Fogarty and Garry Leonard are "unmarked" (as voices) and function within
its texture.

Second, the essay consciously works on discrete levels and in discrete reg-
isters. We have made no effort to smooth over the hiatuses, to muffle the gear
wrenching that goes on between one segment and another. In resisting the temp-
tation of integration, we hope to achieve a double end. On the one hand, there
is a sense in which, discursively, separate parts of the essay remain self-immured.
Again, we would protest that this feature is Joycean, that the wrenchings of gear
in our essay mimic the wrenchings of gear that go on between one chapter of "A
Portrait of the Artist as a Young Man" and "Ulysses" and another and make
the pleasures and satisfactions they have to offer quite different. On the other
hand, just as in "Ulysses" and "Portrait," filaments pass from one to the other;
connecting threads exist. Thus, we remain true to our un-Habermasian per-
suasion, not only that communication does not necessarily take place on a basis
of shared assumptions, but that it does not need the kind of common ground
beloved of Habermas and Arendt, that it may happen obliquely and discreetly,
here and there, sporadically and unpredictably, unconsciously and by chance. In
producing this essay, we felt we communicated very well indeed.

[ANDREW GIBSON]: Anne Fogarty has recently substantially advanced our
understanding of "Ivy Day in the Committee Room." In "Parnellism and
the Politics of Memory: Revisiting 'Ivy Day in the Committee Room,'" she
argues that we should not pin Joyce to a more or less straightforward allegiance to Parnell and critique of the decline of post-Parnellite Ireland. Literary Parnellism was rather a complex and unstable entity. Parnellism in the late
1890s and early 1900s was a site of conflict, controversy, debate. This dis-
sonance was above all the case with the annual commemoration of Parnell's
passing. Joyce is not caught up in a romantic and nostalgic nationalism. In
fact, "the Parnellism that underpins 'Ivy Day' is very much alert to the evolv-
ing nature of the Irish political scene" (Fogarty 2006, 105). Ivy Day itself was

an occasion for playing out contemporary political tensions. Not only that, it also served "as a stimulus for the mobilization of fresh nationalist objectives," indeed, for reformulations of Parnell's legacy itself (ibid., 113). In its very formal intricacy, "Ivy Day" mirrors some of the most crucial political, economic, and cultural divisions and confusions of early-twentieth-century colonial Dublin. But Joyce is also concerned with the unfulfilled utopian ideals of nationalism. Indeed, in counterpointing James Connolly's socialist ideals with Parnell's, he sustains and canvasses the utopian possibilities as well as the problems of both ideologies.

Fogarty's case is powered by the conviction that "Ivy Day" is the story in *Dubliners* whose complexity is most closely related to a sense of "deeply embedded and convoluted political and historical data" (ibid., 104). "Our ability to negotiate the narrative," she argues, "even at the most rudimentary level, is predicated upon the possibility of piecing together the veiled historical debates and complex historical matrix at which it gestures" (ibid.). This statement is precisely right: but Fogarty herself gives most of her attention to the nationalist aspect of the matrix. If we are going to get the full measure of the complexity of the historical matrix to which she refers, we also need to recognize that the Irish politics of labor and/or socialism—the equivocation here is deliberate, for reasons that will become clear—in the late nineteenth and early twentieth centuries is susceptible to the same kind of complex analysis as nationalism. James Fairhall has already provided a careful and scrupulous account of "Ivy Day" with reference to Connolly's socialism (1993, 95–105). But though Fogarty herself cites Fairhall approvingly, his version of the politics of "Ivy Day" now asks to be revised and complicated, given both Fogarty's work and the historical research that has appeared since Fairhall addressed the subject. Joyce scholars have perhaps been a little inclined to assume that, before Jim Larkin, at least, Irish socialism was chiefly James Connolly and a small bunch of men in a dingy room.[1] But Left politics was not exactly a negligible feature of the Dublin in which

1. Compare Dermot Keogh, who notes that historians have tended to set Connolly and Larkin apart from both the union movement and the working-class rank and file in Ireland (1982, 2).

Joyce grew up. The Mayday parade of 1893, for example, numbered twenty thousand people and included Parnellites and Fenians along with socialists and Labour and union men and women (O'Connor 1992, 55). Most Irish towns had their own trade-union councils as early as the late 1880s. The first Irish Trade Union Congress took place in 1895. This larger but less romantic Left politics does not feature much in Joyce, though he was doubtless aware of Nannetti's Labour involvements.[2] But knowing about the Irish Left helps clarify one or two things about Joyce's works, particularly in the case of "Ivy Day." Second, Irish labor and/or socialist politics in the period 1891–1904 was as riven with discord and debate as post-Parnellite nationalism. If we are not aware of that fact, then we miss something of the intellectual mode in which "Ivy Day" is constructed.

"Ivy Day" has long been thought of as built around an absent center, the dead Parnell. It would, however, be better to conceive of it as having two absent centers or, better, two occluded foci: Parnell or nationalist hopes and aspirations, on the one hand, and Labour and socialist hopes and aspirations, on the other. But this conception immediately raises a problem that neither Fogarty nor Fairhall explicitly addresses. The case for Parnell is obvious: from the title of the story to Hynes's poem, Parnell is missing and missed, but also omnipresent. The question of Labour, by contrast, might be thought of as flitting in and out of the story as Hynes flits in and out of the committee room. It would seem to be substantially broached only in the exchange about Colgan (*D*, 148). Why should Fogarty and Fairhall assume it has anything like the major, even pervasive importance they attribute to it? Why should we do so, here? Is this belief not an example of an all too familiar, anachronistic wishful thinking?

There is a clear answer to these questions, and it sheds a good deal of light on the politics of "Ivy Day." Insofar as the story is a form of social, political, and cultural analysis in fiction—insofar as its mode is analytical,

---

2. Nannetti was originally a Labour leader. He was returned as one of the two Labour candidates for the Corporation in 1898. When he was returned as MP, in 1900, it was symptomatic of how far the Irish Parliamentary Party had succeeded in selling itself as also the Irish Labour Party. See Daly 1984, 216, 219.

or "vivisective," in more Joycean terminology (*SH*, 190)—it has three principal aspects. The first one, self-evidently, is national. The issues here are dependence and independence, colonizer and colonized, Home Rule, the British monarchy, and so on. But the other two aspects are economic and class analysis, which are much less readily associated with contemporary Irish nationalism, and smack more of a modern Left politics. "Ivy Day"'s concern with a Left politics is not just confined to the exchange about Colgan. We know it because the story makes so much of economic indicators and class discourse, though it deals with class in a highly specific sense.

Thus, from Jack's fire rake (a "piece of cardboard" [*D*, 144]) to O'Connor's leaky boots and his thoughtfulness about how quickly he uses his tobacco, to the "denuded" condition of the committee room (*D*, 147) and the characters' anxiety about getting paid, to the Mayor's simple tastes—"He'd live on the smell of an oil-rag" (*D*, 156)—and Tierney's "extensive house property in the city and three places of business" (*D*, 160), Joyce puts questions of economic deprivation and economic differences both tiny and large into play, as nationalist discourses often did not, but socialist and Labour discourses repeatedly did. The nontraditional Irish fuel, coal, and specifically a paucity of it are central to the story, and are obviously related to the economic theme. The meager fire in the story is commonly read as a metaphor for the guttering of nationalist hopes. But it is not impossible that, in the spirit of socialist analysis, it also has a more material referent and indicates the frustration of Labour hopes too, specifically, in 1890, the same year as the fall of Parnell.[3] Joyce also links signs of poor health,

3. When, in 1890, John McCormick, one of Dublin's 154 coal merchants, provoked a dispute by banning the unionization of the labor in his dockyard, the district secretary of the gas workers' union, Adolphus Shields, took two thousand men out on strike, shutting down almost every dockyard in the process. Like Parnell, the strike united very different camps, from a range of different Irish unions to Michael Davitt and his supporters to the Orange Order. Coal supplies dwindled, though the strikers ensured that they continued to reach the poor. The strike was the most significant experiment in union power in Ireland before the arrival of Larkin in 1907. It was crucial to the subsequent development of Irish trade unions. It collapsed because of insufficient support from union headquarters in London, though the coal porters walked out again in 1891. The strike provided the famous example both of a Dublin

poor diet, and poverty, as did contemporary commentators on Dublin, and as he himself does repeatedly elsewhere (see, for instance, Cameron 1903, 1904, 1905; and Gibson 2002, especially 36–40). Class consciousness is also pervasively evident in "Ivy Day," if often in rather twisted forms, and in something other than the classical Marxist sense. Jack writes Colgan off as "a tinker."[4] Henchy promotes Tierney's solid bourgeois credentials in public but refers to him as "that little shoeboy" in private (*D*, 155). He is willing to let Hynes off the hook to the extent, at least, that the latter's father "was a decent respectable man" (*D*, 152), and in defending the king cranks up a bit of English posh ("He's a jolly fine decent fellow. . . . Damn it, can't we Irish play fair?" [*D*, 161]).[5] Crofton considers his companions "beneath him" (*D*, 160) and respects Parnell because he was "a gentleman" (*D*, 162), and so on. "Ivy Day" conveys the impression of a society riddled with a consciousness of class. Since it is the consciousness of class that is specifically at issue, that the distinctions are in large part trivial, and sometimes merely notional, is Althusserianly beside the point.

The concern with class and economics is what makes it possible for us to assume that Connolly's thought is relevant to the story as a whole, rather than just a passage and a particular point or two. That is not to say, however, that there are not also precise boundaries to Connolly's relevance, even from within a perspective dictated by the story's "Labour concerns." What follows aims to deepen awareness of Connolly's importance for "Ivy Day," but also to establish its limits as rigorously as possible. Joyce's biographical links with

coal shortage and of an outburst of Dublin working-class solidarity. See Keogh 1982, 101–3. It is worth recalling that Moore described Joyce as "nobody—from the Dublin docks" (Ellmann 1983, 529).

4. The use of *tinker* as a term of class abuse was by no means uncommon in the first few decades of the century, in England as well as Ireland.

5. Compare Gibson 1994, 179–221, especially 194–97. But there the object of my analysis was what I took to be the colonized Dublin unconscious. Here, by contrast, I find it hard to think that Henchy does not pronounce the phrases without some degree of his own (not Joyce's) ironic mimicry of English voices. Of course, it may be that the uncertainty itself illustrates the point (holding political contradictions together). This point remains the same if Henchy's tone is ironical, just a little more complicated.

Connolly are familiar from Costello, Fairhall, and others (see Costello 1992, 215; and Fairhall 1993, 96). Fogarty and Fairhall both note that Connolly's analysis of the influence of drink and the drink industry in Irish politics, and specifically its use to bribe electors and election workers, appears to have influenced "Ivy Day" (Fairhall 1993, 98–99). Fairhall also notes the relevance of Connolly's critique of Mayor Timothy Harrington and his attacks on the political power of slum landlords.[6] In the end, however, Connolly's presence in "Ivy Day" is more intellectual than real. As Fogarty argues, it is above all "Connolly's *writings* . . . [that] are subsumed into the texture and the dominant motifs" of "Ivy Day" (emphasis added).

It is surely Connolly's analysis of the politics of the middle classes that is most relevant to Joyce's work in general and "Ivy Day" in particular. This issue is complex, however, not least because Connolly's analyses owe debts both to Marxism and the British socialism that helped him cut his political teeth and to his politically astute awareness of historically and culturally specific local conditions. There is one particular theme of Connolly's, however, that is crucial to "Ivy Day." What Connolly brilliantly understood in the Irish and above all the Dublin middle class was that it was virtually bound to be divided and caught up in doublethink. This predicament had nothing to do with any supposed Irish character or set of characteristics. It was a feature of a particular phase of the development of colonial Irish society. Parnellism had run its course. Home Rule was stalled. The British government was trying to kill it with kindness. The Dublin petit bourgeoisie was like any other in that it necessarily gave priority to its material interests. But it was also distinctive in that it was part of a colonial culture, and thus vulnerable, insecure, and relatively deprived. In a time of political stagnation, it therefore found itself weathercocking madly between British and nationalist allegiances, depending on how the political wind was blowing.

Connolly was ruthlessly clear about the consequences of this seesawing. His analysis typically fused socialist and nationalist perspectives, as he had done from the start of his Irish career (see Anderson 1994). An article

6. For Connolly's attack on Harrington, see Connolly 1901, reprinted in Connolly 1997, 56.

he published in *Workers' Republic* for September 3, 1898, under the title "Home Thrusts," encapsulates his case and gets the point exactly. In the present set of historical circumstances, the political pragmatism of the Dublin middle class was encouraging a "'broad platform' . . . so broad in fact is it you can neither discover where it begins or ends" (reprinted in Connolly 1997, 24). In other words, the petit bourgeoisie were being forced to seek to keep a foot in different and sometimes opposed political camps, and thereby to hedge their political bets. Connolly was concerned about the direction in which this ambivalence was leading. He saw very clearly its implications for nationalism as much as socialism. He deplored the spectacle of "Home Rule Lord Mayors shaking hands with Tory Lord Lieutenants, Home Rule editors drinking loyal toasts today and writing 'patriotic' articles tomorrow, Home Rule corporations electing Tory Lord Mayors, the conquest of Ireland at last accepted and ratified by her sons" (ibid., 23). The promotion of the Catholic bourgeoisie to significant positions of political and cultural power that had been particularly marked with the Local Government Act in 1898 had at once been a problem. "The middle-class politician . . . cries out as his fingers close upon the plunder: 'No class questions in Irish politics'" (ibid., 21). Ireland should stop identifying middle-class progress with the progress of the nation. It should rather do away "with middle-class leadership, which means middle-class compromise, middle-class trickery [compare "tricky Dicky Tierney"], middle-class time-serving, middle class treachery" (ibid.). In Connolly's account of matters, only the Irish working class could truly and sincerely represent the nationalist cause.

Placed in the context of Connolly's argument, "Ivy Day" reads like an analysis of the shifts and tergiversations of the Dublin petit bourgeoisie, a nationalist analysis, but nationalist with a particular, implicitly socialist, twist. The twist must remain largely implicit, because Joyce is strictly concerned to write about what he knows. Henchy works for the Nationalists but defends the royal visit. Jack thinks the working class should find political representation but is scornful of Colgan. The Conservatives are supporting the Nationalists, and the Nationalist candidate can be made to look eminently congenial to them. Henchy promotes Tierney precisely as standing on Connolly's "broad platform": "*he doesn't belong to any party, good, bad or indifferent*" (*D*, 160–61). Characters assume that political doublethink is ubiquitous, and so Joyce makes it seem. Henchy believes that Hynes is spying for Colgan and that half the "hillsiders and fenians" are "in the pay of the Castle" (*D*, 152). That everyone appears to respect the memory of Parnell only deepens the impression of conflicting loyalties.

By contrast, Hynes would appear to be the character who exposes the others' compromises, passes comment on them, and partly directs our judgment of them. Connolly argued that what Ireland required was not middle-class subterfuge but the "strong, vigorous speech and action" he associated with Labour (1997, 23). Hence the difference between the bold directness of Hynes's speech and the way the other characters talk. Hynes's analysis so closely resembles Connolly's that it is clear that Joyce had Connolly specifically in mind, particularly since Hynes makes his point in the context of a defense of Labour. He expresses his dislike of the political "hunker-sliding" he associates with Tierney—going in "on the nationalist ticket" but "kowtowing to a foreign king"—and derides "those shoneens that are always hat in hand before any fellow with a handle to his name" (*D*, 148). These phrases put Connolly's exact point about middle-class *séoninism* in more vivid form (compare Connolly 1997, 25). Even Hynes, however, is caught in contradiction, as we shall see in a little while.

Connolly's thought, then, is indeed pervasively evident in "Ivy Day." As far as political ideas are concerned, the story takes up a position that is in some ways like the position of Connolly's Marxist Irish Socialist Republican Party. Furthermore, it is specifically like Connolly's as opposed to other Left or leftist positions available on the Irish political scene. Henry Hyndman's Social-Democratic Federation, William Morris's Socialist League, the Irish Labour League, the Dublin Socialist Club, the Progressive Club, the Irish Socialist Union, the Irish Democratic Trade and Labour Federation, the Fabian Society, the Independent Labour Party: all of these organizations had appeared in Ireland in the eighties and nineties, if largely to disappear again soon afterward.[7] They were mainly of British provenance, and Ireland

7. For a full account of these societies, see Boyle 1988, 138 and chap. 8, "The Voice of Dissent," 171–215. The impression of richness and diversity is to some extent misleading. Many of these organizations had more or less the same membership.

almost always came a poor second on their list of priorities. On occasions, their representatives were frankly racist (as in the case of the Webbs).[8] Most important, they were invariably indifferent to the question of Home Rule, declaring it to be irrelevant to the lot of the Irish worker.

Connolly's insistence on thinking socialism and nationalism or anti-imperialism together was therefore quite distinctive. But Fairhall's claim that "beyond doubt Connolly's solid, historical reality underlies the vague, absent figure of the Labour candidate in 'Ivy Day'" is not sustainable (1993, 92). The fact that Colgan is apparently a bricklayer immediately detaches him from Connolly, who was not known in terms of any trade. It is Connolly's ideas that matter in the story. There is no evidence in "Ivy Day" that Joyce was thinking of Connolly the man. If he had wanted to index Connolly's "solid, histori-cal reality," he could and surely would have done so.[9] Joyce may give Hynes a Connolly-based argument, but Connolly's position is not Colgan's. When Connolly himself stood for the Wood Quay Ward, though he was endorsed by the Dublin Trades Council, his revolutionary socialism made him an extremely unusual Labour candidate. Colgan is certainly a much more ordinary one. Numerous such candidates were elected after the Act of 1898 (see Ellis 1985, 169). Nothing in "Ivy Day" suggests that we should distinguish Colgan from them. Connolly had no faith in merely ameliorative or reformist work. Such would not seem to be the case with Colgan (or with Hynes). So, too, that Hynes describes Colgan as a "plain, honest man" who "goes in to represent the labour classes" (*D*, 148) hardly suggests that he is a radical firebrand. Far from establishing his relation to Connolly, the general tone in which Colgan is referred to or discussed makes his distance from Connolly very clear.

Fairhall's argument effectively suggests that "Ivy Day" plays off a fis-sured and fragmented nationalism against a unitary socialism. Yet the Irish

8. As for instance, in a letter to Graham Wallas, July 1892: "The people are charming but we detest them, as we should the Hottentots, for their very virtues. Home Rule is an abso-lute necessity in order to depopulate the country of their detestable race." Sidney Webb wrote most of this letter; Beatrice added the last ten words. See Boyle 1988, 181.

9. Here Joyce's different uses of Connolly and Nannetti are obviously significant. Nan-netti is a good example of the kind of Labour leader in Dublin who was very unlike Connolly. Connolly's ideas get a Joycean treatment. Nannetti actually gets into *Ulysses*.

Left was nothing if not disunited. This fact was very clear to influential Labour outsiders, like Kier Hardie (see Clarkson 1925, 184, 398).[10] First of all, as Fairhall himself remarks, Labour politics was not socialist politics. There were sometimes fierce differences between the two, not least over the relation of the Left with the Irish Parliamentary Party. Second, immediately after the fall of Parnell, the urban working class had indeed united, going "Parnellite to a man" (O'Connor 1992, 56). However, as we have seen, that unity had subsequently fallen apart, with various different socialist, social democratic, or labor parties competing. Third, the Irish trade-union movement was split. The relationship between British and Irish trade unions was very much overdetermined by the colonial relation. On the one hand, most of the Irish trade councils were absorbed by British amalgamated unions in the 1890s. On the other hand, the British unions repeatedly alienated their Irish equivalents by virtue of their superior attitudes, neglect of Irish issues, indifference to religious questions, and so on.[11] Such problems divided Irish labor itself, with some of it seeking an alliance with nationalism, some of it not.[12] Irish unionists also had their own version of the kind of double dealing that Connolly and Joyce recognized in the Dublin middle classes.

There are at least two obvious ways in which "Ivy Day" diverges markedly from Connolly. First, no more than any other of Joyce's works does it appear to credit the Marxist historical narrative, its inexorable logic and the certainty of its inevitable end to which Connolly repeatedly subscribes (see, for example, Connolly 1909, 9–10, 35). One might think of its formal features as effectively constituting a rejoinder to that narrative. Second, and more important here, the story suggests a distinct skepticism regarding both the political will of and the potential for solidarity within the working class,

10. For all his support for Connolly, however, Hardie held views of Ireland that were in many ways disappointingly unenlightened.

11. In Britain, immigrant Irish labor was heavily involved in trade unionism. The British National Union of Dock Labourers was known as "the Irish union." An Irishman, Jim Connor, even composed "The Red Flag." See Keogh 1982, 94; and O'Connor 1992, 48. Yet the British unions were almost paranoically fearful of what they took to be the effects of Irish immigration on the labor market.

12. For a fuller account of this division, see O'Connor 1992, 55–60.

in both of which Connolly had great confidence (see, for instance, Connolly 1901, 56).[13] The abstraction of Connolly's thought was to some extent a weakness. Joyce, by contrast, remains rooted, immersed in particular life and lives. As a result, on the question of the political potential of the working class, he can seem much closer to the pragmatic, experienced realism of the Labour men and union organizers than he does to Connolly. Irish union leaders were not above complaining about the low level of political awareness evident in their followers. Michael O'Lehane, for example, founder of the Drapiers' Assistants' Association in 1901, recalled his early membership as in many ways reactionary, prejudiced against other workers and obsessed with footling and pretentious hierarchical distinctions between virtual economic equals. Indeed, in complaining of the "false notions of respectability" of many of his members—they wanted to dress "like dukes," he wrote, "on the wages of a dustman"—he was effectively identifying a working-class *séoninism.*[14]

Joyce conveys views similar to O'Lehane's in his treatment of Jack the caretaker, a crucial figure in "Ivy Day" and one of Joyce's rare working-class characters. It is through Jack above all that he registers the problem of and for the Irish Left. Like the more middle-class characters in the story, Jack is unresistingly servile or "gratefully oppressed" (*D*, 49). The others tend to treat him rather like a servant, sometimes patronizingly. But he shows no sign of resenting it. Like them, he reserves his most pungent contempt for his own. His dismissal of Colgan is a precise example of the kind of lack of fellow feeling that worried O'Lehane: a worker who suspected another of getting a little above himself was quick to run him down. Through Jack, Joyce suggests that the internal rifts and divisions that this historically specific colonial culture produces are by no means confined to the middle class. They are evident, too, in the very class that the Marxist Connolly assumed would be its nemesis.

If Hynes is anything to go by, the same would hold good of those individuals who speak for labor. The irony of Hynes's poem is not principally its

13. It is Eleanor Marx, however, who best represents the tone: "It is certain that the hope of Ireland a nation [*sic*] lies not in her middle class O'Connells but in her generous, devoted, heroic working men and women" (quoted in Ellis 1985, 174).

14. In his trade journal, *Drapiers' Assistant,* 1918, quoted in Keogh 1982, 65.

backward-looking Parnellism. As we saw earlier, Labour had united behind Parnell's cause at the time of the split. The point, more mundanely, is that *the Parnellism specifically expressed in the poem* denies much of what Hynes had previously argued for. The poem is riddled with class metaphor. Parnell is the true Irish aristocrat, "Our Uncrowned King," Erin's "monarch," the people's "lord," sufficiently seigneurial to have "spurned them in his pride" (*D*, 164). Logically enough, the poem also pours scorn on the "rabble-rout," the "coward hounds / He raised to glory from the mire." It is scathing about modernity, too (or "modern hypocrites," at least). In effect, it reeks of distaste for ordinary Irishmen and -women. This aversion is hardly reconcilable with Hynes's early support for "good honest bricklayer" Colgan. It is to Hynes's credit that he seems aware that the poem now seems anachronistic ("Sure, that's old now" [*D*, 163]). It may even be that his "flushed" silence at the end of the story is not the old emotion it is commonly taken to be, but confusion, even embarrassment at how swiftly history has moved on, and moved him on with it, confusion because his poem is so unmodern, perhaps because his heart is, too. At all events, the point is clear: in late-colonial Ireland, political modernity appears infrequently, in fits and starts, in ambivalent or adulterated forms.

In effect, then, Joyce offers a sober caution to Connolly. "Ivy Day" does not reveal a conflict between Joyce's nationalism and his socialism, as Fairhall suggests. It is rooted in Connolly's political articulation of the two together. It would be more accurate to say that the story registers a conflict between Connolly's analysis and his program, on the one hand, and political reality, on the other. Joyce is acutely aware of the immense difficulty of pursuing a politics like Connolly's in the Ireland it describes with any degree of success. Fogarty, again, is right: Joyce's story seems fueled both by a residual utopianism and by an acute awareness of the obstacles it must face. Joyce was certainly not interested in offering us a moral critique of a group of Irishmen. While most of them would not figure in anyone's list of Joycean favorites, the characters in "Ivy Day" are not dislikable, let alone contemptible. But that is not really the point. The mode of "Ivy Day" is historical and cultural anatomy. As such, it is concerned with a problem that is larger than the characters and can be heard everywhere in what they have to say, a problem, in fact, presented in terms of a discursive configuration.

It is the problem of establishing a modern politics in Ireland, of shifting from an old-fashioned, heroic politics to a new, properly democratic, and egalitarian politics.[15] Colonial history had drastically inhibited the possibility of significant change in at least two respects. It had everywhere turned Irish people against themselves, in the socialist and labor as in the nationalist camp, and it had inspired a mythologization of political experience that was to persist as far as the Easter Rising and well beyond. Connolly himself repeatedly lamented the continuing Irish interest in political ideas "regarded throughout the remainder of the world as outworn and obsolete" (1909, 9). He argued that the middle classes were always inclined to take the heroic view of politics, as the characters do in "Ivy Day," because they believed in individual success rather than class action (ibid., 6). But his view of Irish workers as "the incorruptible inheritors of the fight for freedom in Ireland" was scarcely less romantic (see Connolly 1917, xxxvii–xxxviii). Joyce had little use for political mythologies. Connolly ends his "Platform of the Socialist Labour Party" with the sentence "Speed the day." "Ivy Day" might be thought of as echoing that sentiment, with the rider that the day was certainly not going to come quickly (1909, 3).

[JENNIFER LEVINE]: I take my lead from Jane Jacobs, urban theorist and fellow Torontonian, whose last book, *The Nature of Economies,* draws on an ancient rhetorical tradition: the dialogue. Like her, I know that "a book [and also an essay] is equipped to speak for itself, more so than any other artifact. But to be heard . . . [it] needs a collaborator: a reader with a sufficiently open mind to take in what . . . [it] is saying and dispute or agree, but in any case think about it." Describing her own project, she goes on to say that "insofar as the process is enjoyably interesting as well as possibly useful—as I hope it may be—so much the better" (2001, x). "Enjoyably interesting" is something worth aiming for. And a reader who feels invited to dispute or agree (or perhaps both to dispute and to agree) is exactly the kind of reader Andrew Gibson and I want to engage here.

15. I mean "modern," not "postmodern," and "democratic" and "egalitarian" in a modern, not postmodern, sense.

That we came to this project in different ways will be immediately apparent. When you read the following dialogue, you will notice the sudden shift to a more colloquial register. Who *are* these people? you might ask. We do not even have their last names—let alone their academic affiliations. And what is the overarching argument? Isn't the critic the one who gives shape to a reading? Well, no. As dramatized here, the critic may sometimes be the one who pulls the reading apart, scatters it to observe its various contradictions.

Be patient, reader. Read on.

My imaginary characters are Louisa, Jock, and Selwyn. They first met as students in an introductory literature course like so many others, where *Dubliners* was an assigned text. Now Louisa is involved in theater. She is always looking for new material. Jock, whose favorite author is James Joyce, has just reread *Ulysses*. Selwyn's interests tend to history and politics. He is curious about literature, but has never felt entirely comfortable talking about it.

Louisa, on the other hand, has something to say about "Ivy Day": she is excited by its theatricality, convinced that with minor tweaks here and there, it is perfect for the stage. Why would she think so? Because, she says to Jock, it's largely written like a one-act play.[16] It's all entrances and exits off a single stage set, a central light, coming from the fireplace, and everyone grouped around it. When two candles are lit, the scene expands. But nothing offstage. The doorway functions as an absolute limit. Characters appear and disappear there. No flashbacks. No hidden corners. No interiority. Almost no description. Just talk. It's all there, in the dialogue, and in the timing. (She has noticed how often Joyce specifies how long the wait is before the next rejoinder.) "It's exhilarating to be left alone like that," she says, "no other voice whispering in your ear, telling you what things mean. That's how plays work."

Louisa has also noticed that the story is unusual for *Dubliners*: "I mean the single unblinking, unmoving eye it casts on the scene. All the others swerve back in time, or stop the action and jump forward, or move from place to place—even if only from one room to another. But Joyce just keeps that extraordinarily tight focus all the way through. I was wondering if he

16. Louisa is not the first to think so. See also Warren Beck 1969, 120. Norris makes a strong case for naturalistic drama as the story's shadow genre (2003, 172–84).

was having sly fun with the Aristotelian idea of dramatic structure—you know, the classical unities of place and time?"

JOCK: Well, I did notice how deliberately every entrance and exit is mentioned. But if Joyce is playing that game (which I doubt he is), shouldn't there be a unity of action as well? I'm asking you, because I've always wondered about "Ivy Day." Men talk. I suppose you could add: men wait. How would you define the action?

LOUISA: Isn't it obvious that the key event is Hynes's performance at the end? Doesn't everything move toward that?

JOCK: Perhaps, though hardly in the sense that Aristotle meant it. But then what should we make of Hynes's performance? And another question: why would you want to put "Ivy Day" on stage in the first place?

LOUISA: It has always surprised me that Joyce was less successful as a playwright than as a novelist. He has a director's sense of timing and gesture. Listen to the way he stages Hynes's exit: "He went out of the room slowly. Neither Mr Henchy nor the old man said anything but, just as the door was closing, Mr O'Connor, who had been staring moodily into the fire, called out suddenly: 'Bye, Joe'" (*D*, 151). It's all there: Hynes's marginal position in the committee room—the reasons for which remain ambiguous; the lack of welcome from Henchy and the caretaker; O'Connor's tendency to play follow the leader, but to be, always, a little out of step. So part of me just wants to take advantage of what Joyce makes available. I could make a wonderful little play out of his text. And besides, it would just be another way of reading the story, wouldn't it? Reading is always some kind of translation. Mine would be performed in public, that's all. Anyway, look at the way the reader is situated.

JOCK: What do you mean?

LOUISA: You might as well be at a play. You're observing people you don't know, but who know each other. As soon as a character leaves the room, the others talk about him: a revealing comment on life in Dublin perhaps, but from the reader's point of view essential, because in "Ivy Day," that's how you get your information. You never know a character's name until someone in the committee room mentions it. It's as if the narrating function has been switched off. The descriptions that accompany each character's entry into the scene, attentive to a few details of appearance, sound like a director's casting notes. Almost without exception, the story does not reveal thoughts or motives, or it hesitates. I'm thinking of the way it says about Father Keon that "it was impossible to say whether he wore a clergyman's collar or a layman's" (D, 153). (And did you notice how—as if to underline the theatrical premise—he's described as "resembling a poor clergyman or a poor actor" [D, 153]? His actions are oddly contradictory performances: "He opened his very long mouth suddenly to express disappointment and at the same time opened wide his very bright blue eyes to express pleasure and surprise" [D, 153].)

It's even more hesitant about Hynes, who "did not seem to remember at once the piece" that the others are asking for (D, 163). When he does, he "seemed to be rehearsing the piece in his mind" (D, 163). And when it's over, and the cork flies out of the bottle sitting on the hob, "he did not seem to have heard" the earlier invitation to have a drink (D, 165). Always "seemed"—as if the story cannot be sure of anything beyond what can be seen and heard, or what the characters themselves say.

JOCK: Oh, but surely those *seem*s are ironic. And the way Father Keon's clothes are described: doesn't that imply a fastidious, possibly sardonic, storyteller pulling the strings?

LOUISA: Possibly. But I see it differently: a kind of hands-off policy, as if the narrative is stuck at a theatrical distance.

(Jock wants to point out that this situation is not always in play. The narrative seems confident enough about Crofton: "He was silent for two reasons. The first reason, sufficient in itself, was that he had nothing to say; the second reason was that he considered his companions beneath him" [D, 160]. However, he cannot think of any other example. Louisa goes on.)

LOUISA: Again, this is unique in *Dubliners*. "Counterparts" and "Grace" both begin in the same mode, but after a few pages they both shift toward interiority. All the others either are told through a first-person narrative or eventually align themselves with the point of view of a particular character. But not "Ivy Day."[17] It's a swirl of externalized voices. Staging it would bring the committee room to life, and it would make things clearer, wouldn't it?

17. For a fuller discussion of these issues in *Dubliners*, see Riquelme 1983, 120–22. Of all the stories, "'Ivy Day' eschews the presentation of consciousness most completely" (ibid., 120).

At this point the conversation is interrupted by Selwyn's arrival. Today, by remarkable coincidence, he too has something to say about "Ivy Day." He has just heard a visiting professor from the University of London, Andrew Gibson, speak about the story. At last, he says, someone who deals with the historical context in real detail and sees how the shape of a story and the events of the past might be enmeshed together. (But don't think this is the old-fashioned historical criticism—the type that seals the past off, collecting minute details for their own antiquarian interest. On the contrary. There's something very contemporary in the attention it pays to the divisions and contradictions within classes and political movements.) He has asked for a copy of the lecture and now shares it with his two friends. Jock is the first to respond. His question to Louisa about the appropriate response to Hynes's poem is still on his mind, so he is taken with Andrew Gibson's closing observation that "Joyce was certainly not interested in offering us a moral critique of a group of Irishmen." Gibson extends the point toward a broader, more politicized reading than he would likely make, but still, the statement rings true. There has been a long tradition of reading the canvassers as variously corrupt or inadequate and of contrasting them to Hynes, who honorably if sentimentally keeps alive the memory of Parnell. But Hynes is an ambiguous figure, made more so by his reappearances in *Ulysses*. Jock believes the novel and the short stories form a single expanded text and that we must factor into our understanding of Hynes the fact that, in "Aeolus," he conveniently fails to register Bloom's hint: paychecks are being issued; the money he owes him could be repaid. The impression that lingers is of a man who forgets past obligations just as much as he remembers them. So, yes, there is no moral critique here, and there is also no anointing of heroes.

LOUISA: This *is* interesting. But I'm not sure I agree with what he says at the beginning—that our ability to make sense of things (I guess that's what he means by negotiating the narrative), "even at the most rudimentary level, is predicated upon the possibility of piecing together the veiled historical debates and complex historical matrix at which it gestures." Jock, you know Joyce's work better than I do. Is that a fair assumption?

JOCK: Actually, it's Anne Fogarty who said that.

LOUISA: But Andrew Gibson quotes her because he agrees. Surely, "Ivy Day" isn't just a historical document, dead on the page until the historical explanations arrive? Selwyn, you're interested in history. Does it ring true for you?

SELWYN: Look, we read for different reasons, and we value different things. I, for example, am not particularly interested in psychoanalysis. I don't understand why critics twist themselves into hermeneutical knots looking for symbolic meanings when the obvious is staring them in the face. Here's another essay I picked up. Why, for example, would you need to explain Mr. Henchy's technique for opening bottles as a response to impotence, or to the "phallic signifier" (Leonard 1993, 244)? The simple fact is that there's no corkscrew on the premises, and drinkers of stout know how to get around that when they have to. I like that Gibson recognizes the conditions of material lack that haunt the story and sees them for what they are. He doesn't fetishize the past, but he doesn't interpret it away, either. I felt like cheering when he said that the weak little fire in the committee room isn't necessarily to be read as a metaphor for Ireland's fragile nationalist aspirations. What he says about poverty in Dublin is much more to the point.

LOUISA: Sure. Anyone thinking of staging this would have noticed how sparsely furnished the room is—even if it is only a temporary meeting place. I take it that Father Keon with the "rosy spots" on his "damp-yellow" cheeks is probably dying of tuberculosis, which by 1900 was clearly identified with poverty and malnutrition.

SELWYN: Yes, I think he is. But really, Louisa, your uneasiness with Anne Fogarty's claim is a nonissue. She said it to make a point. For decades the idea that Joyce and politics could be put side by side was unthinkable (apart from the iconic figure of Parnell—who, as Gibson points out, was too easily trotted out as the only possible version of an alternative Ireland). When the connections started being made in the 1980s, there was a tendency to project British or American paradigms onto Ireland. Andrew Gibson in London and Anne Fogarty in Dublin are part of a new wave of scholars who are reconstructing that lost Irish history. Bravo to them, I say.

LOUISA: I still think the point is overstated. Look at Mr. Henchy, for example. Andrew Gibson says that these characters are full of contradictions. I agree with that. For him, though, it's a political symptom. But you don't need to know about veiled historical debates to see that Henchy's an alcoholic desperate for a drink. That's what explains his behavior.

JOCK: How so? Doesn't Gibson talk about the problem of drink?

LOUISA: Yes, but only because James Connolly made it his subject. There's no link to Henchy. Look at him, though: he's a changed man once the drinks arrive. But when he first comes in, he's fit to explode. He rubs his hands "as if he intended to draw a spark from them" (*D*, 149). He spits "so copiously that he nearly put out the fire" (*D*, 151). He interrogates O'Connor. He's filled with bile about Tierney, "the little shoeboy": "Mean little tinker . . . with his little pig's eyes. . . . Blast his soul! Couldn't he pay up like a man. . . . Mean little schoolboy of hell! I suppose he forgets the time his little old father kept the hand-me-down shops". He "always had a tricky little black bottle up in a corner" (*D*, 151). He's so on edge that anything sets him off. He's filled with suspicion about Hynes: the minute Hynes leaves (pointedly unacknowledged), Henchy asks what brought *him* to the committee room. Then, after denouncing Hynes ("he's a spy of Colgan's, if you ask me" [*D*, 152]), Henchy identifies him as a sponger.

JOCK: Well, Henchy's right. Remember how he "forgets" about his debt to Bloom when he turns up again in *Ulysses*.

LOUISA: I know, Jock, but that's not my point at the moment. Let me pin this down. When Mr. O'Connor puts in a good word about "that thing" Hynes wrote, Henchy squelches it: "Some of those hillsiders and fenians are a bit too clever if you ask me. . . . I believe half of them are in the pay of the Castle." He works himself up into a lather, escalating suspicions of betrayal from "I believe" to "I know it for a fact," and accusations from "some" to "half," then to a very particular "certain little nobleman with a cock-eye" named as a lineal descendant of Major Sirr—as deadly an association as you can make in nationalist Ireland (*D*, 152).

JOCK: Yes, but Henchy is strikingly courteous and helpful to Father Keon. Why is that? And that's before the drink turns up. Doesn't that weaken your argument?

LOUISA: Henchy says he thought Keon "was the dozen of stout" (*D*, 155). No surprise if he welcomes him in. The key is that he totally deflates after Keon leaves: "He sat down again at the fire. There was silence for a few moments" (*D*, 154). Then the others pick up the slack and talk about needing a drink. Henchy gets his second wind and takes another shot at Tierney: "I asked that little shoeboy three times . . . would he send up a dozen of stout. I asked him again now. . . . 'About that little matter I was speaking to you about . . .' 'That'll be alright, Mr H,' he said. Yerra, sure the little hop-o'-my-thumb has forgotten all about it." Notice how he can't open his mouth without the angry *little* popping out to cut someone or something down to size. Then the drinks arrive, and the belittling stops dead. No tumblers? "Don't let that trouble you" (*D*, 157). Tierney? "He's not so bad after all" (*D*, 157). King Edward? "A jolly fine decent fellow" (*D*, 161). (I like Gibson's suggestion that he's taking the mickey here: but even if it's satire, it's very different from the enraged tone before.) Look at how Henchy expansively offers a drink to anyone who comes in—Crofton, Lyons, the boy from the *Black Eagle,* and finally Hynes, whose reentry now is to be celebrated: "There's one of them that didn't renege [Parnell]," and whose recitation is welcomed: "Listen to this, now, splendid thing" (*D*, 163). He even shushes the others to ensure a proper reception. Henchy's judgments are maudlin and self-contradictory. After all, as he flatly announces, "He [Parnell] is dead" (*D*, 164). But what remains consistent in his second lubricated incarnation is his good humor: the world's his oyster now. Don't you see that Joyce is tracking a symptomatic moment in an alcoholic's life, the desperate frazzle before the drink arrives, and then the expansive bonhomie that follows?

SELWYN: I do see what you mean—but why stop there? Why don't you link this up with a more historicized view of Irish society? Surely drinking— at least in Joyce's Dublin—is never just a private matter.[18] Don't forget, the porter the men are waiting for is essentially their paycheck. And is it only about drink? Look at the way Henchy talks about Tierney. He wouldn't dream of interrupting him when he's in conversation with Alderman Cowley. Behind his back it's an entirely different matter. There he can't let go of the fact that Tierney's father sold secondhand goods—and illegal booze on Sunday mornings (*D*, 168). It's a classic case of the underling sniffing at the boss when he catches him with his pants down—but at the same time

---

18. In addition to Gibson's discussion, see Lloyd 2000, 128–49. Paul Delany (1995) tracks the relationship between drinking and broader questions of consumption, modernization, and nationalism.

resenting the discovery, because it puts in question the illusions that keep the system going. One of the reasons I found the lecture so interesting is that it differentiates between class distinctions (which may sometimes be trivial, or even notional) and class consciousness. As Gibson says, in "Ivy Day" it is "consciousness of class that is specifically at issue." You mentioned the way Henchy keeps using the word *little*. Isn't that another instance? You know, the condescending verbal tick that puts the lower orders in their place?

JOCK: Well, it's definitely not a tall man's condescension, since he is "a bustling little man" himself (*D,* 149)! Louisa, I hadn't noticed Mr. Henchy in the way you have. But I think you're right about him. It's as if he had been sitting there, in the committee room, just another Dublin hack until this moment when you finally see him, caught in his own private hell. You could read this a dozen times and not see it, or it could jump out at you right away. I love that quality of latency in Joyce. But I'm not persuaded by your main argument that "Ivy Day" belongs on the stage. (That's what we were discussing when you came in, Selwyn.) Something crucial happens on the page.

Do you remember the question I asked you about Hynes's performance? Let me show you what I mean. Consider how information is doled out. First the eager introduction to the poem. Then the poem itself, printed in its entirety. (No account of the performance.) Then the reactions to it. So while you are reading the poem, you are relatively free to make your own judgment and measure it against Mr. Henchy's declaration that it is a "splendid thing" (*D,* 162). Perhaps you want to admire it: it is written for Parnell, after all. Perhaps you're squirming a little: Hynes's verse is pretty standard stuff (though probably a little better than most of what was published in the Dublin papers following Parnell's death).[19] The meter strains and stumbles in the seventh stanza. Does the stumble make it bad? Or is it expressive—the excess of feeling overflowing the line? You know that it's not splendid. When it's over, though, you have the reactions of the men in the committee room, for whom it hits a nerve. Somehow, these stanzas have the power to move. In the theater, you would be swept up in Hynes's performance, in the body language of the people around him, and in the applause that follows. By print-

19. See *United Ireland,* Saturday, October 17, 1891, special edition, with color supplement.

ing the poem in full, Joyce allows alternate responses to surface and keeps them in a delicate equilibrium. Yes, the verse is somewhat clichéd. And yes, it is touching. And yes, quite possibly, as Gibson suggests, Hynes's flushed face comes from embarrassment. Nothing is simple. It gets even more interesting in the last lines. Look at the way the story delivers the final judgment: "What do you think of that, Crofton? cried Mr Henchy. Isn't that fine? What? Mr Crofton said that it was a very fine piece of writing" (*D*, 165). Two things happen here on the page. The first is Mr. Henchy's *cried,* right after Mr. O'Connor takes out his cigarette papers and pouch, "the better to hide his emotion." Nothing special about that, you might think, except that here the story does something new. Whenever there's quoted speech in "Ivy Day," the verb introducing it is almost exclusively *said:* so neutral it might as well be invisible. Henchy's *cried* jumps out. He asks his blustery question, but you are invited to hear something else behind it. The second is that Crofton's words are not quoted directly, as is the norm in "Ivy Day." Instead, you have a report *about* speech.

LOUISA: I don't really see your point here. Why does that matter?

JOCK: Because this is a way of putting a frame around Crofton's words and saying to the reader: come over here with me and look at what this fellow has just said. It's impossible to read the last phrase, "a very fine piece of writing," without puffing oneself up a little, as if momentarily speaking in Crofton's voice, but with a self-conscious edge. How else could you capture the ironic take on the closing words? It is ironic, surely, that the man who "hasn't a word to throw to a dog" has the last word—his imprimatur the kind of thing you say when, in fact, you have nothing to say about what the writing is about, or when you have nothing to say about the writing itself, or when you imagine writing in general as a consumable requiring a sticker price—which is precisely what Joyce's stories are not. The rhetorical shifts at the end are unsettling, but essential.

LOUISA: Have you considered the possibility that the embarrassed fumbling at the end, after Hynes's recitation, represents a very different response? Given the "stage directions" Joyce writes into his story, I'd say that the men in the committee room aren't particularly moved by the poem, but feel they should be. The sequence from "silence" to the "burst of clapping," which lasts only "for a little time" (*D*, 165), capped at the end by the pompous praise, looks to me like an awkward cover-up.

JOCK: Hmm . . . But then you diminish the story: you turn it into an exposé. That is, Dublin is a shallow, forgetful place, and the men in the committee room with the possible exception of Hynes are all inadequate. But so what? That doesn't explain why "Ivy Day" touches us. It touches me, at least—and not only because these men are flustered by their own feelings.

LOUISA: How, then?

JOCK: Because in those last pages this most uncompromising of writers acknowledges the humbling fact that sometimes conventional phrases, predictable turns of phrase, occasionally clumsy verse, imperfect, unsophisticated rhyme, even banal images may move an audience as much—perhaps more—than the most sophisticated and accomplished writing. This is what his meticulously told story lets us see. And that's its kick, too. Of course, what moves the reader is not what moves the men in the committee room. In your staged version, you would have to find some way to re-create that layered effect. It would not happen just by having Mr. Henchy emote his lines in a crying tone, or Crofton voice his opinion directly to the others. If he did, he would definitely have the last word. But he doesn't, really. Instead, he's framed by the narrative: a bit of a pompous ass caught like a deer in the story's headlights. The puzzling thing is that, in the committee room, everybody seems to defer to him. It happens again in *Ulysses*. Why? Crofton is the anti-Bloom: he never says anything, but everyone seems to care about his opinion.

SELWYN: This is exactly the kind of detail Andrew Gibson helps us understand. Political life in the early 1900s is in a self-contradicting tailspin. That the Labour candidate's man is welcomed into the Nationalist candidate's quarters, and that Crofton, the Conservative, is of all men asked for his opinion on a recitation honoring Parnell is a sign of the times.

JOCK: I just remembered that Crofton, almost certainly unlike any of the others, has a steady income coming in. Maybe his financial status adds weight to his opinions? (In "Cyclops" the narrator can never get his name right, but what sticks in his mind is that he draws both a wage and a pension [*U*, 12:1589–92]. Of course, that particular narrator is hardly reliable . . .)

LOUISA: Not everybody in "Ivy Day" defers to Crofton, though. It's almost exclusively Henchy. Joyce is staging a specific little drama between the two.

SELWYN: I don't see it. What do you mean?

LOUISA: Henchy and Crofton have been working the ward together. But Crofton, as Jock reminded us, "hasn't a word to throw to a dog": "he's not worth a damn as a canvasser" (*D*, 158). Obviously, while they are talking to prospective voters, Henchy has to keep the conversational ball in the air and to keep alive the illusion of two thinking units on the job. This juggling means constantly creating openings for his partner. The only question, for me, is whether Henchy's behavior in the committee room is just a continuation—he's a big talker and can't stop himself—or whether by now he's so irritated that he's effectively baiting Crofton: pushing and pushing to see whether he can be made to talk after all. It could be played either way.[20] But again, what strikes me is the rich backstory between the lines.

SELWYN: I can see, Louisa, that your theater experience makes you a skilled reader of character and motivation. But the connections both you and Jock make are always internal—inside the story, or between one story and another. I want to take a wider view. How could you not do so, when the story has a title like "Ivy Day in the Committee Room"?

LOUISA: What do you mean? Is it Ivy Day you're referring to? The anniversary of Parnell's death?

SELWYN: Yes, but also the "committee room." We know the story is set in 1902 or 1903, because they're discussing the new king's visit to Ireland.[21] But the title sends us right back to 1890, when the O'Shea divorce case went to court. Parnell was named as the correspondent and found guilty. He was already vulnerable politically. Gladstone's Liberals had won a majority and no longer needed his Irish party to prop them up in Parliament.

20. Garry Leonard argues that the power dynamic is in fact reversed—that Henchy is being controlled by Crofton, and most particularly by his silence: thus Henchy's "unconscious fixation on what he imagines Crofton to be thinking" (1993, 240).

21. Originally scheduled for 1902, the king's visit was postponed by a year until the war against the Boers was over. It was feared that Irish sympathy with the Boer cause would have provoked embarrassing public protest (O'Brien 1982, 88).

When the adultery became public knowledge, his own supporters turned against him too.

LOUISA: Where are you going with this, Selwyn? Even I know this.

SELWYN: Here's the hook. The Irish party caucus met over a few days in December at Westminster, and what happened there made Committee Room 15, where they met, famous. They confirmed Parnell's leadership, expecting him then to gracefully resign and have his withdrawal from power "reluctantly" accepted. But he didn't. So they effectively deposed him: a majority of the members walked out, leaving him in an impossible position. Joyce's father knew details about that meeting through his close friendship with J. M. Tuohy, the London correspondent for the *Freeman's Journal*, who produced the only official version of events and who also gave him an uncensored personal account of everything that had taken place (J. Jackson and Costello 1998, 161). For Parnell loyalists (among them John Joyce), Committee Room 15 represented the locus classicus of betrayal, leading straight to Parnell's death ten months later. It's a dramatic story. To slide over that cluster of associations in the title would be a kind of cultural illiteracy, wouldn't it? Surely, Joyce was playing off that story with his title, particularly since he would have grown up with it.

JOCK: Oh, sure, I agree it's important—but there are other ways of thinking about the title. Look at the story that follows. (And by the way, Joyce wrote it right after "Ivy Day.") It picks up the word *committee* and runs with it.

SELWYN: How so?

JOCK: In "A Mother" a woman who thinks she can manage the world discovers that she cannot. The minute Mrs. Kearney stops being entirely charming and helpful, "the Society" with which she thought she was dealing morphs into something else: a "committee" of which she had not previously been aware and to which she clearly does not belong, even though—as the first pages of the story are careful to tell us—she has poured her energies into arrangements for the concert. "The committee" becomes the counter to any claim that she might wish to press. Over and over again, she is told, "the committee" has made a mistake (*D*, 170), or a decision (*D*, 170), or must be consulted (*D*, 171), or that it would "move heaven and earth" (*D*, 171) to secure a full house, but always that she must wait for a decision from "the committee." Mr. Holohan and Mr. Fitzpatrick call on those two words again and again, using them like a weapon against her. When she eventually asks the stewards "was any member of the committee in the hall" (D, 173), one of them manages to track down an unlikely "little woman named Miss Beirne," who is clearly no more at the center of power than Mrs. Kearney. At the end, she says "that the committee had treated her scandalously," but after that "her conduct was condemned on all hands; everyone approved of what the committee had done" (D, 182).

SELWYN: It's like Foucault's panopticon, isn't it? The modern regime of power is all seeing (so they claim) but is itself unseeable (see Foucault 1995, in particular the chapter "Panopticism," 195–228).

JOCK: You could put it that way. I'd probably say it's like the Wizard of Oz: rather a sham, but powerful precisely because it is absent. What's important to me is that both stories frame "Ivy Day": one in historical time, the other in reading time. I wouldn't agree with you that Parnell's committee room obviously takes precedence.

LOUISA: Can I jump in here? My way of paying attention to the drama might be helpful. Both halves of the frame are important. They even mirror each other. Look at the dramatic situations: Mrs. Kearney gets squeezed out at the end, like Parnell in Committee Room 15. They walk away from her. Like him, she's left with a shrinking group that just can't measure up. At the end, only her husband and daughter are at her side. Both "committees" stage the moment when power seeps away: wonderful drama. And there's something else that links them together. Remember Crofton's fatuous remark about Parnell: "Our side of the house respects him, because he was a gentleman" (D, 162)?

JOCK: Maybe ironic more than fatuous. As I recall the story of Parnell's fall, it was precisely his not doing the honorable thing and stepping down of his own accord that drove his opponents to walk out.[22]

LOUISA: Exactly: he stood accused of ungentlemanly behavior, just as Mrs. Kearney is "condemned on all hands" because she has not acted like a

22. See John Wyse Jackson and Peter Costello: "It seemed the honourable course to take. . . . But Parnell remained defiantly at the helm" (1998, 160).

lady. "'I thought you were a lady,' said Mr Holohan, walking away from her abruptly" (*D*, 182). A lady always covers up a gentleman's failings.

SELWYN: Hmm. I see what you mean, but how is this double frame relevant to "Ivy Day"? Is somebody being squeezed out there?

LOUISA: No, not at all. It's the contrast that's so telling. If you think only about Committee Room 15, you're likely to cast "Ivy Day" in terms of Parnell's fall, with the idea of betrayal at the forefront. But when you pair it with Mr. Holohan's "committee," something else comes into view. This space in the Royal Exchange Ward is a vacuum of power.

SELWYN: Sorry to interrupt, but did you know that the Royal Exchange Ward was one of the richest, and (considering its small population) best represented, in Dublin (O'Brien 1982, 78)? Yet the canvassers are so clearly not "advantaged." Don't you think that by setting his story there, Joyce was underlining this powerlessness? As I see them, the men in the committee room are a bit like telemarketers: arbitrarily paid and somewhat alienated labor. They're certainly not idealistic volunteers who can subsidize their time on the campaign trail with a reliable salary. It would be wrongheaded to judge them against that standard. There's something else, too, about Dublin's Corporation that may be relevant here. Of all the major cities in the United Kingdom, its municipal government had by far the narrowest powers to do anything for its citizens, and also the most limited tax base (ibid., 73–77, 144–45). So in a way this whole election is about less than it could be.

LOUISA: Exactly. There's the denuded little room in which men (from opposing parties) hang out, avoiding work, looking for company, hoping for pay, but making do with talk and drink—the only currencies that really circulate in Dublin. There is no huge betrayal. No power play. Just the experience of defeat. Power, insofar as it exists anywhere in Dublin, is somewhere else: possibly with the men at the *Black Eagle* who will eventually send over the bottles of stout—but not necessarily. Which side you are on, which party you belong to, doesn't much matter anymore. It's as if the possibility of political difference or political choice has been hollowed out.

SELWYN: Louisa, do you realize that you've just described the story in ways that I think Andrew Gibson could agree with? In fact, your point here seems very similar to one he makes in his paper—yet you and Jock have come at the story with such different questions. Does this mean that there is actually common ground between readers like the two of you and someone like me? Or, to put it another way, does fiction get you to where it wants by a variety of paths?

HERE I STOP DANGLING MY MARIONETTES' STRINGS. I have tried to fill in what Andrew Gibson only gestures toward when (twice) he mentions "Ivy Day"'s formal intricacy. What that intricacy might be, or how one might try to understand it, forms a large part of Jock and Louisa's conversation. Has the narrative function written itself out of the story? Or does "Ivy Day," at its pivotal moment, depend on narration for its peculiar effect on the reader? And what is that effect? Andrew Gibson says, quite rightly, that "Joyce was certainly not interested in offering us a moral critique of a group of Irishmen." I think he has put his finger on the pulse of the story—or almost on the pulse. True, judgment is not its aim. But judgment is, among other things, what "Ivy Day" (and, I will argue, all of *Dubliners*) is about. It is tempting to say of Joyce's Dubliners that they live by the dictum "I judge, therefore I am."

The stories are engaged in a conversation with each other: we need to listen into it. Hynes's poem in "Ivy Day" forms part of a long sequence of closing performances, some more self-conscious than others, followed by a judgment. The pattern is set in "The Sisters" with the old priest's odd behavior in the confession box and Eliza's judgment "that there was something gone wrong with him" (*D*, 20). In "An Encounter" what the strange man does is deliberately *not* looked at, but the narrating boy's judgment is visceral. He responds with a performance of his own when he calls to his friend with a false name. When his friend does come to his aid, he feels ashamed: he had "always despised him a little" (*D*, 32), and so now judgment turns to self-reproach. The performances multiply as we move through the stories. In "Araby" the boy manages to evade his uncle's boozy recitation of "The Arab's Farewell to His Steed," but eventually finds himself listening to an even more frustrating "show": the English-accented banter between the young lady at the bazaar and the two young gentlemen. Here again the judgment is turned back on the judge, overlapping his anger with his anguish.

As the stories move away from childhood, the closing performances are no longer so inscrutable. The question they provoke shifts from "What can it mean?" to "Is it well done?" In "A Little Cloud" Little Chandler reads Byron to himself—triggering his own feelings of uselessness and ineptitude. There is the arm wrestle in "Counterparts"—quickly judged by the curate, to Farrington's rage, and then Farrington's little boy, hoping to evade punishment, offers his own performance of a Hail Mary. In "Clay" Maria sings, the repeated stanza reproduced in full, though "no one tried to show her her mistake" (*D*, 129). In "A Painful Case" Mr. Duffy reads Mrs. Sinico's death notice and makes a rush to judgment. The "threadbare phrases" make him physically ill (*D*, 140). But eventually, accusation and judgment boomerang back: "Why had he sentenced her to death? He felt his moral nature falling to pieces" (*D*, 142).

In the stories that follow, the obituary notice joins a poem ("Ivy Day"), a series of musical turns ("A Mother"), a sermon ("Grace"), and an after-dinner speech and a song ("The Dead")—all either reproduced on the page or described in detail. In "A Mother" they come with a sharp sideswipe. Mr. Duggan "sang his music with great feeling and volume, and was warmly welcomed by the gallery; but unfortunately, he marred the good impression by wiping his nose in his gloved hand once or twice out of thoughtlessness" (*D*, 174). Mr. Bell "was a fair-haired little man who competed every year at the Feis Ceoil. On his fourth trial he had been awarded a bronze medal" (*D*, 174). Of Madame Glynn: "'I wonder where did they dig her up,' said Kathleen Kearney to Miss Healey. 'I'm sure I never heard of her'" (*D*, 175). We are a long way from the committee room, where the responses to Hynes's performance are inarticulate and bear no sting. At the end, it is Mrs. Kearney who gives the main performance. Mr. Holohan judges, and Mr. O'Madden Burke, "poised upon his [moral] umbrella," proclaims his assent: "'That's a nice lady!' he said. 'O, she's a nice lady!' 'You did the proper thing, Holohan'" (*D*, 183).

"The Dead" brings the sequence to an end with Gabriel Conroy's reaction to (Gretta's listening to) Mr. Bartell D'Arcy's song. It may or may not be a liberation to Gabriel that "his own identity [is] fading out," but in his "shy," "generous," unresentful response (*D*, 277), we glimpse a counter to the relentless judging of others, of oneself, that forms part of Dublin's paralysis. The collection closes on a far more humane and sophisticated note than Mr. Crofton's vacuous imprimatur. Yet again, as in "Ivy Day," as at so many points in *Dubliners,* we are poised on uncertainty, balancing alternative readings. There is no moral umbrella to lean on.

AG: I don't think we should try to dialogue our way toward a unifying conclusion, do you? That would not be in the spirit of what you've just said. I found I responded to Louisa, Jock, and Selwyn very much as they responded to me: not by grasping them as wholes, but by valuing little details in their discourse, like Jock's point about the word *committee.* In that sense, they are somehow dispersed from the start, as is the essay itself. What point of leverage could we find from which to haul up a synthesis? Two separate points for you, then, but two that I think belong together: for better or worse, and however successfully I disguise it, I find that students who agree with my work or express their enthusiasm for it quite often interest me less than those students who come, not so much from an opposing position to mine as one that is radically apart from it. Thus, the student that I like most in the dialogue here (though I would never tell them) is not Selwyn but Louisa. I like her because of her commitment to the dramatic principle, which always insists on the hole in the middle. It means suspension: in one of its senses, the word *drama* is about throwing something up in the air and waiting to see what happens. We're going to leave everything suspended, I'd guess? But alas, and here is my second point, I wonder whether there isn't a certain discomfort for me in doing so. Your Jane Jacobs quotation was initially the epigraph to the second half of our essay. In the editing process, I separated it off and stood it at the beginning. Sorry about that, but it seemed to me to be crucial to the effect of what we were trying to do. You see, by the end of the essay, I have become as much one of Jane Jacobs's "imaginary characters" as Louisa, Jock, and Selwyn. I never gave the lecture Selwyn heard. And so my historical essay turns out to have been produced by an imaginary character, too. Perhaps he isn't me. "Who helps to believe? *Egomen.* Who to unbelieve? Other chap" (*U,* 9.1079–80).

JL: Agreed. The unifying conclusion seems beside the point. Still, I remain intrigued by the way our various readings do at certain moments overlap.

When you wonder "whether there isn't a certain discomfort" for you in leaving everything suspended, I hope you don't feel you've been misrepresented, but are too polite to make a fuss. In your half, you mention the formal intricacy of "Ivy Day." Tell me more. Are my various stabs at it (first, Louisa's insistence that this story is essentially a script for performance, and then Jock's counterargument about the closing scene) at all what you had in mind? Or is your discomfort owing to something else: the impossibility of our ever grasping our arguments, let alone each other, as more than a constellation of "details"? I'll risk saying that to imagine we ever really see the whole is an illusion (do you think readers of Joyce are more comfortable with this incertitude than most?).

As to what you've been doing in our dialogue, you're quite right: I have invented you as a character. I needed "you" to hand your lecture over to Selwyn. And as you say, you've taken "my" words, borrowed from Jane Jacobs, and shifted them elsewhere. Now they hover over the whole. I'm glad you did that: the new place suits them better. I wonder whether our back-and-forth doesn't enact the double move underpinning every act of reading and interpretation. I created a fiction around your name. You unraveled the text attached to mine. On the one hand, assembling (invention always entails a stitching together . . . perhaps even a stitch up?), while on the other—the one you play—disassembling, unraveling, rearranging. The double movement repeated, over and over again, Penelope like. Do we ever really stop? Can we stop?

AG: I suggest we stop. But not because I feel misrepresented.

JL: And last: I admire enormously the kind of scholarship you're engaged in. Why, then, don't I offer something like it? Why have my three characters so obviously not spent hours in the library? Why don't they bring to the conversation their own gems mined from the archived past? Why, when I finally speak in my own voice at the end, do I stay inside the cover pages of *Dubliners,* as if mesmerized by the way stories bounce off against each other? When I ask myself this question I see, in clear relief, that my engagement with Joyce's writing has always been mediated through my primary engagement with teaching. I've never actually taught the short stories, but I cannot imagine discussing them without the figure of an eager, somewhat puzzled reader before me. I've learned a great deal from such readers. I may have remained one of them.

From: Gibson A
To: Jennifer Levine
Sent: Wednesday, November 12, 2008 6:59 PM
Subject: last email

Dear Jennifer

And, then, yes, puzzlement. I had been about to lay the remaining questions sweetly to rest with your own point about Joyce and the supreme accommodation to incertitude. And then dissensus, discord, disorder, which we seemed however loosely to have formalized and controlled, broke in upon us, vengefully, via the very electronic medium supposed increasingly to facilitate universal communication. You couldn't read my version of our text. Your version came back to me cluttered with gobbledygook. Briefly, it seemed as if we might not get it together at all. Just when we thought we had it beat, the principle of disintegration abruptly overwhelmed us. But after all, "Ivy Day" is very much about disintegration. Its world is threatened by it with the breakdown of the Parnellite dream. Hynes's fine piece of writing serves as a kind of frail counter to it, a slender thread of fidelity and continuity. This is also, perhaps, what the formal intricacy you mention just barely holds at bay. Like Bloom and Molly. Like our own collaboration. Like teaching class after class. This interests me very much in Joyce: the concept of a broken fidelity that nonetheless survives the break. It was how he sought to struggle with the question of betrayal. I think it relates to your point about remaining with obscurity, original puzzlement. Darkness is in our souls, do you not think. And our media!

From: Jennifer Levine
To: Gibson A
Sent: Saturday, November 15, 2008 4:21 PM
Subject: re: last email

Dear Andrew

I hadn't thought of the puzzlement as an experience of obscurity, but I suppose it is. It is after all a reaction to the dazzle: a temporary kind of blindness (with the stress on temporary). What I'd agree with more whole-heartedly is your sense of "Ivy Day" as very much about disintegration. And then, too, what you say about Hynes's recitation seems just right.

I'll hit SEND now, and hope these words pulsing across the Atlantic to you will hold together, that they'll resist the impulse to come undone and recombine in some unreadable code.

Sorry: I can't quite stop there. Surely it's different for us than for the men in "Ivy Day"? No sense for them that an expert somewhere, perhaps just a phone call away, will talk them through the disintegration and make the systems compatible again. For them History, it seems, will be to blame.

Here: Click: SEND.

13

The Politics of Maternity and Daughterhood in "A Mother"

KIMBERLY J. DEVLIN AND CAROL LOEB SHLOSS

Carol invited Kim to work with her on "A Mother," and Kim wrote her section first. Carol was interested in what Kim had done with the mother-daughter bond in psychoanalytic terms, and she decided to see how that bond might be understood in historical terms, if she read Kathleen as a representation of young Ireland itself. Both Carol and Kim were interested in feminist readings, and these two readings attempt to map such readings in relation to an understanding of the psyche and the history and politics of Ireland, respectively. After rereading both essays, they met at Colleen Jaurretche's house before a party and informally interviewed each other about their arguments and related issues.

Joyce's Snob Story: "A Mother" and the Problem of Contempt, *by Kimberly J. Devlin*

The title character of "A Mother" emerges as the nightmare of patriarchal culture: a mature woman, willing to exercise whatever agency she may happen to have been granted, and not ashamed to express anger in public over a gender-based injustice. The narrator of the story seems to try hard to make the reader dislike Mrs. Kearney, by treating her with due patriarchal contempt.[1]

---

1. For an excellent overview of the critical contempt Mrs. Kearney has received, see Jane E. Miller's summary of the various disapproving interpretations of her, in the relatively

The anonymous but not unbiased narrative voice makes her sound like a braggart: "Every year in the month of July Mrs Kearney found occasion to say to some friend:—My good man is packing us off to Skerries for a few weeks. If it was not Skerries it was Howth or Greystones" (*D*, 167). He also implies that her marriage to this "good man," whom she praises, is love-less—she becomes Mrs. Kearney "out of spite" (*D*, 166)—and in doing so she fails to fill her romantic expectations. She is resigned but innerly disappointed: "After the first year of married life Mrs Kearney perceived that such a man would wear better than a romantic person but she never put her own romantic ideas away" (*D*, 167). The couple develops social and domestic routines, one of which implies Mr. Kearney's polite deference to his wife's wishes, another of which shows her playing the conventional role of the caregiver: "At some party in a strange house when she lifted her eyebrow ever so slightly he stood up to take his leave and, when his cough troubled him, she put the eider-down quilt over his feet and made a strong rum punch" (*D*, 167). The portrait of the marriage initially comes into focus as one of banal respectability and mutual convenience.

A crucial strategy the narrator seems to deploy to evoke feelings of dislike for Mrs. Kearney in the reader is to insinuate that hers is basically a snob story. He establishes Mrs. Kearney, for instance, as a social gaze: when she enters the Antient Concert Rooms, we are informed that "she did not like the look of things" because "none of [the young men] wore evening dress" (*D*, 169). Her attention to visual *and* verbal correctness is underscored when "she noticed that [Mr. Fitzpatrick] wore his soft brown hat carelessly on the side of his head and that his accent was flat" (*D*, 170). When he announces the beginning of the concert on the first night, "Mrs Kearney rewarded his very flat final syllable with a quick stare of contempt" (*D*, 170). On the

---

small range of texts that even deign to analyze the story (1991, 408–9). Miller convincingly characterizes the story as "subintentionally feminist" (ibid., 413), a contention that I hope my arguments will further substantiate. Sherrill E. Grace characterizes a typical interpretation as follows: "The standard 'reading' of the text posits Mrs. Kearney as a mercenary female determined to control everyone around her and implies that Joyce, with wry irony, has sanctioned her inevitable defeat" (1988, 274).

second night of the series, she is critical of the "indecorous" behavior of the audience, who act "as if the concert were an informal dress rehearsal" (*D,* 171). But it is worth noting that such a narrative strategy of emphasizing Mrs. Kearney's contemptuous snobbery may be a ruse of sorts, because the narrator himself is a snob, and a ruthless one at that. When he is giving the musical background of the bass, Mr. Duggan—the elaborate details of which suggest that this description is *not* Mrs. Kearney's point of view—the narrator tells us, "One night, when an operatic *artiste* had fallen ill, [Mr Duggan] had undertaken the part of the king in the opera of *Maritana* at the Queen's Theatre. He sang his music with great feeling and volume and was warmly welcomed by the gallery; but, unfortunately, he marred the good impression by wiping his nose in his gloved hand once or twice out of thoughtlessness. He was unassuming and spoke little. He said his *yous* so softly that it passed unnoticed, and he never drank anything stronger than milk for his voice's sake" (*D,* 174). The explicit recording of the artiste as a stand-in and the visual notice of his midperformance nose wiping both make it clear that the narrator's social gaze is as sharply critical as Mrs. Kearney's. Mr. Duggan's softly spoken "yous" are, according to one annotator, an "ungrammatical form of the plural address which suggests a poor education" (T. Brown 1993, 293). His use of "yous" is supposedly "unnoticed" by his listeners, but the snobbish ear of the narrator obviously has not missed this grammatical faux pas. The narrator then proceeds to damn Mr. Bell, the second tenor, with faint praise: he "competed every year for prizes at the Feis Ceoil. On his fourth trial he had been awarded a bronze medal" (*D,* 174). A third victim of narrative contempt is Madam Glynn, who is criticized for her "faded blue dress which was stretched upon a meagre body" (*D,* 175). Her vocal performance also receives a scathing review, followed by a repeated critique of her visual appearance: "The poor lady sang *Killarney* in a bodiless gasping voice, with all the old-fashioned mannerisms of intonation and pronunciation which she believed lent elegance to her singing. She looked as if she had been resurrected from an old stage-wardrobe" (*D,* 180). In the course of the condescending judgment of Madam Glynn, we learn that Kathleen has picked up her mother's talent for contempt: "—I wonder where did they dig her up, said Kathleen to Miss Healy. I'm sure I never heard of her" (*D,* 175). The rhetorical effect of this series of snobbish remarks is that critical social discernment—such as Mrs. Kearney exercises—comes off as an asset rather than a liability in the implied ethos of the narrative.

The narrative ethos of contempt emerges as early as the second paragraph, when the narrator turns it against its prime practitioner, the titular character: "Miss Devlin had become Mrs Kearney out of spite" (*D*, 166)—that is, as an act of ill will presumably directed at her so-called friends, who "began to loosen their tongues" "when she drew near the limit" (*D*, 166). The motivational claim is arguably somewhat spiteful itself, given Miss Devlin's situation and the curious way it is described. We are told, for instance, that "when she came to the age of marriage she was sent out to many houses where her playing and ivory manners were much admired" (*D*, 166). This seemingly complimentary statement elides but implies key issues. First of all, by using the passive voice, it fails to mention crucial other people in her life, namely who "sent [her] out"—in all likelihood, her parents. "Miss Devlin," after all, before she becomes the daunting "Mother" of the title, is implicitly a "daunted" or carefully controlled daughter. Second, the polite phrasing of the sentence ("she was sent out to many houses") evades the blunt reality of her situation: she is forced onto the marriage market—"houses" is euphemistic—as a commodity whose "accomplishments" are the currency with which to purchase the safety net of an "ordinary" young man. She makes the fatal mistake of not putting up the pretense of being interested in her prospects ("she gave them no encouragement," as the narrator carefully tells us), so she marries the older Mr. Kearney "out of spite." Would it be just as easy—and perhaps more accurate—to say "out of desperation" or "owing to a lack of other options"? The second paragraph of "A Mother" paints a far from neutral portrait of "A Daughter" who can operate only under the constraints and expectations of an overdetermined Other: her parents, her so-called friends, and the proprietary gaze of a patriarchal culture.

Miss Devlin's experience as a daughter may help explain why Mrs. Kearney as a mother is so vehement about her own daughter's rights. She understands—presumably from personal experience—that the combination of femaleness and youth puts daughters in vulnerable positions: "They thought they had only a girl to deal with and that, therefore, they could ride roughshod over *her*. But *she* would show them their mistake. They wouldn't have dared to have treated *her* like that if *she* had been a man. But she would see that her daughter got her rights: she wouldn't be fooled" (*D*, 181; emphasis added). This passage is narrated from Mrs. Kearney's point of view and may be a paraphrase of what she says to her "group." It is significant that all of the female pronouns—up until the last sentence—are ambiguous insofar as they could refer to either Mrs. Kearney or Kathleen. The rhetorical effect is to underscore how thoroughly the mother identifies with the daughter; if she is defending herself from exploitation, she is also clearly defending her female offspring. The preceding is only one of very few explicitly articulated arguments that are critical of sexual biases in a patriarchal culture in the entirety of *Dubliners*.[2]

I want to turn away briefly from the story itself to introduce two interesting and contrasting theories that can be deployed to discuss relationships between mothers and daughters and between women in general. According to one line of psychoanalytical thought, in patriarchal cultures, women are unconsciously encouraged to disidentify with one another owing to the stigma of lack (specifically, lack of the phallus). Feminist psychoanalytic theorist Kaja Silverman summarizes this Freudian version of one course of female development by emphasizing its two stages. Initially, the image of the mother "is not only the girl's love object, but also that which the girl aspires to be. Freud insists upon this convergence of identification and desire at the site of the mother in several key passages in 'Femininity' and 'Female Sexuality.'" When the castration complex occurs, the mother-daughter relationship is radically altered: "The castration crisis can perhaps best be understood as the moment at which the young female subject first apprehends herself no longer within the pleasurable frame of the original maternal imago but within the radically deidealizing screen or cultural image-repertoire, which makes of her body the very image of lack. . . . [It] is synonymous with the moment at which the girl feels herself *seen* in ways . . . which are not those she would choose for herself. She is—as a consequence of this—held to an image which she would otherwise refuse" (1996, 33). This forced identification with lack can lead to a defensive projection of lack onto other women

---

2. Norris provides an excellent example of another antipatriarchal diatribe in her reading of Aunt Kate in "The Dead" (1992, chap. 5).

and to an animosity between females, sometimes veiled, sometimes blatant. Evidence of prickly female relationships that might well be owing to such "negative" female development might include the one between Gerty Mac-Dowell and Cissy Caffrey in "Nausicaa," between Molly and Milly as it is recalled in "Penelope," or between Nora and Lucia Joyce as it is represented by Carol Shloss in her recent biography of Joyce's daughter.

But according to another line of psychoanalytic argument, the castration complex may be only temporarily traumatizing for women, while remaining permanently threatening for men. Margot Norris, using Lacanian theory, describes castration in female subjectivity as a "been-there-done-that" experience:

> Jacques Lacan argues that the knot-like structure of the unconscious castration complex produces a paradox. The psychic terror of loss that produces pathological symptoms in the male is nonetheless necessary for the achievement of gender identity. Lacan writes, "There is an antimony, here, that is internal to the assumption of man (*Mensch*) of his sex: why must he assume the attributes of that sex only through a threat—the threat indeed of their privation" (*Ecrits* 281). Both male and female children unconsciously "experience" the perceptual error that elaborates the presence or absence of the male organ into a narrative of violence and loss whose redemption is accomplished by the compensations and appeasements of the gender identification process. The condition of apparent absence in the female creates a secondary misunderstanding with a *temporal* significance. The little girl mistakenly construes her imagined "lack" as meaning that castration has already occurred and is behind her. For the male child, however, it remains proleptic and in the future, a psychic sword of Damocles that constitutes masculinity as only provisionally unmutilated and perpetually threatened and imperiled. (2003, 69)

If the castration complex for women is an unconsciously shared experience that can be put in the past, then the psychic consequences may be unifying, leading to sympathetic identifications between mothers and daughters—and women in general.

If patriarchal societies do in some ways encourage women to disidentify with one another because of the stigma of lack, Mrs. Kearney's defiance of this gender mandate is arguably admirable. If in other cases, they unwittingly promote identifications between women, then her fierce defense of her daughter makes perfect sense. Joyce does give us evidence that Mrs. Kearney is Kathleen's role model, but with a crucial difference encouraged by the mother herself. As a young woman, Miss Devlin was "educated in a high-class convent, where she had learned French and music" (*D*, 166); in the next paragraph, we are told in deliberately resonant language that Kathleen was sent "to a good convent, where she had learned French and music" (*D*, 167). Consciously or unconsciously, Mrs. Kearney is wise enough to try to avoid seeing in her daughter's life a repetitive pattern of her own case, in which talents were turned into commodities to make her more marketable. Instead, she urges her daughter to make more direct economic use of those talents, in order to give her the gift of choice. Aware of economic realities, Kathleen's father ensures for her a dowry in the event she opts for marriage; her mother provides an alternative or an additional option—the chance of a career—and an appropriate one, given the cachet attached to musical talents in her culture. Jane E. Miller adds, "Mrs. Kearney's desire to establish a public reputation for her daughter is not an indication of a passion for social climbing (she is never shown trying to rise above her class or means), but rather is a practical response to a bleak situation" (1991, 411).

"A Mother" offers a unique portrait of female identificatory bonding: in another interesting use of pronouns in the story, the extent to which Mrs. Kearney puts herself in her daughter's position is once again adumbrated, when she angrily states, "I have *my* contract" (*D*, 176; emphasis added)—the contract, technically I think, is really Kathleen's (see *D*, 168). In the interest of balance, perhaps, the story also offers two smaller portraits of female disidentifications, and even betrayal. In order to elucidate them, it is important to first point out that Mrs. Kearney's contemptuous diatribe against sexual biases in a patriarchal society—the diatribe with its ambiguous use of the pronouns *her* and *she* that I mentioned above—turns out to be not unwarranted. The narrator of the story—who may be gendered as a "she" rather than as a "he"—tells us, after all, "the baritone was asked what did he think of Mrs Kearney's conduct. He did not like to say anything. He had been paid his money and wished to be at peace with *men*" (*D*, 180; emphasis added). We learn shortly afterward that he has not performed yet, that he goes on stage after the intermission ("Mrs Kearney had to stand aside to allow the baritone and his accompanist to pass up to the platform" [*D*, 183]). If he is paid in advance, why shouldn't Kathleen receive equal treatment?

The revealing question to the baritone, which makes clear the engendered injustice at the heart of the story, is asked during the discussion that takes place between Mrs. Kearney's "rival" group, composed of "Mr Holohan, Mr Fitzpatrick, Miss Beirne, two of the stewards, the baritone, the bass and Mr O'Madden Burke" (*D*, 180). After the question to the baritone has been asked and answered, Mr. O'Madden Burke states, "—I agree with Miss Beirne. . . . Pay her nothing" (*D*, 181). The implication may be, I believe, that the proposal for breaking the contract comes from the one identified female member of the amorphously defined "Committee" that we see: namely, the "little woman named Miss Beirne . . . [whose] oldish face was screwed into an expression of trustfulness and enthusiasm" at the beginning of the final concert (*D*, 173)—so much for female solidarity.[3] But the more disturbing lack of female solidarity emerges in the hints that another daughter in the story does not understand the engendered message in Mrs. Kearney's position. Miss Healy hears it only out of a sense of social—as opposed to female—loyalty: "Then [Mrs. Kearney] appealed to Miss Healy. Miss Healy wanted to join the other group but she did not like to do so because she was a great friend of Kathleen's and the Kearneys had often invited her to their house" (*D*, 181). Ultimately, she betrays her so-called great friend by agreeing to take her place (at least in part). What is described adjectivally as a gesture of kindness is, in fact, an act of betrayal: as the narrator tells us with unmistakable contempt and irony, "Miss Healy had kindly consented to play one or two accompaniments" (*D*, 182). Miss Healy appropriately shares her name with the more well-known politician Tim Healy: he was ini-

3. Garry Leonard offers a provocative reading of "A Mother" as a strong critique of the myth of masculinity in his chapter on the story. But the committee that he claims exists as "an abstraction that represents the value of masculinity in the same vague way as the existence of the General Post Office" (1993, 267) is not totally male, as the presence of Miss Beirne makes clear— "masculinized" entities can appropriate female subjects (as Leonard himself elsewhere implies). Jane Miller characterizes this female character as "a supernumerary" of the Eire Abu Society (1991, 418), but the story does imply that she is given a voice when decisions are being made.

tially one of Charles Stewart Parnell's "lieutenants," who later distinguished himself as "one of the leaders of the move to oust Parnell from leadership of the Irish Nationalist Party, [in other words] as Parnell's 'betrayer'" (Gifford 1988, 147). Even small-scale nationalist organizations, such as the Eire Abu Society in "A Mother," can count on having a willing and reliable backstabber, even though the political betrayal here is antifeminist, a young woman implicitly undermining the protest of another.

In her battle with the "Committee" that presumably—and haphazardly—governs the Society, it may appear that Mrs. Kearney is the loser. The final dismissive contemptuous remark is uttered by her foe: "'I thought you were a lady,' said Mr Holohan, walking away from her abruptly" (D, 182). The contemptuous implication of the insult supports both patriarchal and class biases: Mr. Holohan implies that Mrs. Kearney's public display of anger and her sense of injustice ("— I'm asking for my rights, she said" [D, 182]) disqualify her from the status of social decency and "proper" womanhood. In his supposed moment of victory, however, Mr. Holohan finds himself as angry as his snubbed opponent—he does not come out of the battle temperamentally unscathed: "Mr Holohan began to pace up and down the room, in order to cool himself for he felt his skin on fire" (D, 183).

Throughout Mrs. Kearney's battle and in her moment of defeat, Mr. Kearney admirably, I think, stands by his woman: the narrator forces us to rethink this union as a marriage of convenience. But when I presented a shorter version of this essay at a conference, an audience member raised an interesting question about this assertion regarding Mr. Kearney's loyalty: namely, why does he fail to verbally support his wife, to intervene on her behalf? Mr. Holohan at one point explicitly appeals to him, giving him a chance to speak, but he remains silent, continuing to "stroke his beard" (D, 179). I believe the silence is telling and important: he lets his wife speak for herself and refuses the role of the chivalric interloper. Although he at one point asks Mrs. Kearney to lower her voice (D, 178), there is no evidence that he disagrees with her or finds her position unreasonable. "A Mother" may be the only story in Dubliners where we see almost no familial conflict or betrayal, where solidarity perdures to the bitter end—the brief exceptional moment occurring when Mrs. Kearney is justifiably "haggard with rage" (D, 182), but her anger is plainly not felt toward her spouse or her daughter.

Afterward, Mr. Kearney simply follows orders, the family exiting as a unit, just as earlier he had agreed to attend but, as we find out, not in order to intervene. And although Mr. O'Madden Burke confidently proclaims toward the climax of the conflict that "Kathleen Kearney's musical career was ended in Dublin after that" (*D*, 180),[4] *Ulysses* happily assures us that it is not: Molly Bloom thinks of Kathleen—contemptuously, of course—as part of the competition in Dublin's musical culture. Kathleen has the benefit of her mother's identificatory support, and her unconventional father, in turn, supports both wife and female offspring. In the dismal world of daughterhood portrayed in *Dubliners*—think of Polly Mooney or Eveline Hill—these crucial backings may be the conditions for female survival and, God forbid, even success.

Local History and the Birth of a Nation, *by Carol Loeb Shloss*

> But we have all bent low and low and kissed the quiet feet
> Of Cathleen, the daughter of Houlihan.
>   —W. B. Yeats, "Red Hanrahan's Song about Ireland"

When the Irish Revival gained momentum in Dublin, Mrs. Kearney, the protagonist of Joyce's story "A Mother," "determined to take advantage of her daughter's name" (*D*, 167). She arranges for Kathleen, already an accomplished musician, to learn Gaelic; their home becomes a center for Nationalist friends; and in due course Kathleen is invited to accompany various artists at a concert sponsored by the Eire Abu (Ireland to Victory) Society. Quietly, by virtue of a mother's calculation, Joyce conflates an actual young woman with the iconography of an emerging nation, and by charting her damaged fate ("Miss Kathleen Kearney's musical career was ended in Dublin after that, he said" [*D*, 180]) invites us to consider what it means to

---

4. For a good explanation of why O'Madden Burke emerges as "the object of the sharpest satire" in the story, see J. E. Miller 1991, 421. Norris astutely points out that he has "no official connections to the concert except as an unofficially deputized reviewer," and logically inquires, "What gives Mr. Burke the authority to judge a labor dispute?" (2003, 191).

engender both a national culture and a daughter whose life will be circum-scribed by the specific rights, roles, and obligations of that nation as it strug-gles to come into being. Mrs. Kearney is both the mother of a real daughter and, by virtue of her (small, particular) role in Ireland's program for cultural self-definition, the progenitor of a more encompassing way of life. In this story about a pianist-daughter who will not play the role of unpaid accom-panist, the mother helps to set the stage, so to speak, for Kathleen's future.

The ground for this conflation—daughter/Daughter of Ireland—in the mind of a determined mother and in the art of her creator was doubt-less the world of performance art in Dublin during the early 1900s, where "Kathleen" was widely understood to signify national aspirations. W. G. Fay had recently performed W. B. Yeats's *Cathleen ni Houlihan* with the Irish National Dramatic Company, and Richard Ellmann reports that in 1902 Joyce had been scheduled to meet Yeats at the Antient Concert Rooms, where he was supervising its rehearsal (1982, 104). The play was first per-formed on April 2, 1902, and subsequently published in *Samhain* (Octo-ber 1902). These circumstances along with the prevalence of other Yeats poems[5] and popular music like "Oh, Did You Not Hear of Kate Kearney?" (M. Power 1976, 532–34) can be supposed to underlie Mrs. Kearney's desire to exploit her daughter's name, and they lend Joyce's story a subtext that is consonant with Yeats's embodiment of the romance of Irish destiny in the person of a hag whose rejuvenation depends upon the sacrificial recognition of Ireland's youth.

This statement is not to claim, as does critic Ben Collins, that "A Mother" is Joyce's rewriting of the Yeats play, a recasting of the themes of money, music, patriotism, in parallel if ironic terms—but simply that reso-nances exist, faintly, but with effects that Joyce will exploit by implicitly ask-ing us to speculate about the wider implications of the unfolding narrative action. In the Yeats drama a poor old woman (the Shan van Vocht) deflects an anticipated marriage, entering a home in Killala, County Mayo, in the West of Ireland on the eve of a young couple's wedding. The year is 1789.

---

5. See especially "The Countess Cathleen," first performed in Dublin in 1899, and "Red Hanrahan's Song of Ireland," also written in 1899.

She identifies herself as Cathleen ni Houlihan and reminds the bridegroom of those individuals who died for her in the past and the hard service of the ones who help her in the present: "They that had red cheeks will have pale cheeks for my sake; and for all that they will think they are well paid" (ibid.).[6] The union that comes about is not one of a man and wife, but the marriage of the young man's heart to a symbol of Irish independence. He abandons his fiancée for love of Ireland and for the living memory of subsequent generations: "The people shall hear them for ever."

In Joyce's story, set in 1905, there is no love lost on any account, but the issue of who will be "well paid" in the service of Ireland remains essential. In fact, the narrative turns on the issue of pay at an event designed to raise public appreciation of Irish music and to contribute to the cultural self-definition that became increasingly important to nationalists after Parnell's death in 1891 and the defeat of his parliamentary initiatives. Mrs. Kearney devotes considerable time and effort to organizing this local performance before she realizes that the agreement about Kathleen's fee will not be honored. At first she tries to behave well; then she calculates a possible solution; finally she loses her self-control.

Margot Norris's excellent reading of this story, "Critical Judgment and Gender Prejudice in 'A Mother'" (see Collins 1970; Kearney 2001) alerts us to some of the reasons that Mrs. Kearney attributes so much significance to her daughter's contract. Norris analyzes the story as a labor dispute. She points to the importance of contracts in women's history and to the fact

6. Oh, did you not hear of Kate Kearney?
   She lives on the banks of Killarney:
   From the glance of her eye,
   Shun danger and fly,
   For fatal's the glance of Kate Kearney.
   For the eye is so modestly beaming,
   You'd ne'er think of mischief she's dreaming,
   Yet, oh, I can tell
   How fatal the spell
   That lurks in the eye of Kate Kearney.
   Lyrics by Lady Morgan, quoted in Moffat 1897, 180–81.

that until the Married Women's Property Acts of 1870 and 1885, married women, who lived under "coverture," could neither make wills or contracts nor sue or be sued. The protection of the law, so recently extended to Irish women, was the voice of, and guarantor of, due process—a late, hard-won, and hence valued civic achievement. One could expect any knowledgeable woman to chafe at the breach of its protection, as, indeed, Mrs. Kearney does, seeing it both as a violated pact—"I have my agreement and I intend to see that it is carried out" (*D*, 176)—and as a gendered slight: "They thought they had only a girl to deal with and that, therefore, they could ride roughshod over her. . . . They wouldn't have dared to have treated her like that if she had been a man" (*D*, 181).

It is the grace of Norris's essay to rescue the story from the hands of misogyny and to place the narrative events once again on the level of real conflict: there are two points of view in any dispute, though Joyce does not represent them equitably. Norris's analysis shows how Joyce manipulates judgment—both in the narrative voice and in the voices of the critics within the story—and demonstrates clearly how Mrs. Kearney's presentation is prejudiced before we ever see her in action, a prejudice that has been reiterated, amplified, and reinflected according to the various biases of the story's commentators.

The most salient examples of this point, already amply noted by others, are David Hayman and Warren Beck, who simply and malignantly label the protagonist according to their own projected responses to strong women (see Norris 2003, 185–96; J. E. Miller 1991, 407–26; Hayman 1969, 123–41; and Beck 1969, 123–41). Beck finds her "insufferable" (1969, 276) and obsessively demanding, and, rather than explore the social tensions demonstrated in the Antient Concert Rooms, he endorses the judgment of the men who cheat her: "The defeat of Mrs. Kearney is to be fully approved of" (ibid., 262). Hayman (1969) follows suit with equally venomous judgments. To him, Mrs. Kearney is a virago: a "sour presence, a succubus." Linda Rohrer-Paige offers a different kind of condemnation, reading the strong mother as too strong, too controlling, and thus someone who stultifies her daughter, ruining her career in the very act that purports to benefit it (1995, 331). From one perspective, the mother makes men uncomfortable; from the other, she supposedly hurts her own child, but she is consistently blameworthy.

All of these condemnations derive from Mrs. Kearney's disruption of traditional gender roles, and, indeed, we witness in them the reiteration of its unsettling effect on the assembled company of men within the narrative, who expect and laud compliance, malleability, and deference in women who are "ladies." Not only Kathleen, but Mrs. Kearney herself bears the weight of being associated with a pathos-laden icon: the self-denying, long-suffering mother. She is implicitly judged by other kinds of stereotypes like the ones given prominence in Padraic Pearse's poem "The Mother," which identifies the self-sacrifice expected from Irish mothers, who should willingly give up their children (and presumably everything else) to the cause of freedom:

> Lord, thou art hard on mothers:
> We suffer in their coming and their going:
> And tho' I grudge them not, I weary, weary
> Of the long sorrow—And yet I have my joy:
> My sons were faithful, and they fought.

Mrs. Kearney suffers nothing comparable in the Antient Concert Rooms, and the narrative ends not with "long sorrow" but with anger tied to a stone. She is "haggard with rage" (*D*, 182).

If we leave this mode of blameful response and ask what is happening in the concert rooms of Joyce's imagination, if we ask what social tensions are being performed, regardless of our judgment of the performers, we come, I think, to some more interesting ideas about the story. Norris begins to do this by concentrating on the idea of a labor dispute. What is the source of the disagreement, and what are the merits of each side? She, like Jane Miller, places the narrative in the social history of women's lives and explores the awkwardness of a mother when she leaves the domestic sphere and enters into the public arena. Clearly, Mrs. Kearney does not know the implicit rules for public engagement; she does not know how to negotiate effectively, but, setting this aside, is there any validity to her grievance? Norris concludes that there is.

I would argue that this point is an excellent step in reclaiming a balanced reading of the tale, but that something more encompassing than a single contract is at stake in the fraught interaction Joyce represents. Insofar as the concert is given, like Yeats's *Cathleen ni Houlihan*, in the service of

Irish independence, it serves as a small, specific demonstration of how cultural identity is constructed and reproduced: what is at stake is the viability of two different modes of imagining and accomplishing the future (Mrs. Kearney's and the Committee's). What is important is not the music on the stage—the ostensible reason for the gathering—but the various *ways* of collaborating in the service of a common national goal. Thus, my central question is not whether Mrs. Kearney is blameworthy, not whether the narrative voice carries with it or reinforces a certain judgment of this mother, but what is performed in the service of nationalism—by any of the characters. What kind of "mothering" is presented to us? What "birth" of a nation (Victory to Ireland) does this narrative anticipate? And what are the social implications of "birth" in a male-dominated culture, a culture where virtually all narratives of the social are constructed by men?[7] Like Joyce's episode in *Ulysses*, "Oxen of the Sun," where Mrs. Purefoy, in the turmoil of birth pangs, never appears "on stage," all of the important labor in this story (about another mother) happens behind the scenes.

Mrs. Kearney (whose name, O'Cearnaigh, as Mary Power reminds us, derives from the Irish word for "victorious" [1976, 533]) conducts her life according to strict rules for propriety. Her correctness and attention to form, to duty, to "what is right" could not stand in starker contrast to the slapdash ways of Hoppy Holohan, who roams the streets with his pockets full of "dirty pieces of paper," as he tries to put together a series of concerts. From the opening of the story, Joyce establishes that people with extraordinarily different codes of conduct will be trying to work together; their life experiences have given each of them different models of social organization. Mary Power has called this the difference between "gentility and bungling," and wryly observes that neither quality has much to contribute to lively theater (ibid.). But it is precisely this difference that Joyce will explore in the Antient Concert Rooms, offering both characters as aspects of his native culture and using them to typify what Dublin had to contribute to the Irish Revival.

On the one hand, Joyce dramatizes the bourgeois propriety of the Revival, its pretensions toward (and longing for) a kind of general Westernized idea of

7. For an excellent discussion of this subject, as it applies to *Ulysses*, see Duffy 1999, 210–28.

high culture. Mrs. Kearney, though convent educated, is cut from the same cloth as Gabriel Conroy in "The Dead": she has studied music and French, and though she plays an active role in the Gaelic-language movement, the details about her education are meant to suggest a proclivity toward European culture, a pining for cultivation that is anathema to the general population and that Joyce describes as "the chilly circle of her accomplishments" (*D,* 166). She is represented as secretly romantic, disappointed in her marriage proposals, and pragmatic about the husband she finally does choose. Their marriage is defined by reciprocal duties and small horizons: he is a responsible provider, a serious, pious man, and a good father. She is not pious, "but she never weakened in her religion and was a good wife to him" (*D,* 167). She cares for him in illness; he sends her on summer holidays. Their daughters are also convent educated: Kathleen has attended the academy, and both girls have been given dowries. It is marriage by the book if not by the heart; it is not romantic, but neither is it filled with animosity or bad faith. Although Joyce is concerned with simony, the buying and selling of what is sacred, throughout *Dubliners,* this situation is not an example of it. It is simply a falling away from higher hopes, a life compromise, an instance of people carrying on in the face of diminished possibilities.

Out of this diminishment and the formalities that attempt, probably unsuccessfully, to compensate for it (eating Turkish delight does not really go very far), Mrs. Kearney hopes to fashion better possibilities for Kathleen. This desire is part of her motivation for helping to organize the Eire Abu concerts; it is the reason for her hospitality to Mr. Holohan, a man whom she would probably not in other circumstances entertain in her home. Here she is on familiar ground, knowing the symbolic value of the decanter and the silver biscuit barrel: "Now, help yourself, Mr. Holohan!" (*D,* 169). Joyce describes her as "invariably friendly and advising—homely, in fact" (*D,* 169). Equally important, he describes her as good at what she does: tactful, knowledgeable, and quietly authoritative. She is the one who puts together the program, for she understands both grammar and how to pace the entertainment. To this point, she is "the little woman behind the man," working competently, but remaining in the background, letting men take credit for her contributions.

This dynamic changes when the evening of the first concert arrives and Mrs. Kearney enters public space. Here it is Hoppy Holohan who is "at home," though in this case being at home also means bearing "disappointment lightly." The hall is nearly empty, audience members are carelessly dressed, even more carelessly behaved, and the artists are "no good" (*D*, 171). Although Mr. Fitzpatrick and the Committee try to recoup the series, shortening it to three and sending hawkers out on the street, it is an effort that is as careless as the audience. Joyce repeatedly describes Mr. Fitzpatrick's face as "vacant"; he is a man who stands around laughing with friends instead of attending to business, and neither he nor Mr. Holohan will answer questions directly. Where Mrs. Kearney approaches the public performance with vigorous and pointed attention, the men of the Committee seemingly prefer to bring young women lemonades, look at their heaving bosoms, and then retreat to an upstairs room for "a little something" (*D*, 177). Despite the presence of one woman on the Committee, Miss Beirne, it is clear that this group is an Old Boys' Club, Irish style, and that, to them, nothing much rests on the success of the concert. Even the unnamed reviewer, with his "plausible voice and careful manners" (*D*, 177), has something more important to do on Saturday evening and fobs his job off on Mr. O'Madden Burke.

Thus, Joyce opposes two styles of being in the world, portraying contrasting value systems established by lifelong proclivities and experiences. Even before the showdown in which Mrs. Kearney announces that the show *will* go down if Kathleen is not paid, Joyce has set the stage for misprision. Coming from a home environment governed by duty, Mrs. Kearney cannot appreciate the hail-fellow-well-met style of the Committee members—their sub rosa deals, their "insider trading," their evasiveness with those persons not part of the clique, their vacant hope that success will come despite lackluster efforts. Neither Mr. Holohan nor Mr. Fitzpatrick can sympathize with Mrs. Kearney's high standards and insistence on the letter of the law. Seeing women as instrumental to male designs, resentful of the mother's disruptive assertion of what is right, impatient to get back to the bonhomie that is their solace for ineptitude, wanting to pass off their debt, expecting the women to take up the slack, Holohan and Fitzpatrick understand themselves to be the appropriate legislators of culture. Under the weight of the mutual animosity between opposed groups, the social machine collapses. Middle-aged adults are reduced to calling each other names.

But what has really happened? What wider conflict has Joyce asked us to consider? Some readers have concluded that the story is in fact a backstory, the explanation of a botched concert, whose origins reside in memory. Michael O'Neill's 1959 research has been picked up and used in various ways by Donald Torchiana, Jane Miller, and Margot Norris, who all point out that Joyce participated in a concert on August 27, 1904, that was so poorly organized that the audience had to wait interminably, put up with noisy distractions, and listen to a dreadful substitute pianist. Miss Eileen Reidy, who was to have accompanied the real James Joyce, left early, so he had to sit at the piano and accompany himself (see O'Neill 1959, 226–30; and Torchiana 1986). According to these commentators, fiction provides an account of what a newspaper left blank, and in so doing both explains and implicitly shifts the blame for Joyce's improvisation to the shoulders of an irate woman.

Commentary could rest here were it not for the iconographic associations of Mrs. Kearney's daughter's name. But "Kathleen," who is both the symbol of the state and an example of the young women who will inherit it, invites us to examine local history as an exemplar of something broader. And, indeed, when we look at the pattern of social interaction in the narrative, it is possible to see it as a recapitulation of attitudes and misunderstandings that characterized gender relationships in nationalist groups more generally, where strong women were often deprecated at the same time that their services were relied upon to accomplish the very goals that later excluded them.

Situated between several examples important to the organizational history of women in Ireland—the formation of the Women's Land League in 1881, the formation of Inghinidhe na hEireann (Daughters of Ireland) in 1900, and the founding of Bean na hEireann (Women of Ireland), the first women's paper ever produced in Ireland in 1908—the story reminds us that Mrs. Kearney was not the only mother to suffer denigration in the public realm. This chapter is not the place to rehearse the complexities of these various histories, but a few salient comments will serve to establish my point, as follows.[8]

8. See Ward 1995 for excellent discussions of these organizations. See also Hayes and Urquhart 2001.

As Anna Parnell, sister of Charles Stewart Parnell, wrote in her memoir of this period, *The Land League: Tale of a Great Sham,* she was asked by Michael Davitt to take charge of the executive committee for the whole Land League movement on January 31, 1881. The circumstances were extraordinary, as both parties understood, but Davitt recognized that the land movement was at a critical juncture. On March 2, 1880, the British government had passed the Protection of Person and Property (Ireland) Bill, granting itself "absolute power of arbitrary and preventative arrest." Known in Ireland as the Coercion Act, it was designed to permit various leaders of the land agitation to be arrested—and its consequence, as Davitt anticipated, was that he, Parnell, and Devoy (head of the American Fenians) would soon be incarcerated. Either the land agitation would collapse, or they could seek a way around the Coercion Act. Facing the opposition of his colleagues, who feared that they would be open to "public ridicule" (ibid., 11) were they to rely on women, Davitt opted to invite Anna Parnell to assume the executive role in the organization. The ladies' branch of the League was collapsed the following year, with great acrimony on both sides, but its brief access to public power, the problems it encountered, and the bitterness of its demise offer an interesting context for Mrs. Kearney's brief, unsuccessful foray into public life.

The women were good at their jobs, but their competence was met with the ridicule Davitt had feared for himself. The *Times,* for example, commented that "it will hardly be to the ladies that the men will look for real advice and guidance in the crisis at which they now find themselves" (ibid., 22). The Catholic Church followed suit, with Archbishop McCabe of Dublin lambasting women who forgot "the modesty of their sex and the high dignity of their womanhood" by going into the public arena. They were "unworthy of a child of Mary" (ibid., 23).

Defying public judgment, the women continued their efforts on behalf of peasants threatened with eviction, until their activism aroused alarm in both Parnell and the British government. As historian Margaret Ward (1995) observes, former foes united in their opposition, finally finding a mutual bond in their desire to get rid of these unruly women. The government agreed to release the prisoners, deal with the question of rent arrears, and amend the Land Act in exchange for Parnell's agreement that he would prevent further "outrages."

Parnell staked his career on the suppression of the Ladies' Land League. When he and Michael Davitt met after their release from prison, he told Davitt that he would leave public life if the women were not suppressed. He saw the new understanding he had reached with Gladstone as the stepping-stone to Home Rule, and the maneuverings that followed, though not coercive, were designed nonetheless to accomplish the ladies' defeat. Their questions about whether to continue resistance to rent went unanswered; their appeals for funds were ignored. Requests for consultation were simply returned. Anna Parnell recognized this runaround for what it was. Here was male bonding in the face of authority asserted by women, even though their assistance had been sought and, in fact, had been invaluable not only in keeping the movement alive but also in engineering the release of its male leadership; here were numerous refusals to deal straightforwardly; here was name-calling of the most contemptuous kind. The pattern was all too familiar by the time Joyce represented a similar dynamic in "A Mother." "They thought they had only a girl to deal with and that therefore, they could ride roughshod over her. . . . They wouldn't have dared to have treated her like that if she had been a man" (*D,* 181). It did not matter that Anna was Parnell's sister; she was disposed of. It does not matter that Mrs. Kearney is still a useful member of the community; she is outcast, and Kathleen's musical career is pronounced over. "'But I'm done with you,' said Mr. Holohan" (*D,* 183).

Declan Kiberd reminds us that the conditions of struggle define the "lineaments of . . . freedom" (1995, 395). That is, the process by which freedom is sought does not disappear when freedom is obtained, but remains as the condition of continued struggle, a part of the past and a component of the future, since what one knows continues unabated. In these instances—in history and in its re-presented fiction—we find well-bred, competent women relied upon for their competence and then denounced for their exercise of it. We find, in short, self-defeating conflicts, failures to unite different kinds of talents, a marked resistance to cooperation. If this is the model of cultural organization that defines the conditions for the birth of an independent nation, it is also an unhappy, proleptic model of its eventual achievement.

Fanny Parnell, Anna's sister, was a poet who, having seen the damage done to impoverished peasants by an unjust land-tenure system, wrote a poem that advised those individuals damaged by adversity to "set your faces as a flint and swear to hold your own" (Ward 1995, 11). Joyce ends his story with an interesting variation of this trope, which is also, obliquely, a variation on the story of Yeats's *Cathleen ni Houlihan:* Mrs. Kearney "stood still for an instant like an angry stone image" (*D,* 183). She is described as "*haggard,*" a word that gestures toward Ireland as a hag. Which, I think, is Joyce's point. "Kathleen's" future, like Ireland's, is prefigured in her mother's present experience.[9] The conditions of struggle define the lineaments of freedom. We could say that although Mrs. Kearney seems to violate the nationalist version of motherhood, she in fact embodies it in a form not recognized by the men assembled in the concert hall. Not seeing her talents, her hopes, her aspirations or disappointments, not giving credit for her contributions to their effort, she remains the unappreciated hag of Yeats's imagination, the Shan van Vocht untransformed, tied to the blindness of Irish men and stultified by her own responsive rage.

In this sense, "A Mother" can be considered Joyce's prelude to the "Oxen of the Sun" episode of *Ulysses,* where Mrs. Purefoy, literally in labor, performs the act of (re)generation while the "Old Boys' Club" in the anteroom of the hospital muffles around with sacrilegious and uncomfortable repartee about the embarrassments of the very labor she is performing. In both instances, Joyce shows us the ironies of using motherhood as a representation of statehood in an environment where actual mothers are maligned. He shows us the irony of rhetoric used in the face of its diminished opposite behavior, language belying performance, words giving the lie to deeds, words themselves as a kind of deed that will linger in memory and bear retribution. To recall Fanny Parnell once more, his implicit imprecation might well be hers: "Set your faces as a flint and swear to hold your own."

If "Oxen of the Sun" explores a contemporary version of the "crimes against fertility" figured in Homer's *Odyssey* as the murder of sacred cattle, "A Mother" can be said to explore something more akin to a failed relationship that is the prelude to fertility. Literally, motherhood signals new life; tropologically, it can also speak to us about the fertility of imagination,

---

9. For a psychological explanation of this reproduction of gender roles, see Chodorow 1978.

initiative, and organizational skills that are necessary to bring about new social conditions. In the social (and nationalist) tableau presented in "A Mother," we see a divorce of talents rather than a marriage of reciprocal and necessary abilities. Looked at in negative terms, Joyce pits careless sentimentality against rigid calculation in his narrative, but he also gives us ground for considering that they need not occur as inevitable oppositions: orderliness and careful reckoning could, in other circumstances, go hand in hand with smooth sociability. It is in their failure to unite that Kathleen is not given her due on this particular evening of local history; it is in the divisions (and suppressions) of gendered abilities that Ireland is, or was at the turn of the century, ill served in larger terms. No one is willing either to pay the cost of getting a young woman onto the concert stage or to contribute to the next concerted stage of nation building.

Carved stone images of women have, since megalithic times, been considered symbols of fertility in Ireland.[10] In "A Mother," Joyce shows us that, at least in 1905, there were reasons for the stones to be angry.

Final E-mail Exchange

Dialogue: Kim Devlin and Carol Shloss
"A Mother"

KIM: I'm happy you invited me to work on this particular story. I was interested because Mrs. Kearney is the first in a series of women who openly react

---

10. In response to my interest in Joyce's choice of such an arresting image at the end of this story, I did a Google search for *Ireland* and *stone* and *woman,* finding in this way a wealth of information about ancient carved stone images of women known as "Sheela na Gigs." There is controversy over the origin and meaning of the term, but one scholar, Jørgen Andersen, considers that the name is an Irish phrase, *Sighle na gCioch,* meaning "the old hag of the breasts." These effigies, blunt in their anatomical detail, are usually described as both ferocious and gaunt and can often be found on the fronts of churches and castles above portals. They are, quite literally, "angry stone images," and, as they are generally considered to be fertility symbols, they are implicitly symbols of affronted fertility. Anyone interested in pursuing this interesting subject can find more information in two books, Freitag 2004 and Roberts 2001.

when men mistreat them. She's Joyce's first angry woman, and she's also the first to utter a "back answer." Margot Norris shows women giving various back answers. Here we see that Mrs. Kearney anticipates the women of "The Dead." When my students read this story, they readily identify with Kathleen, the daughter, saying, "I would want my mother to do the same thing, to defend me." My first question for you is this: given your knowledge of Joyce's life, is there any evidence why he became interested in discontented and even angry females? Did Joyce realize that Nora and Lucia were angry?

CAROL: How can we contextualize this historically? Nora was a back answerer, but she identified with her son, not with her daughter, so there's not any immediate source for this in the family . . . so if it's not from a family source, it has to be from some other place.

KIM: Did he see any strong mother-daughter bonds in other families?

CAROL: What's the exact date this story was written?

KIM: Late September 1905.

CAROL: Why are you interested in looking for a source?

KIM: Because, in the Joyce canon, female anger becomes increasingly angry. This is his earliest fictional representation of an angry woman.

CAROL: Well, Joyce was angry about his publishing situation. . . . Maybe he projected the anger that was unacceptable to him as a man onto a woman. But I see that we've pointed to the answer of our own question. . . . [T]he anger would have been most apparent to him in his sisters . . . the Dilly Dedaluses of the world.

KIM: And then the sisters also gave him an example of female bonding in the face of female oppression.

CAROL: Let me take this in a slightly different direction: "Kathleen" is also Ireland and the ire of Ireland in the face of another kind of oppression. Maybe that's what's so groundbreaking about this story: there are lots of stories of Irish anger, but usually the anger is expressed by men. Here there's a confluence . . . political anger, made manifest through Kathleen's name, an exemplar of Ireland; Joyce's personal anger about broken literary contracts; and familial anger . . . all expressed through the voice of a particular mother.

KIM: There's another interesting point about anger. At the end Mrs. Kearney makes others angry. . . . [F]inally the lackadaisical ways of conducting business are called on the carpet, and Mr. Holohan finally feels exactly the same emotion that Mrs. Kearney feels. The one point I disagree with you about is that the argument harms Kathleen's fate, for in *Ulysses* Kathleen is doing just fine as a singer. . . . [S]he becomes successful in musical circles in 1904.

CAROL: Do I actually say that Kathleen's fate is damaged or simply that it is temporarily damaged in the story? I meant my essay to mean that it's damaged in the story alone, for I regard *Ulysses* itself as a kind of back answer. In fact, I can't see how this story was read as critical of women for so long. . . . [T]he criticism of the conference organizers is everywhere—both in the mouth of the mother and in the voice of the narrator—and the narrative implicitly asks, "By whom should Ireland's fate be controlled?" Mr. Holohan and the organizers of this patriotic event are screwups. This brings up another question: how can we look at our work in relation to the criticism that preceded it? When I looked back in my research, I was astounded at the sexism, the insistence that Mrs. Kearney was a hag—not haggard, but a hag. For me, writing about the story was a kind of allegory of my own position in the Joyce community. I've been subject to the same kind of sexism, and by some of the very same critics who criticize this story.

KIM: My first book was subject to the same kind of criticism many years ago. . . . [I]t was "too feminist," according to one anonymous reader, who wanted to reject it mainly on that basis. You're right about the sexism on all levels. Mrs. Kearney is another figurative reincarnation of the Medusa: the fierce woman's gaze turns passive men into volatile men; it arouses their anger.

CAROL: There's so very much anger under the surface of the story; the anger's everywhere—attacking with hands—anger turning physical. Even verbal aggression is improper in women, but physical aggression, attacking, is more taboo; verbal aggression seems like an oxymoron. It's interesting that both of us read the anger as positive. When I reread the story, I thought, "It's about time; go for it; say it."

KIM: Students now almost always support Mrs. Kearney's anger.

CAROL: Here's another question: do you think that our reading is class-based or privileged-based? We're educated with the equivalent of Mrs. Kearney's convent education.

KIM: True, but the narrator is also "class educated"—a bit of a snob—which creates one of the interpretive challenges of the story. Still, in this regard, our articles work well together: I emphasize class difference, you emphasize gender difference, but both class and gender are used against women in ways that are unfair. Think of Anna Parnell in your essay: both she and Mrs. Kearney were invited into public life and then turned upon: men offered them proposals, solicited their help, and then refused to honor their commitments. Do you think Joyce knew about that? About Anna Parnell?

CAROL: We'd have to learn how Joyce acquired his knowledge of Irish history, but I suspect that the Sheehy-Skeffingtons, being both nationalists and feminists, would have known, and maybe it was common knowledge among Parnell supporters.

KIM: I have another thing in your essay to discuss: your use of the image of the Shan von Vocht. That's another image of the poor old woman, and it comes up again in "Telemachus" with the milk woman. Joyce's point is that this icon for Ireland is treated with total contempt in reality. Even though Stephen thinks of her as a figure for Ireland, Mulligan insults her, particularly because he knows she won't know he's doing so. She meets only male arrogance and contempt.

CAROL: What's interesting there is that she's in some ways the opposite of Mrs. Kearney. She's ignorant and humble, not convent educated and talented, and she still gets the short end.

KIM: You can't win either way; the contempt is not class bound.

CAROL: It makes the story even more remarkable: the sexism is everywhere. Mulligan and the musicale organizers are typical. So where did the attitudes in this story come from?

KIM: Probably memories of growing up in a patriarchal culture—and maybe of his younger self. I don't think it is true that Joyce as an adult had contempt for educated women. I work at one of the United States' most ethnically diverse schools, and the students' identification with the entire Kearney family is prevalent, I would guess, because they've felt or experienced a similar discrimination in terms of ethnicity or race as well as gender.

CAROL: So it's an early story about responses to oppression. I see it in the same light as Virginia Woolf's work, where the origin of English patriarchal institutions is considered to be the patriarchal family. The family is a haven from public life, but it is also the very place that engenders it. Joyce gets at this idea here, too, by suggesting that the fate of one family in one situation has collective implications.

KIM: I think another interesting aspect of "A Mother" is that it starts out by sounding as if the Kearneys *are* a typical patriarchal family, but then it turns out that they're not. Mr. and Mrs. Kearney listen to each other; Kathleen, I think, understands her mother's position, so it's not typical at all.

CAROL: I totally agree with you in your point about the family. When you read that Mrs. Kearney married out of spite, early reviewers went on to conclude that it was a bad marriage, a marriage of convenience, Mrs. Kearney was a user, and so forth. But given the other marriages we see in *Dubliners,* this one is actually the best.

KIM: And even if the biased narrator is telling the truth about her marrying out of spite, we can infer that they've grown to respect each other; she doesn't feel any marital spite in the narrative present. Mr. Kearney reappears in *Ulysses* as Bloom's guarantor. . . . [H]e supports the outsider Bloom. Not many other people are on Bloom's side in Dublin. He's a decent man.

CAROL: The other thing that's said about Mrs. Kearney's motive for marrying is that Mr. Kearney would "wear well." And she's right. She has good judgment.

KIM: I have one final question. In preparation for this conversation, I reread your essay on Milly and Molly in *Ulysses*: *Engendered Perspectives.* In "A Mother," the mother-daughter bond strikes me as very strong: something unique in the Joycean canon. As I said earlier, Kathleen does not mind her mother's intervention on her behalf. I assume she supports her mother's position. Are Mrs. Kearney's behavior and Kathleen's collusion forms of delinquency? In your other essay, you suggest that Milly's bad behavior may be a good way to survive in a system that treats women as second-class citizens.

CAROL: That was based on de Certeau's comment about what the weak can do in response to power. So my answer is "no" and "yes." Mrs. Kearney is not the typical oppressed: she plans ahead; she's better educated; she's not typical of the downtrodden. If the milk woman in "Telemachus" had spilled the milk over Buck Mulligan's head—that's the type of delinquency de Certeau had in mind—but again, Mrs. Kearney is more intelligent and cagey than those around her. It's her class as a whole that's oppressed, but within her class, she's more in control than most. Nonetheless, it's also clear that she's delinquent, and I think we're both rooting for her.

Pasadena. 31 December 2008. 7:28 p.m. Colleen's house. Cheers to 2009. Clink.

14

"Grace"

Spirited Discourses

R. BRANDON KERSHNER AND MARY LOWE-EVANS

Vicki Mahaffey first approached Brandon Kershner about this project. As it turned out, Kershner had about half an essay's worth of discussion of tea and alcohol in "Grace," an extension of some of his recent work on material culture in Ireland. He thought of asking Mary Lowe-Evans whether she would be willing to write something on that story that might complement his demi-essay, and in fact she had a good deal of unpublished material addressing that story from the standpoint of the church's resistance to modernism. Our essay is the rather unlikely result of the dialogue between these two investigations of discourses. A good part of our effort was to explore why Joyce would choose to attack the issue of the crisis in Catholicism along with his most explicit treatment of the social phenomenon of alcoholism as it was framed by the institution of tea drinking. As it became apparent that the only perspective that could make sense of this issue was the one offered by (post)colonial studies, our essays drew nearer to one another. In the joint process of writing, the distinction between Lowe-Evans's deployment of Catholic intellectual history and Kershner's history of commodities began to lessen, as it became clear that the church's ideas were highly commodified while the substances Kershner treated showed themselves as charged with intellectual implication.

Grace," originally intended to stand as the final *Dubliners* story, is odd in several respects. Although several other story titles (such as "The Sisters") are oblique, seeming only tangentially related to the main themes of the story, here we are certainly drawn to wonder why Joyce chose to embody his treatment of such a significant religious concept in a story about an alcoholic tea taster who happens to be a reluctant convert to Catholicism. Our essay will attempt to explore the ways in which the cultures—we might say the discourses—of religion, tea, and alcohol, all of them imposed upon Ireland by external power, worked to reflect and reinforce one another's effects. Joyce recognized the common features of the three commodities of grace, alcohol, and tea, and their entanglement through the historical specifics of the late nineteenth century and the heritage of colonialism. The story's emissary of grace, Father Purdon, is a thinly disguised version of Father Bernard Vaughan, an Americanized British Jesuit whose interpellation of the Dubliners in attendance at a businessmen's retreat carried the authority of both British and Roman power. As even Bloom recognizes, religion in Joyce's world is an opiate; as such, it parallels tea and alcohol. All these items can function as bribes offered to a potentially rebellious populace, all are pervasive but in a sense invisible; all are dependent upon and also produce the gift of speaking in tongues that is the manifestation of a special type of grace.

Joyce's choice for the title and rather occulted subject matter of "Grace" was partly determined by discourses set into play during the modernist crisis in Catholicism. Emer Nolan has deemed the story "Joyce's most intimate examination of early-twentieth-century Irish Catholicism in *Dubliners*" (2007, 162). But Irish Catholicism itself was dramatically influenced by the broader modernist crisis. From roughly the mid-nineteenth until the mid-twentieth centuries, the reigning popes promulgated numerous doctrines, documents, practices, and devotions meant to stem the tide of various "isms" challenging papal authority and doctrinal certitude. Rationalism, empiricism, liberalism, nationalism, and consumerism represented some of the most serious threats. Among the strategies the church employed to counter these perceived heresies was to vigorously promote neo-Thomism, an updated version of Saint Thomas Aquinas's medieval theological interpretation of Aristotelian rationalist philosophy. Moreover, the papacy specifically singled out the Jesuits to sell neo-Thomism to the faithful, and it was the Thomistic doctrine regarding grace they deployed to bridge the gap between faith and reason.[1] Grace thus became an increasingly valuable commodity in the religious market. As Joyce would have learned from *The Maynooth Catechism,* "Without grace we can do nothing to merit heaven" (*Catechism* n.d., 22). Not coincidentally, that catechism was commissioned by the 1850 National Synod of Thurles, a conference of Catholic clergy in Ireland ordered by the papacy as part of its antimodernist agenda. "Under the stewardship of the formidable Paul Cardinal Cullen, popular spiritual practices, such as patterns, were discouraged, while attendance at Mass and at a range of devotions sponsored by the institutional Church came to be regarded as definitive of Irish Catholic identity" (Nolan 2007, 126). Such devotions included specialized retreats, like the retreat for businessmen featured in "Grace."[2]

Besides displaying these oblique connections to the modernist crisis, "Grace" responds quite directly to the papacy's initiatives. To begin with, it was inspired by a sermon Joyce heard on "the strange subject of actual and sanctifying grace," which, according to Stanislaus, had for years "puzzled and fascinated [his] brother" (*BK,* 227). After listening to the sermon in question, Joyce left the church "angry and disgusted," not about the doctrine of grace itself, but "at the inadequacy of the exposition. . . . It angered him that such shoddy stuff should pass for spiritual guidance" (*BK,* 227). Joyce seems never to have recovered from his fascination with the elusive doctrine of grace, but remained a "gracehoper" all his life, attempting to provide his own eccentric, but apparently more adequate, exposition of the

1. Two works are especially informative about the modernist crisis, Jodock 2000 and McCool 1977.

2. While spiritual retreats for the clergy date back to the Middle Ages at least, it was not until the pontificate of Leo XIII (1878–1903) that retreats for specific types of laymen were inaugurated. The 1911 edition of *The Catholic Encyclopedia* reports that "retreats for laymen have spread greatly throughout the Catholic world during the last twenty-five years. A French Jesuit, Père Henry, was the pioneer in this great revival. In 1882 he gave himself to the task of instituting retreats for working men, and it was not long before houses devoted to this purpose were founded all over Europe. . . . England and Ireland have taken up the movement" (Debuchy 1911, 1).

concept throughout his oeuvre. Indeed, Stanislaus confidently asserts that the relationship of grace to original sin "was to be the subject of *Finnegans Wake*" (*BK,* 226).[3] While inviting readers to consider apparent abuses and misrepresentations of grace, he also conveys a thoroughly orthodox interpretation of it. Like Aquinas, Joyce aspired to instill a certain theological correctness in his readers, albeit his theology is told "slant."

Joyce was reminded of his distasteful experience with the sermon on grace when Stanislaus wrote him in Paris (while Joyce was studying "Aristotle in French and Aquinas in Latin" [*BK,* 198]) about "an absurd incident" in Dublin involving their father, John Joyce, who had agreed to attend a retreat with his friend Matt Kane. As previously mentioned, the subject of the sermon Joyce heard as well as the retreat his father attended represent typical devotional ploys the papacy literally indulged during the modernist crisis. By assigning an increased number of indulgences for the performance of officially sanctioned practices, the papacy enticed the faithful to join its antimodernist crusade. As if anticipating some confusion on the part of the laity about the exact nature of indulgences, *The Maynooth Catechism* devotes a page and a half to explaining and defending them. The simple definition offered, however, is "the remission, through the power of the Church, of the temporal punishment due to sin which sometimes remains after the sin is forgiven" (*Catechism* n.d., 56). Undoubtedly, the indulging of devotional practices contributed to Joyce's interest in simony, an important thematic concern in "Grace" where abuses of ecclesiastical power become associated with their secular counterparts in the world of commerce.

In the persons of Tom Kernan and his wife, Martin Cunningham, Mr. Power, Mr. M'Coy, and Mr. Fogarty, "Grace" portrays the laity, a cast of Catholic characters all of whom are more or less involved in Dublin's commercial or public life. Their collective experience of the Catholic modernist debate, as Joyce represents it, apparently moves them toward a facile, docile acceptance of hegemonic church control and "shoddy" theology (to borrow Stanislaus's term [*BK,* 227]). The story implies, too, that the characters'

3. See Moseley 1968, 3–21, for a comprehensive analysis of Joyce's pervasive use of the Catholic doctrine regarding grace in his works.

religious docility is comparable to, and perhaps even a result of, their unrealized social pretensions and circumscribed commercial aspirations—just as, from another perspective, it mirrors their unthinking submission to the prescribed social ritual of alcohol. Tom Kernan's battered silk hat comes to represent this multifaceted cultural phenomenon, while the retreat, as the word suggests, indicates the church's interest in maintaining a compliant flock. Even the "distant speck of red light which was suspended before the high altar" (*D*, 212) during the men's retreat (which, Mr. Power is convinced, was "sure to be crammed to the doors" [*D*, 199]) signals a particular devotion strenuously promoted and indulged during the modernist crisis.

The devotion signaled by the glowing red light is the exposition of the blessed sacrament or "Real Presence" of Jesus, body and blood, soul and divinity, in the form of a consecrated host displayed on the altar in an elaborate gold case set on a pedestal, appropriately called a monstrance. Joyce no doubt intended to increase the ironic force of his story by emphasizing, on the one hand, that the light is a distant "speck" and, on the other, that it is red, symbolically suggesting Jesus's prostitution. And if Jesus is the accidental prostitute decked out in an ornate monstrance, the pimp of the piece would seem to be Father Purdon, the retreat master whose name recalls Purdon Street, the entrance to the red-light district of Dublin in the last decades of the nineteenth century. As he prepares to lead the retreatants in the upcoming liturgical performance, "Father Purdon knelt down, turned towards the red speck of light and, covering his face with his hands, prayed" (*D*, 213). Inspired by the real-life Father Bernard Vaughan, renowned for his oratorical skills and successful retreats in London and Dublin, the fictional Father Purdon also suggests a parodic Thomas Aquinas, the Aristotelian theologian who had been effectively rendered a procurer by the papacy.

Known as both the "dumb ox," because of his humble demeanor and great size, and "the angelic doctor," owing to his reputed chastity, erudition, and rhetorical gifts, Thomas Aquinas, a thirteenth-century Dominican friar, studied under Aristotle's student Albert the Great, who predicted that "we call this young man the dumb ox, but his bellowing in doctrine will one day resound throughout the world" (Kennedy 1912, 2). Albert's prophesy has been realized largely because of the antimodernist popes and their Jesuit minions. "They're the grandest order in the Church . . . said

Mr. Cunningham, with enthusiasm. The General of the Jesuits stands next to the Pope" (*D*, 201). As for Father Purdon, Mr. Cunningham describes him as a "fine jolly fellow! He's a man of the world like ourselves" (*D*, 202). Yet with his "powerful-looking figure . . . two thirds [of whose] bulk [was] crowned by a massive red face" (*D*, 213), he might very well be viewed as the dumb ox in spite of himself.

Joyce attributes one of only three mentions of the word *grace* in the story to Purdon. Very near the conclusion, Father Purdon avers, "Well, I have looked into my accounts. I find this wrong and this wrong. But, with God's grace, I will rectify this and this. I will set right my accounts" (*D*, 215). Joyce's quite purposeful attribution of the words *with God's grace* not to the narrator (who uses the word in the other two instances) but to Father Purdon reveals a degree of orthodoxy in either or both Joyce and Purdon. In spite of the obvious representation of Father Purdon as a purveyor of "shoddy stuff [that would] pass for spiritual guidance" (*BK*, 227), he expresses a Thomistically correct interpretation of grace. Embedded in the closing words of his accountant's version of salvation is the offhand, even clichéd acknowledgment that grace is a freely bestowed gift from God required for any and all spiritual merit. In perfect alignment with Aquinas's teaching, Father Purdon indirectly admits that under our own natural powers, without the grace God dispenses, we can do nothing to "set right [our] accounts." By assigning this insight to the character who is at once the most likely (because he is a priest) and least likely (because he is a compromised "man of the world like ourselves") suspect in the story, Joyce also supports another tenet of Thomistic theology. Purdon implies that we can never be certain grace will take hold in our souls.[4] This puffed-

---

4. In the *Summa Theologica* under "Law: Question #112, Of the Cause of Grace," Aquinas explains, "Nothing can act beyond its species, since the cause must always be more powerful than its effect. Now the gift of grace surpasses every capability of created nature, since it is nothing short of a partaking of the Divine Nature, which exceeds every other nature. And thus it is impossible that any creature should cause grace. For it is as necessary that God alone should deify, bestowing a partaking of the Divine Nature, by a participated likeness, as it is impossible that anything save fire should enkindle" (Thomas n.d., 1–2). Further along in the chapter, Aquinas states, "Man is compared to God as clay to the potter according to Jer. 18:6:

up retreat master thus also embodies an irony implicit in the papacy's use of Aquinas—a chronicler of incertitude, so to speak—as its bulwark (pun intended) against those individuals who would question its authority or the unassailability of its doctrines.

Leading up to its surprisingly orthodox conclusion, however, "Grace" involves readers in one of the most controversial moments in the history of the modernist crisis in Catholicism, the declaration of the pope's infallibility during the First Vatican Council (1869–70). "Papal infallibility, said Mr. Cunningham, that was the greatest scene in the whole history of the Church" (*D,* 168). Having made this pronouncement, Mr. Cunningham then gives his version of the great scene. According to him, only two cardinals had held out against declaring the pope infallible when speaking ex cathedra. Not surprisingly, he recalls that one had been Irish and the other German. "—John [MacHale] of Tuam . . . was the man. . . . There they were at it, all the cardinals and archbishops from all the ends of the earth and these two fighting dog and devil until at the last the Pope himself stood up and declared infallibility a dogma of the Church *ex cathedra.* On the very moment John MacHale, who had been arguing and arguing against it, stood up and shouted with the voice of a lion: *Credo!*" (*D,* 209). Contrary to Mr. Cunningham's confident assertions, however, the historical record indicates that although only two delegates voted no on the final ballot, a considerable number of attendees, including John Henry Newman, expressed opposition, and approval of the doctrine led to withdrawal from the church not only by a single German cardinal, but also a significant number of German "Old Catholics," as they came to be called (Baumgarten 1911, 1).

'As clay is in the hand of the potter so are you in my hand.' But however much the clay is prepared it does not necessarily receive its shape from the potter. Hence, however much a man prepares himself, he does not necessarily receive grace from God" (ibid., 5). And further along, "For certitude about a thing can only be had when we may judge of it by its proper principle. Thus it is by indemonstrable universal principles that certitude is obtained concerning demonstrative conclusions. Now no one can know he has the knowledge of a conclusion if he does not know its principle. But the principle of grace and its object is God, Who by reason of His very excellence is unknown to us" (ibid., 8).

It is not clear where Joyce acquired his information about the First Vatican Council prior to composing the first draft of "Grace"; however, he was curious enough about the subject to research it during his residency in Rome in 1906. On November 13 of that year, he wrote Stanislaus:

> I was today in the *Biblioteca Vittorio Emanuele,* looking up the account of the Vatican Council of 1870 which declared the infallibility of the Pope. . . . Before the final proclamation many of the clerics left Rome as a protest. At the proclamation when the dogma was read out the Pope said "Is that all right, gents?" All the gents said "Placet" but two said "Non placet." But the Pope "You be damned! Kissmearse! I'm infallible!" . . . I looked up MacHale's life [however] they say nothing of his having voted at the Vatican Council. I shall continue there tomorrow and rewrite that part of the story. *Grace* takes place in 1901 or 2, therefore Kernan at that time 1870 would have been about twenty-five. He would have been born in 1848 and would have been only 6 years of age at the time of the proclamation of the Immaculate Conception dogma 1854. (*SL,* 130–31)

Notably, the benchmarks Joyce sets for Kernan's life are associated with two of the most notorious papal initiatives taken during the modernist crisis— one coercive and one seductive. The declaration of papal infallibility exemplifies a prescriptive, even confrontational, ploy, while the proclamation of the immaculate conception constitutes an exercise in seduction, an exploitation of increasing popular affection for the Virgin Mother that inaugurated a century-long "Golden Era of Mary."[5]

With regard to John MacHale, if Joyce continued his research the next day, as he indicates in the letter to Stanislaus (and as Cunningham's use of the word *Credo* in the story suggests), Joyce may have come across a version

---

5. Maurice Hamington uses this phrase. He observes that the proclamation of the immaculate conception "was a landmark in Catholic ecclesiology because it elevated Mary to a quasi-divine status" (2001, 57). Not only was it the first of only two dogmas ever to be pronounced infallibly (the other, proclaimed in 1950, is the doctrine of Mary's bodily Assumption into heaven), but it was also a means for elevating pontifical status for a pope who had been under political and intellectual siege for the first eight years of his pontificate.

of MacHale's participation in the Vatican Council similar to the one officially sanctioned by the church and recorded in the 1910 *Catholic Encyclopedia:*

> Notwithstanding his very advanced years, Dr. MacHale attended the Vatican Council in 1869. With several distinguished prelates of various nationalities, he thought that the moment had not arrived for an immediate definition of the dogma of papal infallibility; consequently, he spoke and voted in the council against its promulgation. Once the dogma had been defined, Dr. MacHale instantly submitted his judgment to the Holy See, and in his own cathedral he declared the doctrine of infallibility "to be the true Catholic doctrine, which he believed as he believed the Apostle's Creed." (M. Kelly 1910, 4)

Earlier in his tenure as bishop, MacHale had also been an outspoken opponent of the above-mentioned Cardinal Paul Cullen, Pius IX's mouthpiece in Ireland. Because of his involvement in secular politics, especially the Tenant League, the Irish-speaking MacHale was "eventually isolated, and if not crushed, he was at least effectively contained" (Larkin 1972, 640). The *"Credo"* Mr. Cunningham attributes to MacHale thus finds its parallel in the capitulation forced upon him by the pope's minion, Cardinal Cullen. It also reinforces the idea of Irish Catholic enthrallment to the papacy Joyce is intent on establishing here and elsewhere.

Prior to the discussion about the dogma of infallibility in "Grace," the protagonist, Mr. Kernan, hesitantly enters the men's conversation about the Society of Jesus. "I haven't such a bad opinion of the Jesuits," he says. "They're an educated order. I believe they mean well, too" (*D,* 201). Stanislaus tells us that Tom Kernan is a composite of John Joyce, who had experienced a fall down the stairs of a pub, "the accident with which the story begins," and Dick Thornton, "a plump rubicund commercial traveler and tea-taster" (*BK,* 226), who shared John Joyce's love of booze and balladeering. In the story he is represented as a reluctant Catholic at best, one who has converted in order to marry his Catholic wife in the church. Yet, like John Joyce, he respects the Jesuits, the order so enthusiastically championed and empowered by the papacy during the modernist crisis. In rendering Kernan a "commercial traveler and tea taster," however, Joyce seems to have in mind a much more complex agenda than simply to parody his own feckless and irreverent but nonetheless elitist father. Tom Kernan seems carefully designed to be the counterpart of Father Purdon. After all, while it is Tom Kernan who has fallen down the stairs of a public house at the opening of "Grace," it is Father Purdon who "struggl[es] up into the pulpit" (D, 213) of the Jesuit church in Gardiner Street near its conclusion.

Sermons on grace such as the ones preached by Father Bernard Vaughn, SJ, on whom Father Purdon is modeled, may well have included the notion that a special manifestation of grace in one's soul is the gift of tongues. "Tongues are a gift in Greek Charisma meaning grace gift. If it is of grace it cannot be earned so we cannot demand it or even seek it because everything of grace is freely given, God distributes his gifts as he wills" ("Gift of Tongues" n.d., 1). While the gift of tongues refers to the ability to speak in one language while being understood by all listeners, no matter what their language, Joyce capitalizes on the idea in "Grace" by associating two men who live by their tongues—one an impecunious commercial tea taster, the other a commercialized religious orator—to demonstrate the overlap between the various systems they represent, especially with regard to the compromised values those systems apparently engender.[6] As noted above, Father Purdon has the last word on grace in the story. Mr. Kernan, however, indirectly has the first.

The narrator tells us that "Mr. Kernan was a commercial traveler of the old school which believed in the dignity of its calling. He had never been seen in the city without a silk hat of some decency and a pair of gaiters. By grace of these two articles of clothing, he said, a man could always pass muster" (D, 188). One of many ironies here, of course, is the fact that readers have just witnessed Kernan on the floor of a pub lavatory: "His hat had rolled a few yards away and his clothes were smeared with the filth and ooze of the floor. . . . His eyes were closed and he breathed with a grunting noise" (D, 184). We further learn that the gifted tongue with which he supports himself and his family by tasting tea has been rendered temporarily handicapped because he has bitten off a piece of it in his fall. In effect, his tongue

---

6. Brandon Kershner calls attention to the grace and gift of tongues connection (1989, 137).

has dis-graced him. Corrina Del Greco Lobner has provided an insightful interpretation of Joyce's use of "grace" in the story (though, oddly, she does not attempt to interpret Father Purdon's use of the word). Focusing on the ambiguity inherent in the term, she argues, "The theological complexities of grace . . . are multiplied by the word's vicissitudes through the centuries; therefore grace's ability to adapt to various levels of meaning creates an interesting if equivocal scenario" (n.d., 2). Besides recognizing the equivocal nature of the word *grace,* however, Joyce's emphasis on the tendency to interpret grace as something to be purchased or performed constitutes the common denominator of its uses in the story.

As we get to know Mr. Kernan better, we find that his fall from grace could easily have been predicted, since he has had a history of imbibing excessively and running up debts that keep his family in compromised circumstances. We are led to suspect, however, that conditions apparently beyond his control may have had something to do with his degradation. "Modern business methods had spared him only so far as to allow him a little office in Crowe Street" (*D,* 189), where he tasted tea for a London firm. Possibly he is in the midst of a grace period, a time allowing him to settle his debts and find another position. However, there is nothing in the story to indicate he is about to do so. Yet even his wife seems willing to grant him a certain grace. In spite of her obvious disgust with the current behavior of her husband, who, she announces, has "been drinking since Friday" and "never seems to think he has a home at all" (*D,* 190), she, too, dwells briefly on the time when she "had passed out of the Star of the Sea Church in Sandymount, leaning on the arm of a jovial well-fed man who was dressed smartly in a frock coat and lavender trousers and carried a silk hat gracefully balanced upon his other arm" (*D,* 191). Thus, even the otherwise practical Mrs. Kernan allows delusions of former grandeur momentarily to cloud her perception of their current situation. And when the plot to entice her husband into attending the retreat—implicitly to cure his alcoholism—is disclosed to her by Martin Cunningham (a cunning ham who also has a gift of tongues), she immediately agrees, even though it is well known that Cunningham himself is burdened with a hopelessly alcoholic wife.

When presented with his friends' proposal to include him in the retreat, Mr. Kernan resists: "Understanding that some spiritual agencies were about to concern themselves on his behalf, he thought he owed it to his dignity to show a stiff neck [and] took no part in the conversation" (*D*, 201), until the Jesuits are brought into the discussion. At this point, almost exactly midway in the story, the narrative moves away from the apparently secular tale of Tom Kernan's graceless fall down the stairs of a pub and into the debate the church had instigated about pontifical power. Learning that the retreat master is not only a Jesuit but (as his wife recalls Mr. Kernan himself once was) a "jolly . . . man of the world" (*D*, 202), Mr. Kernan becomes more interested. Next, enter Mr. Fogarty the grocer, who "flattered himself, his manners would ingratiate him with the housewives of the district [and who] bore himself with a certain grace" (*D*, 205). Also bearing a gift of tongues in the form of "a half-pint of special whiskey" (*D*, 205), Mr. Fogarty shows great interest in the discussion about Pope Leo XIII's attributes. By association, the pope's reputed talents—he is an intellectual, scholar, poet—seem comically to imbue this inebriated gathering. Mr. Kernan is now hooked. He becomes as involved in the increasingly spirited conversation as his meager knowledge of the popes will allow. He is even prompted to recount having once seen Bishop MacHale, "at the unveiling of Sir John Gray's statue . . . here was this old fellow, crabbed-looking old chap, looking . . . from under his bushy eyebrows" (*D*, 210).

At the end of this animated session, when Mr. Power announces to Mrs. Kernan, "We're going to make your man here a good holy pious and God-fearing Roman Catholic," Mr. Kernan himself agrees. "I don't mind," he says, "smiling a little nervously" (*D*, 210). And though he balks at carrying a candle during the retreat, Mr. Kernan joins the assembly of minor city officials, money lenders, pawnbrokers, journalists, and downtrodden commercial travelers like himself who make up the congregation. "Gradually, as he recognized familiar faces, Mr. Kernan began to feel more at home. His hat, which had been rehabilitated by his wife, rested upon his knees" (*D*, 213). The homily Father Purdon delivers is comforting to this gathering of worldlings. "Jesus Christ was not a hard taskmaster. He understood our little failings, understood the weakness of our poor fallen nature, understood the temptations of this life" (*D*, 215). Mr. Kernan surely recognizes himself in these inclusive characterizations: "our little failings"; "our poor fallen nature." He's an insider now, retreating along with his fellow Dubliners into a state of grace.

Or, to look at it another way, he has fallen out of the state of blissful inebriation that for him constitutes the only state of grace available in a fallen world. If on the spiritual level "Grace" is a story of religious themes unexpectedly debased into issues of power and social position, on the material level it is a tale of potables and their social and historical resonance. "Grace" begins with liquids that are both vividly drawn and rather repellent—the "ooze" of the lavatory floor on which Mr. Kernan is lying and the "thin stream of blood" trickling from his mouth (*D,* 184). He is, of course, in a bar—he has been in and out of bars, we learn, "since Friday" (*D,* 190)—and just before falling down the stairs to the lavatory had been drinking rum. We soon learn that he is an alcoholic given to binges and that although he still holds a position as commercial traveler for a tea company and lays claim to some degree of respectability, his social life is clearly in decline. The story, on one level, concerns the plan a group of his male friends conceive to help "reform" Mr. Kernan by taking him on a religious retreat—in Cunningham's words, to "wash the pot" (*D,* 200). Their assumption is that renouncing the devil and all his works by recommitting themselves to Roman Catholicism will necessarily include a more temperate lifestyle for Mr. Kernan. The hope is that by a kind of sympathetic magic, a new interest in spirituality will reduce his taste for spirits. Given the story's movement from Kernan's alcoholic disgrace to his brief reformation at a businessmen's retreat conducted by a popular Jesuit preacher, it is clear that Joyce is interested in the ways the culture of religion and the culture of alcohol ostensibly oppose and reinforce each other.

In recent years the greater interest in the colonial context of Joyce's stories has brought increased attention to the markers of social and political authority in the story as well. Like all the *Dubliners* stories, this one is about power, and Joyce is careful to mark its differing forms and minute gradations. When the manager appears to investigate Kernan's fall at the story's beginning, the two men who had been with him quickly vanish, we presume in fear of being held responsible, and when the policeman, summoned by the manager, appears, it marks the increased seriousness of the situation. Mr. Power is able to keep the social awkwardness from escalating into a charge of public drunkenness because the constable recognizes him as a man of substance (and also, it is implied, because he bribes the constable). Kernan, embarrassed by the idea that someone has had to pay the constable on his behalf, begins a diatribe against constables brought in from the countryside, asking, "Is this what we pay rates for? . . . To feed and clothe these ignorant bostoons?" (*D*, 197). He mocks "yahoos" from the country presuming to boss sophisticated city people like himself; in his own ignorant way, Kernan is trying to deploy the authority of the metropolis against the periphery, a basic principle of colonial authority. Of course, this attempt is severely compromised by his colonized status: it must embarrass his companions to hear him posturing as a big-city sophisticate when he is only another Dublin "jackeen."

It is by manipulating social pressure that Kernan's companions hope to cajole him into attending the retreat. And in fact both Cunningham and Power are employed by the "Castle," the center of Dublin administrative power, while even the despised McCoy works for the coroner's office. These men are connected to the sources of power in colonial Dublin—Cunningham with his "secret sources of information" (*D*, 195), McCoy with his rather shady past as an inquiry agent. Money, of course, is a major marker of social power, and it is striking how often, during a story putatively centered on religious themes, that a litany of minor debts and loans is invoked. Kernan, it is implied, has actually converted to Catholicism in order to marry his present wife and (perhaps) to gain access to her money. Religious authority, though, is somewhat different, and the men's bedside discussion of Catholicism is really a discussion of that subject—the authority of charismatic churchmen like John MacHale (whose force of personality according to Kernan seems to spring mainly from his aggressive eyebrows), or the authority of the pope over his cardinals, or even the authority of the "old, original faith" over upstart Protestantism. And meanwhile, the discussion itself is something of a battle for authority, as each of the men has a different, equally mistaken detail to add to their communal fantasy of church history. Cunningham seems to win most of these skirmishes, through a combination of social authority and certainty of his position.

It has been argued that the story turns on silence and ellipsis, upon the unspoken and unarticulated, and that alcohol in the story is both pervasive and invisible. Considering the fact that the men have gathered at Kernan's bedside because of his alcoholism, it is stunning how the subject almost never comes up, and in fact only Cunningham has the moral authority to answer Kernan's *faux-naif* question, "How did it happen at all?" with a grave, "It happened that you were peloothered, Tom." Even so, the term *peloothered* adds a jokey, affectionate intonation to the accusation of public drunkenness. But plainly the men are in no position to preach abstinence to their friend, however much he might need this lesson. After all, they are all drinking stout until Fogarty arrives, when they switch to whiskey. Further, there is a direct linkage between the institutions of the Roman Catholic Church, for whom wine is a sacrament, and the institution of social alcoholism in Dublin.

But alcohol is only one of the relevant substances whose history resonates in "Grace." The story is presided over by two complementary liquids, tea and alcohol, and they, with their associated backgrounds, point to the ultimate sources of hidden power and compulsion in the story, through their involvement in colonial history. Kernan is a traveler for a tea company based in London and has also mastered the highly specialized art of tea tasting, which he performs in the company office: "On the mantelpiece of this little office a little leaden battalion of canisters was drawn up and on the table before the window stood four or five china bowls which were usually half full of a black liquid. From these bowls Mr Kernan tasted tea. He took a mouthful, drew it up, saturated his palate with it and then spat it forth into the grate. Then he paused to judge" (*D*, 189). Just as Bloom's family has a predilection for photography, so does Kernan's for tea: one of his two eldest sons is a clerk for a tea merchant in Belfast. Tea is his profession and the support of his family, but alcohol is, we might say, his avocation. The social uses of the two are in some ways identical, in some ways complementary. Both liquids are to some extent addictive, and both have been used in most societies as an accompaniment to conversation and as a medium for social bonding—tea often among women or mixed groups, alcohol primarily among men. Tea (along with coffee) is frequently suggested by prohibitionists as a substitute for alcohol. Mrs. Kernan helps her husband recover from his binge with "beef-tea," a kind of consommé, but then allows the men to reverse her work by sharing their alcohol in front of him.

But for all its relatively innocuous qualities, tea carries with it the cultural memory of imperialism's worst excesses. In the first place, it enabled the British to live relatively healthy lives in foreign climates, thus lowering the human cost of empire. The phenolics in tea can kill bacteria that cause typhoid, cholera, and dysentery. "It was, in effect, an efficient and convenient water-purification technology that dramatically reduced the prevalence of waterborne diseases" (Standage 2005, 179). But an aesthetic dimension was added to the practical one. Tea tasting had become a recognized art in Tang-dynasty China, and the author of *The Classic of Tea*, Lu Yu, was said to be able to identify the source of water used in the tea's preparation by its taste alone (ibid., 181). Mr. Kernan was probably asked to perform no such fine discrimination: representing the tea's final distributor, he was necessary not because the tea had not been sorted at its site of production, but because throughout the nineteenth century the adulteration of tea had become increasingly flagrant at each step along its path to the consumer— much as happens with heroin or cocaine today.

Tea was first imported to Europe from China as a medicinal and a luxury drink, and remained so until the mid-eighteenth century; only by the early nineteenth century did it become a drink common among the working classes as well as the aristocracy. The preponderance of tea consumed in Europe was black tea, which the Chinese rejected as fit only for export (although it was simply made from green tea leaves that had been allowed to oxidize overnight), and this sort seems to be the variety Mr. Kernan tests. By 1820 probably thirty million pounds was being consumed in the United Kingdom annually, and a great deal was reexported as well (Hobhouse 2005, 118). At this point all the tea was produced in Canton, and the Chinese had kept strict control of all information regarding its cultivation and production. But despite their near-total ignorance of the product they handled, the British for years had used or attempted to use it for imperial leverage. A famous miscalculation was their attempt to impose a levy on tea in the American colonies with the Tea Act of 1773. Aside from their preference for smuggled tea from the Netherlands, the Americans also resented the monopoly the British were granting the East India Company, which was in fact an economic behemoth: at its height the company generated more revenue than the

British government, ruled over far more people, and through the duty on tea produced 10 percent of all government revenue (Standage 2005, 203–4). Thus, tea, once merely a luxury beverage, came to serve as a marker for imperial economic excesses.

By the early nineteenth century, the British were finding it difficult to pay for the massive quantities of tea that European demand warranted, since the Chinese government was interested in few goods other than gold and silver, of which there was a limited supply. What could the West offer to maintain the importation of tea?

> The answer was opium, which had been an East India Company monopoly in India since 1758. . . . In 1773 the illicit trade with China was wrested from the Portuguese by the English. China had banned opium in 1729, making its growing, supply or smoking an offence, and ultimately a capital crime. The British nevertheless exported 60 tons in 1776 and five times that quantity in 1790; this was all sold to smugglers or to corrupt Chinese. . . . The growing and preparation of opium in India was a monopoly, carefully controlled by the East India Company, which was at that date not only the monopoly trader within India, but also the government. (Hobhouse 2005, 144–45)

When the Chinese attempted seriously to put a stop to the illegal trade, the result was the Opium War of 1840–42. The military humiliation of the Chinese ensured that the trade in both tea and opium would continue for the foreseeable future, at the cost of widespread opium addiction among the Chinese. It also enabled the British finally to discover the secrets of tea husbandry. A tea industry had been established in Assam by 1860 and in Ceylon and Java by 1890.

For a combination of economic, political, and aesthetic reasons, the main Western tea-drinking nations are Britain, Ireland, Australia, and New Zealand, and the spread of tea drinking within those countries was an immediate sign of the hegemony originally established through British monopoly capitalism. Mr. Kernan the tea taster has his place in the chain binding Ireland to Britain, Britain to India and then to China, a chain of economic dependency whose links are reinforced through the logic of addiction. Intent as they are on ignoring the fact of Kernan's lethal addiction to alcohol, who among his friends would be capable of realizing the irony in his family's apparently benign dependence upon tea? It is as if a mysterious logic of displacement governed the colonial universe of commodities: when tasting and then spitting out tea for his British employers begins to drive the man to distraction, he is compelled to start ingesting the complementary liquid currency of colonial domination: alcohol.

The linkage "Grace" demonstrates between social intercourse and alcohol is traditional in many cultures. The origins of alcohol use are prehistoric, but our earliest records show that the Mesopotamians and Egyptians both had a form of beer and were well acquainted with the use of alcohol to enliven social occasions, to inspire devotees to a religious frenzy, or simply to form a significant part of the diet of men, women, and children. The role of beer, wine, and then distilled spirits in the history of colonization is well known—on the macroeconomic scale as part of the notorious triangular trade involving molasses, slaves, and rum, on the microeconomic scale as the most efficient way of neutralizing resistant Africans, Native Americans, or, indeed, Irish, all of whom were believed to have a racial or ethnic susceptibility to alcohol. By the turn of the century, Dublin was in economic crisis, partially brought on by the fact that British manufacturers had driven nearly all native industry out of the Irish capital—the sole exceptions were printing and publishing, on the one hand, and distilling, on the other (Daly 1984). On taking a census of those characters of Joyce who are lucky enough to be employed, it is remarkable how many of them are involved in either administration or in one of these trades. Alcohol-related jobs range from Stephen's father, who was once "something in a distillery," or Old Cotter in "The Sisters," who brings home technical talk of "faints and worms," to poor Bob Doran, who works for a company that produces altar wine. Joyce frequently associates alcohol and religion as two opiates of the people: Bloom thinks about this parallel when he attends a Roman Catholic service, and "Grace" capitalizes upon the way each can substitute for the other.

When we view the story's events within the historical context of the culture of alcohol, we are soon brought to the possibility that the gathering of men in "Grace" echoes not only the Vatican Council but also the Greek symposium. This ancient model for the all-male drinking party that is purportedly dedicated to the discussion of higher things adds a mock-classical resonance to the painfully inaccurate discussion of church history among Cunningham, Power, McCoy, Fogarty, and Kernan. The symposium, an all-male aristocratic drinking ritual, traditionally took place in the *andron,* a special "men's room" that is ironically echoed both by the lavatory where Kernan is found and by his bedroom, "the air of which was impregnated with a personal odour" (*D,* 192). Although women were not allowed to join the drinking or conversation, they might be present as servers (as is Mrs. Kernan). In Athens three libations were poured before the drinking commenced: one to the gods, one to fallen heroes and ancestors, and one to Zeus (Standage 2005, 57); the modern Dublin parallel here would be the men's salute to the Jesuits, to famous churchmen like Mac-Hale, and to the pope.

Ensuring that the party kept to a middle way between unreasonable abstemiousness and overindulgence like Kernan's would be the job of the *symposiarch*—"either the host, or one of the drinking group, chosen by ballot or a roll of dice" (ibid.). Here, since Kernan is obviously disqualified, Cunningham and Power vie briefly for control of the party, but Power finds himself "out-generalled." The symposium might be an occasion for the invention of witty song and repartee, or a discussion of art and philosophy intended for the education of the young. The party in "Grace," more like what we term an "intervention" in our contemporary therapeutic culture, ironically reflects the Greek tradition. If it is the best thing Kernan's friends can think of, and Father Purdon the best his culture can offer, perhaps we should recall that even the best-intentioned *symposiums* at times degenerated into violence and orgies.

Garry Leonard comments that at the beginning of the story, "Mr. Kernan has not only fallen down the stairs, he has also fallen out of the discourse that sustains the identity of his masculine friends," who "encourage Mr. Kernan to reembrace his ideal image by performing a self-congratulatory ceremony that restores him to 'grace' by celebrating the mutually recognized truth of their own fictional structuration as subjects" (1993, 273–74). While our reading here has been less psychoanalytic than Leonard's, like Leonard's it has been an attempt to locate Kernan within the network of competing social discourses of turn-of-the-century Dublin. Among them, the church's discourse (generated in response to a variety of modernisms) and the discourse of addictive beverages are two of the more suggestive, opening as they do onto satiric echoes of Thomas Aquinas and the Symposium and beyond onto the interplay of power among middle-class Catholic Dubliners upon a massively colonized stage.

15

Dead Again

MARGOT NORRIS AND VINCENT P. PECORA

Our essays reflect the new theoretical perspectives we have acquired in the years since we each first published work on Joyce's story "The Dead" some decades ago. However, we approached these new readings in slightly different ways. Vincent Pecora responded in a revisionist spirit to his own 1986 "PMLA" essay on the story, attempting to come to terms both with certain lacunae in that reading and with his own change in perspective after more than twenty-five years of teaching and reflection. Margot Norris began by specifically engaging with Pecora's 1986 piece as a point of departure—and putting it into dialogue with her own early discussions of the intersection of aesthetics and gender in the work. Here she brings "Possible World Theory," a branch of narratology, to bear on the question of Gabriel and Gretta's relationship to narration and writing in order to address the figures' motives and sensibilities insofar as they shape the reader's engagement with the conundrum of their marriage. The conversation that ensued after we exchanged essays was very much a product of the Internet era: the authors began to correspond via e-mail, quite informally at first, and what is included here as an appendix is more or less the entirety of their dialogue. What is striking in retrospect is the degree to which the e-mail conversation, albeit accidentally, reproduces some of the characteristics of pretelephonic intellectual life, a life once recorded in voluminous epistolary debate. Of course, what was once true about such correspondence—the fact that it was often preserved in "hard copy" for decades, even for centuries—is generally speaking no longer the case. Today we routinely purge servers and hard drives of our written dialogues in ways that would make Samuel Richardson's "Clarissa" an

343

unimaginable work of art. Perhaps, though, we need to reconsider the enormous
potential hidden in once again "writing," rather than speaking, to one another,
a "semantic potential," as Jürgen Habermas might say, that for many years
would seem to have been lost.

The Inkbottle and the Paraclete, *by Vincent P. Pecora*

The invitation to reconsider a story about which I first wrote more than twenty-five years ago has been an occasion for some personal reflection on the whole business of literary criticism, and especially on what I might call the irreducible vicissitudes of interpretation. That the things from which we derive meaning seem to change with time because *we* have changed is of course a truism, and this point applies to places and people just as much as to stories and poems. But at least on this occasion, I found it to be an interesting truism, full of possibilities. And so, like Wordsworth returned to Tintern Abbey, I found myself looking back on what I had written about "The Dead," "with gleams of half extinguished thought, / With many recognitions dim and faint, / And somewhat of a sad perplexity." It is the perplexity I felt on rereading both the story and what I wrote about it that I want to share in what follows—a perplexity much less sad than Wordsworth's, but the consequence of recognitions dim and faint all the same.

The story unfolds with the same nonjudgmental "scrupulous meanness" of Flaubertian realism that distinguishes the earlier tales in the collection, with a heavy use of free-indirect discourse, though many have felt that it also marks a sort of departure for Joyce: it is a deeper, more developed piece of work; it points us toward the mature novels; and it seems to represent a reconciliation of sorts on Joyce's part with an Ireland toward which, throughout the earlier stories, he had shown mostly bitterness and disdain. This last point, best argued by Joyce's great biographer Richard Ellmann, albeit largely on the strength of a partial reading of one of Joyce's letters, has been especially relevant for many critics, since Gabriel Conroy and his wife, Gretta, share characteristics of Joyce and his eventual wife, Nora, and since the narrative pattern of initial bitterness and disdain toward Ireland leading toward a kindlier acceptance seems to be repeated in Joyce's subsequent

A Portrait of the Artist as a Young Man and *Ulysses*. Moreover, the larger political journey taking us from youthful angry shame about one's colonized nation to a more complex and nuance-laden relationship with it would be later elaborated by critics like Declan Kiberd and Vincent Cheng as the sign of the postcolonial condition in Joyce. To be sure, there had already been a long and lively debate about the story's conclusion, defined largely by whether you believed Gabriel's humbled acknowledgment of his mortality at the end was a redemptive triumph of self-awareness and fellow feeling or a sobering, tragic, existential confrontation with death in an uncaring universe. But in either case, what Ellmann called a renewed sense of the "mutuality" with others that comes with being humanly vulnerable was the largely accepted reading of the ending, and no one (at least in print, as far as I could tell) had concluded that Joyce might be treating Gabriel with cruel irony. But to me, back in 1985, it appeared obvious that we should see Gretta at the end as self-deluded about her erstwhile hero, Michael Furey, and Gabriel as equally self-deluded about both Gretta and himself. And that was more or less what I claimed, decades ago.

Now, I did not originally present my argument in such bald terms, but clothed it in the rather thick and heavy folds of literary theory—vaguely deconstructive theory—so that the story seemed to be less about Joyce's ironic intentions than about the illusion of what Derrida had called "self-presence," exemplified by the misguided belief that we could ever make our intentions fully transparent to others, or even to ourselves (see, among many examples, Derrida 1973, 75–77). I thus drew less on earlier critics of Joyce's often-slippery irony, such as Wayne Booth, than on Derrida's more thoroughgoing critique of any notion of intentional consciousness unmediated by preexisting traces of language (see Booth 1961, 323–36). (The omission of Booth was something I tried to correct in the version of the argument that appeared in my first book, where, to the dismay of some of my more theoretically astute reviewers, Booth's older moralistic concerns over unanchored irony were brought back into the discussion; see Pecora 1989, 103–7.) I also borrowed heavily from Nietzsche's critique of Christian asceticism and altruism, which were prime examples for me of the illusion of self-presence. But most of all, I drew on Joyce's stated suspicions both of heroic Christ-like self-sacrifice and of the degree to which his own authorial intentions might be either just "old phrases, sweet only with a disinterred sweetness" (*P,* 233)—that is, sentimental narrative or moral clichés—or perhaps forms of literary plagiarism, that is, unconscious forgeries of someone *else's* language and intentions. This entire problem of language haunted by intentions not one's own, and intentions haunted by language not one's own—which was for me central also to the free-indirect discourse that was Joyce's favorite narrative device—was symbolized most trenchantly by Joyce's later figure of "the Haunted Inkbottle" used by the "pelagiarist" Shem the Penman in *Finnegans Wake* (182). (As Joyce's pun suggests, acknowledging that we are all plagiarists of sorts is, in a sense, a Pelagian release from the taint of primal guilt, from the "original sin" supposedly incurred by betraying our originality, our origins.) The question Stephen Dedalus puts to himself in *A Portrait*—"Could his mind then not trust itself?" (*P,* 233)—was, I argued, precisely the question Joyce was articulating throughout his fiction. And the key to my argument about all this in "The Dead," as the title of my original essay, "'The Dead' and the Generosity of the Word," implied, lay in the word *generosity.*

In brief, I argued that the concept "generosity" had been thoroughly corrupted by numerous earlier moments in the text where it was either a false front for ulterior motives or the sign of a willing self-victimization on the part of the Irish nation as a whole (Ireland being, as Joyce wrote nastily in an earlier story, filled with the "gratefully oppressed"). Thus, when I came to the story's penultimate paragraph, which follows Gabriel's realization that his love for Gretta was trivial by comparison to the love of the heroic Michael Furey and which dramatizes the sudden appearance within Gabriel of a new self-awareness and acceptance of others earned through humiliation, my argument was that the attentive reader could not read the line "Generous tears filled Gabriel's eyes" without feeling that it rang false, or, in simpler terms, that Joyce was being thoroughly ironic about Gabriel's presumed emotional awakening. In my view, the gas worker, Michael Furey, was himself a gaseous creature etherealized by Gretta's overwrought romantic sensibility. Here, my real guide was Hugh Kenner's brilliant reading of the story "Eveline," in which the title character is seen as unable even to comprehend how much she had fictionalized all that she thought she had lost when she decided not to leave Ireland with her suitor, whom Joyce ironically (so Kenner claimed) named Frank (see Kenner 1972, 38). But Gabriel seemed to me even more of a sentimental fool at the end of the story than he was at the beginning, since he was in effect buying into a set of eminently Gaelic folk myths, largely originating in Macpherson's *Poems of Ossian,* which celebrated self-sacrifice, heroic romantic loss, and (last but not least) the saving virtue of a generosity that depended upon, indeed fetishized, one's own victimhood.

That is, Gabriel seemed to be passively and unthinkingly accepting all the cultural stereotypes that Joyce more than once indicated he believed were both the products and the enablers of Ireland's self-induced political and cultural victimization. I thus suggested that Joyce had constructed the story as a sort of narrative trap, one that would demonstrate to the reader just how easy it was to fall prey to such political and cultural clichés. Instead of making his peace with Ireland's unsought failings, and demonstrating a more generous understanding of the tragedy that had so often been Irish life, as Ellmann had argued, I suggested instead that "The Dead" was actually one more rotten egg hurled at the stereotypes of an Irish self-regard that found metaphysical comfort in its ability to endure humiliation, and then make redemptive music from it. The only problem in my reading, of course, was that most other readers did not think it accurately reflected what Joyce was doing, which meant either that in my interpretation Joyce's readers were on the whole as foolish as Gabriel and Gretta, since they so often took those characters at face value at the end rather than as figures of ridicule, or that the story was something of a failure. I opted for the former alternative, thereby earning some praise, but also a fair amount of enmity from a number of my colleagues in turn. Some, like Dennis Taylor, wrote immediately in a letter to *PMLA*'s "Forum" that my account absurdly presented Joyce's story as embodying "a gigantic cultural trap sprung by Christ." In a book published in 2003, Desmond Howard wrote that "reading Pecora reading 'The Dead' is both exciting and unnerving," noting with some irritation that my "menacingly articulate analysis . . . races beyond the borders of Joyce's fiction and into the very act of reading and interpretation" (Harding 2003, 65). The main problem for most of those scholars who objected to my interpretation was understandable enough, however, and it was a consequence of the sort of paradox that Paul de Man once upon a time liked to exploit. If Joyce had designed a story about seemingly hard-won insight that turned out to be just one more version of being duped, and moreover had done so in such a hermetic and obscure fashion that one could never be sure where the joke stopped, then what would ever count as genuine insight, and how would we ever know when we had it, including insight about the story itself? Why wouldn't my own insight into the story then go up in smoke along with Gabriel's awakening? As Taylor cleverly (and I now think correctly) put it, my version of the story actually refused ambiguity, presenting Joycean modernism as "oddly puritanical: it excoriates Gabriel and denies that he has any choice." Nevertheless, for many years I was satisfied that it was enough to have made people nervous about the story. On rereading both the story and my essay, however, I was less satisfied (and this dissatisfaction also embraced the longer book-chapter version, which grounded the text's "cultural trap" in the "iron cage" of Max Weber's modern, administered society). It was not so much that I now feel that I had been wrong about the story, but rather that my own early account fell short in conveying just how perplexing this story really is.

Searching for the key to my perplexity, I began to reflect on the large amount of scholarship over the past forty years or so that has been devoted to the role of the reader in producing the meaning of literary texts. And, not surprisingly, I found that I agreed more fully than I once had with Hans Robert Jauss that an interpretation is a function of a historically defined "horizon of expectations," and with Stanley Fish (or at least with one of his various avatars) that an interpretation is a function of the "interpretative community" that validates it, and even with David Bleich and Norman Holland that an interpretation is a function of the individual reader's "personality," and ultimately the reader's unconscious thought processes, including everything from gender to the effects of trauma. My reading, I decided, was very much of its theoretical time and place, shaped by Derrida's deconstruction, by Foucault's critique of a panoptic modern social order, and by a more broadly based critical obsession, built on figures like Lacan and Althusser, with the various ways by which we had all been interpellated as manageable subjects by a given social order (see Althusser 1971, 170–83; Althusser in fact highlights "Christian Religious Ideology" as his prime example). To a degree, such ideas, like those ideas of reader-response criticism itself, have been quietly absorbed into much critical practice at this point. And although I cannot agree with the strong version of reader-response theory—Wordsworth's "half-create" already seems more than sufficient—I also cannot ignore the large degree to which the rather formalistic notion of an "implied reader" and deconstruction itself played significant roles in my earlier interpretation of Joyce's story, roles that they would not play today.

At the same time, both Wordsworth and Bleich helped me see that my reception of the story was in no sense simply a function of a historical moment or theoretical model, but was also a deeply personal response. Gabriel's sense of superiority and humiliation, and especially Joyce's angry frustration with the religious, national, and familial nets trying to keep him from fleeing everything that (he felt) oppressed him, as recounted in *A Portrait*, had uncanny parallels in my own life: an educated, formerly Catholic son of uneducated working-class parents, one who had been introduced to Joyce in a Jesuit secondary school. If I could not accept that Joyce was being sincere in portraying a fictional version of himself as learning to accept what he most desired to escape, then perhaps the roots of my critical approach could be found in my own unresolved refusal to make a separate peace with my family and its expectations. Moreover, it now seems eminently plausible that if I saw unflinching irony in Joyce's narratives as the mark of the vigilant critical intelligence resisting the lure of unthinking sentimentality, it might be because something similar had become a kind of defense mechanism for me too—that is, aggressive irony as a psychic defense against messy emotional attachments. I began to wonder whether my elaboration of the story's meaning was "menacingly articulate" precisely because articulating unwanted human ties in a menacing fashion was the best way I had at the time to keep them at bay.

Yet on further consideration, nothing in the archive of research into the role of the reader promised true explanatory comfort for my sad Wordsworthian perplexity. And none of it proved adequately explanatory for the simple reason that my predicament was, in fact, not really commensurate with Wordsworth's. That is, I was responding not simply emotionally to a mute landscape, one that (as far as anyone knew) had no intentions embodied in it, but rather to language that had been deliberately organized by a human intelligence like my own and that actually seemed to be trying to communicate something to me. It was surely not all my fault that, having arrived once again at the famously hyperventilated purple prose of the story's conclusion, I no longer had a clear sense of what this piece of literature was finally supposed to *mean*. No matter how much I tried to convince myself that the problem was in *me*, and that any new reading of the story I might produce would be just as personally or historically determined as the old reading had been, I could not quite relinquish my sense that the story itself *did* matter a great deal, and that the difficulties of interpretation finally had to be traceable, in some fashion, back to particulars of the text and not simply explained away by characteristics of the reader or the epoch. If the latter premise were as true as the strong version of reader-response theory implied, then the confusion of daily life on this planet would be far more profound than it already is.

And so I turned to a critic who has been, and still is, rather hostile toward all this Wordsworthian (or deconstructive) talk of a reader's role in creating the meaning of a text, especially when that text is threatened with being reduced to little more than a chain of empty material signifiers resting lifelessly on the page. As it happens, for quite different reasons I had also been reading Walter Benn Michaels's book *The Shape of the Signifier*. Michaels has now combined two of his earlier arguments—that the meaning of any literary work is, and can only ever be, identical with the intention of the author and that the belief in cultural identity is at bottom no different from racism—into one grand unified theory. Not to put too fine a point on it, Michaels now claims that belief in the independence, or at least inevitably errant quality, of the signifier, of the sort that we associate with deconstruction and creative reading, logically entails cultural essentialism, and ultimately racism. "I am arguing," he writes, "that anyone who thinks the text consists of its physical features (of what Derrida calls its marks) will be required also to think that the meaning of the text is crucially determined by the experience of its readers, and so the question of who the reader is—and the commitment to the primacy of identity as such—is built into the commitment to the materiality of signifier" (2004, 13). That is, if you don't believe that authorial intention is the same thing as textual meaning, then you don't believe that people are defined by what they say and by their beliefs, and you must believe that people (not just readers) are defined by what they are, by a cultural essence (that is, something independent of rational beliefs), which effectively makes you a racist.

I do not want to get into the business of parsing Michaels's argument here. It is perhaps enough to say that I do not see why being suspicious of what people claim or think they mean by a given utterance, or wondering whether they really do believe what they say and imagine they believe, or recognizing along with Joyce that our inkbottles are often haunted, and that we often unconsciously plagiarize (which is really all that is technically required to make you a creative reader of some sort, even if not in consciously deconstructive terms)—I do not see why any of these claims necessarily mean that I must also believe that people have a specific and essential cultural or racial identity. Even Michaels himself seems to believe that people do not really always understand what they say they mean; otherwise, deconstructionists who say they are not essentialists could not make the logical error Michaels says they are making. That is, I do not see why Joyce's haunted inkbottle should entail cultural essentialism, though Michaels's argument points in that direction. Still, while I was dismayed by this latest turn in Michaels's larger antitheoretical project, reading his eminently persuasive ridicule of strong versions of creative reading reminded me just how much I agreed with him on certain key points. Indeed, despite my appropriation of strategies borrowed from deconstruction and reader-response theory, my earlier interpretation of "The Dead" was based squarely (as I indicated in my response to Dennis Taylor's *PMLA* letter) on my belief that I had more accurately discerned what Joyce meant us to understand than previous criticism had. Nothing in my original interpretation, I felt, contradicted the idea that, just as Michaels has long argued, the meaning of the story and the author's intention were one and the same. Today I would simply say, minus the theoretical jargon, that I believed then that Joyce was intentionally being far more ironic about his principal characters than most other readers were willing to credit. But it was never easy to square my underlying belief that I could better grasp Joyce's intentions—they were to me, at the time, clearly ironic—with my argument in the essay itself, which was that we should be thoroughly, deconstructively, suspicious about the nature of all intentions, Joyce's as well as Gabriel's, and that this suspicion was a logical consequence of Joyce's own (Pelagian) views of language and society.

As with my turn to Jauss and company for help, I found that Michaels's bracing certainty about the necessary identity of authorial intentions and textual meaning did little to aid my perplexity, for as I have already indicated, my problem today is not that I have discovered a clearer set of intentions in the story different from the ones I found earlier. It is that I am far less certain today what the intended meaning of this story might be, especially of the ending, than I once was, and that this uncertainty is not the consequence of its being badly constructed. Moreover, I think I can also say that I have begun to wonder all over again what these words *intention* and *meaning* are actually supposed to represent where literature is concerned, whether they are in fact adequate concepts when faced with the literary object. I found myself recalling F. R. Leavis's witty dictum about Joseph Conrad's wanting to make "a virtue out of not knowing what he means" (1963, 180), and I have come to believe that it has more to recommend it than we generally are willing to admit. In any case, I have long wondered whether the claims put forward in Michaels and Steven Knapp's original essay, "Against Theory," were of much help in dealing with a situation in which an author foregrounds the necessity of what Conrad calls "singleness of intention," and then proceeds quite deliberately to undermine the phrase's coherence, perhaps getting lost along the way in the thickets of his own rhetorical fancy. I must admit that I am just as perplexed these days when I return, usually in preparation for a class, to Conrad's *Heart of Darkness,* which grows somehow murkier, more incoherent, and more perplexing every time I read it. And don't even begin to talk to me about *Nostromo*!

So where does my perplexity finally leave me? I want to avoid, if I can, descending into a complete textual skepticism, for in fact I believe we know a great many things about texts and how they work. Instead, I want to return to the final paragraphs of Joyce's story, and see if all this reflection and rumination on readers and intentions might not point, just because of the perplexity, to a more adequate response. Above all, I want to address more deliberately now the question of the sentimental in Joyce, an element of his work that I had more or less denied in my earlier reading, and ask how it should be squared with Joyce's radically unsentimental technique. From Stephen Dedalus's overwrought, but very earnestly portrayed, pangs of conscience—his "agenbite of inwit" (*U,* 1.481)—over failing to pray with his sick mother, to Leopold Bloom's sincere belief that "love," as "everybody knows," is "really life" (*U,* 12.1482–85), to Molly Bloom's ingenuous, uninhibited, final "Yes" aimed less at her suitor than at life itself, we have an author who may have learned most of what he knew about narrative from the French (he claimed at one point that he learned nothing from the English novel) but seems to have kept, where sentiment is concerned, a kind of hidden filial allegiance to Charles Dickens, a writer to whom he was at best overtly ambivalent (see Ellmann 1983, 233, 320–21). One simply cannot imagine, for example, Joyce's great stylistic precursor Flaubert earnestly ending a novel with a woman earnestly exclaiming yes to a marriage proposal (even if she does quietly admit "well as well him as another" [*U,* 18.1604–5]), or (worse) seriously portraying her response as the triumph of the life force. From Balzac to Zola, the great French realists simply did not imagine that good novels could do the latter with a straight face.

Yet there are places in French fiction presenting similar interpretive dilemmas where sentimental endings are concerned. I am thinking especially of Flaubert's well-known story "Un cœur simple," written near the end of his alternately successful and disappointing career, a story Joyce knew and was perhaps a bit jealous of. It is a story that, as many have noted, repeats motifs found earlier in *Madame Bovary,* but in a somewhat less obviously ironic key. The ending is especially relevant to my ruminations about "The Dead," for "A Simple Heart" is either one of the very few instances in Flaubert's work where the reader is expected to be overcome with out-and-out tear-filled sentiment, or it is one of the cruelest endings in his entire corpus, one not sublime, but bitingly ridiculous. The "simple heart" of the title is Félicité, an obscure, pious, loyal, and trusting maidservant in the Normandy countryside of Flaubert's birth. She is a character who, had she been Irish, would have been very much at home in *Dubliners.* Her most enduring affection is for her parrot, Loulou, at once a kind of surrogate son and lover, which she has stuffed and mounted when he dies. All of this information is related with the same economy and scrupulous lack of affect that Joyce admiringly imitated in his early writing. Depending on how one reads events like the stuffing of Loulou, however, the story is either dripping with sentiment or dripping with irony.

At the end, after many years of unrequited faith and faithfulness, Félicité, now blind, deaf, and addled, is dying of pneumonia. She enters her death agony with the same vomiting, throaty rattles, and bloody froth at the corners of her mouth, and in the same religious delirium, as had Emma before her. But here, everything has been softened, made more obviously sentimental. As Flaubert ends the tale, his heroine lies dying with the worm-eaten mounted parrot now sitting on an outdoor processional altar set up near her room for the feast of Corpus Christi: "A blue cloud of incense was wafted up into Félicité's room. She opened her nostrils wide and breathed it in with a mystical, sensuous fervor. Then she closed her eyes. Her lips smiled. Her heart-beats grew slower and slower, each a little fainter and gentler, like a fountain running dry, an echo fading away. And as she breathed her last, she thought she could see, in the opening heavens, a gigantic parrot hovering above her head" (Flaubert 1961, 56). Despite the fact that this story quickly became one of Flaubert's most popular works, in which the pathos of Félicité's demise, as well as her Holy Ghost of a parrot, were taken with great earnestness, some critics could not help but note the similarity to Emma Bovary's end, which surely was infused with irony, and they pointed to the bathos, rather than the pathos, of Loulou's dramatic apotheosis. Moreover, we know not only that Flaubert had strong anticlerical feelings, but also that he had a few years earlier read with great enthusiasm Spinoza's *Theological-Political Treatise,* a book that might be said to have laid the foundations for seeing Christianity from the critical perspective of the anthropologist, so that his story might even be understood as subtly demonstrating the confused anthropological basis of religious illusions like the feathery Christian Paraclete. Or perhaps it is a purely linguistic confusion—a Holy Ghost of the inkbottle, as Joyce might say—that most amused him. After all, Flaubert's elegant, sentimental *conte* is at bottom a long, meandering setup for a pun that is evident only in French: in her confusion, Félicité ends up mistaking her *Perroquet* for *le Paraclet.*

Yet, as Robert Baldick notes, Flaubert is also reported to have said that the story "is not at all ironical as you may suppose, but on the contrary very serious and very sad. I want to move tender hearts to pity and tears, for I am tender-hearted myself" (ibid., 15). In fact, there is an uncanny resemblance, or repetition, between the situation prompting Flaubert to write "A Simple Heart" and the one that prompted Joyce to write "The Dead." Flaubert had often been disappointed by the negative response of those readers who understood the point of his irony, and by the misunderstanding praise of those on whom the irony had been lost. George Sand, an old and close friend, had reproached him for "spreading unhappiness" with his books, and there is some evidence Flaubert wrote "A Simple Heart," which is very much a biographically based homage to the narrow, ignorant, provincial environment of his youth, as a way of showing Sand that he could be more generous and accepting of the backwater French national life he had so bitterly satirized in previous novels (see ibid., 12). Even if there were not good reasons to doubt Flaubert's assertions of tenderheartedness, the story itself remains a wonderful example of a sort of narrative split personality. Flaubert's stated hope that "now, surely, no one will accuse me of being inhuman anymore" (ibid., 15), so similar to Joyce's statement in the oft-quoted letter to his brother about wanting to be kinder to Ireland in his final story, itself betrays a certain repressed bitterness. It is as if Flaubert somehow resented having to write a more generously sentimental story in the first place, even as he felt he should. There is certainly something moving about Félicité's miserable fate, with one humiliation following another as she declines, increasingly withdrawn into what is left of her memory. Yet I cannot help laughing when she begins to kneel down and pray to her badly taxidermied parrot as if it were the Holy Ghost, and when, in the last lines, the decrepit, worm-eaten Loulou descends from on high. This fusion of the sublime and ridiculous, this curious admixture of authorial generosity and cutting black humor, is (I am convinced) precisely what Flaubert intended, and one might say it is this deep equivocation between pathos and bathos that becomes one of the distinguishing marks of modernist literature, exemplified most spectacularly by Kafka's hysterical laughter as he read his seemingly tragic novels to his puzzled friends. Beckett too would draw on this particularly unstable rhetorical tone, as if he had figured out how to pare down the story of Félicité's obscure life to nothing but the skeletal structure of the unrelieved, yet mundane, and ultimately somehow ridiculous miseries that punctuate all such obscure lives. One could say too that Julian Barnes's Nabokovian *Flaubert's Parrot* is an obvious postmodern inheritor of this generic mutation.

So the question I want to pose is as follows: should we perhaps see the ending of "The Dead" as similarly structured by an equivocation between pathos and bathos? On the one hand, I am now willing to acknowledge that Gabriel's implied final reverie is a sublime Homeric or Dantean vision of "that region where dwell the vast hosts of the dead," symbolically defined by powerful Christian imagery of "crooked crosses and headstones," "the spears on the little gate," and "the barren thorns" and by that snow lying "on all the living and the dead." But on the other hand, it still seems to me somehow pretentious that Gabriel should think "the time had come for him to set out on his journey westward." That swoon is still vaguely ridiculous, too alliterative, hyperbolic—"his soul swooned slowly as he heard the snow falling faintly through the universe"—a self-induced romantic delirium, not unlike Emma Bovary's at her suicidal death, haunted by ghosts that Gabriel can only glimpse through his self-pitying tears. Thinking of the young Michael Furey, destroyed by a powerful yet thwarted passion, Gabriel's acknowledgment that "he had never felt like that himself towards any woman but he knew that such a feeling must be love" does, I now am willing to admit, have a certain poignancy. Yet I wonder whether Gabriel's delirious meditation on the putative sublimity of a love he has never felt is also a subtle parody of the romantic sublime—and we should recall that Stephen Dedalus "swoons" in the same way over his exaggerated sense of his sinfulness in *A Portrait*. We know from earlier stories just how satirical Joyce (like Flaubert) could be about such religiously amorous swoons. (Just a few months before beginning work on "The Dead," for example, Joyce wrote to his brother, "Perhaps my view of life is too cynical but it seems to me that a lot of talk about love is nonsense" [letter to Stanislaus Joyce, November 13, 1906, *Letters II*, 189].) There is, I now recognize, something deeply human and moving about Gretta and her sorrow, and about her sense of a lost chance for passion in an otherwise dreary existence. But I cannot shake the feeling that, throughout *Dubliners*, it is precisely this preoccupation with the lost or missed passions of the past that is meant to be seen as paralyzing, as usurping the chance for passion in the present—as if we are meant to see Gretta, like Eveline, getting more pleasure out of what she thinks she lost than out of her real husband. And I cannot avoid thinking that Gabriel is somehow repeating the motif, lamenting all that he *could* have had with Gretta, had he only known what he was missing. There is now for me even real pathos in the figure of Michael Furey. Yet I still cannot dismiss the sense that he winds up being not only someone who once *sang* a romantic Irish ballad about unrequited passion, "The Lass of Aughrim," but a quasi-legendary figure in his own right who has stepped right out of the ballad into Gretta's memory. I am more willing now to accept that the word *generous* as applied to Gabriel's tears could be taken at face value, or perhaps simply as meaning "copious." But it still for me reverberates with irony in the context of the story as a whole.

I will not, that is, any longer deny the affecting poignancy of the conclusion, as John Huston's movie captured it. But what, finally, *are* Joyce's intentions, and did he know what they were before or after he wrote those final elevated paragraphs? A story like "Araby" clearly shows that Joyce, who liked thinking of himself as Luciferian, could be every bit as ironic as Flaubert about the power of religiously induced emotion to supply the passion that was missing in the obscure lives of oppressed (and repressed) people. Is something like that going on at the end of "The Dead," too, or is this story one case in Joyce's work where the cross and thorns of Christ's passion, and men angelically named Gabriel and Michael, are to be seen (as Ellmann and many others see them) as the real thing? And if all of it remains unclear, does the obscurity I feel mean that the strong claims of Bleich and Holland about the reader's role inevitably trump the claims of Michaels's pragmatism? I am not sure how to answer such questions. But I would like to conclude by asking you to imagine that "A Simple Heart," with its scrupulously ambiguous ending, might provide a kind of guide. And to illustrate why, I want to cite the thoroughly ambiguous letter Joyce wrote to his brother Stanislaus in 1906 that, in my view, has so often been misread in evaluating the meaning of "The Dead":

> I have often confessed to you surprise that there should be anything exceptional in my writing and it is only at moments when I leave down somebody else's book that it seems to me not so unlikely after all. Sometimes thinking of Ireland it seems to me that I have been unnecessarily harsh. I have reproduced (in *Dubliners* at least) none of the attraction of the city for I have never felt at my ease in any city since I left it except in Paris. I have not reproduced its ingenuous insularity and its hospitality. The latter "virtue" so far as I can see does not exist elsewhere in Europe. I have not been just to its beauty: for it is more beautiful naturally in my opinion than what I have seen of England, Switzerland, France, Austria or Italy. And yet I know how useless these reflections are. For were I to rewrite the book as G. R.

[Grant Richards] suggests "in another sense" (where the hell does he get the meaningless phrases he uses) I am sure I would find again what you call the Holy Ghost sitting in the ink-bottle and the perverse devil of my literary conscience sitting on the hump of my pen. And after all *Two Gallants*—with the Sunday crowds and the harp in Kildare street and Lenehan—is an Irish landscape. (September 25, 1906, *Letters II,* 164, quoted in Ellmann 1983, 231)

It is remarkable how often the first part of this letter has been either cited alone or unduly emphasized in Joyce criticism to explain the significance of the story it describes. Written some months before Joyce began work on "The Dead," the letter has been used by Ellmann and many others (even very astute contemporary critics like Michael Levenson a few years ago [1996, 426]) to suggest Gabriel's, and by implication Joyce's, decision to grant (in Ellmann's words) "a kind of bondage, of acceptance, even of admiration to a part of the country and a way of life that are most Irish" (1983, 250). In my earlier reading of the story, I responded with a frankly oppositional critique that overemphasized the second part of the letter and focused on the passages that I felt proved that Joyce's story was anything but the generous reconciliation with family and nation that most of his readers thought it was.

Today I want to take the letter as a contradictory whole, to come a bit closer to that binocular, rather than monocular, perspective that Joyce emphasized so trenchantly in the "Cyclops" episode of *Ulysses.* If I had to decide afresh what Joyce really did mean at the story's end, I would say that I am not sure even he knew. Perhaps he tried to eat his cake and have it too, creating a character who finally gives in to the more generous impulses that Joyce himself obviously felt, all the while mischievously undermining that character, subtly parodying the larger spirit of reconciliation—which is, of course, what the Holy Ghost (the Paraclete, the Flaubertian Parrot) in his inkbottle is all about—with ambiguous details and rhetorical overkill. Joyce did not resort to the kitsch of a giant stuffed parrot welcoming his protagonist into the afterlife. But I believe that the author of *Dubliners* was somehow quietly at cross-purposes, if I can put it that way, with the beautiful, redemptive language of its finale, which even rhetorically occupies for me some strange middle ground between free-indirect discourse and omniscient description. I think Joyce was finally so troubled and frustrated by the impossible morass of personal and political claims Ireland made on him that he could not decide whether he should reconcile with it or turn his back on it, and I think the end of the story with its swoon into the comforts of oblivion is the surest sign of Joyce's own deep and irresolvable ambivalence. Instead of deciding what he really felt about Ireland, I now believe, Joyce remained confused and uncertain and wrote an awfully good story about his perplexity. But perhaps that is just what all great storytellers do.

Art and Artlessness in the Possible Worlds of "The Dead," *by Margot Norris*

Vincent Pecora's reading of Joyce's "The Dead" offers us perhaps the most acute interrogation of the signal conundrum at the heart of the story: does Gabriel experience an authentic or inauthentic epiphany at its end? Instead of offering an easy answer, Pecora concludes with an explanation of why it may be so difficult for us to challenge the significance and grandeur of Gabriel's gestures of heroism, generosity, self-sacrifice, and spiritual transcendence at the end of story. "If Gabriel fools himself, if in the very process that we accept as self-discovery, he only reimplicates himself blindly in the cultural conditions he longs to transcend, then we may simply be doing the same thing, in our reading, in our lives" (1986, 243). I take this statement to suggest that Gabriel and the reader share similar stakes in seeking some escape from what Pecora calls the "metaphysical discontent" (ibid.) of ordinary life, and those stakes lie in the most deeply embedded institutions of culture. This highly sophisticated formulation of the issues and perils at the heart of the story has rightly become one of our interpretive norms for reading "The Dead," and I would neither wish nor be able to challenge it. Vincent Pecora's essay "'The Dead' and the Generosity of the Word" appeared in the March 1986 issue of *PMLA*. My own essay on "The Dead" first appeared under the title "Stifled Back Answers: The Gender Politics of Art in Joyce's 'The Dead'" in the Autumn 1989 issue of *Modern Fiction Studies* and was subsequently reprinted in revised form in my 1992 *Joyce's Web: The Social Unraveling of Modernism.* This early reading of mine concurs with Pecora's argument that the story clearly demonstrates that art is not above politics—although I locate Joyce's critique of Gabriel's self-idealizing gestures in his relationship to the women in his life, including the seemingly insignificant Julia Morkan and her sister Kate. My strategy in these essays was to link Gabriel's valorization of poetry, music, and culture to his aesthetic objectification of women, and particularly of Gretta, at the same time that he contributes to the cultural conditions that mandate woman's domestic and artistic silencing. My revised title for this study asked the seemingly facetious question "Who killed Julia Morkan?" and provided a simple answer that sounded like a joke: "the pope." Specifically, I argued, Pope Pius X's November 1903 *Motu Proprio,* making women ineligible to sing in church choirs, destroyed Julia Morkan's career and possibly hastened her death within the next six months, since Leopold Bloom verifies in *Ulysses* that she is dead by June 16, 1904. Although Gabriel does not directly create oppressive institutional conditions for women, my reading would agree with Pecora that in his idealistic fatuity, Gabriel "reimplicates himself blindly in the cultural conditions he longs to transcend." I would further agree with Pecora that the reader too is implicated in Gabriel's blindness. But more than a decade and a half later, I am curious to explore how an alternative theoretical approach to the question of Gabriel's motives might address the issues—and sustain or challenge readerly discomfort and peril in joining Gabriel, or refusing to join him, in his escapist enterprise.

The approach to "The Dead" that I would like to test in this respect is situated in the field of narratology and goes by the name of "Possible Worlds" theory. I am intrigued by the possibility of recoding escapist impulses and desires for transcendence (such as the ones felt by Gabriel in the story) as inscribed in private or alternative worlds whose conflict with what might be called the actual worlds in the domain of fiction is constitutive of narrative plots. After first sketching out the premises and conceptual framework of Possible Worlds theory, I hope to apply them to "The Dead" with the aim of demonstrating their usefulness for providing an alternative formulation to Vincent Pecora's conclusion. Possible Worlds theory came to prominence in the 1990s in the work of three narratologists. Marie-Laure Ryan published *Possible Worlds, Artificial Intelligence, and Narrative Theory* in 1991, followed in 1994 by Ruth Ronen's *Possible Worlds in Literary Theory* and in 1998 by Lubomir Dolezel's *Hetercosmica: Fiction and Possible Worlds.* Ruth Ronan explains the theory's aim: "The development of a conceptual

framework of possible worlds hence at first glance seems to offer a new out-
look on the problem of fictionality, on the ontology of fictional worlds and
fictional objects, and on generic problems such as realism" (1998, 21). Possible Worlds theory is therefore less a theory of fiction than a theory of *fictionality*, of what is nonactual, nontrue, pretended, made up, nonexistent,
and the like, in narrative stories. But if fiction—as opposed to nonfiction—is
by definition a domain composed of fictionality, its fictionality is nonetheless
complicated by its tendency (especially in realism) to *pretend* that elements in
its domain are true or actual. As Ronan points out, "Fiction poses a problem
for philosophers because unlike other possible but non-actual occurrences,
fictional states of affairs dissimulate their fictionality and may be presented
as *facts*" (1994, 31). Thus, Joyce's story "The Dead" is set in a fictional 1904
Dublin that with its references to Usher's Island, Phoenix Park, the *Daily
Express*, assorted statuary, and the Gresham Hotel *pretends* an actuality that
can, presumably, be historically and geographically verified. Possible Worlds
theory can address the phenomenon of a fictional Gresham Hotel and a historical Gresham Hotel by formulating criteria for what is called "trans-world
identity" (ibid., 57) between the actual world and fiction. But what interests
me more than the relationship between our world and actual worlds in fiction is the ability of Possible Worlds theory to address what are sometimes
referred to as modal operators. These are the factors of possibility, probability, necessity, and impossibility that not only underlie some taxonomies
and distinctions of the fictional genre, but also make it possible to explore
ontologies within a specific kind of literary mode, such as realism. For Marie-
Laure Ryan, these modalities underlie the private worlds of human thought
within the semantic domain of fiction—private worlds that she calls APWs,
or Actual Possible Worlds.

But although Ruth Ronan implicitly suggests that Ryan's unproblema-
tized Textual Actual World may be naive (ibid., 69–70), this point is not an
issue for me because I am much more interested in Ryan's private or Alternative Possible Worlds. These worlds strike me as extremely useful for identifying a variety of ontological conditions that together play a role in the plot of
"The Dead." Ryan's APWs (Alternative Possible Worlds in a modal system
of reality) are "constructs of the human mind. The virtual in the narrative universe exists in the thoughts of characters" (1991, 110). Ryan divides

these possible worlds, existing in the minds of fictional characters, into such categories as Knowledge-worlds (knowledge, belief, and ignorance [ibid., 114]), Obligation-worlds (commitments and prohibitions defined by social rules and moral principles [ibid., 116]), and Wish-worlds (desired states and actions [ibid., 117]). If we consider the fictional universe of "The Dead," all three of these possible worlds come quickly into view. The discussion of opera stars and musical performance around the Morkan dinner table brings into play the Knowledge-world of many of the secondary characters in the story. On the other hand, Kate Morkan's bitter comments about the injustice of Pope Pius X's *Motu Proprio* banning women from choirs voice her frustration with the implacability of the Obligation-world created and enforced by the Roman Catholic Church. And Gabriel Conroy's romantic memories and yearnings—"He longed to recall to her those moments, to make her forget the years of their dull existence together and remember only their moments of ecstasy" (*D*, 265)—appear to express Gabriel's Wish-world. "The Dead," like any work of fiction, contains a posited empirical or Actual World that, in this case, is set in Dublin, Ireland, in January 1904, in the upstairs rooms of a house on Usher's Island and, later, in a room at the Gresham Hotel. The played piano, the danced lancers, the sung aria, the consumed goose, and the exchanged conversations all belong to this Textual Actual World. But this Actual World is shot through with private worlds—most invisible, although they might be inferred, and some made manifest to us through the narration. These private worlds—the sources of Lily's and Kate Morkan's bitterness, Miss Ivors's political convictions, Gabriel's feelings about his wife—are themselves fictional (or nonfactual) within the context of the fictional domain of "The Dead," although Ryan's categories would allow us to differentiate them into a variety of modalities. Ryan's Possible Worlds may therefore make it possible to explore one of the questions raised for me by Vincent Pecora's reading of "The Dead": namely, the ontological status of "the mythomania that so characterizes Dublin life" (1986, 241). This question is perhaps best tackled by first sorting out the roles that private or alternative worlds in fiction play in the constitution of the story plot.

Ryan writes, "For a move to occur and a plot to be started, there must be some sort of *conflict* in the textual universe. Plots originate in knots—and knots are created when the lines circumscribing the worlds of the narrative universe, instead of coinciding, intersect each other. In order to disentangle the lines in their domain, characters resort to plotting, with the almost inevitable effect of creating new knots in some other domain" (1991, 120). This formulation runs into an immediate problem when it is tested in "The Dead" because of the distribution of external and internal focalization. We can certainly posit that there is some sort of tangle in the boundaries of their private worlds when Gabriel encounters Lily and Miss Ivors. In the case of Lily, the external focalization—describing only her actions and words rather than her thoughts—gives us no access to her private world except by inference. However, the implication of "The men that is now is only all palaver and what they can get out of you" (*D*, 219) suggests that Lily's Knowledge-world has suffered what we nowadays call a "reality check." She seems to have experienced a shift in her belief in the truth-value of sweet or flattering language with a consequent shift in her esteem of seemingly gracious men. Given that Gabriel Conroy is an incorrigible producer of sweet and flattering language (*"Is it because there is no word tender enough to be your name?"* [*D*, 266]), the Knowledge-worlds of Lily and Gabriel not only will not coincide but will tangle. Pecora describes, "Gabriel's response to being caught so nakedly by a caretaker's daughter, to being so neatly unmasked, is to reaffirm the cultural, bourgeois vision he would like to project to the world" (1986, 238). Thus, Gabriel uses the gold coin, symbol of his generosity, to contradict Lily's cynicism and prove not only that he is not trying to get anything out of her, but that, on the contrary, he means to be her benefactor. Whether Gabriel's gesture produces a "knot" in Lily's Knowledge-world is again made unknowable by the external focalization. But the encounter establishes Gabriel's pattern of responding to "knots" created in his own Knowledge-domain by the beliefs of others with self-mythologizing maneuvers designed to restore his role as the steward of the "health, wealth, long life, happiness and prosperity" he wishes for everyone (*D*, 254).

Vincent Pecora analyzes this maneuver as Gabriel Conroy's need to continually transform the sense of victimization that afflicts the Dubliners of "The Dead" into a noble situation, a self-sacrifice that he can code as a "princely failing" (1986, 238). The feudal, fairy-tale trope resonates with Marie-Laure Ryan's description of the implicit end and goal of narrative striving: "The best of all possible states of affairs for a system of reality is one in which the constitutive propositions of all private worlds are satisfied in the central world. In such a system, everybody's desires are fulfilled, all laws are respected, there is a consensus as to what is good for the group; what is good for the group is also good for every individual, everybody's actions respect these ideals, and everybody has epistemic access to all the worlds of the system" (1991, 120). Both Gabriel's efforts—to put galoshes on his wife and shore up the health of his children—and the narrator's determination to predict the total success of the Christmas party ("Never once had it fallen flat. For years and years it had gone off in splendid style as long as anyone could remember" [D, 216]) work in the service of this utopian goal. But Gabriel's failure to effect this best of all possible worlds can be traced to some extent to his refusal to take advantage of "epistemic access" to the Knowledge-, Obligation-, and Wish-worlds of others—a refusal enacted also by the narrative focalization. Both Kate Morkan's rage at the victimizing Obligation-world imposed on Ireland by Catholicism ("I suppose it is for the good of the church if the pope does it. But it's not just, Mary Jane, and it's not right" [D, 241]) and Molly Ivors's efforts to create a political Obligation-world of Irish nationalism remain impenetrable both to Gabriel and to the narrator whose character-bound focalization extends only to Gabriel's thoughts and feelings. And this blindness extends to such other private worlds as the Knowledge-world as well. No one at the party is interested in something that Freddy Malins knows and seeks desperately to communicate—namely, that there are black tenors whose voices might rival the voices of the "legitimate" white singers enshrined in the musical pantheon created at the dinner table. This double indifference, by Gabriel and the narrative perspective, could indeed be troped as a "princely failing"—though in a sense of moral hauteur rather than as an excess generosity, as Gabriel would have it. It further accounts for both the inauthenticity of the best of all possible worlds Gabriel seeks rhetorically to restore with his after-dinner speech and the inauthenticity of his epiphany at the end.

We might suggest, then, that Gabriel Conroy's attempt to create the best of all possible worlds for himself, his family, and his community is produced by his complex—if unconscious—manipulation of the relationships between his various private worlds and their intersection with the people around him. Marie-Laure Ryan's model does not fully address such manipulations, and

"The Dead" could therefore serve to introduce some complications into Possible Worlds theory. For example, Ryan concedes that Knowledge-worlds can be either incomplete or partial, and she makes a distinction between these two terms. "An incomplete K-world fits on its reference world like a cover with some holes in the middle; the location of the holes is determined, and the character knows where his or her knowledge is defective. A partial K-world is like a cover that is too small, the regions beyond the cover remaining unsurveyed" (1991, 115). Gabriel Conroy might be thought of as a consciousness that deliberately punches holes in the Knowledge-world—not intending to make it incomplete, but in order to improve it by patching the holes with elements imported from his Wish-world. This might be a way of explaining the operation of Gabriel's mythologizing impulse, as a "private-world-exchange maneuver" that is most clearly visible in his dealings with Gretta. Her Galway life is one of the holes Gabriel punches into his Knowledge-world—presumably prompted by his mother's denigration of the provincialism that makes her call her daughter-in-law "country cute" (*D*, 231). Although Gabriel mentally protests this characterization ("that was not true of Gretta at all" [*D*, 231]), he appears nonetheless to have exiled Gretta from her place of origin and—judging from his ignorance of her early romantic life—to have discouraged her from discussing it with him. "She's from Connacht, isn't she?" Miss Ivors asks about Gretta. "'Her people are,' said Gabriel shortly" (*D*, 234). Gretta's own response to Miss Ivors's suggestion that the Conroys take a trip to the West of Ireland betrays her longing for the place. "His wife clasped her hands excitedly and gave a little jump. 'O, do go, Gabriel,' she cried. 'I'd love to see Galway again'" (*D*, 236–37). But instead of exploiting this opportunity to remedy a self-created hole in his Knowledge-world, Gabriel elects to paper it over with his Wish-world. His ignorance of Gretta's actual past is rehabilitated with material from his own memories—or, at least, his imagined memories. "Like the tender fires of stars moments of their life together, that no one knew of or would ever know of, broke upon and illumined his memory. He longed to recall to her those moments, to make her forget the years of their dull existence together and remember only their moments of ecstasy" (*D*, 265).

Not until Gabriel seems to concede near the end that "he had never felt like that himself towards any woman but he knew that such a feeling must be love" (*D*, 277) are we free to wonder if that ecstatic memory might perhaps belong to what Ryan would call a "Pretended-world." She writes, "The complete semantic description of a character's domain thus includes both authentic and inauthentic constructs—beliefs and mock beliefs, desires and mock desires, true and faked obligations, as well as genuine and pretended intents" (1991, 118). Gabriel's desire for what I would characterize as a "lyrical" existence, an aesthetic construction of memories, sentiments, and values that allow themselves to be expressed in markedly beautiful language, appears sincere and appears to represent his true Wish-world. Yet his curious confession after Gretta's outburst opens the possibility that the narration, so thoroughly complicit with Gabriel's self-imaginings, has given his mental performances an aura of sincerity and genuineness without guaranteeing their authenticity. One could redeem the discrepancies and inconsistencies in Gabriel's Wish-world by arguing that the lyrical existence he covets is the Wish-world he *wishes* he could inhabit because it would remove him further from the Actual World of indelicately clacking heels and shuffling soles. Gabriel might therefore not only punch holes into his Knowledge-world and paper them over with pieces of his Wish-world, but do the same with his Wish-world: punching holes in it and papering them over with chunks of a Pretended Wish-world. This Pretended Wish-world, then, might be considered the source of Gabriel's mythomania, although I would find its inspiration in a different mythic arena than does Vincent Pecora. Pecora identifies the myth enacted by Gabriel's generosity and self-sacrifice as religious, that of Christ, while I see specifically aesthetic myths as shaping the lyrical Wish-world Gabriel creates as the ostensible object of his desire. I have discussed these intertextual models previously in my earlier work on "The Dead" and would continue to insist on the legitimacy they draw from either primary or secondary allusions in the text. The most notable is, of course, Shakespeare's *Romeo and Juliet,* whose balcony scene is represented in Julia Morkan's embroidered picture (*D*, 230)—a scene Gabriel reenacts as he watches Gretta listening on the stairs. Another is the reverse of the myth of Pygmalion and Galathea—possibly embedded in the references to Robert Browning, author of "My Last Duchess," about a man whose princely failing is to turn a living wife into a work of art. These are not moral myths of saviors whose suffering and sacrifice redeem the world, but rather aestheticizing myths about men who transform the women they ostensibly love into ecstatic lyrics or beautiful pictures—"*Is it because there is no word tender enough to be your name?*" (*D*, 265); "*Distant Music* he would call the picture if he were a painter" (*D*, 260).

Pecora's sense of the nature of Gabriel's mythomania and my own are not unrelated, of course, since the myths we postulate as Gabriel's models and inspirations deal—in a very general way—with the redemptive power of love. But my focus on the specifically dramatic or theatrical nature of the sources that inspire Gabriel's enactments is useful for pointing up the way the theatrical or the aesthetic legitimates insincerity or inauthenticity as art and artifice. Ever since Aristotle exonerated drama and theater from charges of lying, artistic representation has enjoyed an ethical license presumably detached when acting moves off the stage and into ordinary behavior. Yet when ordinary behavior mimics art, as it does in Gabriel's soliloquies, it seems to acquire some of art's legitimacy as an expressive medium of emotion and value. This point may help to explain how Gabriel could fail to realize that he postures not only in his words and speeches but even in his most intimate thoughts—a realization that comes to him as an acutely mortifying *anagnorisis* after Gretta's revelation. "He saw himself as a ludicrous figure, acting as a pennyboy for his aunts, a nervous wellmeaning sentimentalist, orating to vulgarians and idealising his own clownish lusts, the pitiable fatuous fellow he had caught a glimpse of in the mirror" (*D*, 273). Gabriel's Pretended Wish-world of a lyrical life conceals an actual Wish-world that we might characterize as one focused on patriarchal privilege and filled with desire for class, gender, and cultural superiority. The vulgarity of this Wish-world is one Gabriel shares with many of the other guests and one that consequently contributes to his "metaphysical need." The dream of wishing for something finer, something higher, the kinds of longings and aspirations embodied in poetry and works of art, in turn shapes his Pretended Wish-world. And it allows him to replace the prosaic fictionality of his *actual* Wish-world, with its crude desire for prestige and superiority, with the pretended poetic fictionality of spiritually princely longings. Given the layering or imbrication of fictional constructs that constitute this secondary Pretended Wish-world, this complex and intensely private domain of Gabriel's world should be immune to challenge. Yet it will be stunningly challenged in

"The Dead" when it becomes tangled and knotted with Gretta's own layered and multidimensional private worlds.

When Gretta erupts with her Michael Furey story, Gabriel's private worlds become assaulted with the force of another constellation of Possible Worlds not yet dreamed in his philosophy. The patches he had glued over the Galway portion of his Knowledge-world are ripped off, and he has to confront the existence of an actual provincial world in which boys toil in the gasworks, go out walking with young girls, contract tuberculosis, and die. It is a world in which galoshes, dumbbells, and stirabout would seem incapable of keeping disease, death, and tragedy at bay. But Gretta's Knowledge-world appears itself to have been reworked in aesthetic wools, as it were, like Julia Morkan's domestic appropriation of Shakespeare's balcony scene, and is thereby also transformed into a poignant Wish-world. Both Gabriel and Vincent Pecora construe Gretta's wish as the desire to transform herself into a romantic heroine. "So she had had that romance in her life: a man had died for her sake" (D, 276), Gabriel thinks. And Pecora writes, "Gretta transforms Michael Furey into the one grand passion of her life by idealizing both his death and her love: he dies—not, as Gabriel suggests, from consumption—but for her" (1986, 241). Pecora then attributes two fictional models for the "legend" Gretta builds around Michael Furey: "The Lass of Aughrim" and, once again, Christology. "The suggestion of Christ's death in her phrase is only accented by his standing in a garden 'where there was a tree,' as if crucified for her sake" (ibid., 241–42). In Pecora's reading, Gabriel not only embraces Gretta's romantic mythologizing of the story, but elaborates it, intensifies it, and appropriates it for his personal redemption. "In the name of Michael Furey, his legendary hero and personal saint, Gabriel sacrifices himself to the past, and to the dead, more profoundly than any of his compatriots does" (ibid., 243). But perhaps Gretta's private world—so long suppressed by Gabriel—should not be so quickly suppressed by our criticism. Gretta does appear to transform Michael Furey's death from a prosaic event in the Actual World into a symbolic act or gesture: "I think he died for me" (D, 274). But does this sentiment belong to her Wish-world or to a Pretended Wish-world? Is her mythomania of the same order as Gabriel's or different?

What does Gretta wish in her private Wish-world? The narration's internal focalization on Gabriel, with its consequent lack of access to Gretta's

thoughts, makes this question difficult to answer except by speculative inference. But one might hazard the possibility that Michael Furey offered Gretta
something her husband does not: namely, love without palaver. We know
only Gretta's verbal account of her courtship by Michael Furey, if we can
even call it a courtship, and in it he speaks only once, the words that become
her evidence that he died for her: "But he said he did not want to live"
(*D*, 275). Without artful words of the kind Gabriel masters in abundance,
Michael Furey conveyed to Gretta a world of lyrical expression, in his song,
in his eyes, and in his simple final words. "'I can see him so plainly,' she said
after a moment. 'Such eyes as he had, big dark eyes! And such an expression
in them—an expression!'" (*D*, 272). Can eyes express anything other than
sincerity? Gretta clearly construes them as incapable of the kind of palaver
that a literary sensibility can construct rhetorically—"In one letter that he
had written to her then he had said: *Why is it that words like these seem to me
so dull and cold? Is it because there is no word tender enough to be your name?*"
(*D*, 265). Gretta, unbeknownst to Gabriel, too knows something about love
letters and, like him, is capable of remembering what she wrote to someone
for whom she cared. But her letter is rendered poignantly expressive by what
it does not say and by what she eschews in expression. "He was much worse
and I wouldn't be let to see him so I wrote him a letter saying I was going
up to Dublin and would be back in the summer and hoping he would be
better then" (*D*, 274–75). This letter without palaver moves Michael Furey
off his sickbed on a rainy night so that he can say good-bye to her. Neither
Michael Furey nor Gretta appears to have suffered from princely longings,
from desires to elevate their feelings to some loftier and spiritually weight-
ier plane. We might therefore be forgiven to ask why the story might not
have transpired as Gretta remembers and tells it, and why the dying Michael
Furey's sentiment—that he did not wish to live without her—could not have
been sincere.

What the story conveys of Gretta's Wish-world might be no more than
that she wishes that the life she touched so many years ago not be forgotten
by at least one person—by her. And it may be important to remember that it
is Gabriel who turns her story into a love story ("he knew that such a feeling
must be love" [*D*, 277]). Three times Gabriel asks her if she was in love with
the person who used to sing the song. "'Someone you were in love with?' he

asked ironically" (*D*, 272); "'O then, you were in love with him?' said Gabriel" (*D*, 272); "'I suppose you were in love with this Michael Furey, Gretta,' he said" (*D*, 273). Gretta never concurs with his expression, conceding only that "I was great with him at that time" (*D*, 273). There is no evidence that Gretta's mythomania, if we can even call it such, is the desire to turn herself into the romantic heroine of a Pretended Wish-world. Her Michael Furey story may reflect merely a desire to remember, belonging to her Knowledge-world; a desire to grieve, belonging to her Wish-world; and a desire to memorialize, belonging to her Obligation-world. The story of Michael Furey is, after all, an effectively buried story, one never intended to be told or offered to an interlocutor—as the accidental events that force it into the open make clear. Gretta is caught off guard twice in the course of the late evening: by unexpectedly hearing "The Lass of Aughrim" and by Gabriel breaking into her melancholy with an amorous advance. The explanation that she must offer so that Gabriel will not produce a faulty interpretation of her mood ("Tell me what it is, Gretta. I think I know what is the matter. Do I know?" [*D*, 271]) is impromptu, artless, and uncontrived. In this matter I would disagree with Vincent Pecora, who characterizes the story as a fiction, "an unexpected fiction that dashes Gabriel's hopes for the evening" (1986, 241). It is precisely the artlessness of Gretta's story that ties Gabriel's private world into a knot, I would argue. What terrifies Gabriel in Gretta's story is his need to confront the possibility of a genuinely lyrical existence, a world of feeling and caring never elevated to self-consciousness or dressed in beautiful language designed to rebound to the greater glory of its producer. What Gabriel hears in Gretta's story are beautiful words that are *not* palaver—a discovery that confounds him, and, we might add, confounds the narrative voice as well. It is important to remember that the narrative voice gets no credit or share in either the sincerity or the style of Gretta's story that is conveyed entirely as reported speech. "I implored of him to go home at once and told him he would get his death in the rain. But he said he did not want to live. I can see his eyes as well as well! He was standing at the end of the wall where there was a tree" (*D*, 275).

Vincent Pecora construes this reference to reinforce Furey's religious function—"the suggestion of Christ's death in her phrase is only accented by his standing in a garden 'where there was a tree,' as if crucified for her sake" (1986, 242). But perhaps it is precisely the imposition of myth to give meaning to the story that the reader is invited to resist. Unlike that of Christ, or even Romeo, Michael Furey's death is not voluntary, and the power of his love may have failed as a redemptive gesture if it left Gretta chiefly with a feeling of the insufficiency of love to protect, heal, and save. Narratologically, Gretta's story is itself about a knot produced by the tangle of two private worlds, and the knot it produced in hers may have had effects Gabriel cannot divine. Gretta's glimpse into Michael Furey's world may have prompted her to pursue a utopian progress of only the most prosaic kind: marriage to a man who provides galoshes, dumbbells, and stirabout to keep his wife and children healthy and safe. Gabriel may therefore totally misconstrue and underestimate his role in the plot of Gretta's story when he thinks "how poor a part he, her husband, had played in her life" (*D*, 276). In Gretta's experience, love cannot save, except on the most prosaic level, and Gabriel's role as a good man, a generous man in the most ordinary and nonheroic sense, may be the fulfillment of her highly realistic Wish-world. But Gabriel patently fails to see this possibility, and hence he remains confounded. What response can either Gabriel or the narrative voice possibly make to Gretta's story— particularly in light of a plot pressure that requires Gabriel to restore a utopian equilibrium to all their worlds? My response coincides with Pecora's, I believe, though I would formulate it in the language of Possible Worlds theory. Gabriel has glimpsed in his wife's private worlds his own Pretended Wish-world but without the pretense—and he has no response to such a world of sincere feeling except an initial imitation, followed by a blizzard of palaver. His own humble memorialization of Julia Morkan's proleptic death seems initially to concede the failure of his palaver—"He would cast about in his mind for some words that might console her and would find only lame and useless ones" (*D*, 277). But the pressure of his Pretended Wish-world is not long kept at bay, and soon his sentiments become loftier and grander, reaching cosmic proportions—"Other forms were near. His soul had approached that region where dwell the vast hosts of the dead" (*D*, 277). If Gretta memorializes one dead person, Gabriel memorializes hosts of dead persons—resorting to the metaphor of the snow to seal the universe with his

Pretended Wish-world. "His soul swooned slowly as he heard the snow falling faintly through the universe and faintly falling, like the descent of their last end, upon all the living and the dead" (*D*, 278).

Like Pecora, I too believe it is risky and uncomfortable for the reader to resist joining Gabriel in his escapism from the humiliations of his Dublin life. But I would identify "the very institutions that produce and maintain the viability" of Gabriel's motives at the end of the story (1986, 243), and that readers share, as the institution of art rather than religion. The social function of art as an "affirmative culture," to use the Marxist term, that papers over our Actual World with a Pretended World of transcendence and utopian possibility is one I explored at length in *Joyce's Web*. I would stand by the argument that Peter Buerger inspired in my thinking in that work—that, unlike many of the other modernists, the target of Joyce's critique is not merely mass culture and popular art but the high art of modernism itself, including his own. If we accept this auto-critique, or self-critique of modernist art at its most powerful, disciplined, and beautiful, then our own relationship to high art becomes highly problematic. If the exquisite prose at the end of "The Dead" is to be equated with the most effective and seductive sort of palaver, then the reader risks becoming as imperiled and feminized as the victim of Flaubert's critique of romantic novel consumption. To my mind it is the cultural ideology of high art—the subject of discussion around the Morkan dinner table, incidentally—that is much more critically important to the twentieth-century secular imagination than the religious ideology Pecora finds at base of the anchoring institution in "The Dead." The reading I have attempted here, using Possible Worlds theory, illuminates for me *why* the critique of high art is so threatening to the story's reader. Art—particularly the highest forms of art—represents a collective, secular, twentieth-century Wish-world, not only within poetry and literature, but also beyond. Art may still offer the best possibility for transcendence, for a loftier, more cosmic, more disinterested vision of the universe in our struggle with the metaphysical discontents of ordinary existence. The notion that it might function as a Pretended Wish-world—an affectation designed to merely confer social, intellectual, and cultural superiority to our impaired vanity—may be a bitterer pill than we can swallow.

Dialogue on the Preceding Essays

vp: First, I would like to address the question of "sentiment." This is perhaps more my terminology than yours, but I do think one of the important issues you raise is the (for you) authenticity of Michael's and Gretta's sentiments—that is, sentiment free from the distortions of "palaver," or insincere rhetoric—and the inauthentic nature of Gabriel's sentiment, that is, sentiment always already predetermined by rhetorical models. I think this is an issue that runs throughout Joyce's subsequent work, and that has often been the underlying content of numerous arguments about what he is doing. As you have no doubt noticed, I am now closer to your point of view—or at least more on the fence, more willing to give Gretta her due—but I still think Joyce is deliberately treading on very thin ice where sentiment in the story is concerned, and I still think there is an almost inexorable tendency in his thinking and in his work to turn against his own authentic sentiments and perhaps see them, at a second glance, as no more than received wisdom, "palaver," or rhetorical plagiarism.

Second, there may be a point of intersection between us about the French realism from which Joyce learned so much, or at least about Flaubert. You put your finger on something important at the end of your paper—that Flaubert (like others in the modern French intellectual tradition) generally saw sentiment, and religious belief too, as the weakness of women (in "Un cœur simple" as well as in *Madame Bovary*), and that this weakness extended for him to the desire for, and susceptibility to, sentiment in novels as well. I think you want to see Joyce as revising this tradition, as being more of a feminist than Flaubert ever was, in the sense that Joyce is allowing space for authentic sentiment on the part of women and innocent boys (and more "feminine" men, such as Leopold Bloom), and satirizing the lack of it in egoistic men, such as Gabriel Conroy. This is a cogent argument. But I think I will remain on the fence, and not only because of counterevidence such as the "Nausicaa" episode of *Ulysses* and the treatment of Molly Bloom in that novel, or because of the letter that I cite at the end of my essay, but because I still think the potentially irresolvable issue of the degree to which all authentic sentiments, all earnest intentions, are ultimately inseparable from rhetorical coding is a rather salient one in Joyce's subsequent work—*A Portrait* would make no sense without this issue, I think.

But then, your notion of "possible worlds" may be a way around the problem. . . .

MN: I think your second observation, about Joyce's relation to French realism (or, perhaps, more broadly, Continental realism), offers us a particularly promising point of discussion. One of the points you made caused me to think back on some other earlier thoughts of mine on Joyce's stories. I do indeed think that Joyce was more feminist than Flaubert. In my Bedford series essay on "The Dead," I try to argue that Joyce's Continental inspiration and intertext for "The Dead" was Ibsen's "A Doll's House." We know from one of Joyce's conversations with Arthur Power that he regarded Ibsen's play as a kind of feminist manifesto. "The purpose of *The Doll's House,* for instance, was the emancipation of women, which has caused the greatest revolution in our time in the most important relationship there is—that between men and women; the revolt of women against the idea that they are the mere instruments of men" (1974, 35). "The Dead" and Ibsen's play have in common the seasonal setting: the climax occurring at a Christmas party set in January, with the husband's amorous advance on the wife disrupted by her disclosure of a secret from the past. Even small details like the husband's controlling solicitude toward the wife (Torvald barring macaroons for Nora and Gabriel pushing galoshes on Gretta) are paralleled. I would argue neither Ibsen nor Joyce fails to see the ironies in the husband's rather than the wife's fatuity about the marriage. My other quarrel with a thematic Flaubertian reading of Joyce came out in my challenge of Kenner's view of "Eveline" in my recent book, *Suspicious Readings of Joyce's "Dubliners."* I join other critics (such as Katie Mullen) whose evidence disagrees with his conclusion. (My essay reads "Eveline" as a story about legitimate emigration anxieties rather than a girl's romantic delusion.) But this challenge certainly doesn't neutralize the other evidence of Flaubertian influence you mention, such as "Nausicaa," and doesn't necessarily speak to Gretta's response to Michael Furey in "The Dead."

VP: I certainly agree about Ibsen's role in Joyce's thinking—for me, as for others, Ibsen may indeed be the most important influence on Joyce—so your reading of the way "The Dead" is shadowed by *A Doll's House* makes plenty of sense. But, as you indicate, there is no Michael Furey in *A Doll's House* (which is to say there is no "Lass of Aughrim" either); nor, I think, do most readers of Joyce feel that Gretta simply wants out of an oppressive marriage with Gabriel (Joyce is not quite, I think, Ibsen on this score). That is, you can reset *A Doll's House* in Ireland, but then it isn't exactly *A Doll's House* anymore. In any case, your reading still requires that we read the final narrative focus on Gabriel with irony—which most readers, and certainly most of my students, always find hard to do. Which brings us back to the big question of intent: if Joyce agreed with Ibsen as much as you say he did, then why would he confuse his readers by putting all the nice and moving poetry in the mind of the Torvald figure? It is authorial perversity, to my mind, at the very least.

MN: You're quite right to point out that *A Doll's House* doesn't map perfectly on to "The Dead." It's not clear that Gretta—in spite of her "There's a nice husband for you, Mrs. Malins"—recognizes how controlling Gabriel is, and you're quite right that there's no suggestion that she finds the marriage intolerable, as Nora does. But the question of why Joyce would deliberately confuse the reader in the end is easier for me to consider. I think Joyce deliberately confuses the reader at the end of most—if not all—of the stories in *Dubliners*. (Is the priest in "The Sisters" guilty of something or not? Is Eveline caught in an insoluble dilemma, or is she a silly, fatuous girl, as Kenner thinks? And so forth.) And I think the reason he confuses us is not authorial perversity, to my mind, but to warn readers not to trust stories and narrators and their artful palaver too much. This is pretty much the same lesson we could attribute to Flaubert's *Madame Bovary*—only I think Joyce does something much more subversive, and that's to turn the critique not just against junk, but against high art as well, and—most radically—against his own art.

Works Cited

Index

Works Cited

The edition of *Dubliners* referred to throughout is James Joyce, *Dubliners*. New York: B. W. Huebsch, 1916.

Agamben, Giorgio. 1993. *Stanzas: Word and Phantasm in Western Culture*. Translated by Ronald L. Martinez. Minneapolis: Univ. of Minnesota Press.

Althusser, Louis. 1971. "Ideology and Ideological State Apparatuses: Notes Toward an Investigation." In *Lenin and Philosophy, and Other Essays*, 121–73. London: New Left Books.

American Heritage Dictionary of the English Language. 1992. 3rd ed. Boston: Houghton Mifflin.

Anderson, W. K. 1994. *James Connolly and the Irish Left*. Dublin: Irish Academic Press.

ApRoberts, Robert P. 1967. "'Araby' and the Palimpsest of Criticism; or, Through a Glass Eye Darkly." *Antioch Review* 26, no. 4: 469–89.

Aquinas, Saint Thomas. n.d. "Law: Question #112, Of the Cause of Grace." In *Summa Theologica*. http://www.loang.com/exlibris/Aquinas/sum12112.htm.

Arac, Jonathan. 1997. "Shop Window or Laboratory: Collection, Collaboration, and the Humanities." In *Politics of Research*, edited by E. Ann Kaplan and George Levine. New Brunswick, NJ: Rutgers Univ. Press.

Arendt, Hannah. 1958. *The Human Condition*. 2nd ed. Chicago: Univ. of Chicago Press.

Aristotle. 1934. *Nicomachean Ethics*. Translated by H. Rackham. Loeb Series. Cambridge, MA: Harvard Univ. Press, 1982.

Attridge, Derek. 2000. "Touching Clay: Reference and Reality in *Dubliners*." In *Joyce Effects: On Language, Theory, and History*, 35–52. Cambridge: Cambridge Univ. Press. Originally published in *Le dit et le non-dit (Tropismes 6)*. Edited by Jean-Hacques Lecerise. Paris: Univ. of Paris X–Nanterre, 1993.

————. 2004. "Reading Joyce." In *The Cambridge Companion to James Joyce*, 1–27. 2nd ed. Cambridge: Cambridge Univ. Press.

Attridge, Derek, and Marjorie Howes, eds. 2000. *Semicolonial Joyce*. Cambridge: Cambridge Univ. Press.

Backus, Margot Gayle. 2008. "Odd Jobs: Joyce, Wilde, and the Scandal Fragment." In *Joyce Studies Annual, 2008*, 105–45. New York: Fordham Univ. Press.

Baudrillard, Jean. 1970. *The Consumer Society: Myths and Structures*. Translated by Chris Turner. Los Angeles and London: Sage, 1998.

————. 1981. *For a Critique of the Economy of the Sign*. Translated by Charles Levin. St. Louis: Telos Press.

Baumgarten, Paul Maria. 1911. "Old Catholics." In vol. 11 of *The Catholic Encyclopedia*. http://www.newadvent.org/cathen/11235b.htm.

Beck, Warren. 1969. *Joyce's "Dubliners": Substance, Vision, and Art*. Durham, NC: Duke Univ. Press.

Beja, Morris. 1989. "Farrington the Scrivener: A Story of Dame Street." In *Coping with Joyce: Essays from the Copenhagen Symposium*, edited by Morris Beja and Shari Benstock. Columbus: Ohio State Univ. Press.

Benjamin, Walter. 1968. *Illuminations*. Edited by Hannah Arendt. Translated by Harry Zohn. New York: Schocken, 1969.

Bleich, David. 1978. *Subjective Criticism*. Baltimore: Johns Hopkins Univ. Press.

Booth, Wayne. 1961. *Rhetoric of Fiction*. Chicago: Univ. of Chicago Press.

Borch-Jacobsen, Mikkel. 1982. *The Freudian Subject*. Translated by Catherine Porter. Stanford, CA: Stanford Univ. Press.

Bourke, Joanna. 1993. *Husbandry to Housewifery: Women, Economic Change, and Housework in Ireland, 1890–1914*. Oxford: Clarendon Press.

————. 1999. "The Ideal Man: Irish Masculinity and the Home, 1880–1914." In *Reclaiming Gender: Transgressive Identities in Modern Ireland,* edited by Marilyn Cohen and Nancy J. Curtin. New York: St. Martin's Press.

Bowen, Zack. 1969. "After the Race." In *James Joyce's "Dubliners": Critical Essays*, edited by Clive Hart. New York: Viking.

————. 1970. "Hungarian Politics in 'After the Race.'" *James Joyce Quarterly* 7 (Winter).

————. 1982. "Joyce's Prophylactic Paralysis: Exposure in *Dubliners*." *James Joyce Quarterly* 19, no. 3: 257–73.

Boyle, John W. 1988. *The Irish Labour Movement in the Nineteenth Century*. Washington, DC: Catholic Univ. of America Press.

Brivic, Sheldon. 2001. "Dealing in Shame: Gender in Joyce's 'Circe.'" In *European Joyce Studies 10.* Amsterdam: Rodopi.

Brooker, Joseph . 2004. *Joyce's Critics: Transitions in Reading and Culture.* Madison: Univ. of Wisconsin Press.

Brown, Richard. 2008. *A Companion to James Joyce.* New York: Blackwell.

Brown, Terence. 1992. *Introduction to "Dubliners."* New York: Penguin.

———. 1993. Notes to *Dubliners,* 237–317. New York: Penguin.

Bulson, Eric. 2006. *The Cambridge Introduction to James Joyce.* Cambridge: Cambridge Univ. Press.

Burke, Joanna. 1993. *Husbandry to Housewifery: Women, Economic Change, and Housework in Ireland, 1890–1914.* Oxford: Clarendon Press.

Cameron, Sir Charles A. 1903. *Report upon the State of Health in the City of Dublin for the Year 1902.* Dublin: Cahill.

———. 1904. *Report upon the State of Health in the City of Dublin for the Year 1903.* Dublin: John Falconer.

———. 1905. *Report upon the State of Health in the City of Dublin for the Year 1904.* Dublin: John Falconer.

Castle, Gregory. 2006. *Reading the Modernist Bildungsroman.* Gainesville: Univ. Press of Florida.

Catechism: Ordered by the National Synod of Maynooth and Approved by the Cardinal and the Archbishop and the Bishops of Ireland for General Use Throughout the Irish Church. n.d. Reprint, Galway, Ireland: Firinne Publications.

Cheng, Vincent J. 1995. *Joyce, Race, and Empire.* Cambridge: Cambridge Univ. Press.

Chodorow, Nancy. 1978. *The Reproduction of Mothering: Psychoanalysis and the Sociology of Gender.* Berkeley and Los Angeles: Univ. of California Press.

Cixous, Hélène. 1972. *The Exile of James Joyce.* Translated by Sally Purcell. New York: David Lewis.

Clarkson, J. Dunsmore. 1925. *Labour and Nationalism in Ireland.* New York: Longmans, Green.

Cohen, Ed. 1993. *Talk on the Wilde Side: Toward a Genealogy of a Discourse on Male Sexualities.* New York: Routledge.

Collins, Ben L. 1970. "Joyce's Use of Yeats and of Irish History: A Reading of 'A Mother.'" *Eire-Ireland: A Journal of Irish Studies* 5, no. 1: 45–66.

Connolly, James. 1898. "Home Thrusts." *Workers' Republic,* Sept. 3.

———. 1901. "Home Rulers and Labour: A Remonstrance." *Workers' Republic* (Oct.).

———. 1909. *The New Evangel, Preached to Irish Toilers.* Dublin: H. W. West.

———. 1910. *Labour in Irish History*. Dublin: Maunsel.

———. 1997. *The Lost Writings: James Connolly*. Edited by Aindrais Ó Cathasaigh. London: Pluto.

Costello, Peter. 1992. *James Joyce: The Years of Growth, 1882–1915*. London: Kyle Cathie.

Curtin, Nancy J. 1999. "'A Nation of Abortive Men': Gendered Citizenship and Early Irish Republicanism." In *Reclaiming Gender: Transgressive Identities in Modern Ireland*, edited by Marilyn Cohen and Nancy J. Curtin. New York: St. Martin's Press.

Daly, Mary E. 1984. *Dublin: The Deposed Capital: A Social and Economic History, 1860–1914*. Cork: Cork Univ. Press.

Dante Alighieri. 1980. *Inferno*. Translated by Allen Mandelbaum. New York: Bantam.

———. 2006. *The Divine Comedy, I: Inferno*. Translated and edited by Robin Kirkpatrick. London: Penguin.

Deane, Seamus. 2000. "Dead Ends: Joyce's Finest Moments." In *Semicolonial Joyce*, edited by Derek Attridge and Marjorie Howes. Cambridge: Cambridge Univ. Press.

Debuchy, Paul. 1911. "Retreats." In vol. 11 of *The Catholic Encyclopedia*. http://www.newadvent.org/cathen/12795b.htm.

Delany, Paul. 1995. "'Tailors of Malt, Hot, All Round . . .': Homosocial Consumption in *Dubliners*." *Studies in Short Fiction*: 381–98.

Deleuze, Gilles. 1993. "Bartleby ou la formule." In *Critique et Clinique*. Paris: Editions de Minuit.

Deleuze, Gilles, and Félix Guattari. 1987. *A Thousand Plateaus: Capitalism and Schizophrenia*. Translated by Brian Massumi. Minneapolis: Univ. of Minnesota Press.

de Man, Paul. 1971. *Blindness and Insight: Essays in the Rhetoric of Contemporary Criticism*. New York: Oxford Univ. Press.

Deming, Robert H., ed. 1970. *James Joyce: The Critical Heritage*. Vol. 1. London: Routledge and Kegan Paul.

Derrida, Jacques. 1973. *Speech and Phenomena, and Other Essays on Husserl's Theory of Signs*. Translated by David B. Allison. Evanston: Northwestern Univ. Press.

———. 1992. "Force of Law: The 'Mystical Foundation of Authority.'" In *Deconstruction and the Possibility of Justice*, edited by Drucilla Cornell, Michel Rosenfeld, and David Gray Carlson, 3–67. New York: Routledge.

———. 2000. *Of Hospitality: Anne Dufourmantelle Invites Jacques Derrida to Respond*. Translated by Rachel Bowlby. Stanford, CA: Stanford Univ. Press.

———. 2001. *On Cosmopolitanism and Forgiveness*. Translated by Mark Dooley and Michael Hughes. London: Routledge.

de Voogd, Peter. 2000. "Imaging Eveline: Visualised Focalisations in James Joyce's *Dubliners.*" *European Journal of English Studies* 4, no. 1: 39–48.

Doherty, Gerald. 2004. *"Dubliners"' Dozen: The Games Narrators Play.* Madison, NJ: Fairleigh Dickinson Univ. Press.

Dolar, Mladen. 2006. *A Voice and Nothing More.* Cambridge, MA: MIT Press.

Dolezel, Lubomir. 1998. *Heterocosmica: Fiction and Possible Worlds.* Baltimore: Johns Hopkins Univ. Press.

DuBois, W. E. B. 1965. *The Souls of Black Folk.* In *Three Negro Classics,* introduced by John Hope Franklin. New York: Avon.

Duffy, Enda. 1999. "Interesting States: Birthing and the Nation in 'Oxen of the Sun.'" In *"Ulysses"—En-gendered Perspectives: Eighteen New Essays on the Episodes,* edited by Kimberly J. Devlin and Marilyn Reizbaum. Columbia: Univ. of South Carolina Press.

Eagleton, Terry. 1996. *Literary Theory: An Introduction.* Minneapolis: Univ. of Minnesota Press.

Ehrlich, Heyward. 2006. "'Araby' in Context." In *Dubliners,* by James Joyce, edited by Margot Norris, 261–83. New York: W. W. Norton.

Ellis, Peter Berresford. 1985. *A History of the Irish Working Class.* London: Pluto.

Ellmann, Richard. 1966. *Letters of James Joyce.* 3 vols. New York: Viking.

———. 1982. *James Joyce.* Rev. ed. Oxford: Oxford Univ. Press.

———. 1983. *James Joyce.* Oxford: Oxford Univ. Press.

———. 1988. *Oscar Wilde.* New York: Vintage.

Fairhall, James. 1993. *James Joyce and the Question of History.* Cambridge: Cambridge Univ. Press.

Fargnoli, A. Nicholas, and Michael Patrick Gillespie, eds. 2006. *A Critical Companion to James Joyce: A Literary Reference to His Life and Work.* Rev. ed. New York: Facts on File.

Fish, Stanley. 1980. *Is There a Text in This Class? The Authority of Interpretive Communities.* Cambridge, MA: Harvard Univ. Press.

Flaubert, Gustave. 1924. *Oeuvres Complètes Illustrés: Correspondance.* Edited by M. René Descharnes. Paris: Librairie de France.

———. 1961. *Three Tales.* Translated by Robert Baldick. London: Penguin.

Flynn, Elizabeth. 1983. "Gender and Reading." *College English* 45, no. 3: 236–53.

Fogarty, Anne. 2006. "Parnellism and the Politics of Memory: Revisiting 'Ivy Day in the Committee Room.'" In *"Our Mixed Racings": Joyce, Ireland, and Britain,* edited by Andrew Gibson and Len Platt. Gainesville: Univ. Press of Florida.

Foucault, Michel. 1988. *History of Sexuality*. Translated by Robert Hurley. Vol. 1. New York: Vintage Books.

———. 1995. *Discipline and Punish: The Birth of the Prison*. Translated by Alan Sheridan. New York: Vintage Books.

Freire, Paulo. 1970. *Pedagogy of the Oppressed*. Translated by Myra Bergman Ramos. New York: Continuum, 2000.

Freitag, Barbara. 2004. *Sheela-na-Gigs: Unraveling an Enigma*. London: Routledge.

Freud, Sigmund. 1917. "Trauer und Melancholie." In *Psychologie des Unbewussten*, edited by Angela Richards. Vol. 3 of *Studienausgabe*. Frankfurt: Fischer, 1975.

———. 1953–74. *The Complete Psychological Works of Sigmund Freud*. Edited by James Strachey. Standard ed. 24 vols. London: Hogarth Press.

———. 1963. *A General Introduction to Psychoanalysis*. Translated by Joan Riviere. New York: Washington Square Press.

———. 1989. *Introductory Lectures on Psychoanalysis*. Translated by James Strachey. New York: W. W. Norton.

———. 1997. "A Child Is Being Beaten." In *Sexuality and the Psychology of Love*. New York: Macmillan.

Gazalé, Midhat J. 1999. *Gnomon: From Pharoahs to Fractals*. Princeton: Princeton Univ. Press.

Gibbons, Luke. 2000. "'Have You No Homes to Go To?': Joyce and the Politics of Paralysis." In *Semicolonial Joyce,* edited by Derek Attridge and Marjorie Howes, 150–71. Cambridge: Cambridge Univ. Press.

Gibson, Andrew, ed. 1994. *Reading Joyce's "Circe."* European Joyce Studies 3. Amsterdam and Atlanta: Rodopi.

———. 2002. "Macropolitics and Micropolitics in 'Wandering Rocks.'" In *Joyce's "Wandering Rocks,"* edited by Andrew Gibson and Steven Morrison, 27–56. European Joyce Studies 12. Amsterdam and Atlanta: Rodopi.

Gifford, Don. 1982. *Joyce Annotated: Notes for "Dubliners" and "A Portrait of the Artist as a Young Man."* 2nd ed. Berkeley and Los Angeles: Univ. of California Press.

———. 1988. *"Ulysses" Annotated*. Berkeley and Los Angeles: Univ. of California Press.

"Gift of Tongues." n.d. http://www.letusreason.org/Pent3.htm.

Giles, Jana. 1997. "The Craft of 'A Painful Case': A Study of the Revisions." In *European Joyce Studies 7: New Perspectives on Dubliners*. Amsterdam: Rodopi.

Girard, René. 1961. *Deceit, Desire, and the Novel: Self and Other in Literary Structure*. Translated by Yvonne Freccero. Baltimore: Johns Hopkins Univ. Press, 1965.

———. 2000. "Do You Believe in Your Own Theory? 'French Triangles' in the Shakespeare of James Joyce." In *A Theater of Envy: William Shakespeare*. New York: Oxford Univ. Press.

Grace, Sherrill E. 1988. "Rediscovering Mrs. Kearney: An Other Reading of 'A Mother.'" In *James Joyce: The Augmented Ninth*, edited by Bernard Benstock, 273–81. Syracuse, NY: Syracuse Univ. Press.

Greene, Graham. 1971. *A Sort of Life*. London: Bodley Head.

Griffith, Arthur. 1904. *The Resurrection of Hungary: A Parallel for Ireland*. Dublin: James Duff & Co., M. H. Gill & Son, Sealy, Bryers & Walker.

Hamington, Maurice. 2001. "Gender and the Challenge of Social Construction: Mary the Mother of Jesus." In *Women's Studies: An Interdisciplinary Anthology*, edited by Roberta Rosenberg, 49–59. New York: Peter Lang.

Hansen, James. 2009. *Terror and Irish Modernism: The Gothic Tradition from Burke to Beckett*. Albany: SUNY Press.

Harding, Desmond. 2003. *Writing in the City: Urban Visions and Literary Modernism*. New York: Routledge.

Harris, Susan Cannon. 2002. *Gender and Modern Irish Drama*. Bloomington: Indiana Univ. Press.

Hayes, Alan, and Diane Urquhart, eds. 2001. *The Irish Women's History Reader*. London: Routledge.

Hayman, David. 1969. "A Mother." In *James Joyce's "Dubliners": Critical Essays*, edited by Clive Hart. New York: Viking.

Herr, Cheryl. 1986. *Joyce's Anatomy of Culture*. Urbana: Univ. of Illinois Press.

Herring, Phillip. 1982. "Structure and Meaning in Joyce's 'The Sisters.'" In *The Seventh of Joyce*, edited by Bernard Benstock, 131–44. Bloomington: Indiana Univ. Press.

Herzog, William R., II. 1994. *Parables as Subversive Speech: Jesus as Pedagogue of the Oppressed*. Westminster: John Knox Press.

Hobhouse, Henry. 2005. *Seeds of Change: Six Plants That Transformed Mankind*. Rev. ed. London: Shoemaker & Hoard.

Holland, Norman N. 1975. *5 Readers Reading*. New Haven, CT: Yale Univ. Press.

Jackson, John Wyse, and Peter Costello. 1998. *John Stanislaus Joyce*. New York: St. Martin's Press.

Jackson, John Wyse, and Bernard McGinley, eds. 1993. *James Joyce's "Dubliners": An Illustrated Edition, with Annotations*. New York: St. Martin's.

Jackson, Roberta. 1999–2000. "The Open Closet in *Dubliners:* James Duffy's Painful Case." *James Joyce Quarterly* 37 (Fall–Winter).

Jacobs, Jane. 2001. *The Nature of Economies*. Toronto: Vintage Canada.

Jauss, Hans Robert. 1982. *Toward an Aesthetic of Reception*. Translated by Timothy Bahti. Minneapolis: Univ. of Minnesota Press.

Jay, Martin. 1998. "Experience Without a Subject: Walter Benjamin and the Novel." In *Cultural Semantics: Keywords for Our Time*, 47–61. Amherst: Univ. of Massachusetts Press.

Jodock, Darrell, ed. 2000. *Catholicism Contending with Modernity*. Cambridge: Cambridge Univ. Press.

Joyce, James. 1963. *Stephen Hero*. Edited by Theodore Spencer. Additional pages edited by John J. Slocum and Herbert Cahoon. New York: New Directions.

———. 1968. *A Portrait of the Artist as a Young Man: Text, Criticism, and Notes*. Edited by Chester G. Anderson. Viking Critical Library. New York: Viking.

———. 1976a. *Finnegans Wake*. New York: Penguin.

———. 1976b. *Selected Letters*. Edited by Richard Ellmann. New York: Viking.

———. 1977. *A Portrait of the Artist as a Young Man*. Edited by Chester G. Anderson. New York: Penguin Books–Viking Critical Edition.

———. 1977–79. *James Joyce Archive*. Edited by Michael Groden. 63 vols. New York: Garland.

———. 1986. *Ulysses*. Edited by Hans Walter Gabler with Wolfhard Steppe and Claus Melchior. New York: Vintage Books.

———. 1991. *Dubliners: An Illustrated Edition with Annotations*. New York: St. Martin's.

———. 1992. *Dubliners*. Edited by Terence Brown. New York: Penguin.

———. 1993a. *Dubliners*. Edited by Hans Walter Gabler with Walter Hettche. New York: Garland.

———. 1993b. *Dubliners*. Edited by Hans Walter Gabler with Walter Hettche. New York: Vintage.

———. 1993c. *Dubliners: An Annotated Edition*. Edited by John Wyse Jackson and Bernard McGinley. London: Sinclair-Stevenson.

———. 2000a. *Dubliners*. Edited by Jeri Johnson. Oxford World's Classics. Oxford: Oxford Univ. Press. "The Sisters," 3–10. "The *Irish Homestead* Version of 'The Sisters,'" 190–93.

———. 2000b. *Occasional, Critical, and Political Writing*. Edited by Kevin Barry. Oxford: Oxford Univ. Press.

———. 2006. *Dubliners*. Edited by Margot Norris. Text edited by Hans Walter Gabler with Walter Hettche. New York: W. W. Norton.

Joyce, Stanislaus. 1958. *My Brother's Keeper: James Joyce's Early Years*. New York: Viking.

Kant, Immanuel. 1951. *Critique of Judgement.* Translated by J. H. Bernard. New York: Macmillan.

Kearney, Martin F. 2001. "Robert Emmet's 1803 Rising and Bold Mrs. Kearney: James Joyce's 'A Mother' as Historical Analogue." *Journal of the Short Story in English* 37 (Autumn): 49–61.

Keats, John. 1988. "The Eve of St. Agnes." In *Complete Poems of John Keats,* edited by John Barnard. London: Penguin.

Kelly, Linda. 2006. *Ireland's Minstrel: A Life of Tom Moore: Poet, Patriot, and Byron's Friend.* London and New York: I. B. Tauris.

Kelly, M. T. 1910. "John MacHale." In vol. 9 of *The Catholic Encyclopedia.* http://www.newadvent.org/cathen/09499a.htm.

Kennedy, D. J. 1912. "Saint Thomas Aquinas." In vol. 14 of *The Catholic Encyclopedia.* http://www.newadvent.org/cathen/14663b.htm.

Kenner, Hugh. 1955. *Dublin's Joyce.* London: Chatto and Windus.

———. 1956. *Dublin's Joyce.* Bloomington: Indiana Univ. Press.

———. 1972. *The Pound Era.* London: Faber and Faber. First published by Berkeley and Los Angeles: Univ. of California Press, 1971.

Keogh, Dermot. 1982. *The Rise of the Irish Working Class: The Dublin Trade Union Movement and Labour Leadership.* Belfast: Appletree.

Kermode, Frank. 1979. *The Genesis of Secrecy: On the Interpretation of Narrative.* Cambridge, MA: Harvard Univ. Press.

Kershner, R. B. 1989. *Joyce, Bakhtin, and Popular Literature: Chronicles of Disorder.* Chapel Hill: Univ. of North Carolina Press.

———. 1992. "Mr. Duffy's Apple." *James Joyce Quarterly* 29 (Winter).

———. 2008. "Joyce, Music, and Popular Culture." In *A Companion to James Joyce,* edited by Richard Brown, 270–85. New York: Blackwell.

Kiberd, Declan. 1995. *Inventing Ireland: The Literature of the Modern Nation.* London: Jonathan Cape.

Kipp, Julie. 2003. *Romanticism, Maternity, and the Body Politic.* New York: Cambridge Univ. Press.

Knapp, Steven, and Walter Benn Michaels. 1985. "Against Theory." In *Against Theory: Literary Studies and the New Pragmatism,* edited by W. J. T. Mitchell, 11–30. Chicago: Univ. of Chicago Press.

Knowlton, Eloise. 2005. "Showings Forth: *Dubliners,* Photography, and the Rejection of Realism." *Mosaic* 38, no. 1: 133–50.

Kukla, Rebecca. 2005. *Mass Hysteria, Medicine, Culture, and Mothers' Bodies.* Lanham, MD: Rowman and Littlefield.

Lacan, Jacques. 1977. *Ecrits: A Selection*. Translated by Alan Sheridan. New York: W. W. Norton.

——. 2005. *Le séminaire livre XXIII, le sinthome*. Edited by Jacques-Alain Miller. Paris: Seuil.

Lamos, Colleen. 1995. "James Joyce and the English Vice." *Novel* 29 (Fall).

——. 2001. "Duffy's Subjectivation: The Psychic Life of 'A Painful Case.'" In *European Joyce Studies 10: Masculinities in Joyce/Postcolonial Constructions*, edited by Christine Van Boheemen-Saaf and Colleen Lamos. Amsterdam: Rodopi.

Lane, Leeann. 2004. "Female Emigration and the Cooperative Movement in the Writings of George Russell." *New Hibernia Review* 8, no. 4: 84–100.

Larkin, Emmet. 1972. "The Devotional Revolution in Ireland, 1850–1875." *American Historical Review* 77, no. 3: 625–52.

Law, Jules David. 1987. "Joyce's 'Delicate Siamese' Equation: The Dialectic of Home in *Ulysses*." *PMLA* 102: 197–205.

Lawrence, Karen R. 1990. "Joyce and Feminism." In *The Cambridge Companion to James Joyce*, edited by Derek Attridge, 237–58. Cambridge: Cambridge Univ. Press.

——. 2003–4. "Close Encounters." *James Joyce Quarterly* 41 (Fall–Winter): 127–42.

Leavis, F. R. 1963. *The Great Tradition*. New York: New York Univ. Press.

Leonard, Garry M. 1989. "The Question and the Quest: The Story of Mangan's Sister." *Modern Fiction Studies* 35: 459–78.

——. 1993. *Reading "Dubliners" Again*. Syracuse, NY: Syracuse Univ. Press.

——. 1998. *Advertising and Commodity Culture in Joyce*. Gainesville: Univ. Press of Florida.

Levenson, Michael. 1996. "Living History in 'The Dead.'" In *Dubliners*, by James Joyce, edited by Robert Scholes and A. Walton Litz, 421–38. New York: Penguin.

Levi, Primo. 1947. *If This Is a Man*. Translated by Stuart Woolf. Reprint, London: Vintage, 1996.

Levinas, Emmanuel. 1985. *Ethics and Infinity: Conversations with Philippe Nemo*. Translated by Richard A. Cohen. Pittsburgh: Duquesne Univ. Press.

Levine, Jennifer. 1998. "James Joyce, Tattoo Artist: Tracing the Outlines of Homosocial Desire." In *Quare Joyce*, edited by Joseph Valente, 101–20. Ann Arbor: Univ. of Michigan Press.

Lloyd, David. 2000. "Counterparts: Dubliners, Masculinity, and Temperance Nationalism." In *Semicolonial Joyce*, edited by Derek Attridge and Marjorie Howes. Cambridge: Cambridge Univ. Press.

Lobner, Corrina Del Greco. "Equivocation as Stylistic Device: Joyce's 'Grace' and Dante." n.d. http://www.brown.edu/Departments?ItalianStudies/LD/numbers/04/lobner.html.

Lynd, Helen. 1958. *On Shame and the Search for Identity.* New York: Harcourt Brace.

Lyotard, Jean-François. 1988. *The Differend.* Translated by G. van den Abbeele. Manchester: Manchester Univ. Press.

Macpherson, James. 2001. "'Ireland Begins in the Home': Women, Irish National Identity, and the Domestic Sphere in the *Irish Homestead, 1896–1912." Éire-Ireland* 36, nos. 3–4: 131–52.

Mahaffey, Vicki. 1988. *Reauthorizing Joyce.* Cambridge: Cambridge Univ. Press.

———. 1991. "The Case Against Art: Wunderlich on Joyce." *Critical Inquiry* 17, no. 4: 667–92.

———. 2007. *Modernist Literature: Challenging Fictions.* Oxford: Blackwell.

Mandel, Jerome. 1984. "The Structure of 'Araby.'" *Modern Language Studies* 15, no. 4: 48–54.

Mandelbrot, Benoit B. 1983. *The Fractal Geometry of Nature.* San Francisco: W. H. Freeman.

Manganiello, Dominic. 1980. *Joyce's Politics.* London: Routledge and Kegan Paul.

Marx, Karl. 1867. "The Fetishism of the Commodity and Its Secret." In vol. 1 of *Capital.* Harmondsworth: Penguin.

Masiello, Francine. 2004. "Joyce in Buenos Aires: Talking Sexuality Through Translation." *Diacritics* 34: 55–72.

McCool, Gerald A. 1977. *Catholic Theology in the Nineteenth Century.* New York: Seabury Press.

McEwan, Ian. 2001. *Atonement.* New York: Random-Anchor.

McGann, Jerome J. 1988. *The Beauty of Inflections: Literary Investigations in Historical Method and Theory.* Oxford: Clarendon.

Melchiori, Giorgio. 1984. "The Genesis of *Ulysses.*" In *Joyce in Rome: The Genesis of "Ulysses,"* edited by Giorgio Melchiori. Rome: Bulzoni Editore.

Michaels, Walter Benn. 2004. *The Shape of the Signifier: 1967 to the End of History.* Princeton: Princeton Univ. Press.

Milesi, Laurent. 1997. "Joyce's Anamorphic Mirror in 'The Sisters.'" In *European Joyce Studies 7: New Perspectives on "Dubliners,"* edited by Mary Power and Ulrich Schneider, 91–113. Amsterdam and Atlanta: Rodopi.

Miller, J. Hillis. 2005. *Literature as Conduct: Speech Acts in Henry James.* New York: Fordham Univ. Press.

Miller, Jane E. 1991. "'O, She's a Nice Lady!': A Rereading of 'A Mother.'" *James Joyce Quarterly* 28, no. 2: 407–43.

Moffat, A., ed. 1897. *The Minstrelsy of Ireland*. London: Augener.

Moseley, Virginia. 1968. "The Coincidence of Contraries in 'Grace.'" *James Joyce Quarterly* 6: 3–21.

Mullin, Katherine. 2000. "Don't Cry for Me, Argentina: 'Eveline' and the Seductions of Emigration Propaganda." In *Semicolonial Joyce*, edited by Derek Attridge and Marjorie Howes, 172–200. Cambridge: Cambridge Univ. Press.

————. 2003. *James Joyce, Sexuality, and Social Purity*. Cambridge: Cambridge Univ. Press.

Nietzsche, Friedrich. 1998. *The Genealogy of Morality*. Translated by Maudemarie Clark and Alan J. Swensen. New York: Hackett.

Nolan, Emer. 2007. *Catholic Emancipations: Irish Fiction from Thomas Moore to James Joyce*. Syracuse, NY: Syracuse Univ. Press.

Norris, Margot. 1992. *Joyce's Web: The Social Unraveling of Modernism*. Austin: Univ. of Texas Press.

————. 1998. "A Walk on the Wild(e) Side: The Doubled Reading of 'An Encounter.'" In *Quare Joyce*, edited by Joseph Valente. Ann Arbor: Univ. of Michigan Press.

————. 2003. *Suspicious Readings of Joyce's "Dubliners."* Philadelphia: Univ. of Pennsylvania Press.

Norton, Lady Caroline. 2006. "The Arab's Farewell to His Steed." In *Dubliners*, by James Joyce and edited by Margot Norris, 214–15. New York: W. W. Norton.

O'Brien, Joseph. 1982. *"Dear, Dirty Dublin": A City in Distress, 1899–1916*. Berkeley and Los Angeles: Univ. of California Press.

O'Connor, Emmet. 1992. *A Labour History of Ireland, 1824–1960*. Dublin: Gill and Macmillan.

O'Neill, Michael J. 1959. "Joyce's Use of Memory in 'A Mother.'" *Modern Language Notes* 75.

Ovid. 1955. *The Metamorphoses of Ovid*. Translated by Mary M. Innes. Baltimore: Penguin.

Owens, Cóilín. 2008. *James Joyce's "Painful Case."* Gainesville: Univ. Press of Florida.

Pecora, Vincent P. 1986. "'The Dead' and the Generosity of the Word." *PMLA* 101, no. 2: 233–45.

————. 1989. *Self and Form in Modern Narrative.* Baltimore: Johns Hopkins Univ. Press.

Perrault, Charles. 2002. "Donkeyskin." In *The Annotated Classic Fairy Tales,* edited by Maria Tatar, 212–28. New York: W. W. Norton.

Phillips, Adam. 1996. *Monogamy.* London: Faber.

Platt, Len. 1995. *Joyce and the Anglo-Irish.* Amsterdam: Rodopi.

Potts, Willard. 2000. *Joyce and the Two Irelands.* Austin: Univ. of Texas Press.

Pound, Ezra. 1970. *Guide to Kulchur.* New York: New Directions.

Power, Arthur. 1974. *Conversations with James Joyce.* London: Millington.

Power, Mary. 1976. "The Naming of Kathleen Kearney." *Journal of Modern Literature* 5 (Sept.).

Rabaté, Jean-Michel. 1982. "A Portrait of the Reader as a Young Dubliner." In *James Joyce: Authorized Reader,* 20–49. Baltimore: Johns Hopkins Univ. Press, 1991. Originally published as "Silence in Dubliners." In *James Joyce: New Perspectives,* edited by Colin MacCabe, 45–72. Bloomington: Indiana Univ. Press.

Redmond, John Edward. 1910. *Home Rule: Speeches of John Redmond, M.P.* London: T. Fisher Unwin.

Reynolds, Mary. 1981. *Joyce and Dante: The Shaping Imagination.* Princeton: Princeton Univ. Press.

Rich, Adrienne. 1972. "The Phenomenology of Anger." In *The Fact of a Doorframe: Poems, 1950–1984.* New York: W. W. Norton.

————. 1980. "Compulsory Heterosexuality and Lesbian Experience." *Signs: Journal of Women in Culture and Society* 5 (Summer): 631–60.

Riquelme, Paul. 1983. *Teller and Tale in Joyce's Fiction: Oscillating Perspectives.* Baltimore: Johns Hopkins Univ. Press.

Roberts, Jack. 2001. *The Sheela-na-Gigs of Ireland and Britain: Divine Hag of the Christian Celts.* London: Mercier Press.

Rohrer-Paige, Linda. 1995. "James Joyce's Darkly Colored Portraits of 'Mother' in *Dubliners.*" *Studies in Short Fiction* 32 (Summer): 329–41.

Ronan, Ruth. 1994. *Possible Worlds in Literary Theory.* Cambridge: Cambridge Univ. Press.

Ruoff, James. 1957. "'A Little Cloud': Joyce's Portrait of the Would-Be Artist." *Research Studies of Washington State College* 25 (Sept.).

Russell, John. 1966. "From Style to Meaning in 'Araby.'" *College English* 28, no. 2: 170–71.

Ryan, Marie-Laure. 1991. *Possible Worlds, Artificial Intelligence, and Narrative Theory*. Bloomington: Indiana Univ. Press.

Saint-Amour, Paul K. 2007. "'Christmas Yet to Come': Hospitality, Futurity, the *Carol*, and 'The Dead.'" *Representations* 98 (Spring): 93–117.

Saint-Amour, Paul K., Michael Groden, Carol Shloss, and Robert Spoo. 2007. "James Joyce: Copyright, Fair Use, and Permission—Frequently Asked Questions." *James Joyce Quarterly* 44 (Summer): 753–84.

Scholes, Robert, and A. Walton Litz, eds. 1996. *Dubliners: Text and Criticism*. Rev. ed. New York: Viking Penguin.

Senn, Fritz. 1986. "'The Boarding House' Seen as a Tale of Misdirection." *James Joyce Quarterly* 23 (Summer): 405–15.

Shashaty, Jill. 2010. "Reading *Dubliners* Parabolically." *James Joyce Quarterly* 47 (Winter).

Shloss, Carol Loeb. 2003. *Lucia Joyce: To Dance in the Wake*. New York: Farrar, Straus, and Giroux.

Silverman, Kaja. 1996. *The Threshold of the Visible World*. New York: Routledge.

Small, Nathaniel. 2006. "The Ineluctable Modality of the Triangle: Shaping Desire in Joyce." Unpublished paper written for Maud Ellmann's course on Irish modernism at Northwestern Univ.

Spoo, Robert. 1987. "'Una Piccola Nuvoletta': Ferrero's *Young Europe* and Joyce's Mature *Dubliners* Stories." *James Joyce Quarterly* 24, no. 4: 401–11.

Standage, Tom. 2005. *A History of the World in Six Glasses*. New York: Walker.

Stevens, Wallace. 1990. "The Snow Man." In *The Palm at the End of the Mind*, edited by Holly Stevens. New York: Vintage.

Stokes, John. 1999. "Wilde the Journalist." In *The Cambridge Companion to Oscar Wilde*, 69–79. Cambridge: Cambridge Univ. Press.

Stone, Harry. 1965. "'Araby' and the Writings of James Joyce." *Antioch Review* 25, no. 3: 375–410.

Stornmonth, James. 1885. *A Handbook of Scientific Terms*. Edinburgh: Machlachlan and Stewart.

Szarkowski, John. 1988. *Winogrand: Fragments from the Real World*. New York: Museum of Modern Art.

Taylor, Dennis. 1986. "Forum." *PMLA* 101, no. 5: 862–63.

Thomson, D'Arcy. 1966. *On Growth and Form*. Edited by John Tyler Bonner. Cambridge: Cambridge Univ. Press.

Torchiana, Donald T. 1971. "Joyce's 'After the Race,' the Races of Castlebar, and Dun Laoghaire." *Éire-Ireland* 6, no. 3: 119–28.

———. 1986. *Backgrounds for Joyce's "Dubliners."* Boston: Allen and Unwin.

Valente, Joseph. 1995. "The Myth of Sovereignty: Gender in the Literature of Irish Nationalism." *ELH* 61, no. 1: 189–210.

———. 1998a. "Joyce's (Sexual) Choices." In *Quare Joyce*, edited by Joseph Valente, 1–16. Ann Arbor: Univ. of Michigan Press.

———, ed. 1998b. *Quare Joyce.* Ann Arbor: Univ. of Michigan Press.

———. 2000. "'Neither Fish nor Flesh': The Double-Bind of Irish Manhood." In *Semicolonial Joyce,* edited by Derek Attridge and Marjorie Howes, 96–127. Cambridge: Cambridge Univ. Press.

Vesala-Varttala, Tanja. 1999. *Sympathy and Joyce's "Dubliners": Ethical Probing of Reading, Narrative, and Textuality.* Tampere, Finland: Tampere Univ. Press.

Walshe, Eibhear. 2005. "The First Gay Irishman? Ireland and the Wilde Trials." *Eire/Ireland* 40, nos. 3–4: 35–57.

Walzl, Florence. 1966. "Gabriel and Michael: The Conclusion of 'The Dead.'" *James Joyce Quarterly* 4: 17–31.

Ward, Margaret. 1995. *Unmanageable Revolutionaries: Women and Irish Nationalism.* London: Pluto Press.

Webb, Robert C. 1999. *Psychology of the Consumer and Its Development: An Introduction.* New York: Kluwer/Plenum.

Weber, Max. 2001. *The Protestant Ethic and the Spirit of Capitalism.* Translated by Talcott Parsons. London: Routledge.

Werner, Craig Hansen. 1988. *Dubliners: A Pluralistic World.* Boston: G. K. Hall-Twayne.

Wilde, Oscar. 1988. *The Portable Oscar Wilde.* Edited by Richard Aldington and Stanley Weintraub. New York: Penguin.

———. 2000. *A Woman of No Importance.* In *The Plays of Oscar Wilde.* Hertfordshire: Wordsworth Editions.

Williams, Keith. 2004. "Short Cuts of the Hibernian Metropolis: Cinematic Strategies in *Dubliners.*" In *A New and Complex Sensation: Essays on Joyce's "Dubliners,"* edited by Oona Frawley, 154–67. Dublin: Lilliput Press.

Williams, Michael A. 2010. "The Rubric of Guilt in 'The Sisters.'" Paper presented at the Twenty-Second International James Joyce Symposium in Prague, June 15.

Williams, Trevor L. 1991. "No Cheer for the 'Gratefully Oppressed' in Joyce's *Dubliners.*" *Style* 25, no. 30: 416–39.

Wright, Richard. 1963. *Lawd Today.* New York: Walker.

Žižek, Slavoj. 1989. *The Sublime Object of Ideology.* London and New York: Verso.

———. 1997. "From Joyce-the-Symptom to the Symptom of Power." *Lacanian Ink* 11 (Fall): 12–35.

———. 2000. "Melancholy and the Act." *Critical Inquiry* 26, no. 4.

Index

www.ingramcontent.com/pod-product-compliance
Lightning Source LLC
Chambersburg PA
CBHW012000050726
47499CB00010BA/3226